Trauma and Coping Mechanisms among
Assemblies of God World Missionaries

Evangelical Missiological Society Monograph Series

Anthony Casey, Allen Yeh, Mark Kreitzer, and Edward L. Smither
SERIES EDITORS

A Project of the Evangelical Missiological Society
www.emsweb.org

Trauma and Coping Mechanisms among Assemblies of God World Missionaries

Towards a Biblical Theory of Well-Being

Valerie A. Rance

PICKWICK *Publications* · Eugene, Oregon

TRAUMA AND COPING MECHANISMS AMONG ASSEMBLIES OF GOD WORLD MISSIONARIES
Towards a Biblical Theory of Well-Being

Evangelical Missiological Society Monograph Series 12

Copyright © 2021 Valerie A. Rance. All rights reserved. Except for brief quotations in critical publications or reviews, no part of this book may be reproduced in any manner without prior written permission from the publisher. Write: Permissions, Wipf and Stock Publishers, 199 W. 8th Ave., Suite 3, Eugene, OR 97401.

Pickwick Publications
An Imprint of Wipf and Stock Publishers
199 W. 8th Ave., Suite 3
Eugene, OR 97401

www.wipfandstock.com

PAPERBACK ISBN: 978-1-7252-8958-1
HARDCOVER ISBN: 978-1-7252-8959-8
EBOOK ISBN: 978-1-7252-8960-4

Cataloguing-in-Publication data:

Names: Rance, Valerie A., author.

Title: Trauma and coping mechanisms among Assemblies of God world missionaries : towards a biblical theory of well-being / by Valerie A. Rance.

Description: Eugene, OR: Pickwick Publications, 2021 | Evangelical Missiological Society Monograph Series 12 | Includes bibliographical references.

Identifiers: ISBN 978-1-7252-8958-1 (paperback) | ISBN 978-1-7252-8959-8 (hardcover) | ISBN 978-1-7252-8960-4 (ebook)

Subjects: LCSH: Assemblies of God—Missions. | Psychic trauma—Religious aspects—Christianity. | Suffering—Religious aspects—Christianity.

Classification: BV2595.A8 R36 2021 (print) | BV2595.A8 (ebook)

12/10/21

To my wonderful family who lived with me through the traumas of the mission field and to my Lord who brought us through each traumatic event stronger than before.

"Trust in the Lord with all your heart and lean not on your own understanding; in all your ways submit to him, and he will make your paths straight." (Prov 3:5–6)

Contents

List of Tables | xi
List of Figures | xiii
Preface | xv
Acknowledgments | xvii
List of Abbreviations | xviii

1. **Introduction to the Problem** | 1
   Background   3
   Purpose   3
   Problem Statement   4
   Research Questions   4
   Significance of the Study   4
   Goals   6
   Limitations and Delimitations   7
   Definitions   7
   Assumptions   9

2. **Trauma and Coping: Psychological and Coping Issues Impacting Missionary Well-Being** | 10
   Introduction   10
   Trauma and Its Outcomes   11
       A Brief History of the Development of Psychological Trauma   12
       A Description of Trauma   14
       Reactions to Trauma   16
   Coping and Its Outcomes   27
       Well-Being   27
       Coping   35

Post–Traumatic Growth　50
　　　The Concept of Pain and Suffering　52
　Missionary Trauma　60
　　　Missionary Related Trauma　60
　Conclusion　71

3. **Biblical Personalities and Trauma: Towards a Theology of Well-Being | 73**
　Introduction　73
　Biblical Personalities and Trauma　74
　　　Traumatic Accident　74
　　　Natural Trauma　75
　　　Violent Crime　76
　　　War Related Trauma　77
　　　Hostage Event　78
　　　Child/Adulthood Physical or Sexual Abuse　79
　　　Vicarious or Secondary Events　81
　　　Psychological/Physical Trauma　83
　　　Trauma Types　89
　　　Biblical Characters Presenting PTSD Symptomatology　89
　Biblical Personalities and Coping　96
　　　Trusting in God　96
　　　Asking Assistance from God　102
　　　Praise and Worship to God　107
　　　A Sense of Purpose/Call　111
　　　Working with God　112
　　　Expressing One's Complaints to God　114
　　　A Theology of Suffering　118
　　　Receiving Assistance from Family and Friends　120
　A Biblical Theology of Well-Being　122
　　　Trusting in God　123
　　　Asking Assistance from God　123
　　　Praise and Worship　124
　　　A Sense of Purpose/Call　125
　　　Working with God　125

Lamenting/Venting   126
　　　A Theology of Suffering   126
　　　Assistance from Friends and Family   127
　Conclusion   129

4. Contemporary Missionary Well-Being Regardless of Trauma | 130
　Introduction   130
　Methodology   131
　　　Research Design   131
　　　Selection of Participants   132
　　　Instruments   132
　　　Permission to Survey   137
　　　Ethical Agreement and Practice   137
　　　Research Procedure   138
　　　Data Processing and Analyses   138
　Results   139
　　　Preliminary Analysis   139
　　　Participant Characteristics   139
　　　How Many AGWM Missionaries Live through
　　　Traumatic Events?   145
　　　What Types of Trauma Do AGWM Missionaries Endure?   146
　　What Coping Skills Minimize the Negative Impact of Trauma in Missionaries Lives and Enhance AGWM Missionary Well-Being?   198
　　　　Adventurousness (ERS)   199
　　　　Social Resiliency (RAS)   199
　　　　General Resiliency (RS)   200
　　　　Call (CVQ)   200
　　　　Satisfaction with Life (SWLS)   202
　　　　Positive Religious Coping (B-RCOPE-P)   204
　　　　Negative Religious Coping (B-RCOPE-N)   205
　　　　Respondent Demographic and Training Factors   213
　　Discussion   215
　　　Study Limitations   218
　　　Future Research Suggestions   219
　　Conclusion   219

5. Conclusion: A Biblical Theory of Well-Being | 222
   Overview of Trauma and Coping Survey   222
   Overview of Biblical Theology of Well-Being   223
   A Biblical Theory of Well-Being   224
      Trust in God   224
      Asking God for Help   226
      Praise and Worship   227
      Sense of Purpose/Call   229
      Working with God   230
      Lamenting/Venting   231
      Theology of Suffering   232
      Assistance from Friends and Family   233
      Education/Training   237
   Conclusion   241

Appendix A: Biblical Character Trauma Overview | 243

Appendix B: Biblical Character Coping Overview | 245

Appendix C: PTSD Diagnoses for Biblical Characters Using the DSM-V Criteria | 247

Appendix D: Survey Trauma Explanation | 255

Appendix E: Trauma and Coping Survey | 257

Appendix F: Informed Consent | 291

Bibliography | 293

Tables

Table 2.1. Broad Outlines of Possible Developmental Shifts in Means of Coping | 41

Table 3.1. Biblical Personalities TEQ Trauma | 88

Table 4.1. Demographic Characteristics | 140

Table 4.2. Country of Service | 140

Table 4.3. Missionary Experience | 141

Table 4.4 Education | 142

Table 4.5. Percent of Missionaries Who Experienced Trauma by Category | 147

Table 4.6. Violent Crimes | 149

Table 4.7. Types of Violent Crimes | 154

Table 4.8. Traumatic Natural Disaster | 155

Table 4.9. Traumatic Accident | 157

Table 4.10 Danger of Losing Life | 161

Table 4.11. Received News of Mutilation, Serious Injury, or Violent/Unexpected Death of a Close Friend or Family Member | 164

Table 4.12. Traumatic Missionary Conflict | 167

Table 4.13. Traumatic Missionary Conflict | 168

Table 4.14. Vicarious Trauma | 171

Table 4.15. Living in a War Zone | 173

Table 4.16. Ages of Childhood Physical or Sexual Abuse | 176

Table 4.17 Childhood Physical or Sexual Abuse | 178

Table 4.18. Other Traumatic Events | 180

Table 4.19. Traumatic National Church Conflict | 187

Table 4.20. Traumatic National Church Conflict | 188

Table 4.21. Adult Physical Abuse | 190

Table 4.22 Traumatic Events that Cannot be Spoken | 192

Table 4.23. Adult Sexual Abuse | 194

Table 4.24. Taken Hostage | 196

Table 4.25. Pearson Correlation | 201

Table 4.26. Coping Scales Frequency | 202

Table 4.27. SWLS Pearson Correlation | 203

Table 4.28. B–RCOPE–N Pearson Correlation | 206

Table 4.29. B–RCOPE–P and B-RCOPE-N Pearson Correlation | 208

Table 4.30. PTSD Groupings and B-RCOPE-N ANOVA | 209

Table 4.31. PTSD and Trauma Groupings and B-RCOPE-N One-way Descriptives | 210

Table 4.32. Respondent Demographic and Training Factors in Relationship to PTSD Sum and Trauma Sum Variables Person Correlation | 214

Figures

Figure 1.1. Conceptual Flow Chart | 5

Figure 1.2. Conceptual Diagram of the Research | 6

Figure 3.1. A Biblical Theology of Well-being Produces Post-Traumatic Growth | 128

Figure 4.1. Missionary Training: Cross-Cultural Training | 142

Figure 4.2. Missionary Training: Trauma Management | 143

Figure 4.3. Missionary Training: Stress Management | 143

Figure 4.4. Missionary Training: Conflict Management | 144

Figure 4.5. Missionary Training: Helpfulness | 144

Figure 4.6. Comparison of Missionary Trauma Studies | 147

Figure 5.1. Trauma Comparison of Biblical Personalities and AGWM Missionaries | 224

Figure 5.2. Biblical Personalities and AGWM Missionaries Biblical Theory of Missionary Coping | 237

Preface

Statistics on missionary attrition conclude that one in fourteen missionaries leave the mission field each year and two-thirds of all missionary attrition is preventable.[1] Robert Bagley's research on missionary trauma finds that 94 percentof the missionaries surveyed reported experiencing traumatic events, most multiple times within the year surveyed.[2] Numerous studies, performed with mission agencies and missionaries still on field, reveal various causes for missionary attrition. However, not one report analyzed the correlation between trauma and how missionaries coped with these traumatic events.

This dissertation examined the effects of trauma and coping mechanisms of Assemblies of God World Missions (AGWM) missionaries in the seven regions (N= 1,907), to create a theoretical foundation for the prevention of attrition and to enable well-being and longevity among missionaries. This research is unique in that it investigated the traumatic events that both biblical personalities and missionaries suffered and analyzed the coping skills utilized to bring about well-being.

The research investigated the lives of 23 biblical characters and from their stories, developed a biblical theology of well-being. The key component of this biblical theology is trust in God. From this center, seven other coping mechanisms emerge forming petals that begins in trust and fosters that trust. From this research, a Biblical Theory of Well-being emerged that can assist missionaries to deal with the trauma they will face on field.

This study hypothesized that missionaries who suffered high amounts of trauma and showed low PTSD symptomology would be utilizing good coping techniques and those who underwent lower amounts of trauma yet displayed high PTSD symptoms would be employing poor or negative coping skills. The results of the survey found no statistical difference between Low Trauma/High PTSD and High Trauma/Low PTSD participants

---

1. Hay et al., *Worth Keeping*, 72.
2. Bagley. *Trauma and Traumatic Stress*, 104.

and their coping ability in the areas of adventurousness, social support, resiliency, calling, or positive religious coping. The majority possessed and implemented these skills while dealing with trauma. Yet, the survey did reveal statistical differences in the development of PTSD and the missionaries' satisfaction with life (optimism) and negative religious coping.

Acknowledgments

I LIKE TO JOKE that I started my doctoral journey because of fashion; I wanted a "blinged out" robe. The fashionista in me quickly faded away as I plunged into the academic rigor the doctoral program required. I could not have finished this passage without the help of some amazing people. First, I would like to thank my husband DeLonn. He is the only reason I have a PhD after my name. I never liked school, but he always encouraged me to continue my education while we lived in El Salvador. Then, when God led us to AGTS, he told me I had the ability to do graduate studies. I also want to thank my children, LaDawn and Chad, Jorel and Natalie, and Shayla and Brandon; and my grandchildren James Kalel, Blake Charles, Eli Timothy, Hunter Jacobsen, Judah Alexander, Zoey Lovie, and Ruth Jolie. You have been with me every step of the way, and in discouraging times always told me "Mom, you can do it!" Special thanks to Shayla for editing my papers and dissertation.

To all my doctoral professors, you have taught me so much and encouraged me at every opportunity. Dr. Joe Castleberry, thanks for being so kind to me with my first doctoral paper. I did not think I had it in me to write academically, then you told me "Val, that was a great paper, you have what it takes to earn a PhD." Those words have helped me through many a paper thereafter. I can never thank my committee chair Dr. Johan Mostert enough for his never-ending optimism, encouragement, and praise. Thanks to my other committee members Dr. Paul Lewis, who with patience and laughter helped me navigate biblical exegesis; and Dr. Melody Palm, whose Spirit-filled counseling classes taught me in words and example how to be a Spirit-led counselor. I also want to deeply thank Dr. Bryan Kelly. Without you, I would still be trying to figure out SPSS and putting all that data into the correct format. I saved the best thank you for last; "Lord, I felt your presence beside me through each class, each book I read, and each word I wrote. It is only because of the power of your Spirit that I am walking down the aisle, accepting my diploma, in my 'blinged out' robe."

Abbreviations

AG	Assemblies of God
AGWM	Assemblies of God World Missions
ASD	Acute Stress Disorder
B-RCOPE	The Brief Religious Coping Scale
CVQ	The Calling and Vocation Questionnaire
DV	Dependent Variable
DSM	The Diagnostic and Statistical Manual
EC	AGWM Executive Committee
ERS	The Ego-Resiliency Scale
GAS	General Adaptation Syndrome
HPA	Hypothalamic-pituitary-adrenocortical
IV	Independent Variable
PTG	Post-Traumatic Growth
PTS	Post-Traumatic Stress
PTSD	Post-Traumatic Stress Disorder
PTSDC	PTSD Checklist Civilian
RAS	The Resilience Appraisal Scale
RS	The Resiliency Scale
SOC	Sense of Coherence
SRG	Stress-Related Growth
STS	Secondary Traumatic Stress
SWLS	The Satisfaction with Life Scale
TEQ	Trauma Event Questionnaire

1

Introduction to the Problem

As I lay face down on the cold, hard floor of our missionary apartment in El Salvador, a man held a gun to the back of my head as his three companions took away our meager possessions. Thankfully, the babies stayed asleep despite the clothes thrown upon them as the robbers looked for treasure. The three informed the last man to "take care" of us. However, as he left, he whispered, "It is only because of your God" and shut the door. This story describes one of many traumatic events DeLonn, my husband, and I faced during our missionary career starting in 1984. Yet, we not once thought of leaving the field.

David Smith,[1] a new missionary to the country of Honduras, sat in his new missionary Speed the Light[2] car waiting for the light to change at a busy intersection. A man ran up to his driver's side car door, pointed a gun at him, and demanded the car. Smith opened the door and stepped out of the vehicle. The thief entered the automobile and drove away. The next week Smith and his family boarded a plane, leaving the land of their calling forever.

Trauma and life changes lace the missionary career. Missionaries change culture and locations frequently, leaving established friends and social structures behind. Often, they reside in areas of civil unrest and endure life-threatening situations. When these intercultural ministers experience natural disasters, they must go beyond simply surviving to assisting the national church and the local community in rescue, survival, and recovery efforts. Often these situations reoccur over the course of the missionary's career. Many missionaries can withstand multiple stressors and not only survive but thrive. Others, though, cannot manage the pressure, returning home with feelings of failure.

---

1. Name and location changed for privacy reasons.
2. Speed the Light is an Assemblies of God World Missions (AGWM) program where young people raise money to equip AGWM missionaries with ministry vehicles.

Attrition rates and reasons vary from study to study. Stanley Lindquist reports as high as 50 percent attrition among first term missionaries, mostly due to psychological trauma.[3] Keri Barnett et al. claims one career missionary in twenty (5.1 percent) leaves the field every year.[4] Rob Hay and associates lowers this number to one in fourteen.[5] These cross-cultural workers walk away from their career for different reasons. Researchers consider acceptable attrition to include retirement, issues with children or stateside family, change of jobs, or health problems. Preventable or unacceptable attrition constitutes lack of home support, interpersonal conflict (with nationals, co-workers, or agency), marital problems, emotional problems, lack of calling, inadequate pre-field equipping/training, poor cultural adaptation, unfulfilled expectations, and low self-esteem/stress.[6]

Wycliffe Bible Translators' research into missionary attrition reveals missionaries seldom admit the actual reason for leaving the field, and even though stress could be seen as an element in the decision-making process, it seldom receives recognition as the tangible motive.[7] Nevertheless, stress is a constant companion to all cross-cultural workers. When missionaries take the Holmes/Rahe Stress Scale, they average 600 points of stress per year. According to the scale, when a person reaches 300 points of stress, he or she has a high potential for physical illness.[8] Lindquist affirms, "The combination of relational, spiritual, and occupational problems can create an environment of stress, which may eventually cause the missionary to leave the field."[9] Joanne Schwandt and Glendon Moriarty maintain the stress and high demands of the missionary occupation, as well as familial, physical, emotional, and spiritual factors all contribute to increased attrition rates.[10] The missionary reality of survival while facing trauma causes chronic stress. When the stress becomes unmanageable, destructive symptomatic responses ensue.[11]

This chapter will offer a synopsis of the problem intended for doctoral research, connecting the relationship between trauma and missionary

---

3. Lindquist, *Prediction of Success*, 22.
4. Barnett et al., "Psychological and Spiritual Predictors," 27.
5. Hay et al., "Organizational Values," 216.
6. Allen, *Coping with Trauma*, 421; Jones, *Trauma and Grace*, 56; Taylor, "Challenging the Missions Stakeholders," 9–10.
7. Gardner, "Proactive Care of Missionary Personnel," 436–37.
8. Schwandt and Moriarty, "What Have the Past 25 Years," 320–21.
9. Lindquist, *Prediction of Success*, 320.
10. Schwandt and Moriarty, "What Have the Past 25 Years," 320–21.
11. Lindquist, "Mission Agency Screening," 243–44; Richardson, "Psychopathology in Missionary Personnel," 93.

coping skills in the lives of Assemblies of God World Missions (AGWM) missionaries. The association of the author's background and interest in the subject will be investigated, along with communicating the study's proposed purpose, significance, and goals. To direct the range of the research, the problem statement and research questions will be introduced. The delimitations of the study, definitions of terms, and the author's assumptions will complete the chapter.

Background

Called at age five, missions remain the focus of my life to this day. I wanted to help people, so perusing a bachelor's degree in psychology seemed a logical choice. DeLonn, my husband, and I served as AGWM missionaries since 1984. We spent 20 years in the country of El Salvador, living the first nine years in a civil war.

During those years, I experienced many traumatic occurrences involving war, gang-related violence, and natural disasters. Nontheless, traumatic events did not seem to bother me. I remained calm and did not exhibit Post-Traumatic Stress Disorder (PTSD). I thought this a normal response until I witnessed how fellow missionaries reacted to what I perceived as lesser traumatic episodes. For example, days after surviving an in-home armed robbery, a fellow missionary recounted the traumatization of his family when they had to move from one apartment to another in the same building.

The realization that people react differently to trauma made me curious as to what factors cause some missionaries to stay and others to leave the field. I contemplated that with the knowledge of these reasons, counseling intervention could assist missionaries broken by crisis to remain on field. I desire to support missionaries, not only through the normal stress of missionary life, but also in coping with inevitable traumatic situations. To prepare myself for this task, my post-graduate counseling Master's focused on trauma and PTSD.

Purpose

The purpose of this study is to identify a hypothetical basis for missionary well-being by examining the relationship between trauma and coping mechanisms among AGWM missionaries.

Problem Statement

The problem to be investigated in this study involves evaluating the experience and perceptions of trauma among AGWM missionaries and their coping abilities, by exploring the following three areas:

Research Questions

1. What defines human well-being in and through traumatic experiences in biblical/theological contexts, and in what ways does this inform today's contemporary missionary?
2. What psychological issues related to trauma and coping impact missionary health and well-being?
3. What coping skills minimize the negative impact of trauma in missionaries' lives and enhance AGWM missionary well-being?

Significance of the Study

The significance of this research will be as follows:

1. This study will relate to the call God placed in my heart to assist missionaries in times of trauma. The results of this research will better prepare me to educate missionaries for the trauma they might face in their field of service and give wise counsel after a crisis event.
2. Understanding how missionaries cope with traumatic experiences could possibly assist AGWM in promoting missionary well-being. Tools such as pre-field trauma education, crisis management, trauma response teams, and short-term counseling could be recommended to better fortify AGWM's member care system.
3. Much of the previous research about missionary trauma focused on the amount of trauma missionaries endured or the reasons for missionary stress. To date, little research has concentrated on coping skills leading toward missionary well-being. This coping component can lead toward better member care for missionaries on field.

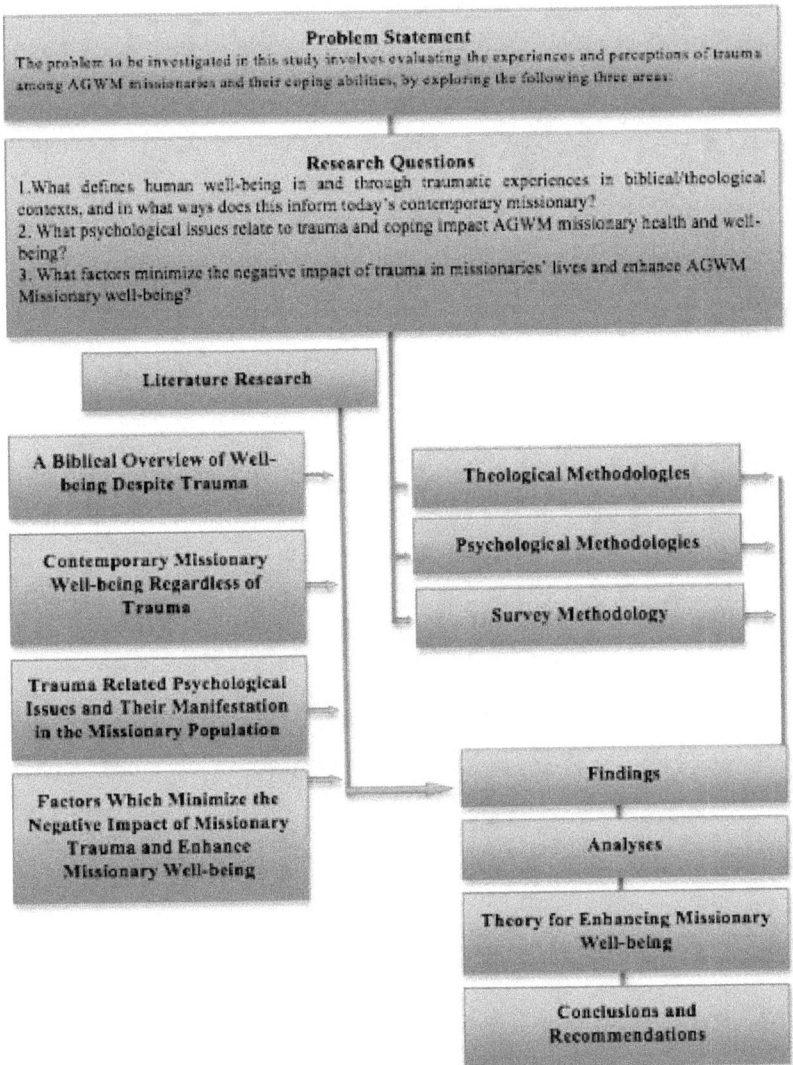

Figure 1.1. Conceptual Flow Chart of the Methodology

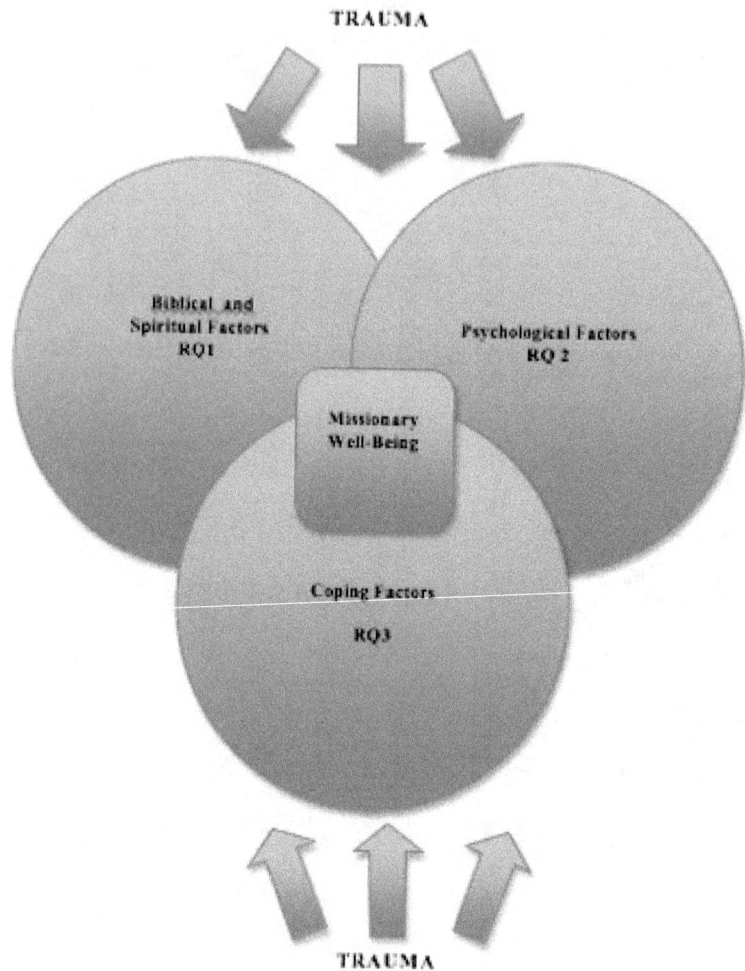

Figure 1.2. Conceptual Diagram of the Research

Goals

The goals of this study include:

- A description of appropriate coping that can assist missionaries as they struggle with trauma they may encounter while serving on field by: 1) articulating a theology of well-being as seen in the lives of biblical

characters; 2) identifying the secular and religious insights into trauma, coping and well-being; and 3) investigating the trauma AGWM missionaries endure and what coping skills they utilize to remain healthy in their field of service.
- The enumeration of a Biblical Theory of Well-being to fortify AGWM's member care system.

Limitations and Delimitations

In the survey research, I realize my personal ability to maintain well-being despite traumatic experiences and remain on field may bias my interpretation of the data. It may also be difficult to measure missionaries' levels of trauma and PTSD with what may be years separating them from the original field trauma. With no theology of well-being in existence, this research should be viewed as an endeavor at theological expression. Psychological research into the effects of trauma on the general population continues to expand; however, few studies touch the unique missionary population.

Missionary trauma can happen in any country and be caused by many variables. This research will be limited to missionaries serving with AGWM in the regions of Africa, Asia, Eurasia, Europe, International Ministries, and Latin American and Caribbean, and will focus on what missionaries consider traumatic experiences in their lives and how they coped with these events. This does not infer other types of trauma or crisis do not also produce missionary stress and attrition.

Definitions

A definition for each key term in this study follows:

Anxiety—"The apprehensive anticipation of future danger or misfortune accompanied by a feeling of worry, distress, and/or somatic symptoms of tension. The focus of anticipated danger may be internal or external."[12]

Assemblies of God (AG)—A Pentecostal denomination formed in the United States in 1914, as a cooperative fellowship of ministers and congregations, for the purpose of doctrinal integrity and missional activity.[13]

---

12. American Psychiatric Association, *Diagnostic and Statistical Manual*, 818.
13. Rance, *Empowered Call*, 7.

Assemblies of God World Missions (AGWM)[14]—Founded in the same 1914 meeting as the denomination, the AGWM continues its engagement in the missionary endeavor to evangelize the world through its Bible-based, Spirit-empowered, and Christ-centered message. AGWM's methodology stands on the four biblical pillars of: reaching, planting, training, and serving.[15]

Attrition—The English term as it applies to mission service refers simply to the departure from field service by missionaries, regardless of cause.[16]

Burnout—"A psychological strain representing a process of the depletion of personal coping resources in reaction to prolonged exposure to stress at work."[17]

Coping—"The ongoing transactional process between a person and his or environment, a process impacted by both cognitive appraisal and coping behavior."[18]

Depression (or depressivity)—A psychological disorder involving the body, mood, and thoughts. "Feelings of being intensely sad, miserable, and/or hopeless. Some patients describe an absence of feelings and/or guilt; feelings of inferior self-worth; and thoughts of suicide and suicidal behavior."[19]

Hardiness—This allows a person to take the crisis elements and, with control and commitment, can find meaning, personal development, purpose, and the belief that he or she has the power to change the outcome.[20]

Member care—Consists of the preparation, equipping, and empowering of missionaries for effective and sustainable life, ministry, and work. It addresses all aspects of missionary well-being (i.e., spiritual, emotional, relational, physical, and economic). The responsibility for member care resides with the sending agency, the sending church, the receiving church, leadership (home and field), the team, families, and the individual missionary themselves.[21]

---

14. Through the years, the missions' arm of the AG has been called the Foreign Missions Department (FMD), the Department of Foreign Missions (DFM), and most recently AGWM.

15. AGWM, "Assemblies of God World Missions."

16. Taylor, "Revisiting a Provocative Theme," 69.

17. Solcova and Kebza, "Personality Characteristics," 64.

18. Maynard et al., "Religious Coping Style," 65.

19. American Psychiatric Association, *Diagnostic and Statistical Manual*, 820.

20. Arndersson-Arnten, et al., "Influence of Affective Personality Type," 140–41; Eschleman et al., "Meta-Analytic Examination of Hardiness," 278.

21. Mobile Member Care, "Crisis Intervention."

INTRODUCTION TO THE PROBLEM

Post-Traumatic Growth (PTG)—"The positive change that the individual experiences as a result of the struggle with a traumatic event."[22]

Post-Traumatic Stress Disorder (PTSD)—Listed as a Trauma and Stressor-Related Disorder in the *Diagnostic and Statistical Manual of Mental Health Disorders* (DSM-V), PTSD affects a person's memory, emotional responses, intellectual processes, and nervous system due to one or more traumatic experiences. To diagnose PTSD the following criteria must be exhibited: exposure to one or more traumatic events, re-experiencing of the event, psychic numbing and avoidance, symptoms of increased arousal, and duration of symptoms for four weeks or longer.[23]

Resilience—"The ability . . . to maintain relatively stable, healthy levels of psychological and physical functioning . . . as well as the capacity for generative experiences and positive emotions."[24]

Stress—"The pattern of specific and nonspecific responses a person makes to stimulus events that disturb his or her equilibrium and tax or exceed his or her ability to cope."[25]

Trauma—Trauma involves a sudden and life-threatening event, which produces painful memories that overwhelms one's ability to cope.[26]

Well-being—"Well-being includes the presence of positive emotions and moods (e.g., contentment, happiness), the absence of negative emotions (e.g., depression, anxiety), satisfaction with life, fulfillment and positive functioning . . . In simple terms, well-being can be described as judging life positively and feeling good."[27]

Assumptions

With the available data indicating the quantity of traumatic events missionaries experience, and the high attrition rates reported by mission agencies, I assume a correlation between High Trauma/Low PTSD and good coping mechanisms. A missionary's success on field directly links with his or her resilience and well-being; hence, proper training and member care will aid in missionary retention. This research will ascertain the validity of these assumptions.

22. Calhoun and Tedeschi, *Facilitating Posttraumatic Growth*, 17.
23. American Psychiatric Association, *Diagnostic and Statistical Manual*, 217–80.
24. Bonanno, "Grief, Trauma, and Resilience," 42.
25. American Psychiatric Association, *Diagnostic and Statistical Manual*, 829.
26. Figley and Figley, "Stemming the Tide of Trauma," 173.
27. Center for Disease Control and Prevention, "Health-Related Quality of Life."

2

Trauma and Coping

Psychological and Coping Issues Impacting Missionary Well-Being

Introduction

THE BIRTH OF THE current discussion on trauma happened between the years 1866 to 1870 when Jean-Martin Charcot witnessed "the effects on the nervous system of powerful disturbances following railroad accidents."[1] Yet, people experienced trauma throughout history.[2] The Bible recounts the traumatic stories of many of its principle characters. The first recorded missionary of the gospel, the Apostle Paul, dealt with many obstacles during his missionary service. Paul writes about being overworked, imprisoned, sleep deprived, and starved. He lacked adequate clothing, faced harsh physical elements, and had near-death experiences from: beatings, stoning, robberies, and shipwrecks. Paul received threats from believers and non-believers alike (2 Cor 11:23–29).

People currently continue to experience traumatic events in their lives. One study reports that 39.1 percent of its North American respondents witnessed one or more traumatic events.[3] Whereas, a study of West African missionaries shows that missionaries go through crises and trauma more than the general United States population.[4] Robert Bagley's study on missionary trauma realizes that 94 percent of the missionaries surveyed reported experiencing traumatic events, most multiple times within the survey year.[5] When stress levels from these accumulated incidents exceed a person's coping abilities and resilience mental breakdown will likely occur.[6] Dorothy Plackett,

---

1. Fassin and Rechtman, *Empire of Trauma*, 30.
2. van der Kolk et al., "History of Trauma in Psychiatry," 3.
3. Breslau et al., "Traumatic Events," 217.
4. Carr and Schaefer, "Trauma and Traumatic Stress," 279.
5. Bagley, "Trauma and Traumatic Stress Among Missionaries." 104.
6. Carr and Schaefer, "Trauma and Traumatic Stress," 280.

missionary William Carey's first wife, suffered jealous delusions on field, which remains a well-documented case in point.[7] These types of situations can cause missionaries to give up and leave the field prematurely.

Attrition among contemporary career missionaries is disheartening. Statistics confirm one out of twenty missionaries return home each year and early prevention can stop two-thirds of all missionary attrition.[8] The missionary lifestyle often includes such stressors as: cultural adjustment, loneliness, overwork, harsh living conditions, lack of recognition, high mobility, and multiple separations in conjunction with crisis or trauma such as: war, robbery, and national disasters.[9] Reasons for the exodus may vary, but most stem from stress related disorders, resulting from unresolved stressful or traumatic experiences.[10] Coping abilities greatly influence a person's capability to overcome cultural stressors and trauma.

People cope with stress and trauma in different ways mainly because of diverse personality types, previous coping experience, or social support.[11] One's culture also influences how he or she will respond and interact with crises and stress.[12] This chapter will examine the historical growth of the psychological and physical issues of trauma and coping, explore the understanding of secular and biblical suffering, and how these subjects interfere or assist with missionary well-being.

Trauma and Its Outcomes

People cannot live in this world without encountering one or more traumatic incidents during their lifetime. Events such as these often leave the victim feeling depressed, anxious, and/or unable to concentrate. These symptoms and others can last for many years.[13] Authors, including Homer, William Shakespeare, and Charles Dickens noted the effects of trauma on human behavior.[14] Nineteenth-century psychologists argued on how trauma affected the human body. Some considered traumatic behaviors derived

---

7. Schwandt and Moriarty, "What Have the Past 25 Years," 317.
8. Barnett et al., "Psychological and Spiritual Predictors," 27.
9. Schwandt and Moriarty, "What Have the Past 25 Years," 321.
10. Grant, "Trauma in Missionary Life," 72–73.
11. Hobfoll, "Influence of Culture 2001," 352; Wright, "Recognizing and Understanding Troubled Children," 33.
12. McNally, "Panic and Posttraumatic Stress Disorder," 131.
13. Bonanno, "Resilience in the Face of Potential Trauma," 135; Brunet et al., "Effects of Initial Trauma Exposure," 97.
14. Friedman et al., "Classification of Trauma," 738.

from the heart, calling these actions Soldier's Heart, DaCosta's Syndrome, or Neurocirulatory Asthenia. Others focused on the nervous system naming the disorder Railway Spine or Shell Shock. Still others contemplated the psychological bases of these disruptive behaviors branding such conduct as Nostalgia or Traumatic Neurosis.[15] The Diagnostic and Statistical Manuals (DSM) I through II deemed the reaction to extreme stress and trauma to be temporary and reversible naming this clinical condition Gross Stress Reaction.[16] With the extreme trauma of the Vietnam War, many clinicians needed a new diagnostic construct for soldiers suffering from "severer, chronic and sometimes irreversible syndromes following exposure to catastrophic events."[17] Thus, the DSM-III through V proposed the Post-Traumatic Stress Disorder (PTSD) diagnostic criteria used today.

Whatever type or context of the trauma, a person will react in various ways. He or she can respond with psychological problems such as: anxiety, stress, culture shock, burnout, depression, and PTSD. This section will survey the development of trauma and the possible byproducts of this life-threatening crisis giving a foundation of understanding as to how these issues affect missionary life.

A Brief History of the Development of Psychological Trauma

Throughout history most people understood the physical effects of traumatic events. The pain and suffering of open wounds or disease could easily be seen, and, with time and medical assistance, this distress could most often be healed. The comprehension of psychological trauma, however, has been a long and sometimes painful process. Charcot became interested in the accounts of London doctors about people's reactions to train accidents in the years of 1866 to 1870.[18] Doctors and psychologists of the day believed the hysteria developed from small legions on the spine caused by the accident, thereby calling this syndrome Railway Spine or Railway Brain.[19] Scholars report that Charcot, through his study of traumatized patients, developed a theory of what he called hysteron-traumatic auto suggestion. He saw that the trauma put the victims into a hypoid state, much

---

15. Friedman et al., "Classification of Trauma," 738; van der Kolk et al., "History of Trauma in Psychiatry," 47.
16. Friedman et al., "Classification of Trauma," 738–39.
17. Friedman et al., "Classification of Trauma," 739.
18. Fassin and Rechtman, *Empire of Trauma*, 30.
19. van der Kolk et al., "History of Trauma in Psychiatry," 48.

like hypnosis thus defining for the first time the dissociative complications resulting from shocking incidents.[20]

Researchers chronicle the history of trauma through the significant discoveries of Herman Oppenhelm, James J. Putman, Edouard Stierlin, Pierre Janet, Sigmund Freud, Abram Kardiner, Chaim Shatan, and Robert Lifton. Oppenhelm (1889), a German psychologist, suggested that delicate molecular deviations in the central nervous system created traumatized people's functional complications and named the condition Trauma Neurosis.[21] Putnam (1881), a neurologist from the United States, understood psychic traumatization to be when a person regresses toward a primitive, thoughtful, simplified, and reactive ways of living life.[22] In Switzerland, psychiatrist Stierlin (1909) became the first person to research disaster psychiatry. He found that a substantial number of people who survived traumatic events developed enduring post-traumatic stress symptomatology.[23]

Janet (1887) became one of the most influential psychiatrists in trauma when he developed the idea that because of traumatic emotional upheaval a person became unable to connect their terrifying experience with prevailing rational patterns. He found that the victim reacted to memories of the trauma as violently as he or she did to the original event. Psychology slowly forgot his extensive research in memory, trauma, and dissociative treatment. Yet, psychologists reestablished his legacy and included it with modern knowledge of PTSD in the 1980s.[24] Freud at first agreed with Charcot and Janet's understanding of trauma's dissociative scheme but later Freud determined that hysterical memory disruptions did not stem from the inability to assimilate new information into old patterns, but "from the active repression of conflict-laden sexual and aggressive ideas and impulses, centering around the Oedipal crisis at about age five."[25]

Trauma research developed quickly because of the horrors and trauma of war. First World War doctors diagnosed traumatized soldiers exhibiting irregular or fast heart palpitations, chest pain, or shortness of breath as Soldier's Heart. If military men showed symptoms of fatigue, tremors, or ticks physicians identified they had Shell Shock.[26] At the beginning of

20. van der Kolk et al., "History of Trauma in Psychiatry," 49–50.
21. Fassin and Rechtman, *Empire of Trauma*, 31; van der Kolk et al., "History of Trauma in Psychiatry," 48.
22. van der Kolk et al., "History of Trauma in Psychiatry," 49.
23. van der Kolk et al., "History of Trauma in Psychiatry," 50–51.
24. van der Kolk et al., "History of Trauma in Psychiatry," 52–53.
25. As stated in van der Kolk et al., "History of Trauma in Psychiatry," 54.
26. Jones and Wesley, "Psychological Trauma," 219.

World War II, Kardiner reassessed his unsuccessful psychoanalytic theory of war neuroses and, in 1941, published his findings in *The Traumatic Neuroses of War*. In this work, he defined PTSD and, even though he realized the healing power of psychotherapy, he also warned of the hazards and complications the soldiers underwent to speak of these terrifying events.[27] In the Second World War, medics most often considered the psychological trauma of war caused ulcers.[28] During the Vietnam War, two prominent New York psychiatrists, Shatan and Lifton started what they called rap groups to help returning veterans talk about their war experiences. Rap groups became very successful and spread throughout the United States. Shatan and Lifton combined what they learned from these war vets and research on Holocaust, burn, and accident survivors and made a list of the 27 most common traumatic neuroses. These later became the start of the PTSD classification system of the DSM-III.[29]

A Description of Trauma

Trauma involves a sudden and life-threatening event, which produces painful memories that overwhelms one's ability to cope.[30] These events can be "unexpected, perceived as undesirable and uncontrollable, out of the ordinary, and threatening to one's life and general well-being."[31] Bessel van der Kolk deems psychological trauma as, "the loss of faith that there is order and continuity in life" which "results in a state of helplessness."[32] The DSM-V defines a traumatic stressor to be, "Any event (or events) that may cause or threaten death, serious injury, or sexual violence to an individual, a close family member, or a close friend."[33] Traumatic events can destroy a person's trust in the world, other people, and even his or her self-identity.[34]

Trauma does not go away. Its memory alters the course of the individual's life and how he or she interacts with family and society.[35] The way

---

27. van der Kolk et al., "History of Trauma in Psychiatry," 56–58.
28. Jones and Wesley, "Psychological Trauma," 219.
29. van der Kolk et al., "History of Trauma in Psychiatry," 61.
30. Beste, *God and the Victim*, 5; Figley and Figley, "Stemming the Tide of Trauma Systemically," 173.
31. Calhoun and Tedeschi, "Posttraumatic Growth," 216.
32. van der Kolk, "Psychological Consequences," 31.
33. American Psychiatric Association, *Diagnostic and Statistical Manual*, 830.
34. Bonanno et al., "Coping Flexibility and Trauma," 117; Brison, *Aftermath*. 40; Grant, "Trauma in Missionary Life," 73.
35. Beste, *God and the Victim*, 5; Rambo, *Spirit and Trauma*, 2; Wise, "Introduction," 1–3.

a person perceives and recounts the traumatic event determines his or her role as a casualty or survivor.[36] Jennifer Beste defines four categories of factors that will determine how traumatized a person will become. These include: 1) the nature of the trauma, its length of time, how often it happens, and severity; 2) the proneness of the individual to PTSD (e.g., one's biological nature, genetic susceptibility to traumatic stress, psychological issues, how the trauma affected the central nervous system, previous occurrences, and the pre-trauma developmental level, power of emotional defenses, and awareness of self); 3) one's family support and dynamics; and 4) the person's cultural, societal, and political framework.[37]

Types and degrees of trauma vary from Type I trauma (single-blow events) to Type IV trauma (many different types of traumatic incidents over a life span). Car accidents, fires, tornadoes, hurricanes, burglary, rape, the sudden death of a family member, or homicide constitute Type I trauma. This trauma type can also occur because of the event happening to a person's friend or family member (also known as secondary or vicarious trauma). It usually transpires only once. Type II trauma comprises war, or sexual, physical, and emotional abuse, or if several Type 1 incidents strike repeatedly over a short time span in the past but then stopped. Type III trauma consists of trauma that continues to happen such as racism or discrimination. The cumulative effects of traumatic victimization over a life span produces Type IV trauma.[38]

Trauma can be classified into two other categories, natural trauma and human-made trauma. Natural trauma can be witnessed in acts of God: earthquakes, tornadoes, avalanches, floods, fires, hurricanes, and volcanic eruptions. A person's reaction to this one-time crisis depends on the extent of exposure to the event. Human-made trauma can include: violent crimes, traffic accidents, war, political violence, domestic violence, and child abuse.[39] Trauma can also be defined in terms of physical (i.e., body injury), psychological (i.e., an incident that causes strong emotional reactions), social (i.e., oppressive social conditions; e.g. war, poverty, discrimination, violence), historical (i.e., past personal or social violence), ongoing (i.e., daily violence), and vicarious or secondary trauma (e.g., trauma experienced by mental health helpers called Compassion Fatigue).[40] Contact with profound traumatic in-

36. Jobson and O'Kearney, "Cultural Differences in Personal Identity," 96.

37. Beste, *God and the Victim*, 6–7.

38. Allen, *Coping with Trauma*, 7; Figley, *Helping Traumatized Families*, 7; Floyd, *Crisis Counseling*, loc. 435–44; Ibrahim et al., "Dynamics of Posttraumatic Growth," 122.

39. Allen, *Coping with Trauma*, 13–16.

40. Wise, "Introduction," 3–4.

cidents can produce an immediate and long-term (up to two generations) negative impact on the person, the family, and the society.[41]

Alexander McFarlane attempts to grade exposure to trauma. He ranks trauma starting with the lowest exposure and moving to the highest exposure as: "awareness of destruction and loss, safe by chance–guilt, duration of exposure, absence of control, dissociation, risk of injury, panic, threat to life, witnessing injury, actual injury, survival by freak circumstances, and seeing death." He considers this ranking a good start but understands that it must be contemplated considering a large range of variables.[42] Most certainly, the type and one's exposure to trauma will determine how he or she will react and what kind of psychological functionality will follow.

Reactions to Trauma

When trauma happens, people react in many ways. Trauma, because of its sudden and unexpected nature, will produce stress. This stress can cause a person to become fearful of how this traumatic event will change his or her future or if it will happen again thus creating anxiety. As stress and anxiety wear on a person, burnout, or depression can occur. These reactions can be a healthy way to work through trauma, however, if a person becomes stuck in feelings of stress, anxiety, and depression, he or she will be diagnosed as having PTSD.

Stress

People, no matter their career, experience stress many times during their lifetime. Anything that puts conflicting or heavy demands on a person produces stress. A Harvard physician-researcher, Walter Cannon, studied the stress response at the beginning of the twentieth century. Yet, Hans Selye became known as the "Father of Stress" with his research into the predictable response to stress, which he termed the General Adaptation Syndrome (GAS).[43] This syndrome has three distinctive stages: an alarm reaction, resistance, and exhaustion.[44]

---

41. Dybdahl, "Psychosocial Assistance to Civilians in War," 134.
42. McFarlane, "Severity of the Trauma," 41.
43. Quick et al., *Stress and Challenge*, 24.
44. Monat and Lazarus, "Stress and Coping," 5–6.

Stricts, the Latin word for stress, means "to be drawn tight."[45] The human body contains a defense system allowing one to cope with real or imagined threatening events. The perception of danger floods the body with the catecholamine, epinephrine, and norepinephrine. Stress also employs the hypothalamic-pituitary-adrenocortical (HPA) axis that discharges corticosteroids, causing heightened arousal to determine if one should stand and attack (fight), or run away (flight).[46]

The DSM-V defines stress as, "The pattern of specific and nonspecific responses a person makes to stimulus events that disturb his or her equilibrium and tax or exceed his or her ability to cope."[47] Robert Woolfolk and Frank Richardson describe stress to be, "a perception of threat or expectation of future discomfort that arouses, alerts, or otherwise activates the organism."[48] Other researchers explain a stressful situation as when a person becomes unbalanced with his or her environment because of perceived overly demanding life conditions.[49] Humans experience stress, yet frequently they do not comprehend why.

Stress has three basic types: systemic or physiological (i.e., disruptions of the tissue systems), psychological (i.e., thought processes that lead to assessment of the danger), and social (i.e., the disruption of the family or social system).[50] It is not only a function of the environment but also the "internal characteristics of the individual (whether psychological, hormonal, or immunological)."[51] Psychological stress has two main properties: 1) anticipating—expecting future danger, and 2) cognition dependence—learning, judgment, perception, thought, and memory.[52]

Stress can be understood in terms of length of time and severity. One can comprehend chronic stress as a continuing problem found in the surrounding environment (i.e., natural or social) or the individual (e.g., long-term illness, prior traumatization, genetic predisposition). This stress also occurs through daily minor stressors within a short time frame (e.g., arguments,

---

45. Wright, *Beating the Blues*, 93.
46. Taylor, "Affiliation and Stress," 88; Wright, *Beating the Blues*, 93.
47. American Psychiatric Association, *Diagnostic and Statistical Manual*, 829.
48. Woolfolk and Frank Richardson, *Stress, Sanity, and Survival*, 8.
49. Abu-Raiya and Pargament, "Religious Coping Among Diverse Religions," 25; Appley and Trumbull, "On the Concept of Psychological Stress," 58; Carlson, "Stress and Coping Approach," 292; Lazarus and Folkman, *Stress, Appraisal, and Coping*, 21.
50. Monat and Lazarus, "Stress and Coping," 1–2.
51. Lazarus, *Psychological Stress*, 42.
52. Lazarus, *Psychological Stress*, 83.

family problems, traffic jams, financial problems).[53] A person exposed to chronic stress increases his or her possibility for illness.[54]

Some people adapt to stress better than others because of personality, ways of thinking, socially and somatically based resources, lifestyle, social connectedness, relationship competence and/or physical health,[55] yet most appraise stress into four general types: "benign, threats of future stressors, harm or loss, and challenges."[56] Richard Lazarus and Susan Folkman's cognitive theory of stress identifies three types of stress appraisals: primary, secondary, and reappraisal. Primary appraisal considers whether the stressor is irrelevant, benign-positive, or stressful (i.e., harm/loss [danger already happening], threat [future possible problems], challenge [good outcomes]).[57] Secondary appraisal deems what should be done in the situation. Reappraisal changes the first appraisal because of new information.[58]

Stress presents in a myriad of ways. The perception of not being in control is a major source of stress. This can be loss of control in major life events (e.g., death of loved one, accidents, natural disasters) or minor incidences (e.g., waiting in line, riding in the passenger seat, losing things).[59] People under extreme stress can present many potentially long-term psychological conditions (e.g., depression, pathological grief, and phobias).[60] Extreme stress "affects both acute and chronic adaptation: it permanently alters how an organism deals with its environment on a day-to-day basis, and it interferes with how it copes with subsequent acute stress."[61] Cultural stress or cultural shock happens when a person does not know the rules of a new culture.[62] Culture can be viewed as a social game with unwritten rules only the members of the society comprehend and uphold.[63]

---

53. Aldwin, "Stress and Coping Across the Lifespan," 18; Norris, "Epidemiology of Trauma," 416; van der Kolk, "Psychological Consequences," 10–12.

54. Eschleman et al., "Meta-Analytic Examination." 280; Schlotz et al., "Perceived Stress Reactivity Scale," 1; Taylor, "How Psychosocial Resources Enhance Health," 65.

55. Kebza and Solcova, "Trends in Resilience Theory," 17; Zwickel, *Workplace Stress*, 11.

56. Aldwin, "Stress and Coping Across the Lifespan," 17; Arndersson-Arnten et al., "Influence of Affective Personality Type," 140.

57. Lazarus and Folkman, *Stress, Appraisal, and Coping*, 53.

58. Gardner et al., "Cognitive Therapy and Behavioral Coping," 138.

59. Mukherjee and Alpert, "Overview of Psychological Interventions," 5; Tan, *Experiencing God's Peace*, 162; Wright, *Beating the Blues*, 104.

60. Shalev, "Stress Versus Traumatic Stress," 94.

61. van der Kolk, "Body Keeps the Score," 223.

62. Kraft, *Communication Theory*, 103.

63. Hofstede and Hofstede, *Cultures and Organizations Software of the Mind*, 4.

When stressful challenges overwhelm a person, he or she can be diagnosed with Acute Stress Disorder (ASD). With many of the same criteria as PTSD, ASD should only last two days to four weeks after which PTSD should be identified.[64] Even with the commonality of acute stress in these traumatic situations, the stress response remains short lived because most people naturally adapt to their experience.[65] Not all stress is negative; human beings need a small amount of pressure to maintain momentum. In manageable amounts, stress can promote growth and personal development.[66] Good or bad, everyone perceives the diverse sources of stress uniquely.

Anxiety

The threat of impending trauma causes a state of arousal called anxiety.[67] The DSM-V describes anxiety as "The apprehensive anticipation of future danger or misfortune accompanied by a feeling of worry, distress, and/or somatic symptoms of tension. The focus of anticipated danger may be internal or external."[68] Charles Spielberger (1972) defines anxiety as "an undesirable emotional state characterized by subjective feelings of stress, apprehension, and worry, and by arousal of the autonomic nervous system" while Timothy Leary (1982) identifies it as "a cognitive-affective response characterized by physiological arousal and apprehensions regarding potentially negative outcomes that the individual perceives as pending."[69] Many view anxiety and stress as synonymous, yet Myron Loss explains that stress results from external pressures whereas internal tension produces anxiety.[70] These external pressures create the variable of uncertainty, which many consider the antecedent of anxiety.[71] Momentary anxiety assists people readying them to cope when life becomes unpredictable, uncontrollable, and unfamiliar. Chronic anxiety, on the other hand, hinders managing life's chaotic situations.[72] Therapists diagnose

---

64. Bryant, "Acute Stress Disorder," 17–18.

65. Bryant, "Acute Stress Disorder," 16.

66. Aldwin, *Stress, Coping, and Development*, 270; Rassieur, *Stress Management for Ministers* 126; Wright, *Beating the Blues*, 94.

67. Allen, *Coping with Trauma*, 51–52; Carr, "Crisis Intervention for Missionaries," para. 5; Dulin and Passmore, "Avoidance of Potentially Traumatic Stimuli," 298.

68. American Psychiatric Association, *Diagnostic and Statistical Manual*, 818.

69. Abbassi and Stacks, "Culture and Anxiety," 26.

70. Jones, *Psychology of Missionary Adjustment*, 31.

71. Monat et al., "Anticipatory Stress and Coping Reactions," 237.

72. Allen, *Coping with Trauma*, 51–52.

PTSD by looking for anxiety symptomatology (i.e., Cluster E: increased arousal, hypervigilance, and/or fear of death).[73]

An individual's personality attributes to his or her level of anxiety. People inclined to view life negatively (i.e., negative affectivity or Type D personality) tend to exhibit more "distress, anxiety, irritability, pessimism, and worry."[74] Type D people also display "a negative view of oneself, the world, the future, and others."[75] This trait anxiety before a traumatic event predisposes a person to exhibit higher post-traumatic symptoms.[76] Magnus Larsson, Martin Backstrom, and Aki Johanson concluded that people with trait anxiety have, "a disposition to experience anxiety," that results in a higher "risk-factor of post-trauma symptoms of anxiety and insomnia when exposed to traumatic situations."[77] Nevertheless, a self-fulfilling affective personality views the worst situations with a positive optimism and a high estimation of his or her ability to cope.[78] The personality factor of neuroticism closely mimics the same psychological and emotional states as trait anxiety (i.e., anxiety, hostility, depression, impulsiveness, and self-consciousness).[79] How a person innately views the world and his or her circumstances often defines his or her reactions when the anticipated trauma actually happens.

Feelings of apprehension and anxiety are universal; however, the way a person experiences and manifests fretfulness depends not only on his or her personality, but also on his or her cultural upbringing.[80] Besides these internal factors, external traumatic experiences from a one's past can predispose him or her to anxiety when exposed to critical events.[81] Gender also affects people's anxiety levels. Research indicates that women fall prey to stress and worry more than men, regardless of culture.[82] People do not like the feeling of nervousness and try to avoid or minimize its effects. Anxiety buffers

---

73. Bryant, "Acute Stress Disorder," 17–18; Carr, "Trauma and Post-Traumatic Stress Disorder," 249–50.

74. Pulley and Wakefield, *Building Resiliency*, 681.

75. Polman et al., "Type D Personality," 681–82.

76. Larsson et al., "Interaction Between Baseline Trait Anxiety and Trauma Exposure," 447; Schottenbauer et al., "Religious Coping Research," 501.

77. Larsson et al., "Interaction Between Baseline Trait Anxiety and Trauma Exposure," 447, 449.

78. Arndersson-Arnten et al., "Influence of Affective Personality Type," 159–60.

79. Schlotz et al., "Perceived Stress Reactivity Scale," 2.

80. Abbassi and Stacks, "Culture and Anxiety," 27.

81. Regehr et al., "Previous Trauma Exposure," 681; Richards et al., "Religious and Spiritual Assessment of Trauma Survivors," 92–93.

82. Abbassi and Stacks, "Perceived Stress Reactivity Scale," 34.

include emotional numbing, hyper-vigilance, avoidance, religious zealotry, social withdrawal, or the use of drugs and alcohol.[83]

During a traumatic event, one study witnessed that between 10–25 percent of survivors responded with "inappropriate" behavior, which included anxiety (others include: hysterical crying or screaming, marked confusion, and a break with reality).[84] Traumatic incidents can include the death of loved ones that can open the door to separation anxiety.[85] Trauma victims can display a variety of psychological disorders (e.g., panic disorder and major depressive disorder) including generalized anxiety disorder (i.e., excessive anxiety and worry lasting at least six months).[86]

Burnout

First introduced in the early 1970s by Herbert Freudenberger, burnout became a common word for stress. Nevertheless, burnout and stress constitute two different issues. Stress involves a universal problem all of humanity experiences at some point in life. Burnout, on the other hand, occurs with highly committed and motivated idealists who work with other human beings.[87] Called a nervous breakdown in years past, burnout will produce physical and emotional exhaustion.[88]

Freudenberger originally labeled burnout as, "a state of fatigue or frustration brought about by devotion to a cause, way of life, or relationship that failed to produce the expected reward."[89] Gerald Corey et al. defined burnout to be "a state of physical, emotional, intellectual, and spiritual exhaustion characterized by feelings of helplessness and hopelessness"[90] and Richard James and Burl Gilliland describe it as a, "state of physical, mental and emotional exhaustion caused by long-term involvement in emotionally demanding situations. It is accompanied by an array of symptoms including physical depletion, feelings of helplessness and hopelessness, disillusionment, negative self-concept, and negative attitudes toward work, people,

---

83. Benight, "Understanding Human Adaptation," 5.
84. Wilkinson, "Management and Treatment of Disaster Victims," 175.
85. Raphael, "Interaction of Trauma and Grief," 35.
86. American Psychiatric Association, *Diagnostic and Statistical Manual,* 222; McFarlane, "Severity of the Trauma," 35.
87. Pines, "Burnout," 387; Tan, *Rest,* 180–81.
88. Quick et al., *Stress and Challenge at the Top,* 29.
89. Freudenberger, *Burnout,* 13.
90. Corey et al., *Issues and Ethics in the Helping Profession,* 60.

and life itself."[91] Burnout happens when a person feels hopeless or ineffective in dealing with his or her profession due to job related stressors.[92] Long-term, chronic stress can also lead to burnout.[93]

A multifaceted process, burnout permeates five areas of life: emotional, spiritual, physical, intellectual, and social.[94] Normally, the first physical symptom of burnout is total fatigue. Other bodily indicators can comprise: headaches, recurrent and persistent colds, ulcers, sleep issues, weight gain or loss, gastrointestinal problems, and the returning of old medical concerns. Intellectually a person loses sharpness in problem solving; emotionally he or she becomes negative, cynical, and depressed; socially he or she feels isolated; and spiritually he or she loses meaning to life.[95] The person feels total hopelessness and cannot effectively complete his or her work.[96] Burnout slowly creeps into people's lives to the point that many have problems distinguishing its symptomatology from what they now consider normal feelings.[97] It can also mask other psychological disorders.

People can be genetically susceptible to burnout. One's personality influences his or her "attitudes (work engagement), behaviors (coping), and 'typical' environmental variables (social support)" which may or may not lead to burnout.[98] During traumatic events, especially natural disasters, people who work with the victims can develop Compassion Fatigue or Secondary Traumatic Stress (STS), which contributes to burnout.[99] In most cases, trauma workers develop burnout instead of Compassion Fatigue or STS.[100]

---

91. James and Gilliland, *Crisis Intervention Strategies*, 480.

92. Craig and Sprang, "Compassion Satisfaction," 322; Devilly et al., "Vicarious Trauma," 383; Solcova and Kebza, "Personality Characteristics Related to Resilience," 64.

93. Floyd, *Crisis Counseling*, loc. 1125; Zwickel, *Workplace Stress*, 143.

94. Wright, *Beating the Blues*, 113–14.

95. Craig and Sprang, "Compassion Satisfaction," 322; Pines, "Burnout," 387; Polman et al., "Type D Personality," 683; Schaefer, "Resources for Effective Support: Personal Resilience," loc. 2428; Wright, *Beating the Blues*, 113–14.

96. Craig and Sprang, "Compassion Satisfaction," 322.

97. Floyd, *Crisis Counseling*, loc. 2948; Hobfoll, *Stress, Culture, and Community*, 196.

98. Maas and Spinath, "Personality and Coping with Professional Demands," 378; Papousek and Genullter, "Don't Take an X for a U," 16.

99. Collins and Long, "Too Tired to Care?," 19; Deighton et al., "Factors Affecting Burnout and Compassion Fatigue," 65; Maloney, "Critical Incident Stress Debriefing," 111.

100. Devilly et al., "Vicarious Trauma," 383.

Yet, burnout differs from Compassion Fatigue in that Compassion Fatigue and STS produce secondary symptoms of PTSD.[101]

Depression

The most frequent mental health problem worldwide is depression. Jon Allen states, "Anxiety is a state of readiness to cope (take flight), whereas depression is a state of giving up the attempt to cope-in effect, a kind of collapse."[102] The DSM-V defines depression as, "A psychological disorder involving the body, mood, and thoughts."[103] For clinical depression to be diagnosed, symptoms must present daily for at least two weeks and consist of: depressed mood, fatigue, feelings of worthlessness/guilt, insomnia or hypersomnia, impaired concentration, diminished interest in life, irritability, restlessness, wanting to die, and weight loss. Depression produces the highest risk of suicide than any other psychological disorder.[104]

Biologically, depression seems to occur in people with a smaller hippocampus, which consequently has fewer receptors for the brain calming chemical serotonin. Depressed people also seem to produce more cortisol (i.e., the stress hormone) than the non-depressed. Cortisol has a toxic effect on the hippocampus and can cause depression. Women, usually during puberty, tend to develop depression more often than men.[105]

Biology alone, however, is not the only contributing factor for depression. Personality can also play a role. One study associated higher levels of depression with people who have a self-destructive personality type (i.e., showing low positive and high negative affect).[106] A stressing life event plays a critical role in the development of this multifactorial disorder; 75 percent of all cases of depression include an environmental stressor (i.e., a traumatic event).[107] Karen Carr suggests that normal

---

101. Craig and Sprang, "Compassion Satisfaction," 322.

102. Allen, *Coping with Trauma*, 62.

103. American Psychiatric Association, *Diagnostic and Statistical Manual*, 820.

104. Carr, "Resources for Effective Support: Normal Reactions after Trauma," loc. 1581; Floyd, *Crisis Counseling,* loc. 1278; Jensma, "Critical Incident Intervention," 132; Minirth and Meier, *Happiness is a Choice*, 25–26; WebMD, "Depression Health Center".

105. Carr, "Resources for Effective Support: Normal Reactions after Trauma," loc. 1335; WebMD, "Depression Health Center"; Young and Korszun, Sex, "Trauma, Stress Hormones and Depression," 23–26.

106. Arndersson-Arnten, et al., "Influence of Affective Personality," 159–60; Frankl, *Man's Search for Meaning*, 160.

107. Balswick and Balswick, *Families In Pain,* 216–21; Dulin and Passmore, "Avoidance of Potentially Traumatic Stimuli," 298; Gaudiano and Zimmerman, "Relationship

depression after trauma can become clinical depression because of family history, previous depression, a breakdown of coping because of chronic stress, or unforgiveness/bitterness.[108]

Even though researchers focused on how traumatic events produced PTSD, these occasions also trigger other disorders like depression.[109] The more traumatic events one withstands increase the possibility of depression.[110] After a disaster, those most likely to suffer depression include those who: "1) have high levels of intrusion and avoidance in the first week after a community disaster, 2) are closest to the danger, 3) have lower levels of social support, and/or 4) have been community members the longest."[111] Several theorists argue that the re-experiencing (or rumination) symptom of PTSD also causes the development and preservation of depression.[112] Thomas Ehring, Silke Frank, and Anke Ehlers make a distinction between rumination and worry by defining rumination as thoughts about past events while worry corresponds to fearful thoughts about the future.[113] Thus, future concern does not generate depression. Depression, a normal function of trauma, helps a person in "separating from and adjusting to significant losses."[114] Healthy depression progresses through the grief and allows time for one to make sense of the trauma.[115]

PTSD

Doctors during World War I witnessed the effects of war on many soldiers. The panic and fear of imminent death often moved men towards combat madness or trauma insanity. The European military at the time desired one and not the other).[116] With the military's desire against combat madness, a French doctor, Clovis Vincent, built a machine called the *torpille*

Between Childhood Trauma History," 468; Young and Korszun, "Sex, Trauma, Stress Hormones and Depression," 26.

108. Carr, "Resources for Effective Support: Effective Community Support," loc. 1567; Foy and Drescher, "Faith and Honor in Trauma Treatment," 237–38.

109. Kaltman et al., "Trauma, Depression, and Comorbid PTSD," 35; Peres et al., "Spirituality and Resilience in Trauma Victims," 344.

110. Schaefer et al., "Traumatic Events and Posttraumatic Stress," 537.

111. Ursano et al., "Prevention of Posttraumatic Stress," 443.

112. Ehring et al., "Role of Rumination and Reduced Concreteness," 489.

113. Ehring et al., "Role of Rumination and Reduced Concreteness," 490.

114. Floyd, *Crisis Counseling*, loc. 1215.

115. Floyd, *Crisis Counseling*, loc. 1267.

116. Fassin and Rechtman, *Empire of Trauma*, 42.

(torpedo) with a shock so strong no solider wanted to endure the trauma insanity treatment and, thereby, returned to combat and bravely gave his life for his country.[117]

The United States military also witnessed the "emotional pressures of trench warfare," which they described as Shell Shock.[118] Doctors determined that "a microscopic cerebral hemorrhage caused by either the concussive or the toxic effects of an exploding shell" caused this syndrome.[119] The military did not want to award pensions to traumatized soldiers so it outlawed the term Shell Shock stating that "well-led, highly trained units with high morale would be virtually immune from post-trauma illness."[120] The Diagnostic and Statistics Manual-I1 (DSM-I), published in 1952 contained a new term, Gross Stress Reaction, for military personnel who had negative psychological reaction to the Korean War. The second DSM came out in 1968 during the Vietnam War, introducing the term Transient Situational Disturbance that included all severe responses to stressful war experiences. They determined that this distress would be short-lived and heal naturally.[121] If psychological issues persisted, the person either had a weak constitution or came from a "degenerate family" leaving total responsibility at the feet of the individual.[122] In 1980, the DSM-III changed the terms Post-Vietnam Syndrome or Delayed Stress Syndrome to the contemporary term for strong reactions to traumatic experiences, Post-traumatic Stress Disorder (PTSD).[123]

Human beings appear to be predisposed to acknowledging the negative over the positive events in life. When people confront equal amounts of loss and gain, loss will have a significantly greater impact on the psyche.[124] All humanity can be exposed to trauma, but some undergo more than others. Studies reveal that 39 percent of people in the United States experience at least one traumatic event in their lifetime[125] and of these, 21 percent suffered a traumatic event within the year of the study.[126] Diagnosis of PTSD requires

---

117. Fassin and Rechtman, *Empire of Trauma*, 49.
118. Jones and Wesley, *Psychological Trauma*, 217.
119. Jones and Wesley, *Psychological Trauma*, 217.
120. Jones and Wesley, *Psychological Trauma*, 217–18.
121. Jones and Wesley, *Psychological Trauma*, 218.
122. Jones and Wesley, *Psychological Trauma*, 217.
123. Jones and Wesley, *Psychological Trauma*, 218.
124. Hobfoll, "Influence of Culture," 341.
125. Breslau et al., "Traumatic Events and Post Traumatic Stress Disorder," 217; Norris, "Epidemiology of Trauma," 415.
126. Norris, "Epidemiology of Trauma," 415.

that a person's symptomatology follow the strict criteria stated in the *Diagnostic and Statistical Manual–Fifth Edition (DSM-V)*.

Stressful or traumatic occurrences release adrenaline causing a fight or flight response. Sometimes, unable to expel all the energy, a person internalizes this force. This naturally produces a stress reaction called Post–traumatic Stress (PTS); nontheless, if PTS does not diminish after four to six weeks, Post–traumatic Stress Disorder (PTSD) will be diagnosed.[127] For one to have PTSD, exposure to a traumatic event defined as involving an actual or perceived threat of psychical death or injury to self or another must have occurred. Symptoms consist of: reliving the event with flashbacks, nightmares, or intrusive thoughts; hyperarousal such as difficulty concentrating, staying asleep, or exaggerated startle response; and avoidance and withdrawal from normal life activities.[128]

Prolonged and repeated contact with danger, violence, and threat of such seem to cause more serious psychiatric disorders in the victims that "impact emotional, behavioral, cognitive and social functioning."[129] The severity of the effect of trauma does not just depend on the amount of trauma experienced. Traumatic factors such as type and context remain imperative to negative pathology.[130] Trauma not only affects human beings socially, emotionally, and physically, it affects their spirituality. The multifaceted interplay between one's body, environment, personality, cultural and social engagement, and spirituality determines how he or she will respond and cope with traumatic events. It can either promote spiritual well-being or decay.[131]

Memories of the traumatic event often trigger PTSD because these remembrances generate an emotional response, which can range in intensity from neutral to powerful.[132] People who develop PTSD establish their lives around the disturbing memory of the trauma.[133] PTSD can strip a person of his or her sense of self or identity[134] and affects his or her need for relationship to reactivate his or her security.[135] Yet, not everyone who lives through a traumatic event develops PTSD. Richard McNally hypothesizes two causes

---

127. Bonanno and Mancini, "Bereavement-Related Depression and PTSD," 182.
128. American Psychiatric Association, *Diagnostic and Statistical Manual*, 271–80; Breslau, "Cultures of Trauma," 115.
129. Crenshaw, "Neuroscience and Trauma Treatment," 23.
130. Allen, *Coping with Trauma*, 6.
131. Kusner and Pargament, "Shaken to the Core," 220.
132. Allen, *Coping with Trauma*, 90.
133. McFarlane, "Severity of the Trauma," 42.
134. Grant, "Trauma in Missionary Life," 73.
135. Allen, *Coping with Trauma*, 149.

why this happens. First, every person possesses unique vulnerabilities, and second, Criterion A stressors have broadened; therefore, even minor crises can be considered within the guidelines. Thus, one can fit the PTSD criterion and not exhibit the PTSD symptomatology.[136]

Trauma can generate stress, anxiety, burnout, depression, and PTSD. These psychological pressures, though uniquely perceived and displayed by each individual, remain universal to all cultures. Most people do not develop these disorders because of natural resilience. Even with enduring great suffering, people can come to a place of well-being.

Coping and Its Outcomes

People tend to cope naturally per Richard Lazarus and Susan Folkman's general coping theory.[137] This theory views humanity as "proactive, goal-directed beings who search constantly for meaning and significance in their lives."[138] When trauma happens, people appraise the situation and apply coping strategies to not only survive but also thrive.[139] This section will investigate the areas of well-being, coping, Post-Traumatic Growth, and the concept of pain and suffering.

Well-Being

Most agree the definition of well-being includes a person having positive emotions such as happiness or contentment, the lack of negative emotions like fear and depression, and satisfaction with life.[140] David Myers states, "Well-being outlasts yesterday's moment of elation, today's buoyant mood, and tomorrow's hard time; it is an ongoing perception that this time of one's life, or even life as a whole, is fulfilling, meaningful, and pleasant."[141] Well-being, or human flourishing can be described "as someone engaged in the process of living vigorously, and whose biological, psychological, emotional, intellectual, social, economic and political parts are integrated into a

---

136. McNally, "Panic and Posttraumatic Stress Disorder," 131.
137. Lazarus and Folkman, *Stress, Appraisal, and Coping*, 53.
138. Abu-Raiya and Pargament, "Religious Coping Among Diverse Religions," 24–25.
139. Lazarus and Folkman, *Stress, Appraisal, and Coping*, 53.
140. Center for Disease Control and Prevention, "Health-Related Quality of Life."
141. Myers, *Pursuit of Happiness*, 24.

functioning whole."[142] In a broad sense, a person can only determine well-being subjectively by assessing his or her life experience and health. Well-being can be conceptualized in two ways: subjective well-being, which focuses on how a person feels (e.g., contentment with life, pleasant affect, infrequent unpleasant affect, hope, zest, humor, love, perseverance) and psychological well-being, which focuses how well a person perceives his or her functioning (e.g., depression, anxiety, self-control).[143]

The concept of well-being dates back to two philosophical mores: eudemonism and hedonism. Aristotle believed that a person living according to his or her virtues defined a good life, which became eudemonism (i.e., "a life dedicated to seeking meaning, engagement with the existential challenges of life, and the actualization of human potential"). Aristippus, on the other hand, claimed that the search of desire described the good life, which became hedonism (i.e., "a life dedicated to seeking pleasure, happiness, and enjoyment").[144] Thus, Arthur Stone and Christopher Mackie developed eudaimonic well-being (or psychological well-being) which comes from the Greek word εὐδαιμονία (eudaimonia) meaning achievement of happiness through "purpose, challenges, and growth."[145] Therefore, eudaimonic well-being refers to one's "perceptions of the meaningfulness (or pointlessness), sense of purpose, and value of life."[146] Hedonic well-being or subjective well-being refers to a person's satisfaction with life or their happiness.[147] A person who has well-being has an abiding sense that no matter the crisis or trauma, all will be well.

Human well-being or human flourishing can be seen in humanistic psychology. Abraham Maslow coined the term Self-actualization, which he viewed as human well-being. He believed that people desire well-being and therefore move toward Self-actualization. To be self-actualized a person must fulfill the hierarchy of needs starting with physiological (i.e., food, water, sleep, sex), safety (i.e., security of body and family, employment, resources, health), love/belonging (i.e., friendship, family, sexual intimacy), esteem (i.e., confidence, achievement, respect), and ending with self-actualization (i.e., morality, creativity, spontaneity, problem solving).[148]

142. Devenish, "Contribution of Spirituality," 53.

143. Gow et al., "Religious Orientation," 143; Li and Zheng, "Adult Attachment Orientations," 1258; Martinez-Marti and Ruch, "Character Strengths and Well-being," 7; Stone and Mackie, *Subjective Well-Being*, 15.

144. Joseph, *What Doesn't Kill Us*, loc. 406.

145. Joseph, *What Doesn't Kill Us*, loc. 438.

146. Stone and Mackie, *Subjective Well-Being*, 19.

147. Joseph, *What Doesn't Kill Us*, loc. 438.

148. Maslow, *Motivation and Personality*, 72–75.

Maslow believed that a person must fulfill each level of the hierarchy before reaching the next, however, one can be Self-actualized and override the lower needs when he or she chooses (e.g., fasting for spiritual purposes).[149] He also deemed that true learning could not happen without tragedy, which required people to view life from a new viewpoint.[150] Self-esteem (i.e., the positive or negative view of the total self) effects contentment and has become one of the greatest predictors of well-being.[151] Maureen Miner and Martin Dowson devised a model of flourishing that encompassed two facets: internal aspect—actualization and an external aspect—altruism. Actualization comprises a person's internal developmental journey towards his or her best human potential (i.e., physical, emotional, intellectual and spiritual domains). Altruism represents one's desire and potential to help others (i.e., moral and relational domains).[152]

Some equate well-being with spirituality. This existential well-being comes from the "supernatural, the sacred, or the transcendental."[153] For others, a religious belief system encourages psychological well-being by upholding "feelings of self-esteem and mastery, as well as positive emotions and beliefs such as meaning, forgiveness, optimism, and gratitude."[154] Gratitude especially can foster well-being in that it helps a person to grow and is growth itself by teaching him or her to appreciate life and draw closer to family and friends.[155] Spiritual well-being can be defined as, "the affirmation of life in a relationship with God, self, community and environment that nurtures and celebrates wholeness."[156]

Well-being not only involves one's psychological, private, or personal feelings of wellness, but it also has a social aspect. For most individuals, the foundation for well-being started with their childhood relationships with parents, siblings, and friends.[157] Adebayo Adejumo reveals, "Well-being even for individuals requires interdependence among people who tacitly

---

149. Miner and Dowson, "Spirituality as a Key Resource for Human Flourishing," 13.
150. Joseph, *What Doesn't Kill Us*, loc. 354.
151. Li and Zheng, "Adult Attachment Orientations and Subjective Well-Being," 1258.
152. Miner and Dowson, "Spirituality as a Key Resource for Human Flourishing," 15.
153. Blaikie and Kelsen, "Locating Self and Giving Meaning to Existence," 137.
154. Ellison et al., "Religious Resources," 288; Gow et al., "Religious Orientation," 143.
155. Rendon, *Upside*, 101.
156. Moberg, "Development of Social Indicators of Spiritual Well-being," 5; Wintermyer, *Weaving a Tapestry*, 13.
157. Gus et al., "Emotion Coaching," 31; Li and Zheng, "Adult Attachment Orientations," 1258; Miner, Dowson, and Malone, "Attachment to God," 327.

agree to approve and support each other in particular ways that have been shaped by culture and history." [158]

Resilience

Resilience offers the power to recover quickly from crisis and trauma and relies on contextually dependent resolution of tensions encountered across cultures and contexts.[159] The word resilience comes from two Latin words, *salire* (to spring, jump up, emerge, to grow fast) and *resilire* (to rebound, bounce back).[160] Psychologists in the 1970s first used this term to describe children who overcame their poverty affected childhood and became well-adjusted adults.[161]

Anthony Mancini and George Bonanno define resilience as "the ability . . . to maintain relatively stable, healthy levels of psychological and physical functioning . . . as well as the capacity for generative experiences and positive emotions."[162] The American Psychological Association Task Force on Promoting Resilience in Response to Terrorism describes resilience as "the process of adapting well in the face of adversity, trauma, tragedy, threats, or even significant sources of stress."[163] Edward Rynearson calls resilience the "psychological 'offense' of great utility after violent dying, which allows a sense of calmness, self-control, detachment, and hope. Resilience performs the crucial function of psychological stabilization so the individual can effectively process and respond to the challenge(s) of trauma and grief."[164] Outcomes differ depending on the individual's personality and his or her relational, communal, cultural, and contextual factors.[165]

Resilience after a traumatic incident does not necessarily signify an outcome trajectory of recovery because both are "discrete and empirically separable outcome trajectories."[166] Recovery signifies a journey from nor-

158. Adejumo, "Need for Cultural Contextualization," 216.

159. Fazio and Fazio, "Growth Through Loss," 245; Ho, "Resilience, Growth, and Distress," 90; Pulley and Wakefield, *Building Resiliency*, 7; Ungar et al., "Unique Pathways to Resilience," 288.

160. Kebza and Solcova, "Trends in Resilience Theory," 13–14.

161. Joseph, *What Doesn't Kill Us*, loc. 1213.

162. Mancini and Bonanno, "Resilience in the Face of Potential Trauma," 42.

163. Foy and Drescher, "Faith and Honor in Trauma Treatment," 234.

164. Rynearson, "Introduction," loc. 513.

165. Harney, "Resilience Processes in Context," 76; Ho, "Resilience, Growth, and Distress," 89; Kebza and Solcova, "Trends in Resilience Theory," 16; Ungar et al., "Unique Pathways to Resilience," 301.

166. Bonanno, "Resilience in the Face of Potential Trauma," 135.

malcy through psychopathology for a period of time and then returning gradually to pre-event levels. Resilience, on the other hand, preserves an unchanging steadiness throughout the traumatic event and beyond.[167] Some trauma researchers do not like using vocabulary such as healing or recovery because of the connotation that the person will return to his or her "old self."[168] A resilient person may exhibit a brief period of psychological distress, but, in the long run, he or she succeeds to function efficiently at his or her normal level. Interestingly, most people exhibit resiliency after traumatic events.[169] These individuals view adversity as "opportunities for growth and development as opposed to threats to well-being."[170]

George Bonanno, one of the top researchers on resilience, contends that no single type or way leads to resiliency.[171] After much study, he catalogued resiliency-promoting factors into two categories: adaptation (i.e., supportive relationships and personality dispositions of elasticity) and pragmatic coping. In Bonanno et al.'s research after September 11, 2001, he concluded that predictors of resilience included: income change, social support, absence of chronic disease, and additional life stressors.[172] He also concluded that religion can promote resilience because of its "providing a stable, shared belief system and by providing affiliation and social support from the religious community."[173] Thomas Kelley disagrees with Bonanno's idea of "multiple pathways to resilience" claiming that the human mind has the natural ability to think it's way out of life's problems.[174]

Other researchers studied resilience and affirmed or added to Bonanno's work. Frederic Flach established a list of psychological resilience factors that include: an aptitude to learn from traumatic encounters, discernment of oneself and others, an elevated tolerance for suffering, creativity, a flexible sense of self-esteem, courage, an inability to behave outrageously, open mindedness, personal discipline, integrity, a sense of humor, a meaningful life, and a future hope.[175] Resilient people "were those with insight into the

167. Bonanno, "Loss, Trauma, and Human Resilience," 101–2.

168. Hess, *Sites of Violence, Sites of Grace*, 66.

169. Bonanno, "Resilience in the Face of Potential Trauma," 136; Bonanno, "Loss, Trauma, and Human Resilience," 104; Bonanno et al., "Self-Enhancement Among High-Exposure Survivors," 985; Mucci, *Beyond Individual and Collective Trauma*, 194–95.

170. O'Rourke, "Psychological Resilience and the Well-Being," 268.

171. Bonanno, "Grief, Trauma, and Resilience," 38–38; Mancini and Bonanno, "Resilience in the Face of Potential Trauma," 976.

172. Bonanno et al., "What Predicts Psychological Resilience After Disaster?," 679.

173. Bonanno et al., "Resilience to Loss and Chronic Grief," 1153.

174. Kelley, "Natural Resilience," 265.

175. Flach, "Resilience Hypothesis," 40.

emotional impact of what they had just been through and who were able to express their feelings to another immediately following the event."[176] Iva Solcova and Vladimir Kebza found that a combination of control, efficacy, competency, energy, involvement, physical strength, and commitment to be part of resilient behavior.[177] Jeanne and Jack Block conceptualized resilience as ego-resiliency.[178] This personality trait indicates that both the inter- and intra-individually has the adaptability to calm outward and inward stressors.[179] Aaron Antonovsk (1987) created the theory, Sense of Coherence (SOC), which consists of three factors: comprehensibility (i.e., cognitively making sense of life events), meaningfulness (i.e., views life's problems as a challenge), and manageability (i.e., utilizes available resources). High SOC individuals appear to be more resilient under stress.[180] Michele Tugade developed the automatic processes of resilience, which operates by either creating a positive effect to downplay the stressful event (e.g., a cup of tea, a smile from a stranger) or using implicit goals for coping.[181]

Another way to understand resilience is to look at it through a developmental perspective where adaptation evolves over time. "Most forms of stress are not simply a short-term, single stimulus, but a complex set of change conditions with a past history and a future course" thus, resilience traits must also change.[182] Frauke Schaefer takes a biological approach to resiliency by advocating reducing baseline stress with "regular aerobic exercise, sufficient sleep, eating resilience-enhancing foods, and having a balanced lifestyle with regular downtimes."[183]

Bonanno disputes what he considers a misconception that resiliency resides only within the individual. He argues, "resilience is a complex phenomenon resulting from a mix of factors including personality, interpersonal variables, such as supportive relationships, and the temporal characteristics of the stressor."[184] These supportive relationships can be found in society or the family unit. The family system can decrease risk and cultivate

---

176. Flach, "Resilience Hypothesis," 40.

177. Solcova and Kebza, "Personality Characteristics Related to Resilience," 76.

178. Block and Block, "Role of Ego-control and Ego-resiliency," 47–51.

179. Philippe et al., "Ego-Resiliency as a Mediator," 392; Schaefer and Moos, "Context for Posttraumatic Growth," 115.

180. Peres et al., "Spirituality and Resilience," 346; Ruddick, "Promoting Mental Health," 36; Tedeschi and Calhoun, *Trauma and Transformation*, 52–53.

181. Tugade, "Positive Emotions and Coping," 194.

182. Pulley and Wakefield, *Building Resiliency*, 13.

183. Schaefer, "Resources for Effective Support," loc. 2387.

184. Bonanno, "Grief, Trauma, and Resilience," 33.

resources.[185] It "is a primary resource of resilience because of the ingredients of kinship resilience, familiar stabilizing patterns of verbal and nonverbal interactions that restore the sense of safety, cohesion, and hope for survival that have developed over years within the family matrix."[186]

According to Hamilton McCubbin et al.'s Resilience Model of Family Stress Adjustment and Adaptation, for a family to be resilient it must develop in four areas: interpersonal relationship and development, well-being and spirituality; community relationships and nature; and structure and function.[187] This model assumes that: 1) all families will go through trauma and hardships; 2) they will naturally develop ways to increase growth for each member; each will cultivate unique protective abilities; 3) they will add too and take from the network of ethnic and cultural affiliations and assets; and 4) they will change to reestablish stability, congruence, and equilibrium.[188]

Resilience must also be viewed from an ecological perspective, which looks at "the interplay between occurrences within families and the political, economic, social, and racial climates in which individuals and their families perish or thrive."[189] A family's worldview will assist them to pull together (i.e., cohesiveness), reframe the crisis (i.e., meaning-making), and continue normal rituals (e.g., family time, eating together, chores), thus reinforcing a sense of belonging and significance.[190]

Resilient families have caring, empathic adults (especially an involved male presence) who have an authoritative parenting style and spend quality time with their children. It reduces stress by creating organized family routines and rituals and providing a healthy network of friends and extended family.[191] Each person in the family unit must be willing to be part of the healing process by being flexible, communicating well, and making sacrifices for each other.[192]

---

185. Pulley and Wakefield, *Building Resiliency*, 15.

186. Salloum and Rynearson, "Family Resilience After Violent Death," loc. 1489.

187. Greeff and Wentworth, "Resilience in Families," 303; Lahad and Leykin, "Introduction," 12–13; McCubbin et al., "Families Under Stress," 7–9.

188. Greeff and Wentworth, "Resilience in Families," 303.

189. Pulley and Wakefield, *Building Resiliency*, 13.

190. Greeff and Wentworth, "Resilience in Families," 304–5; Pulley and Wakefield, *Building Resiliency*, 26.

191. Kumpter et al., "Engendering Resilience in Families," 485–88; Van Horn and Lieberman, "Early Intervention with Infants," 118.

192. Greeff and Wentworth, "Resilience in Families," 312; Pulley and Wakefield, *Building Resiliency*, 106; Walsh, *Strengthening Family Resilience*, 133.

Hardiness

Suzanne Kobasa first coined the term hardiness when researching the association amid personality, stress, and health.[193] Hardiness allows a person to take the crisis elements and, with control and commitment, can find meaning, personal development, purpose, and the belief that he or she has the power to change the outcome.[194] Considered a personality trait, hardiness predisposes a person toward well-being in stressful or traumatic situations.[195] Other personality traits such as good self-esteem, flexibility, tolerance for ambiguity, and introversion/extroversion also factor into hardiness.[196]

Hardy people form strong relationships with coworkers, family, and friends (commitment); they usually feel that they influence the situations of their lives (control); and they see problems as tests not a threat (challenge).[197] Bonanno describes hardiness as consisting of three beliefs: "being committed to finding meaningful purpose in life, the belief that one can influence one's surroundings and the outcome of events, and the belief that one can learn and grow from both positive and negative life experiences."[198] These attitudes assist individuals to make stressful events less frightening and give them more self-assurance to use their coping skills.[199] Hardy people have less stress because they see fewer stressors in life and they proactively cope with the ones they encounter.[200]

People want to live a life of well-being. They want to be happy and satisfied with their existence. However, when trauma happens, some will have a harder time returning to contentment than others. Those who have a natural resiliency may bend but will not break when the storms of life hit them and will remain the same as before. Some who have hardy personalities will naturally be able to control traumatic circumstances and with the help of friends and family returning to a state of well-being. Yet, others find coping a difficult task and either struggle to survive or present destructive psychopathology that ruins any hope of well-being.

---

193. Kobasa, "Stressful Life Events," 3.

194. Arndersson-Arnten et al., "Influence of Affective Personality," 140–41; Eschleman et al., "Meta-Analytic Examination of Hardiness," 278.

195. Eschleman et al., "Meta-Analytic Examination of Hardiness," 277.

196. Quick et al., *Stress and Challenge at the Top*, 41.

197. Eschleman et al., "Meta-Analytic Examination of Hardiness," 277–78; Kebza and Solcova, "Trends in Resilience Theory and Research," 20; Quick et al., *Stress and Challenge at the Top*, 38.

198. Bonanno, "Loss, Trauma, and Human Resilience," 108.

199. Bonanno, "Loss, Trauma, and Human Resilience," 108.

200. Eschleman et al., "Meta-Analytic Examination of Hardiness," 301.

Coping

Researchers became very interested in why some people could handle traumatic situations and others seemed devastated by the same event. As the researchers studied this phenomenon, they determined that personal characteristics (e.g., coping style, personal values, locus of control, religious/spiritual beliefs, personality, attributional style/cognitive schemas) and environmental factors (e.g., social support, family stability) decided one's coping ability.[201] Coping with trauma can differ from dealing with everyday stressors in that: 1) people dealing with trauma have less conscious control over their coping strategies, 2) they have more need to confide in another person, 3) they acknowledge that their coping will last longer, and 4) they will have greater transformation of self if they cope well.[202]

Coping's roots began with Anna Freud's psychodynamic psychological approach, which concentrated on defense mechanisms.[203] Coping is, "the ongoing transactional process between [a person's] environment, a process impacted by both cognitive appraisal and coping behavior."[204] Lazarus and Folkman define coping as, "constantly changing cognitive and behavioral efforts in managing specific external and/or internal demands that are appraised as taxing or exceeding the resources of the person."[205] Coping involves various ways (i.e., behavioral and emotional avenues unique to the individual and the situation) to manage stress and trauma.[206]

The ability to cope relies not only on how people sense a traumatic event, but also their internal and external resources which define their vulnerability.[207] Coping involves an individual activating his or her ability to care for him or herself, to be able to find social support, and rely on protection from outside sources.[208] Some individuals trust their inner strength to cope with stress and trauma. Yet, others realize that they cannot face this suffering alone and depend on spirituality to assist them on their journey to recovery. This section will review both the secular and religious views of coping.

201. Palucka et al., "Social and Emotional Intelligence," 48; Wright, "Recognizing and Understanding Troubled Children," 33.

202. Aldwin, *Stress, Coping, and Development*, 188.

203. Aldwin, *Stress, Coping, and Development*, 21.

204. Maynard et al., "Religious Coping Style," 65.

205. Lazarus and Folkman, *Stress, Appraisal, and Coping*, 141.

206. Bonanno et al., "Coping Flexibility and Trauma," 118; Hambrick and McCord, "Proactive Coping," 69; Tan, *Rest*, 162.

207. Balswick and Balswick, *Families In Pain*, 36.

208. van der Kolk, "Complexity of Adaptation to Trauma," 185.

Secular Coping

Secular psychology has considered the how and why people cope with stress and trauma. Kenneth Pargament introduced eight assumptions about the coping process. 1) "People seek significance," People take different roads in life pursuing significance. Without it, one would not have a fruitful existence. 2) "Events are constructed in terms of their significance to people." People construct significance to both positive and negative events and thus perceive them as stressful or not. 3) "People bring an orienting system to the coping process." This orienting practice helps a person's worldview and how he or she works with it. 4) "People translate the orienting system into specific methods of coping." One's orienting system has the possibility to help or harm his or her coping process depending on choices made for each stressful or traumatic event. 5) "People seek significance in coping through the mechanisms of conservation and transformation." Most people want to first survive the traumatic event and then they can realize their significance in the event and hopefully grow from it. This is done in the four stages of preservation, reconstruction, re-evaluation, and re-creation. 6) "People cope in ways that are compelling to them." With all the ways of coping with a situation, people tend to "select the most compelling option, the strategy expected to bring the greatest gain and the least loss of significance through the use of the fewest resources and the accumulation of the least burden." 7) "Coping is embedded in culture." Culture not only forms a person's coping style, sometimes a person coping strategy can influence culture. 8) "The keys to good coping lie in the outcomes and the process."[209] No single strategy clenches effective coping. One's personality, culture, and situation will determine how successful he or she copes.

Ronnie Janoff-Bulman contends that an individual's coping method has three discrete classifications: involuntary habits for managing new data, determination to reinterpret and make the new data fit one's worldview better, and the collaborations with friends and family that contribute or encumber recuperation.[210] From years of study, researchers have developed many theories[211] and coping strategies to assist in the understanding of the coping

---

209. Pargament, *Psychology of Religion and Coping*, 91, 95, 99, 104, 106, 111–13, 114, 117, 119.

210. Janoff-Bulman, *Shattered Assumptions*, 95.

211. The following list of theories is not exhaustive but it catalogues some of the most influential coping models: General Coping Theory (Abu-Raiya and Pargament, Religious Coping, 25), Constructivist Self Development Theory (Janoff-Bulman, *Shattered Assumptions*, 83), Social Cognitive Theory (Benight, "Understanding Human Adaptation," 2), Terror Management Theory (Chatard et al., "Extent of Trauma Exposure." 47), Transactional Theory (Benight, "Understanding Human Adaptation,"

process. The theories created suggest "the why"[212] people deal with traumatic events and the strategies relate "the how." General Coping and Transactional Theories deduce that people appraise the dangers of life and if it threatens them, they will then determine how to cope with them. Constructivist Self Development theory claims a person filters threatening situations through his or her worldview. Social Cognitive Theory suggests that people do not simply respond to threats but shape their surroundings to accommodate them. Terror Management Theory assumes a person experiences inescapable fear when confronted with his or her own mortality; whereas Conservation of Resources Theory considers the loss of property to terrify humanity. Emotional Processing theory determines one's personality affects how he or she processes trauma. Social Support and Attachment Theories assert the importance of familial and societal ties in how and individual will deal with traumatic events. From these diverse theories one can come to understand why people react so differently to life's problems.

COPING STRATEGIES

How a person copes is just as important as why. Psychologists have recognized several coping strategies people use to combat the effects of trauma. Understanding how humanity copes provides counselors tools to help individuals cope better. Shelley Taylor considers three psychosocial resources to be of upmost importance in coping: optimism (emotional), personal control or mastery (problem-solving), and high self-esteem (personality).[213] From the literature, coping strategies can be divided into five categories: internal resources, external resources, meaning-focused coping, coping ugly, and negative coping.

Internal Resources

Jack Balswick and Judith Balswick expressed the need of a person's internal and external resources to help with their coping skills.[214] Internal

---

3), Conservation of Resources Theory (Benight, "Understanding Human Adaptation," 4), Emotional Processing Theory (Benight, "Understanding Human Adaptation," 5), Social Support Theory (Benight, "Understanding Human Adaptation," 4), Attachment Theory (Schottenbauer et al., "Attachment and Affective Resolution," 449).

212. Theories investigate people's "assumptions, schemas, meaning systems, or worldviews" (Chatard et al., "Extent of Trauma Exposure," 48).

213. Taylor, "How Psychosocial Resources Enhance," 66.

214. Balswick and Balswick, *Families In Pain*, 34–36.

negative and positive dispositions assist or hurt a person's outlook of the tragedy.[215] Internal (i.e., personality and emotions) and external (i.e., family, friends, society) resources profoundly determine one's ability to move from victim to thriver.

Internal resources include a person's personality and emotional fortitude. These assets can be either negative or positive in nature. Internal negative dispositions tend to recognize little control in a crisis; thereby exacerbating fear and anxiety.[216] On the other hand, internal positive characteristics aid a person in a traumatic situation. A positive attitude allows change, wants to learn, and has a sense of identity and purpose.[217]

Being positive reduces negative psychological emotions.[218] The concepts of emotional intelligence (i.e., the capability to monitor, understand, and manage one's emotions about self and others and use this knowledge to solve life's problems) and social intelligence (i.e., the ability to recognize another's feelings and objectives) direct people in: "(a) how to express and manage emotions in ways that do not damage or destroy relationships or lead to self-destructive behaviours; (b) how to implement one's goals and persist in face of frustration and adversity, and (c) how to cope in ways that are flexible and promote personal growth and development."[219]

Research has found that "personality is fundamental to the understanding of coping ability."[220] Coping can also be labeled as "personality in action under stress."[221] Personality and temperament can be described as, "characteristic patterns of thoughts, feelings, and behaviors over time and across situations."[222] Yet, personality and temperament differ from each other in that temperament denotes the hardwired, innate, biological essence of a person that regulates emotional reactivity and self-regulation and personality refers to the influences that environment such as culture and experience lend to his or her being.[223]

---

215. Balswick and Balswick, *Families In Pain*, 201; Gilbar et al., "Coping, Mastery, Stress Appraisals," 559; Greeff and Wentworth, "Resilience in Families," 312; Taylor et al., "Culture and Social Support," 355.

216. Pargament et al., "God Help Me!," 505; Schottenbauer et al., "Religious Coping Research," 500.

217. Pulley and Wakefield, *Building Resiliency*, 10–21.

218. Schottenbauer et al., "Religious Coping Research," 500.

219. Palucka et al., "Social and Emotional Intelligence," 49.

220. Hambrick and McCord, "Proactive Coping," 74.

221. Connor-Smith and Flachsbart, "Relations Between Personality and Coping," 1080.

222. Connor-Smith and Flachsbart, "Relations Between Personality and Coping," 1080.

223. Gardner et al., "Developmental Correlates of Emotional Intelligence," 75–76.

Jennifer Connor-Smith and Celeste Flachsbart believe personality affects one's coping approach "directly, by constraining or facilitating use of specific strategies, or indirectly, by influencing the nature and severity of stressors experienced or the effectiveness of coping strategies."[224] Also, coping strategies that work for one personality type may be detrimental to another.[225] The five personality traits that assist in growth consist of: neuroticism (i.e., self-consciousness, behavioral inhibition, negative emotionality, and reactivity to stress), extraversion (i.e., sociability, high activity levels, assertiveness, sensitivity to reward, and positive emotionality), agreeableness (i.e., compliance, trust, tendermindedness, and altruism), conscientiousness, and openness (i.e., curiousness, creativeness, imaginative, and intellectual involvement in many areas of interest).[226] A negative personality type that seems to perform better under stress and trauma is self-enhancement. This personality type can be self-serving, self-centered, and narcissistic; nevertheless, it possesses a high level of self-esteem that people need during traumatic events.[227] As mentioned before, people with a flexible personality can cope better than individuals with a rigid personality because they can vary their coping style to match the situation.[228] Self-confidence and an easy-going personality help people cope.[229]

Positive emotions such as laughter, humor, and cheerfulness assist people in reducing their levels of distress by undoing negative emotions.[230] Optimists tend to utilize better coping skills and convey better results following traumatic events, whereas, pessimists lean toward poorer coping techniques and communicate undesirable emotional affect.[231] Michele Tugade in her studies, found that the "experiences of positive emotions are transformative and have long-lasting consciences for individuals, even if

224. Connor-Smith and Flachsbart, "Relations Between Personality and Coping," 1081.

225. Connor-Smith and Flachsbart, "Relations Between Personality and Coping," 1082.

226. Connor-Smith and Flachsbart, "Relations Between Personality and Coping," 1080–83; Geisler et al., "What Coping Tells about Personality," 289–90.

227. Bonanno, "Resilience in the Face of Potential Trauma," 137; Bonanno et al., "Self-Enhancement Among High-Exposure Survivors," 985, 994.

228. Bonanno et al., "Coping Flexibility and Trauma," 118; Joseph, *What Doesn't Kill Us,* loc. 2267.

229. Schaefer and Moos, "Context for Posttraumatic Growth," 113.

230. Bonanno, "Loss, Trauma, and Human Resilience," 109; Bonanno and Kaltman, "Toward an Integrative Perspective on Bereavement," 766; Papousek and Genullter, "Don't Take an X for a U," 14; Segerstrom et al., "Optimism is Associated with Mood," 1646.

231. Davis et al., "Making Sense of Loss," 563; Rendon, *Upside,* 129; Schaefer and Moos, "Context for Posttraumatic Growth," 113.

the positive emotions themselves are rather mild and short-lived."[232] According to Viktor Frankl, "A positive attitude enables a person to endure suffering and disappointment as well as enhance enjoyment and satisfaction. A negative attitude intensifies pain and deepens disappointments; it undermines and diminishes pleasure, happiness, and satisfaction; it may even lead to depression or physical illness."[233]

External Resources

Human beings are social and need the external resources of family, friends, and society to survive times of suffering.[234] The family unit models the most helpful or detrimental coping strategies to its members. Families who cope as a functional unity tend to be resilient.[235] For families to cope well they must be flexible yet stable in their predictability, consistent in rules, roles, and patterns of interaction.[236]

Temperament distinctions in childhood and adolescence mold a child's "adaptation to the world and continue throughout adulthood."[237] Psychosocial Ego-Resilient individuals come from families who have a "loving, patient, competent and integrated mother" who has "sexual compatibility" with the father. A family who exhibits a "free interchange of problems and feelings," who agrees on values, and who has concern for "philosophical and moral issues" tends to have better coping abilities.[238]

The key domains of character, trauma exposure, and home or school environments affect how a child will cope with trauma.[239] Nonetheless, the parent or primary caregivers largely determine how a child will handle stressful situations. Parents who offer their children emotional and physical support facilitate positive coping.[240] Caregivers and the family atmosphere comprise an essential role in teaching children how to increase their positive emotional regulation.[241] Therefore, when parents have con-

---

232. Tugade, "Positive Emotions and Coping," 191.
233. Frankl, *Man's Search for Meaning*, 160,
234. Balswick and Balswick, *Families In Pain*, 201.
235. Walsh, *Strengthening Family Resilience*, 14.
236. Walsh, *Strengthening Family Resilience*, 79–80.
237. Gardner et al., "Developmental Correlates of Emotional Intelligence," 75–76.
238. Block and Block, "Role of Ego-control," 51.
239. Garfin et al., "Children's Reactions," 568.
240. Garfin et al., "Children's Reactions," 564.
241. Gardner et al., "Developmental Correlates of Emotional Intelligence," 76.

flict with their children or cannot discuss the trauma, the children will have trouble coping.[242]

Ellen Skinner and Melanie Zimmer-Gembeck investigated and charted possible developmental coping from infancy to adolescence (see Table 2.1.).[243] Babies cope with stress by crying so that an adult will satisfy their needs. The parent copes for the baby (interpersonal co-regulation). As the child grows, he or she develops better coping and regulation skills. The parents hopefully learn to step back and gradually release coping responsibilities to their children. When this happens, children will learn positive coping skills that will aid them throughout their lifetime.

Table 2.1. Broad Outlines of Possible Developmental Shifts in Means of Coping[244]

Developmental Period	Approximate Ages	Nature of Coping	Role of Social Partners	Nature of Regulation
Infancy	Birth to 18 months	From reflexes to coordinated action schema	Carry out coping actions based on infant's expressed intentions	Interpersonal co-regulation
Preschool	Ages 2-5	Coping using voluntary *direct actions*	Available for direct help and participation	Intrapersonal self-regulation.
Middle-childhood	Ages 6-8	Coping using *cognitive means*	Cooperate with and support child's coping efforts	Coordinated self-regulation
Early adolescence	Ages 10-12	Coping using *meta-cognitive means*	Reminder coping	Proactive self-regulation
Middle adolescence	Ages 14-16	Coping based on *personal values*	Backup coping	Identified self-regulation
Late adolescence	Ages 18-22	Coping based on *long-term goals*	Monitoring coping	Integrated self-regulation

242. Garfin et al., "Children's Reactions," 564.

243. Skinner and Melanie Zimmer-Gembeck, "Perceived Control and the Development of Coping," 46.

244. Skinner and Zimmer-Gembeck, "Perceived Control and the Development of Coping," 46.

To assist child caregivers in times of trauma, Phyllis Kilbourn developed the STOP model.[245] These steps give parents the tools they need to help children cope with difficult situations. S stands for Structure. Children must continue their daily routines, especially in chaotic times so that they feel normal and secure.[246] T represents Talk and Time. Families go through traumatic events together, yet the parent must put aside his or her traumatized emotions and make time to be with his or her children and listen to their stories (whether in speaking, drawing, or play) about the event.[247] O signifies Organized Play. Children need to play during stressful situations and parents should play with them.[248] P denotes Parental Support and Caring. Children must know that their parents will take care of them to the best of their ability.[249] Also, children take their emotional cues from the parents. "Adults who reflect calmness, confidence, honesty and an attitude of taking charge in spite of adversity will help children retain their grip on reality and strengthen their reactions to it."[250]

People not only need a supportive family in tough times, they also require friends and society. Healing comes through "community, connections, and relationships."[251] Family and community "are natural 'shock absorbers' in times of crisis."[252] Taylor et al. defines social support as, "the perception or experience that one is loved and cared for, esteemed and valued, and part of a social network of mutual assistance and obligations."[253] The societal culture often influences coping by determining which events would be considered stressful, by appraising the event through prevalent beliefs and values, and by defining appropriate coping styles.[254] Society's cultural rituals often provide a visual and emotional meaning to trauma.[255]

Social support can be broken down into three subcategories: information support (i.e., assistance to comprehend traumatic events and decide what type of coping and assets might be required), instrumental support (i.e., the giving of needed resources), and emotional support (i.e., the offering

---

245. Kilbourn, "Introduction to the STOP Sign Model," 133–46.
246. Kilbourn, "S = Structure," 147–56.
247. Wright, "T = Talk and Time," 157–74.
248. Heard, "O = Organized Play," 175–96.
249. Blomquist, "P =Parental Support," 197–214.
250. Blomquist, "P =Parental Support," 200.
251. Fazio and Fazio, "Growth Through Loss," 221.
252. Pulley and Wakefield, *Building Resiliency*, 105.
253. Taylor et al., "Culture and Social Support," 354–55.
254. Aldwin, *Stress, Coping, and Development*, 215.
255. Perren-Klingler, "Integration of Traumatic Experiences," 50.

of empathy and encouragement).²⁵⁶ Throughout the coping research, social support has proven to be a key ingredient in assisting people in traumatic situations.²⁵⁷ However, the type of assistance must be considered. "The kind of support that emphasizes dependence, that tells the survivor what to do instead of enabling them to choose their own path, can be counterproductive. Instead, friends and family members need to allow survivors to find their own path, to support them in that effort and help them rebuild their lives in their own way."²⁵⁸ To cope with traumatic experiences, one must have strong internal and external resources.

Meaning-focused Coping.

Nietzsche claims, "He who has a Why to live for can bear almost any How."²⁵⁹ For people to cope well, they must find meaning in the stress or trauma they face.²⁶⁰ "Meaning comprises not only beliefs, but also identity, values, goals, and sense of purpose."²⁶¹ Meaning can focus on the ultimate (e.g., intimacy, death, freedom), the mundane (e.g., work, parenting, hobbies), or the spiritual (e.g., beliefs, sense of purpose).²⁶² Meaning-focused coping changes the "appraised meaning of a situation to be more consistent with an individual's beliefs and goals."²⁶³ Antonovsky considers meaningfulness as the key to coping because "it provides the individual with the motivation to search for order in the world, use the resources available, and seek out new resources for managing the demands."²⁶⁴ Irwin Yalom realized meaning of life came from suffering when he wrote, "A real confrontation with death usually causes one to question with real seriousness the goals and conduct of one's life up to then."²⁶⁵

A person's sense of meaning can help him or her to avoid danger by being attentive to negatively veiled encounters, but this can also produce

---

256. Taylor et al., "Culture and Social Support," 355.
257. Rendon, *Upside*, 88.
258. Rendon, *Upside*, 91.
259. Frankl, *Man's Search for Meaning*, 21.
260. Davis et al., "Making Sense of Loss," 572; Riley and Park, "Problem-Focused vs. Meaning-Focused Coping," 587–88; Thompson, "Finding Positive Meaning," 280.
261. Slattery and Park, "Spirituality and Making Meaning," 128.
262. Slattery and Park, "Spirituality and Making Meaning," 128.
263. Riley and Park, "Problem-Focused vs. Meaning-Focused Coping," 589.
264. Solcova and Kebza, "Personality Characteristics Related to Resilience," 66.
265. Joseph, *What Doesn't Kill Us*, loc. 357.

stress and anxiety.²⁶⁶ Most people reevaluate and interpret traumatic events in several ways. They assess significant lessons learned, look at the traumatic event's benefit to themselves and others, imagine themselves in worse situations, and forget the negative.²⁶⁷ Crystal Park states, "Resolving stressful events entails reducing discrepancies between appraised meanings and global meanings."²⁶⁸ Therefore, meaning making can be conceptualized in two ways, global meaning (i.e., one's world expectations, beliefs, goals, and fundamental assumptions) and situational meaning (i.e., appraisal of the situation and how global situational meanings revise the coping process).²⁶⁹ Distress happens when the meaning ascribed to the traumatic event disrupts one's global meaning.²⁷⁰

The Jewish, Austrian psychologist Viktor Frankl survived the Nazi concentration camp at Auschwitz. From his experience, he developed logotherapy based on meaning making. Logotherapy "focuses on the meaning of human existence as well as on man's search for such a meaning."²⁷¹ This meaning can change from person to person, hour to hour, and day to day. "What matters, therefore, is not the meaning of life in general but rather the specific meaning of a person's life at a given moment."²⁷² Frankl found three sources of meaning: "in work (doing something significant), in love (caring for another person), and in courage during difficult times."²⁷³ He saw suffering as meaningless, which only found meaning through how one responded to it.²⁷⁴ Yet, he also realized that suffering was as much a part of life as death, therefore, if life had meaning, so did suffering.²⁷⁵ He believed that life had meaning no matter the circumstances and that one's attitude of hope would pull him or her through.²⁷⁶

Frankl viewed optimism as a strong determinant of meaning making. He witnessed that it assisted in changing suffering into achievement and

266. Slattery and Park, "Spirituality and Making Meaning," 130.

267. Janoff-Bulman, *Shattered Assumptions*, 135; Thompson, "Finding Positive Meaning in a Stressful Event," 281–82.

268. Park, "Meaning, Coping," 230.

269. Aten, "Disaster Spiritual and Emotional Care," 132; Park, "Meaning, Coping," 228; Park and Folkman, "Meaning in the Context of Stress and Coping," 116; Slattery and Park, "Spirituality and Making Meaning," 132–33.

270. Park, "Meaning, Coping," 231.

271. Frankl, *Man's Search for Meaning*, 98–99.

272. Frankl, *Man's Search for Meaning*, 108.

273. Frankl, *Man's Search for Meaning*, 29.

274. Frankl, *Man's Search for Meaning*, 29.

275. Frankl, *Man's Search for Meaning*, 67.

276. Frankl, *Man's Search for Meaning*, 83–84.

accomplishment, taking from guilt the chance to change oneself for the better, and from life's transitory nature an incentive to take responsible action.[277] A successful search for meaning gives a person happiness and a way to cope with suffering.[278]

People make meaning of their world through stories. "Life stories guide behavior and decision making, and they speak to how people create meaning in their lives."[279] Stephen Joseph declares, "Trauma triggers within us the need to tell stories to make sense of what has happened. These stories may take the form of conversations with family, friends, and colleagues.... Transformation arises through the stories we tell."[280]

Narrative refers to the listening, the telling, and the retelling of stories. These narratives involve the difficulties people face. By changing the story, a person can change his or her life.[281] Humanity employs mental narratives to organize, understand, and predict their experiences. Individuals shape their choices through meanings attributed to life's events. Predicaments in life can be personal, socio-cultural, psychological, biological, or a mixture of the four. On occasion others impose hindrances on the individual, but that person chooses how he or she will manage each situation.[282] This narrative can be beneficial in both verbal and written formats.[283]

Irvin Yalom and Morlyn Leszcz, leading proponents of group psychology, discovered several therapeutic factors as their clients shared their stories. People realized that as they disclosed their traumatic experiences, they could relate with one another (i.e., "universality"). Group members could take risks by telling their horrific narratives to help other members recognize that they could do the same (i.e., "identification"). Participants came to understand the unfairness of life and that no one can escape life's pain and sorrow (i.e., "external factors"). Group members associated with each other (i.e., altruism) by "instilling hope" to new members and giving "guidance." "Group cohesiveness" gives people feelings of security and belonging so that they can grow through their narratives. The group becomes family (i.e., "family reenactments") and they help each other produce "self-understanding" and "interpersonal learning." Their stories generate relief

---

277. Frankl, *Man's Search for Meaning*, 137.
278. Frankl, *Man's Search for Meaning*, 139.
279. McAdams, "Role of Narrative," 25.
280. Joseph, *What Doesn't Kill Us*, loc. 2169.
281. Phipps and Vorster, "Narrative Therapy," 32.
282. Drake, "Art of Thinking Narratively," 285; Freedman and Combs, *Narrative Therapy*, 42–44.
283. Mancini and Bonanno, "Resilience in the Face of Potential Trauma," 982.

from emotional distress.[284] Jeanne Slattery and Crystal Park sum up meaning making well when they say, "People's appraised meanings determine how they comprehend and bear the trials and sorrows of the human condition. Their religious and spiritual views, as part of their global meaning, may inform their understanding of trauma and direct their responses."[285] When one finds meaning in life's traumas, suffering becomes bearable and from the horror, then growth can happen.

Coping Ugly

Bonanno observed that many people used coping mechanisms in traumatic situations that would not work or would even be maladaptive in other situations.[286] He described this as pragmatic coping or "coping ugly." He found that repressive coping (i.e., emotional dissociation) often helped people cope with trauma and loss.[287]

After a traumatic event, people need to think about the incident. Psychologists call this thought process rumination. This can be counterproductive when people only contemplate on regrets or linger on self-blame.[288] Rumination happens in two ways: reflective and brooding. "Reflective rumination is characterized by a purposeful turning inward to engage in adaptive problem solving and emotion-focused coping, whereas, ruminative brooding is characterized by maladaptive thinking patterns."[289] Coping happens when a person incorporates his or her reflective ruminations into his or her life narrative.[290]

The coping strategy of avoidance, though part of the fourth stage of trauma recovery, can be a maladaptive coping style if one routinely utilizes denial and does not move forward.[291] Like avoidance, denial, normally seen as detrimental to mental health, can be used positively in coping with stress.[292] Coping ugly can be seen as a negative coping style, however, if used correctly it can lead to constructive results and a healthy outcome.

---

284. Yalom and Leszcz, *Theory and Practice of Group Psychotherapy*, 82–85.
285. Slattery and Park, "Spirituality and Making Meaning," 135.
286. Bonanno, "Grief, Trauma, and Resilience," 39.
287. Bonanno, "Loss, Trauma, and Human Resilience," 109.
288. Calhoun and Tedeschi, "Posttraumatic Growth," 227.
289. Joseph, *What Doesn't Kill Us*, loc. 1890.
290. Calhoun and Tedeschi, "Posttraumatic Growth," 232.
291. Creamer, "Cognitive Processing Formulation," 61.
292. Aldwin, *Stress, Coping, and Development*, 168.

Negative Coping

Coping ability relies on not only how people sense a traumatic event, but also their internal and external resources which determine their vulnerability.[293] Sometimes people cope poorly when facing traumatic events. Negative dispositions tend to recognize little control in a crisis, therefore, concluding the situation to be dangerous exacerbating fear and anxiety.[294] Self-blame negatively effects people when they criticize themselves for making mistakes that in their minds caused the traumatic event.[295]

Trauma shatters one's fundamental worldview about self and others. Coping helps him or her to rebuild a new view of life, "a task that requires a delicate balance between confronting and avoiding trauma-related thoughts, feelings and images."[296] People come into life with a personality prone to positive or negative coping capabilities, honed by culture and experience. Family, friends, and society can also help or hurt the coping process. Individuals must find meaning for the suffering that happens in life or they will emotionally implode. One can cope ugly but cannot utilize negative coping if he or she wants to overcome traumatic events.

Religious Coping

In extreme uncontrollable situations, most people turn toward spiritual or religious power to help with their coping.[297] A person's religion helps in the coping process by "providing a stable, shared belief system and by providing affiliation and social support from the religious community."[298] It also brings meaning and purpose to life's unexpected tragedies.[299] Researchers have found that how religious coping can assist or hinder a person depends on two factors: his or her devotion or relationship to God and personal conservatism or commitment to discipleship.[300]

---

293. Balswick and Balswick, *Families In Pain*, 72.

294. Pargament et al., "God Help Me!," 509; Schlotz et al., "Perceived Stress Reactivity Scale." 2; Schottenbauer et al., "Attachment and Affective Resolution," 451–52.

295. Hess, *Sites of Violence, Sites of Grace*, 48.

296. Janoff-Bulman, *Shattered Assumptions*, 169.

297. Banziger, Van Uden, and Janssen, "Praying and Coping," 102; Pargament et al., "Patterns of Positive and Negative Religious Coping," 720.

298. Bonanno et al., "Resilience to Loss and Chronic Grief," 1153; Bryant-Davis et al., "Religiosity, Spirituality, and Trauma," 306.

299. Bormann et al., "Spiritual Wellbeing Mediates PTSD," 497.

300. Bonanno et al., "Resilience to Loss and Chronic Grief," 1153; Feldman and Cravat, *Supersurvivors*, loc. 136.

Investigators have made distinctions between spirituality and religiosity. They claim that spirituality relates to a person's search for the sacred, capturing it, and having it transform his or her life. Religiosity can be defined as an individual's "commitment to the beliefs and practices endorsed by a specific organized sacred institution such as a church, synagogue, or mosque."[301] Both concepts can be practiced together or separately. Religious coping has been found to decrease symptoms of depression, give greater self-esteem, and support higher life satisfaction.[302] Adults, adolescents, and children all use religious coping. It assists with healthy growth during developmental stress. It offers them a sense of community, self-esteem, and sense of purpose that aid them during times of trauma.[303]

Kenneth Pargament and his colleagues observed that many people use three types of religious coping skills. The first involves a self-directing style where the person actively solves the problem on his or her own. Second, the deferring style happens when one gives the problem in its entirety to God. Third, the collaborative style involves the individual and God working together in the problem-solving process.[304] Ana Wong-McDonald and Richard Gorsuch offer a more mature Christian coping style, that of surrendering. They propose that the surrender coping style allows people and God to work together towards a solution; yet, when their solution differs from God's they surrender their will and follow the path God sets before them.[305]

The way a person uses spiritual coping varies across religions.[306] Some religions support the idea of a personal God actively involved with each human being while others serve a distant God who lets fate determine the destiny of humanity. Individual and collective worldviews differ according to religious tradition. Christianity, an individualistic religion recognizes personal sin and responsibility for salvation. Islam, conversely, has a collectivistic identity viewing salvation as a communal activity. Therefore, Christians tend toward intrapersonal, individualistic coping strategies (i.e., accommodation, self-reliance, problem-solving, escape, submission, and helplessness) while Muslims move toward interpersonal, collectivistic

---

301. Bryant-Davis et al., "Religiosity, Spirituality, and Trauma," 307.
302. Bryant-Davis et al., "Religiosity, Spirituality, and Trauma," 308.
303. Bryant-Davis et al., "Religiosity, Spirituality, and Trauma," 308.
304. Pargament et al., "Patterns of Positive and Negative Religious Coping," 720–21.
305. Wong-McDonald and Gorsuch, "Surrender to God," 149.
306. Osborne and Vandenberg, "Situational and Denominational Differences in Religious Coping," 121.

approach (i.e., delegation, support seeking, opposition negotiation, and external information seeking).[307]

Spiritual coping can have a negative or positive aspect. Negative coping manifests in one's spiritual disposition. This negative spiritual coping mirrors the spiritual pain, struggle, frustration, and turmoil of a person's response to traumatic events.[308] People cope negatively when they believe that God is punishing or abandoning them; when they put all blame on the devil; when they walk away, withdraw, or question God; when they lash out at God; or when they ask God for revenge.[309] Spiritually positive coping skills include: drawing closer to and working with God; believing he or she has God given guidance, support, and life purpose; praying for others; seeking spiritual support from faith communities; and asking God and others for forgiveness.[310] Individuals see God as benevolent and trustworthy.[311] Positive religious coping most often develops Post-Traumatic Growth (PTG) and negative religious coping can lead toward PTSD.[312] Jeanne Slattery and Crystal Park conclude, "Faith and spirituality provide this greater sense of purpose for many people, shaping their view of the world, making suffering understandable and bearable, while providing a sense of coherence, commitment, hopefulness, meaning, purpose, and trust that allow them to make it through difficult times."[313]

To survive trauma and suffering, people can utilize secular and religious coping strategies. Some individuals cope well naturally because of personality characteristics. Others must work harder to overcome their inbred negative biology. Nevertheless, everyone can learn to: think positively, allow friends and family to help, find meaning in tragedy and incorporate it into the story of their lives, cope ugly if need be but never cope negatively, and allow God to be part of the coping process.

---

307. Fischer et al., "Relationship Between Religious Identity and Preferred Coping," 365–66.

308. Kusner and Pargament, "Shaken to the Core," 217.

309. Bryant-Davis and Wong, "Faith to Move Mountains," 676–77; Kusner and Pargament, "Shaken to the Core," 218.

310. Kusner and Pargament, "Shaken to the Core," 217.

311. Bryant-Davis and Wong, "Faith to Move Mountains," 676–77.

312. Gerber et al., "Unique Contributions of Positive and Negative Religious Coping," 303–4.

313. Slattery and Park, "Spirituality and Making Meaning," 134.

Post-Traumatic Growth

Steven Joseph illustrates the differences between resilience, recovery, and Post-Traumatic Growth (PTG). He suggests imagining a tree growing on a hill being battered by the wind yet standing strong and unbending. It looks unchanged after the storm. This is resilience. Another tree bends from the force of the wind but does not break. After the storm, it returns to its original state. This is recovery. A third tree also stands on the hill. It too bends because of strong wind. Yet, this tree does not return to its original shape, the storm has changed it. It will retain its scars and look completely different, but it continues to grow.[314] This is Post-Traumatic Growth.

Trauma does not generate negative post-trauma psychopathology in all people—less than 10 percent develop PTSD; whereas, 90 percent resume pre-trauma equilibrium. Nevertheless, some of the 10 percent who develop PTSD can move on to PTG.[315] Trauma often motivates people to "decrease in their functioning (dive), return to normal levels of functioning (survive), or experience an increase in function (thrive).[316]

In 1996, psychologists Lawrence Calhoun and Richard Tedeschi coined the term Post-Traumatic Growth (PTG) to describe this transformation.[317] They define PTG as "the positive change that the individual experiences as a result of the struggle with a traumatic event."[318] Post-Traumatic Growth denotes: "a reorganization of people's basic beliefs and main assumptions in terms of the way they perceive the world, their identity as individuals, and their relationship with other people."[319]

Even though change occurs differently with everyone, Becca Barnett views three broad categories of PTG: "(a) enhanced perception of self and one's personal resources; (b) enhanced interpersonal relationships, social resources, and spiritual relationships including one's relationship with God; and (c) enhanced philosophy of life."[320] Joseph views three core existential themes in PTG: 1) the uncertainty of life, 2) psychological mindfulness (i.e., how one's feelings, reflections, and actions relate), and 3) personal agency

---

314. Joseph, *What Doesn't Kill Us,* loc. 1230–48.
315. Ibrahim et al., "Dynamics of Posttraumatic Growth." 121.
316. Fazio and Fazio, "Growth Through Loss," 224.
317. Barnett, "How Christian Trauma Survivors Construct Models of God," 192; Figley and Figley, "Stemming the Tide of Trauma Systemically," 175.
318. Calhoun and Tedeschi, *Facilitating Posttraumatic Growth,* 17.
319. Kastenmuller et al., "Posttraumatic Growth," 478.
320. Barnett, "How Christian Trauma Survivors Construct Models of God," 196; Khechuashvili, "Comparative Study of Psychological Well-Being," 54.

TRAUMA AND COPING

(i.e., responsibility for choices made).[321] PTG happens when people make sense of a traumatic incident through storytelling.

> If post-traumatic growth is to take place, we must be active agents in the creation of our own lives. It is through storytelling that we ultimately make sense of our experiences, piece together what happened to us, assimilate information that is concordant with our views of self and the world, and accommodate other information that is discordant—while at the same time rebuilding our worldview and our understanding of ourselves.[322]

People can go through the same trauma and some will develop PTSD and others will cultivate PTG. The people who develop PTSD seem to organize their lives around the trauma, whereas, those who exhibit PTG find meaning by telling their traumatic stories examining the growth they have made between the pre- and post-trauma event.[323] They tend to have a hopeful and optimistic disposition and can adapt coping styles to each situation.[324]

Researchers have used different terms for PTG such as Stress-Related Growth (SRG), thriving, adverbial growth, and benefit findings; their findings commonality being the positive changes and growth that happens to some people after trauma.[325] Yet, one study showed that PTG and SRG did not correlate. People did not connect SRG with any trauma type; they only linked it with normal everyday stress.[326] Differences can also be found between PTG and resiliency. A resilient person returns to pre-trauma balance and may plateau in growth. People exhibiting PTG come through the trauma healthier than before and continue to grow and thrive.[327] Resilient people do not always grow because "there is less struggle, no significant meaning is given to the event, and no relationship develops."[328]

PTG comprises religious and spiritual components. Research has linked PTG with religious and spiritual practices, prayer, positive religious

---

321. Joseph, *What Doesn't Kill Us*, loc. 479.

322. Joseph, *What Doesn't Kill Us*, loc. 2410.

323. Barnett, "How Christian Trauma Survivors Construct Models of God," 202, 204; Calhoun and Tedeschi, "Posttraumatic Growth," 232.

324. Calhoun and Tedeschi, "Posttraumatic Growth," 223–26; Gerber et al., "Unique Contributions of Positive and Negative Religious Coping," 298; McMillen, "Better for it," 460; Westphal and Bonanno, "Posttraumatic Growth and Resilience," 424.

325. Ho, "Resilience, Growth, and Distress," 90.

326. Ibrahim et al., "Dynamics of Posttraumatic Growth," 135.

327. Ho, "Resilience, Growth, and Distress," 93.

328. Schuettler and Boals, "Path to Posttraumatic Growth," 190–91.

coping, negative religious coping, and religious orientation.[329] Mary Beth Werdel et al.'s research confirmed that people who have a faith in God do not emerge from traumatic experiences just "sadder and wiser" but have "increased levels of positive affect."[330] This happened by having a mature faith that did not see a God who abandoned or punished them but a God present in their struggles.

Ryan Denney, Jamie Aten, and Kari Leavell found that PTG occurred when their cancer patients "fully surrendered control of their lives to God" and when they "increased spiritual support from their family and friends."[331] These trauma survivors felt that their trust in God deepened through the struggle because they sensed a divine purpose in their suffering, thereby intensifying their "quality and depth of their payers" and increasing their desire to evangelize.[332] Participant's spirituality directly correlated with their sense of well-being.[333]

People cope in a myriad of ways. Some regress, others merely survive, while others grow and thrive because of the traumatic experience. PTG seems to be more often associated with one's spiritual maturity. This strong spirituality, especially in the area of trauma, often happens because of the person's concept of pain and suffering.

The Concept of Pain and Suffering

The perceptions of pain and suffering, often linked together, have unique differences. Pain has the connotation of a conscious experience of physical, emotional, or spiritual ache. This discomfort, usually beyond one's control, disrupts normal life. Suffering, on the other hand, extends beyond the mere consciousness of pain and contains the understanding of pain's influence on one's life, which causes a mind-set of tolerance, denial, or apathy.[334] Suffering, like gas, "completely fills the human soul and conscious mind, no matter whether the suffering is great or little. Therefore the 'size' of human suffering is absolutely relative."[335] To comprehend suffering, one must investigate the definitions of, the reason for, and the secular and Christian views of pain and suffering.

329. Werdel et al., "Unique Role of Spirituality," 58.
330. Werdel et al., "Unique Role of Spirituality," 67.
331. Denney et al., "Post Traumatic Spiritual Growth," 378, 380.
332. Denney et al., "Post Traumatic Spiritual Growth," 378–82.
333. Denney et al., "Post Traumatic Spiritual Growth," 378.
334. van der Poel, *Wholeness and Holiness*, 35.
335. Frankl, *Man's Search for Meaning*, 44.

Definition of Pain and Suffering

As stated earlier, pain correlates with physical, emotional, or spiritual discomfort. People comprehend physical pain caused from disease or bodily harm, which can be cured by medication. Psychological or spiritual pain occurs with a real or perceived threat of life, or loss of loved ones or possessions.[336] Harder to cope with, this pain presents physical discomfort that only time will remedy. A society or culture can also impose what Mary Mills calls political pain. When a government inflicts violence and annihilation on members of its community, pain becomes an atrocity and evil. The individual usually cannot assuage political pain; it requires others to intervene.[337]

Pain commonly causes suffering but not suffering results from pain. Excessive or unending pain produces suffering. This agony tends to relate with calamity or misfortune and becomes more a psychological rather than a physical pain.[338] Dorothee Soelle proposes three stages of suffering: In the first stage, the sufferer feels numb and isolated; in the second stage, he or she begins to experience feelings of lament or protest; and in the third stage, he or she logically analyzes the situation, enters into solidarity with others, and begins to make plans for action.[339]

Reasons for Pain and Suffering

Humanity does not like to suffer, especially when they do not recognize why. The "riddle of suffering" tries to use logic surrounding the three claims of: God is good, God is powerful, and evil is real. Yet, trying to logically answer the riddle fails because of its distance from human reality.[340] C. S. Lewis declares that people's inhumanity towards each other accounts for four-fifths of human suffering. Goodness cannot come from suffering, but suffering can produce goodness in certain circumstances.[341] Walter Lowe offers three critical functions for suffering: first, it establishes a critical standard; second, it establishes a universal human solidarity; and third, it establishes a religious context.[342]

---

336. van der Poel, *Wholeness and Holiness*, 48.

337. Mills, "Spirituality as a Key Resource," 147.

338. Gigliotti, "Qoheleth," 87; Jeffery, *Evil and International Relations*, 19; Jervis, *At the Heart of the Gospel*, 3-4.

339. McWilliams, *Where is the God of Justice?*, xxii.

340. Brueggemann, "Epilogue," 11.

341. Lewis, *Problem of Pain*, 86.

342. Lowe, *Theology and Difference*, 10.

Establishment of a Critical Standard

Secular and religious societies often view suffering as just punishment for crimes committed. Suffering inflicted by God or a society can reform the individual, protect the society, and deter others from committing the same act.[343] The idea of justly deserved punishment leads to the notion of redemption. People who endure their deserved suffering will be redeemed and allowed back into a right relationship with their community. Christianity views this suffering in light of Christ's suffering, which allowed humanity to be redeemed back into a right relationship with God.[344]

Establishment of a Universal Human Solidarity

Suffering exists as part of life and cannot be escaped without destroying life itself. Carl Jung claimed suffering developed personal growth by allowing people to recognize and deal with their psychological and physical limitations.[345] The realization of the universality of suffering helps humanity to cope. It brings people together to encourage and uphold each other through the trial and anticipate the end of pain and suffering.[346]

Establishment of a Religious Context

The religious arena responds with abundant reasons for suffering. Jewish theology recognizes eight meanings for suffering: retributive, disciplinary, revelational, probational, illusory or transitory, mysterious, eschatological, and meaningless.[347] Walter Kaiser also reveals eight types of suffering in the Old Testament: 1) Retributive (reward or punishment), 2) educational, 3) disciplinary, 4) vicarious (suffering servant), 5) empathetic (empathy with those who suffer produces suffering), 6) doxological (to give glory to God), 7) evidential (faithfulness to God through suffering), and 8) revelational (deeper knowledge and relationship with God and humanity).[348] Erhard Gerstenberger and Wolfgang Schrage narrow the Old Testament reasons

---

343. Jeffery, *Evil and International Relations*, 25–26.
344. Jeffery, *Evil and International Relations*, 27.
345. Jeffery, *Evil and International Relations*, 27.
346. Tillich, *Systematic Theology*, 71.
347. Jeffery, *Evil and International Relations*, 25.
348. Kaiser, *Biblical Approach to Personal Suffering*, 122–29.

for suffering to four: 1) judgment and punishment, 2) divine education, 3) God's will, and 4) the work of Satan.[349]

The New Testament offers six different reasons for suffering: 1) fellowship with Christ (a sign of belonging to Christ), 2) *vis aliena* (i.e., strange power; causing a dependence on God), 3) disillusionment and eschatological reserve (i.e., suffering points a person away from his or herself and toward God), 4) testing (i.e., of faith, resistance, and steadfastness), 5) hope (i.e., looking forward to the end of suffering), and 6) witness (i.e., the answer to suffering produces testimonies).[350] Authors of the New Testament view suffering as a significant component of a Christian's life. The believer draws closer to God and others through anguish.

Hebrew theologians offer the reason for suffering as the consequence of sin and evil. Humanity cannot comprehend a good God would have anything to do with pain and unjust suffering.[351] Christians distinguish between moral and natural evil. Moral evil results from human activity—sins that individuals with free will, inflict on themselves or others. These injustices include slavery, human trafficking, child abuse, and discrimination. Natural evil comprises disasters such as hurricanes, earthquakes, floods, and diseases.[352] Moral and natural suffering, as well as sin, can cause people to question God's character and hence cause damage to their relationship with the Father.[353] Some theologians argue that suffering cannot always be equated with sin and evil because torment can also be caused by love.[354]

The Secular and Christian Views of Pain and Suffering

Suffering happens to the just and the unjust alike (Matt 5:45). No human can escape its existence. Yet, how one views suffering affects how he or she survives. Two distinct positions on suffering preside, secular and Christian.

---

349. Gerstenberger and Schrage, *Suffering*, 207–39.

350. Gerstenberger and Schrage, *Suffering*, 207–39.

351. Brueggemann, "Epilogue," 213; Forde, *On Being a Theologian of the Cross*, 86-97; Rauschenbusch, *Theology for the Social Gospel*, 180–81.

352. Jervis, *At the Heart of the Gospel*, 114; McWilliams, *Where is the God of Justice?*, xvi.

353. Jervis, *At the Heart of the Gospel*, 131–32.

354. Jeffery, *Evil and International Relations*, 30–31.

Secular View of Pain and Suffering

Little writing pertains to the secular viewpoint of suffering. For the most part, modern society rejects the idea that suffering should be a part of life. Pain hurts and must be avoided. Western society deems each individual controls his or her own destiny. "The decline of religion is a function of a rise in the apparent predictability of life, which is accompanied by the hope that human beings can be in charge of their own future without divine assistance."[355] Westerners feel relative safety in this assumption until they encounter a traumatic incident, which shatters their illusions and lessens their ability to cope.[356] Often societies cause great suffering to their own citizens, justifying it as being a religious or cleansing act to better the society. Many cultures that experienced past anguish retain a suffering memory, which lingers for years and hinders the growth of the community.[357]

The secular view of suffering possesses no redemption. Even Frankl realized the need for belief in something to give a meaning to the suffering the prisoners of the Holocaust withstood. The Apostle Paul in 1 Thessalonians 5 noted that non-believers do not experience joy in distress. They do not sense the faith, hope, or love that can happen in stressful times. Paul did not want to observe the unbeliever in torment.[358] Only the Christian's theology of suffering atones for the misery and pain.

Christian View of Pain and Suffering

True followers of Christ understand life generates suffering and God utilizes this anguish to produce character.[359] Theologians have struggled with humanities' suffering, especially afflictions towards the innocent and faithful. Theodicy defends a good and omniscient God in a world of inexcusable suffering and evil.[360] Early Greek theologians justified suffering with the controversial idea that God, through Jesus' death on the cross, suffered for humanity (i.e., the Theopaschite controversy).[361] Theologians like Thomas Aquinas felt that mercy could be attributed to God, but not

---

355. McFarlane and Yehuda, "Resilience, Vulnerability," 26.
356. Barnett, "How Christian Trauma Survivors," 2–3, 80.
357. Lowe, *Theology and Difference*, 9–10.
358. Jervis, *At the Heart of the Gospel*, 30.
359. Allender and Longman, *Cry of the Soul*, loc. 2250.
360. O'Collins and Farrugia, *Concise Dictionary of Theology*, 262.
361. O'Collins and Farrugia, *Concise Dictionary of Theology*, 265–66.

suffering.[362] Nonetheless, other theologians suggested that God wanted to feel humanities suffering. Martin Luther taught the *theologia crucis* (the theology of the cross) as the right way to do theology. He stated that a "saving and merciful, God is known as hidden in Christ crucified and in experiences of suffering and temptation that reveal the nothingness of human beings before God."[363] Jurgen Moltmann argued the cross as the central theme of Christianity. He believed that a God who could not suffer was a deficient God. The Creator revealed his love for his creation by allowing their acts to cause suffering in his being.[364]

The Bible portrays a triune God who suffers with his creation. Jesus as the suffering servant depicts this attribute. God willingly disclosed himself to humility as a man to minister and suffer for the sake of all.[365] The Holy Spirit also grieves when God's creation inflicts violence on each other; and yet, God loves both victim and predator alike.[366]

This suffering God not only offers solidarity, meaning, and dignity to human agony, it also gives a model for Christians to follow. The disciples of Christ should live as obedient servants ready to minister and, at times, suffer for others.[367] Though often difficult for Christians to reconcile the trials of life as being good, it is frequently through suffering that they grow, mature, and conform to the image of Christ.[368] The attitude of Christians should be to embrace suffering as the way of the cross and consider its significance to spiritual development.[369]

The Old Testament addresses human suffering. Psalms 44, 69, and Jeremiah 15 do not equate suffering as punishment, but something one endures for service to God. The testing of Job reveals a follower of God who would not waver in his faith despite waves of trials and torment. The wisdom of Ecclesiastes discloses that the pain of faith exists when one suffers with unanswered questions. The book of Daniel illustrates that one must

---

362. McGrath, *Christian Theology an Introduction*, 275.

363. O'Collins and Farrugia, *Concise Dictionary of Theology*, 262.

364. Livingston et al., *Modern Christian Thought*, 284; McGrath, *Christian Theology an Introduction*, 277.

365. Ladd, *Theology of the New Testament*, 155; Rendon, *Upside*, 144.

366. Linahan, "Grieving Spirit," 45.

367. Grenz, *Theology for the Community of God*, 339; McGrath, *Christian Theology an Introduction*, 275.

368. Hiebert et al., *Understanding Folk Religion*, 163.

369. Dunn, *Theology of Paul the Apostle*, 496; Jervis, *At the Heart of the Gospel*, 33; Lewis, *Problem of Pain*, 110.

serve God even if it leads to martyrdom; knowing that even in suffering, hope of deliverance exists in a powerful God.[370]

Many New Testament authors spoke of suffering. These writers reveal the way of the cross to be a road of suffering. Jesus said, "Whoever wants to be my disciple must deny themselves and take up his cross and follow me" (Mark 8:34).[371] The Bible discloses a God who "overturns pain by experiencing it" and who expects His followers to do the same.[372] "God suffers; Jesus suffers; the apostles suffer; and those subsequent disciples who are called to be leaders and exemplars in the church and world are likewise called to suffer."[373] Suffering then becomes a vital part of discipleship.[374]

Matthew recorded the reality that through God's sovereignty, human suffering will be alleviated either in the present or future (Matt 4:24; 8:5–7; 15:21–23; 17:14–16). Peter spoke about suffering as a normal part of the Christian walk, and it should not be allowed to destroy one's faith (1 Pet 4:12).[375] Paul articulated, in 1 Thessalonians and Philippians 1, his own suffering as being an unavoidable part of a believer's life. He suffered in joy, not because he enjoyed affliction, but because he believed that Christ-like suffering would produce the end of anguish and death. Paul viewed suffering as an integral part of the process of salvation. He did not endure it alone, not only did Jesus walk with him, but other believers joined him in his distress and shared in his pain.[376] Paul's love for Christ drove his life and ministry. The Apostle understood that in every traumatic event, he shared in the sorrow of Christ.[377] Paul makes no distinction between the distressing events brought on by ministry or personal suffering (his thorn in the flesh).[378] He did not ask, "Why?" or try to find a reason for his travail. He embraced unavoidable trauma and encouraged the churches to identify with the suffering Christ, and by staying positive and trusting that in God's love they would find well-being.[379] For Paul states, "Who shall separate us from the love of Christ?

---

370. Mathews, "When We Remember Zion," 115.

371. All Scripture quotations, unless otherwise noted, are from the New International Version.

372. Allender and Longman, *Cry of the Soul*, loc. 2248.

373. Devenish, "Contribution of Spirituality," 58.

374. Dunn, *Theology of Paul the Apostle*, 496.

375. Sweetland, "Suffering in the Gospel of Matthew," 140–41.

376. Dunn, *Theology of Paul the Apostle*, 494–96; Jervis, *At the Heart of the Gospel*, 24–30.

377. Barnett, *Paul Missionary of Jesus*, 165; Roetzel, *Paul*, 170.

378. Hooker, "Interchange and Suffering," 80.

379. Adewuya, "Sacrificial-Missiological Function," 97; Clinton et al., *Caring for People God's Way*, 404; Jervis, *At the Heart of the Gospel*, 65.

Shall trouble or hardship or persecution or famine or nakedness or danger or sword? . . . No, in all these things we are more than conquerors through him who loved us" (Rom 8:35, 37). He continues to write in Romans that the source of suffering is sin. Both believers and non-believers live in an evil world and therefore suffer. The difference becomes visible when believers suffer in Christ and thus have hope.[380]

Hope at the end of suffering, either on earth or in heaven, facilitates a Christian's survival. Believers realize God often uses suffering for their benefit, and he has the power to work all things out for the good of those who love him (Rom 8:28).[381] Even though Christians know severe trials produce growth, most do not seek tribulation. In fact, the absence of conflict should be cause for concern in a believer's life.[382] Yet, for many people, suffering equates failure, evil, or a form of punishment. Scripture states that suffering for Jesus' sake serves to glorify God.[383] Nevertheless, like the thief on the cross, Jesus does not always rescue a person from suffering.[384] This can lead to the temptation not to trust God. Believers often view trials as enduring this life's agony, not as preparing for the life to come. As a result, people try to justify God's present actions and fall into despair when they do not realize the bigger picture of eternity.[385]

Every human being, at some time in his or her life, will confront pain and suffering. Physical pain starts early as babies cry at the pain of hunger, gas, or a soiled diaper. Suffering troubles some more than others, yet all humanity encounters this affliction. Western culture desires pleasure and tries to deny suffering exists. However, other cultures understand the ravages of suffering and build religions around this core concept. Suffering can be used to punish crime and, therefore, Christians often view distress as God's chastisement for sin. Yet, when one investigates Scripture deeper, he or she comes to realize that God chose to identify with humanity by suffering. Therefore, he or she can identify with Jesus through suffering. This anguish produces Christ-like character and stronger discipleship. Christians recognize hope comes from knowing God walks with them through the hard times and a home without suffering awaits them.

---

380. Jervis, *At the Heart of the Gospel*, 114–15.

381. Hiebert et al., *Understanding Folk Religion*, 163.

382. Dunn, *Theology of Paul the Apostle*, 496; Forde, *On Being a Theologian of the Cross*, 83–84.

383. Bromiley, *International Standard Bible Encyclopedia*, 512.

384. Shaffer, *Faith and the Professions*, 70.

385. Sheed, *Theology and Sanity*, 441–42.

Missionary Trauma

Missionaries face a variety of traumas throughout their field career. Some can be life threatening (e.g., robbery, rape, war, evacuations, imprisonment, kidnappings, torture, natural disasters, and medical emergencies). Other traumas can be psychologically intimidating (i.e., missing meaningful home-country family events, government opposition, death threats, multiple goodbyes, betrayal of friends, false accusations, team conflicts, and role changes).[386] These events can cause a missionary to react in a variety of negative ways which can lead to him or her leaving the field. The World Evangelical Fellowship Missions Committee conducted one of the most influential studies on missionary attrition and found that 5.1percent of career missionaries leave the field every year and of those 71percent do so for preventable reasons.[387] To avoid attrition, missionaries must learn to cope well for both themselves and their families. This section will examine how stress, culture shock, burnout, compassion fatigue, anxiety, depression, and PTSD can affect the missionary population.

Missionary Related Trauma

Trauma outcomes can include anxiety, stress, depression, burnout, and PTSD. Being a missionary, compounds these psychological maladies with the added stress of a new culture and the additional traumatic outcomes of culture shock and Compassion Fatigue. "The stress and high demands of the missionary occupation as well as familial, physical, emotional, and spiritual factors all contribute to the increased attrition rates that are reported by mission agencies."[388] This section will look at stress, culture shock, burnout, Compassion Fatigue, anxiety, depression, and PTSD, through a missionary lens.

Stress

Missionaries have one of the most stressful ministry occupations.[389] Clair Camp et al. states, "Missionaries are a unique population because individuals, couples, and families devoted to a missionary cause for religious and/or spiritual reasons are often commissioned to live in international

---

386. Carr, "Crisis Intervention for Missionaries," para. 9.
387. Taylor, "Introduction," 13.
388. Schwandt and Moriarty, "What Have the Past 25 Years," 321–22.
389. Bjorck and Kim, "Religious Coping," 612–13; Williams, "Model for Mutual Care in Missions," 47.

contexts where they may be faced with a myriad of interactive and dynamic stressors."[390] Patricia Miersma compares missionary stress to that of combat veterans[391] while Jeanne Jersma equates this stress to that of an FBI agent.[392] One study determined two of the top five reasons for preventable missionary attrition were self-esteem and stress.[393] Physical and emotional health ranked number one for attrition by missionaries serving in the Evangelical Alliance Mission, the Christian and Missionary Alliance, the Conservative Baptist Foreign Mission Society, and the World Gospel Mission.[394] With stress being one of the top reasons for missionary attrition, one must look at the reasons for missionary stress, the stress of acculturation, and the warning signs of acute stress.

Reasons for Missionary Stress

Missionary stress comprises work priorities and overload, financial and support maintenance, confrontation, cross-cultural communication, and culture shock.[395] This stress starts before the missionary leaves for the field. It begins with missionary preparation (Bible school or seminary), time of pastoral ministry, seeking the best fitting missions agency, and the uncertainty of being found suitable by that agency. Then, the candidate missionary family often must move, live in transitional housing, and travel from church to church to raise their funds. When they finally have their financial support, they must plan their trip, pack their household, say goodbye to family and friends, and leave all they consider familiar.[396]

Building and sustaining a financial base is one of the most stress filled duties of a missionary.[397] Dorothy Gish found that those missionaries who had to raise their own support had more stress than those who had denominational support.[398] A chief cause of significant stress among missionaries is the unconscious feeling of unworthiness of their financial support. Rob Hay and associates state, "To be worthy of financial support,

---

390. Camp et al., "Missionary Perspectives," 350.
391. Miersma, "Understanding Missionary Stress," 93.
392. Jersma, "Critical Incident Intervention," 135.
393. Blocher, "ReMAP I," 13.
394. Allen, "Why Do They Leave?," 425–30.
395. O'Donnell, "Member Care on the Field," 29; Schwandt and Moriarty, "What Have the Past 25 Years," 321.
396. Dodds and Dodds, "Love and Survival," 3.
397. Keckler, "Comprehensive Missionary Wellness," 28.
398. Gish, "Sources of Missionary Stress," 241.

they [missionaries] receive, they must live at the level of their poorest supporter and work as hard as their most workaholic supporter—obviously an almost impossible combination of demands."[399] Faith based fund raising and support maintenance weighs heavy on both new and experienced missionaries.[400] Marge Jones declares,

> New candidates are often put in the position of having to raise a budget within a limited amount of time, which greatly increases the pressure during deputation. Helen Herndon feels that missionaries who leave because of lack of funds have been 'pushed out' because no church or board is willing to be financially responsible for them. She decries the often-used phrase 'Trust in the Lord for your needs,' believing it shows irresponsibility on the part of these agencies. No pastor would serve a church unless it was willing to be financially responsible for him or her. Added to the pressure to raise the stipulated funds in a limited amount of time is the 'tin-cup' image... Daniel Bacon contends that this image has become a major barrier to many young people contemplating career missions.[401]

Several studies have looked at field stress and reported that the issues that become most stressful for missionaries include: confronting others when necessary, dishonesty among nationals, communicating across language-cultural barriers, poverty of the nationals, shortage of supplies, time and effort maintaining donor relationships, being considered rich by nationals, and work priorities.[402] Miersma says, "Witnessing famine, epidemics, oppression and violence is something for which missionaries are ill-prepared. When such things occur in their experience, a very high toll is exacted from them emotionally and psychologically."[403]

Carr categorizes missionary stress into seven groupings: 1) Violent crime—Missionaries most often have direct experience, but they can also witness it done to others. The most frequent consists of carjacking and robbery with or without assault. Missionaries commonly cannot report these transgressions because of a corrupt or non-existent police force. 2) Violence related to war—Missionaries experience stress in this situation because of the constant possibility of being caught in crossfire, being close to a bomb when it goes off, being caught in civil protests or riots,

---

399. Hay et al., "Organizational Values," 216.
400. Foyle, *Honorably Wounded*, loc. 1046.
401. Jones, *Psychology of Missionary Adjustment*, 27.
402. Bagley, "Impact of Trauma," 83; Gish, "Sources of Missionary Stress," 239.
403. Miersma, "Understanding Missionary Stress," 94–95.

and being evacuated. 3) Cultural adjustment issues—Missionaries have to learn a new language and cultural rules. They must deal with poverty, difficult living (e.g., lack of potable water, electricity, phone, and internet) and traveling conditions, lack of infrastructure, and government corruption. 4) Health and sanitation—Missionaries often have to contend with poor hospital facilities, no doctor availability, and threats of diseases like typhoid, parasites, malaria, meningitis, typhoid, and AIDS. 5) Job stress—Missionaries must be able to do whatever work the nationals ask them to do whether part of their skill set or not. They live under constant demands and pressures from the sending agency, home, and national church. They take very little time off and never seem to have enough people or money to do the asked for job. Congruence between self-expectations and one's actual role produces another missionary strain. When a person can choose his or her ministry and work, well-being occurs.[404] 6) Interpersonal crises—Multigenerational and multicultural missionary teams live and work together in very high-pressure situations. This often causes interpersonal conflict, which can be devastating to all involved. Duane Elmer considers missionary conflict to be the number one stressor because of philosophical, generational, proximity and cultural differences.[405] 7) Grief and loss—Missionaries contend with grief and loss all the time. They say goodbye to friends and family when they leave their home country. Many have to send their young children to boarding school and not see them for months at a time. They often feel the loss of "security, safety, familiarity, possessions, hopes, dreams, and constant changes of friends and living situations"[406] A missionary lives from one stressor to another never being able to find equilibrium. The constant psychological stress "means living years with increased adrenalin, which adds to physical changes in the brain and other body systems," and can lead to physical illnesses.[407]

---

404. Lewis-Hall and Duvall, "Married Women in Missions," 311.

405. Elmer, *Cross-Cultural Servanthood*, 87–90.

406. Carr, "Mobile Member Care Team," 79; See also: Donovan and Myors, "Reflections on Attrition in Career Missionaries," 43–48; Foyle, *Honorably Wounded*, loc. 1023; Jensma, "Critical Incident Intervention with Missionaries," 130.

407. Dodds and Dodds, "Love and Survival," 3–4; Foyle, *Honorably Wounded*, loc. 437.

The Stress of Acculturation

The process of learning the appropriate behavior and cultural characteristics of a new culture is acculturation.[408] Acculturative stress occurs when one must learn a new language, establish new social ties, and learn new community rules. This tension can cause emotional pain, perceived alienation and discrimination, and feelings of loneliness, inferiority, and powerlessness.[409] Healthy acculturation, though demanding, does not last forever. Many missionaries mistakenly consider acculturation denotes "going native." Living, dressing, and eating like a national can present a false sense of stability in the culture. Yet, missionaries must value and accept the reasoning process and methodology of the nationals to adjust to the new culture.[410]

Missionaries often struggle with a sense of identity. According to Paul Hiebert they belong "to two or more worlds" yet, cannot fully identify with either.[411] To prevent an identity crisis, missionaries often do one of these three things: consider only one culture home, "going native," or becoming cultural chameleons. Nevertheless, each of these options presents maladaptive identity issues. Heibert suggests missionaries develop transcultural identities where they can navigate being both insiders and outsiders in any cultural setting. "Good mediators are the in-betweeners who often feel they have no home or identity because they live in two or more worlds and must constantly change their identities as they move from one to another."[412] Missionaries must appreciate their identity so that they can better acculturate to their new home.

Geert and Gert Hofstede describe an acculturation curve that happens to people as they adjust to another culture. During phase one (the honeymoon stage), a person enjoys all the excitement of being a part of a new country. Then, in phase two (the culture shock stage), real-life starts happening and feelings of insufficiency, annoyance, worry and irritation start happening. One starts to have to deal with confusion of learning new rules and adjusting old ideas and customs. In phase three, acculturation starts to happen. A person incorporates some of the local worldview, becomes confident in his or her new environment, and integrates into a new

---

408. Grunlan and Mayers, *Cultural Anthropology*, 80; Hwang and Ting, "Disaggregating the Effects of Acculturation," 147.

409. Flaskerud and Uman, "Acculturation and its Effect," 123; Hwang and Ting, "Disaggreating the Effects of Acculturation," 148; Yeh and Inose, "International Students," 17.

410. Jones, *Psychology of Missionary Adjustment*, 14.

411. Hiebert, "Missionary as Mediator," 300.

412. Hiebert, "Missionary as Mediator," 301.

social network, the acculturation stage. Finally, in phase four, stability is accomplished.[413]

Acculturation permeates all areas of a person's life. Dealing with acculturation frequently complicates good family relations. Deficient marital satisfaction and unhealthy interpersonal parent/child relationships can lead to conflict between professional and spiritual obligations.[414] Parents need to be aware that their children also experience stress. A key symptom of childhood stress is "loss of previously learned skills."[415] As the missionary family acculturates each member must give each other grace because no matter how stress arrives, no two humans will observe it identically.

Interestingly, people react to pressure distinctively, what one person observes as stressful another might not.[416] Selye detected circumstantial causes that affect stress reactions. Internal aspects include genetics, temperament, inherited personality characteristics, age, sex, and past experiences. External factors comprise medications, climate, and diet.[417] Even though people identify stress dissimilarly, everyone eventually encounters tension. The psychological results of dealing with constant stress include personality disorders, Acute Stress Disorder (ASD), PTSD, anxiety, and depression.[418] Therefore, missionaries need to comprehend and watch for warning signs of acute stress.

Acute Stress Warning Signs

Prevention becomes a key component in dealing with stress. When a missionary recognizes the warning signs (e.g., fatigue, insomnia, gluttony, irritability, anxiety, anger, and sadness), stress can be avoided. Mission's leaders and missionaries alike should also be aware of unconscious adjustment mechanisms. Missionaries from all cultures apply psychological defense mechanisms when under extreme stress. Examples of these maladaptive coping mechanisms include: denial (often displayed as jokes about nationals), conscious suppression or unconscious repression (i.e., keeping unpleasant memories or thoughts out of mind), reaction-formation (i.e., one's actions are opposite than feelings), displacement (i.e. repressed emotion discharged

---

413. Hofstede, *Cultures and Organizations Software of the Mind*, 324.
414. Foyle, *Honorably Wounded*, loc. 240; Schwandt and Moriarty, "What Have the Past 25 Years," 319–20.
415. Foyle, *Honorably Wounded*, loc. 2465.
416. Wright, *Beating the Blues*, 94.
417. Zwickel, *Workplace Stress*, 11.
418. Carr, "Mobile Member Care Team," 79–80.

in an unrelated act), projection (i.e., attributes to others one cannot accept of him or herself), rationalization (i.e., every reaction must have a logical reason), compensation (i.e., competing to compensate for perceived failure), withdrawal (i.e., excessive reading, sleeping, daydreaming), insulating (i.e., avoids interaction with others), and regression (i.e., the past becomes more important and glorious).[419] Missionaries will experience stress in all areas of their lives. They need to learn to not just live with stressful demands of their missionary career, but to cope well so that they can thrive.

Culture Shock

Anthropologist Kalvero Oberg first coined the term culture shock. He determined six facets of this experience:

> 1) Strain due to the effort required to make necessary psychological adaptations, 2) A sense of loss and feelings of deprivation in regard to friends, status, profession, and possessions, 3) Being rejected by and or rejecting members of the new culture, 4) Confusion in role, role expectations, values, feelings, and self-identity, 5) Surprise, anxiety, even disgust and indignation, after becoming aware of cultural differences, and 6) Feelings of importance due to the inability to cope with the new environment.[420]

Culture shock, or cultural stress, "results from the insecurity people feel who know well the rules of one cultural game, but find themselves in another game in which they are constantly unsure of whether obedience to the rules they know will result in an effective interaction or in being penalized for breaking some rule of which they may be unaware."[421] Judith and Sherwood Lingenfelter define culture shock as, "an emotional state of stress, depression, and varying degrees of impaired function caused by constant exposure to people whose way of life conflicts with our own."[422] It is the "psychological disorientation resulting from being in an unfamiliar culture."[423] Many missionaries deny ever experiencing culture shock;[424]

---

419. Folger-Dye, "Decreasing Fatigue and Illness," 80–85.
420. Jones, *Psychology of Missionary Adjustment*, 40.
421. Kraft, *Communication Theory for Christian Witness*, 103.
422. Lingenfelter, *Teaching Cross-Culturally*, loc. 1248–52.
423. Steffen and McKinney-Douglas, *Encountering Missionary Life and Work*, loc. 1081.
424. Folger-Dye, "Decreasing Fatigue and Illness," 80–85.

yet, Hofstede and Hofstede claim, "studying culture without experiencing culture shock is like practicing swimming without water."[425] Culture shock commonly happens to anyone spending six months or more in a new culture. Some individuals have culture shock for a short period, but for others it can last much longer.[426]

The acculturation process requires the process of culture shock. Though considered negative, adoption of new cultural attitudes, values, and behaviors cannot ensue without cultural stress.[427] Nonetheless, to truly acculturate, a missionary must face and overcome culture shock during each cultural transformation. Culture shock, a necessary part of acculturation, moves through several phases. First the "sojourners experience" happens as the new missionary's fascination and enthusiasm overcomes the encountered hardships of day-to-day life. The missionary then moves into the "crisis" phase when the differing values between his or her host and home culture produces feelings of anger, anxiety, inadequacy, and frustration. Missionaries can become concerned with eating or drinking local food and water, excessively washing their hands, overly worried with cleanliness, and endure incredible homesickness. The last "recovery" phase sees the missionary able to live successfully and work in the host culture.[428] Not only do missionaries have to comprehend new cultural norms and rules, they also must often learn to communicate in a new language and this stress can make culture shock even worse.[429]

Missionaries experience stress again when they return to their cultural home called reversed culture shock. They frequently do not realize this will happen and feel surprised by their emotions of confusion, fatigue, insecurity, and loneliness. Missionaries do not expect home to change but many things have altered socially, and within the extended family. The missionary families have lost their ministry roles, have resettlement problems, and have returned to feeling like beggars as they raise their support again.[430]

---

425. Hofstede and Hofstede, *Cultures and Organizations Software of the Mind*, xi.

426. Lingenfelter and Lingenfelter, *Teaching Cross-Culturally*, loc. 1252.

427. Furnham and Bochner, *Culture Shock*, 197–98.

428. Hofstede and Hofstede, *Cultures and Organizations Software of the Mind*, 324; Rogers and Steinfatt, *Intercultural Communication*, 213; Savicki et al., "Intercultural Development," 158.

429. Foyle, *Honorably Wounded*, loc. 911.

430. Foyle, *Honorably Wounded*, loc. 2993–3035; Pierce, "Holistic View of the Missioning Process," 38–41; Rogers and Steinfatt, *Intercultural Communication*, 213.

Burnout

Jarrett Richardson says that burnout "is a phenomenon frequently experienced by missionary personnel. It develops from exposure to chronic stress that gradually exceeds the individual's physical, emotional, and spiritual coping mechanisms."[431] Burnout occurs with highly committed and motivated idealists who work with other human beings[432] and as, "a state of fatigue or frustration brought about by devotion to a cause, way of life, or relationship that failed to produce the expected reward."[433] Missionaries are highly dedicated and driven crusaders who work with other human beings. They must be "all things to all people" and "there is never any time when they are free from their duties; their duties are often not clearly defined and criteria for knowing when they have done their duty are often ambiguous."[434] They most often do not receive recognition or reward for the excessive work they do. This makes them prime candidates for burnout.[435]

A missionary's age may also influence burnout. "We have observed that younger missionaries are often at higher risk for emotional trauma or burnout. Lack of life experience and unresolved psychosocial tasks leave them vulnerable, especially when their much needed technical skills entice their agencies to place them in positions of heavy responsibility."[436] Young or old, burnout can happen to missionaries unless they recognize the stress that produces it and have the tools to cope with it.

Compassion Fatigue

When a natural disaster happens, not only do missionaries live through the trauma they also are usually first responders to give aid to the national victims. People who work extensively with trauma victims can be susceptible to Compassion Fatigue or secondary traumatic stress.[437] The cost of caring can be high for health care workers and missionaries.[438] Compassion Fatigue happens when the missionary engages with another person

---

431. Richardson, "Psychopathology in Missionary Personnel," 97.
432. Pines, "Burnout," 387; Tan, *Rest*, 180–81.
433. Freudenberer, *Burnout*, 13.
434. Gish, "Sources of Missionary Stress," 237.
435. Donovan and Myors, "Reflections on Attrition in Career Missionaries," 49; Foyle, *Honorably Wounded*, loc. 2691.
436. Miersma, "Understanding Missionary Stress," 98.
437. Maloney, "Critical Incident Stress Debriefing," 111.
438. Collins and Long, "Too Tired to Care?," 19.

"in an empathic relationship characterized by the identification with and understanding of their emotional experience," which emotionally impacts the missionary on both a conscious and subconscious level. Psychology labels this countertransference.[439]

A history of personal trauma makes the missionary more vulnerable to Compassion Fatigue.[440] The symptoms of Compassion Fatigue (e.g., depersonalization, emotional exhaustion, and reduced personal accomplishment) mimic burnout; nonetheless, burnout gradually wears down workers, which differs from the sudden and acute onset of Compassion Fatigue symptomatology.[441] Though a concern, not all missionaries fall prey to Compassion Fatigue. These individuals tend to derive great satisfaction from working with trauma survivors and this compassion satisfaction becomes a protective factor.[442] Missionaries must be careful not to fall prey to Compassion Fatigue by maintaining good personal, spiritual, and physical health.

Anxiety

Missionaries often experience feelings of anxiety. "This frequent experience, often felt as pervasive uneasiness, a specific fear, or a dread associated with particular circumstances or events, is perhaps an area where we [missionaries] all stand on common ground but negotiated quite differently."[443] The average missionary tends to worry more than others because he or she may live in unpredictable circumstances, may not complete his or her goals, and/or may become frustrated with the process of acculturation.[444] Hofstede and Hofstede claim, "extreme ambiguity creates intolerable anxiety."[445] This ambiguity defines a missionary's life as he or she learns the language and rules of the new culture. Often problems such as war, governmental coups, gangs, political demonstrations cause missionaries' anxieties concerning safety for family and team, concerns about if and when they would be evacuated, apprehensions for the national church and friends, and worries over

439. Collins and Long, "Too Tired to Care?," 372; Devilly et al., "Vicarious Trauma," 37.

440. Deighton et al., "Factors Affecting Burnout," 65.

441. Collins and Long, "Too Tired to Care?," 19; Maloney, "Critical Incident Stress Debriefing," 111.

442. Collins and Long, "Too Tired to Care?," 19.

443. Powell, "Short-term Missionary Counseling," 128.

444. Folger-Dye, "Decreasing Fatigue," 79; Schwandt and Moriarty, "What Have the Past 25 Years," 318.

445. Hofstede and Hofstede, *Cultures and Organizations Software of the Mind*, 165.

possessions.[446] Foyle believes feelings of anxiety could signal the beginning of one's failing coping ability.[447] No matter the circumstances, missionaries will not be able to avoid anxiety or stress.

Depression

With the high stress and trauma filled lifestyle of missionaries, depression becomes a very common malady.[448] "Depression is probably the most common psychopathology present in missionary personnel. A wide variety of stressors express themselves through the final common pathway of the depressive syndrome and its variants."[449] Depression can result from acculturation or as the Lingenfelter's call it "becoming a 150 percent person" is difficult and can cause depression.[450] Also, missionary wives have a higher risk of depression and low self-esteem because they are not perceived as missionaries on the same level as their husbands.[451] Missionaries face physical elements and encounter spiritual warfare which produce anger and depression.[452] Nevertheless, missionaries rarely admit depressive symptomatology because they view depression as a sin or lack of faith.[453] Only as missionaries learn the physical, emotional, and spiritual aspects of depression will they be able to counteract its destructive power and avid burnout and leaving the field.

Post-Traumatic Stress Disorder

Even with the strong exposure to stress and trauma, very few missionaries exhibit PTSD symptomatology. Bagley found in his study of missionary trauma that only 24 percent of the missionaries surveyed reported PTSD symptoms at "the most difficult period of adjustment to their most stressful

---

446. Carr, "The Mobile Member Care," 81–82; Carr, "Critical Incident Stress Debriefings," para. 12.

447. Foyle, *Honorably Wounded*, loc. 315.

448. Carr and Schaefer, "Coping with Stress and Trauma," para. 12; O'Donnell, "Member Care on the Field," 291; Schaefer et al., "Traumatic Events and Posttraumatic Stress," 529.

449. Richardson, "Psychopathology in Missionary Personnel," 97.

450. Lingenfelter and Lingenfelter, *Teaching Cross-Culturally*, loc. 1248–52.

451. Crawford and DeVries, "Relationship Between Role Perception," 188; Schwandt and Moriarty, "What Have the Past 25 Years," 318.

452. Love, *Muslims, Magic and the Kingdom of God*, 151–55.

453. Foyle, *Honorably Wounded*, loc. 570.

experience on the mission field" and that none reported PTSD symptomatology at the time of the survey. Also, 72.4 percent of the missionaries reported not suffering any PTSD symptoms.[454] In another study of European missionaries, only 2 percent showed PTSD symptoms, whereas West African missionaries revealed a bit higher rate at 5 percent. Missionaries in the Ivory Coast, Guinea, and Nigeria experienced the highest levels of PTSD at 28 percent.[455] Foyle surveyed 150 missionaries and found that only 10 percent had been involved in extremely violent situations and of these only four mentioned PTSD symptoms.[456] These surveys tend to show that despite the increased stress and trauma missionary life causes, most missionaries do not fall prey to PTSD.

People who decide to become missionaries must realize that they have chosen a life that can be filled with danger and stress. The application process, support raising, saying goodbye to friends and family, and moving to a country starts the stress accumulation that can cause the missionary to leave before the end of his or her first term. The stress builds with language learning and acculturation. During this process, all missionaries, whether they know it or not, go through not only culture shock in their host country but also reverse culture shock when returning home. As the missionary toils with the national church and missionary team, conflict and lack of recognition for his or her hard work can lead to burnout. Missionaries live through traumatic events and can fall prey to Compassion Fatigue, anxiety, and depression. Trauma can also cause missionaries to suffer PTSD, however, most seem to display resiliency to this psychological disorder.

Conclusion

Researchers continue to investigate physical and psychological trauma, discovering and refining new courses of treatment. Trauma can vary from Type I (single-blow events) to Type IV (many types of or repeated trauma over a lifetime), or from human made to acts of God. People can react to traumatic situations by experiencing stress, anxiety, burnout, depression, or PTSD.

Missionaries, probably more than the average North American citizen, must cope with extreme and reoccurring stress and trauma. They not only deal with human and natural disasters, heightened crime, hostile governments, and ministry concerns; they have to do it all in a new culture. Missionaries endure more stress than the average person because of

---

454. Bagley, "Impact of Trauma," 151–52.
455. Carr and Schaefer, "Trauma and Traumatic Stress," 280–81.
456. Foyle, *Honorably Wounded*, loc. 2910.

excess ministry and cross-cultural expectations. They must endure culture shock to truly acculturate into their field of service. Burnout can happen more easily for missionaries because of their high commitment to God, their support base, their idealistic view of what can be accomplished on the field, their need to work with co-missionaries and nationals, and their perceived worth. They often fall victim to Compassion Fatigue because they not only live through the traumatic events, they also serve as first responders to the country's survivors. Missionaries can easily have anxiety over their financial, living, and social situations. This stress, burnout, anxiety, and Compassion Fatigue often cause missionaries to experience depression, which can lead to attrition.

3

Biblical Personalities and Trauma

Towards a Theology of Well-Being

Introduction

SINCE ADAM AND EVE sinned in paradise, humanity has suffered. Today, newspapers and televisions proclaim humankind's enduring trauma from natural disasters (e.g., earthquakes, floods, and hurricanes); yet, most traumatic events come from social and economic exploitation (e.g., war, disease, poverty, pestilences, and famine).[1] C. S. Lewis, in his thesis, *The Problem of Pain*, states that human history "is largely a record of crime, war, disease, and terror, with just sufficient happiness interposed to give them [the victim] while it lasts, an agonized apprehension of losing it, and, when it is lost, the poignant misery of remembering."[2]

Human beings cannot exist without pain and suffering, and there could be no life with its omission.[3] Nevertheless, people rail against the seemingly injustice of suffering. They point to God claiming that a just God would not allow traumatic events that cause suffering. Lewis writes: "If God were good, He would wish to make His creatures perfectly happy, and if God were almighty, He would be able to do what He wished. But the creatures are not happy. Therefore, God lacks either goodness, or power, or both. This is the problem of pain in its simplest form."[4]

This problem of pain and suffering caused theologians throughout history to question how a good God could allow people to suffer. Yet God, through biblical stories, provided people clues to not only how to survive traumatic events, but also how to move from suffering to well-being. Noah built an ark, per God's instruction, and then witnessed the total destruction of the world (Gen 6–7). Sold into slavery by his brothers, Joseph overcame

---

1. Farmer, *Pathologies of Power*, 42–50; Heubach, *Problem of Human Suffering*, 5–7.
2. Lewis, *Problem of Pain*, 14.
3. van der Poel, *Wholeness and Holiness*, 35.
4. Lewis, *Problem of Pain*, 26.

betrayal, abuse, and imprisonment to become second in command in Egypt (Gen 37–40). Daniel lived through captivity, slavery, and near death from hungry lions (Dan 1–6). These biblical characters and many others resided through multiple traumatic events, persevered, and in many ways thrived (Heb 11:32–38). This chapter will observe the trauma experienced by several biblical characters to determine how they coped with the suffering they endured, and from these clues start the process of determining a biblical theology of well-being.

Biblical Personalities and Trauma

The Bible is full of narratives of men and women who suffered a lifetime of trauma. It seems that after choosing to leave the idyllic and peaceful life in the Garden of Eden, humanity began their struggle with the natural and human disasters of earth. This study focuses on 23 biblical characters[5] as representatives of trauma in Scripture. Their lives will be observed to determine the types of trauma they suffered by using the trauma categories of the Trauma Event Questionnaire (TEQ).[6] The TEQ categories include: Traumatic accident, natural trauma, violent crime, war related trauma, hostage event, child/adulthood physical or sexual abuse, vicarious or secondary events, and psychological/physical trauma. These people will then be divided into the trauma classifications of Type I, II, III, and IV (see Appendix A). Then, by utilizing the symptom criteria of the DSM-V, a determination will be made if any suffered with PTSD. Since these observations can only be pulled from the biblical text and not by having the subject take the TEQ or the PTSD Checklist Civilian (PTSDC)[7] the results will be my interpretation of their stories.

Traumatic Accident

The first TEQ category is traumatic accident, which includes the single-blow type trauma of car accidents, fires, and explosions. Only one of the 23 biblical

---

5. I chose the following 23 biblical characters: Daniel, David, Elijah, Elisha, Gideon, Hagar, Hannah, Jeremiah, Jesus, Job, John the Baptist, Jonah, Joseph, Lot, Mary Mother of Jesus, Moses, Naomi, Noah, Paul, Peter, Rehab, Sarah, and Stephen. My dissertation committee and I selected these characters because they had sufficient stories to extrapolate trauma suffered and coping skills used.

6. Vrana and Lauterbach, "Trauma Events Questionnaire."

7. Weathers et al., "PTSD Checklist (PCL)."

characters experienced this type of trauma (see Table 3.1.). Paul endured three shipwrecks on his missionary journeys.

In Second Corinthians, Paul gives an overview of all the traumatic experiences he overcame. In this statement, he includes his traumatic accidents, "Three times I was shipwrecked, I spent a night and a day in the open sea . . . in danger at sea" (2 Cor 11:25). In Acts 27, Paul gives a more detailed account of the shipwreck on his trip to Rome. From the start, Paul experienced problems with this voyage. The winds did not cooperate, causing them to slowly sail close to the coastline. Paul tried to warn the centurion of the perils of continuing the trip, but the guard listened to the ship owner and sailed on to Crete. A storm with "hurricane force" (Acts 27:13) winds hit the ship. The tempest lasted 14 days and, at one point, they "gave up all hope of being saved" (Acts 27:20). The ship finally ran ashore on the island of Malta (Acts 28:1). These traumatic accidents caused so much suffering that Paul "despaired even of life" (2 Cor 1:8).[8]

Natural Trauma

The second TEQ category includes natural disasters such as earthquakes, tornadoes, avalanches, floods, fires, hurricanes, and volcanic eruptions. Of the 23 biblical characters, 12 suffered these "God made" traumas (see Table 3.1.). Natural trauma along with vicarious or secondary trauma tied as the second most suffered biblical trauma.

Moses and Jonah suffered the most natural trauma of the 12 biblical characters. Though God had different reasons to send these disasters (Moses—to get Pharaoh to release the Israelites; Jonah—to encourage him to be obedient), they still had traumatic outcomes to those who underwent them. Moses along with the Israelites and Egyptians endured all eight plagues. These disasters built one upon the other until the final plague when the death angel killed every first born unless lamb's blood adorned the doorpost (Exod 11–12). This "great cry in Egypt surely was an outcome of this extensive trauma."[9] Moses also walked through the Red Sea (Exod 14:21) and experienced another plague among the Israelites because of sin with the Moabites, which killed 24,000 people (Num 25:9). Jonah withstood a violent storm at sea (Jonah 1:4) and suffered heat stroke from the scorching east wind and sun (Jonah 2:8).

The Bible recounts other traumatic natural experiences endured by some of its main characters. Drought and famine traumatized Elijah (1 Kgs

---

8. Adewuya, "Sacrificial-Missiological Function of Paul's Sufferings," 90.

9. Floyd, *Crisis Counseling*, loc. 482.

17), Jeremiah (Jer 14), and Naomi (Ruth 1:1). A lion and bear attacked David (1 Sam 17:37). Jesus and Peter endured a violent storm on the Sea of Galilee (Matt 8:23–27; Mark 4:36–41; Luke 8:22–37). Both Lot and Job witnessed fire from heaven, which devastated Lot's home in Sodom (Gen 19:16-23) and killed all of Job's sheep and the servants watching them (Job 1:16). Noah watched a cataclysmic event as water fell from the sky and springs below the earth erupted to create a flood that destroyed the earth (Gen 7:11)[10] and Paul lived through an earthquake while in a Philippian prison (Acts 16:26). Natural disasters and acts of God seem to be prevalent throughout the Bible and they negatively affected some who lived through them.

Violent Crime

The third trauma category of the TEQ is Violent Crimes. This type includes the traumas of rape, robbery, and assault. This second highest trauma affected 11 of the 23 biblical characters (see Table 3.1.).

Peter seemed to have suffered the most in this classification, with Jeremiah and Jesus a close second. Peter not only endured crimes against himself, such as being imprisoned by the Sanhedrin (Acts 4:3; 5:18) and Herod (Acts 12:4), flogged (Acts 5:40), and threatened with death (Acts 5:33), but he also assaulted the high priest's servant by cutting off his ear at Jesus' arrest (John 18:10). Commonly accepted church tradition says he later died by being crucified upside down in Rome.[11]

Jeremiah withstood many beatings and imprisonment by the priest Pashbur (Jer 20:2), the captain of the guard Irijah (Jer 37:14-16), and King Zedekiah (Jer 37:20–21). The king's officials tried to kill him by lowering him into a muddy cistern and leaving him to starve (Jer 38:6). Many times, during these traumatic events, Jeremiah felt he would die.

Violent crime filled Jesus' last hours on earth. The High Priest illegally[12] arrested Him (Matt 26:47-56; Mark 14:43-50; Luke 22:47-53) and the

---

10. Roop, *Believers ChurchBible Commentary: Genesis*, 70.

11. Barclay, *Master's Men*, 27.

12. Roger Hahn asserts the Jewish legal codes that one can read today "were written 150 years later in Mishnah" so no one really knows the code at the time of Jesus' trial (Hahn, *Matthew*, 317–18). However, Craig Keener expresses that the Sanhedrin needed 23 members to establish quorum for any capital offense trail. In Jesus' case the Sanhedrin gave no advanced notice, they held it at night in the high priest home instead of the temple's Chamber of Hewn Stone. Keener maintains, "Such a meeting is illegal on all these counts, although they would no doubt have explained it as only a preliminary inquiry before a real investigation. The lack of advance notice could have been excused because it is during a feast and all necessary officials are in town; but because Jewish law

Sanhedrin blindfolded then spit on Him and repeatedly beat Him (Matt 26:57-68; Mark 14:53-65; John 18:12, 13, 19-24). The Romans stripped, mocked, and flogged Jesus. They then crowned Him with a crown of thorns and hung Him on a cross (Matt 27:27-56; Mark 15:16-41; Luke 23:33-49; John 19:17-30).

Ferocious offenses such as rape, murder, robbery, and beatings affected many other biblical characters. Sexual trauma transpired when the men of Sodom surrounded Lot's house and demanded to have sexual relations with his guests (Gen 19:4-5). Then threaten him with death and tried to force their way into his house (Gen 19:9). Robbery and murder affected Job when the Sabeans and Chaldeans killed his servants, and stole his oxen, donkeys, and camels (Job 1:14-17). Joseph's brothers hated him so much that they threw him into a cistern while deciding how to kill him (Gen 37:20).

Kings and high officials committed violent crimes against several biblical personalities. David survived numerous attacks from King Saul (1 Sam 18:10—19:16). Mary, Joseph, and baby Jesus escape the genocide of baby boys caused by King Herod (Matt 2:13-18). This king also imprisoned and killed John the Baptist (Matt 14:3-10; Mark 6:17-27). Potiphar sent Joseph to prison (Gen 39:20). Paul survived stoning in Lystra (Acts 14:19), and several whippings and beatings with rods in Caesarea and Philippi (Acts 16:22; 2 Cor 11:23-38). He also endured imprisonment in Philippi (Acts 16:23), Jerusalem (Acts 21-23), and Rome (Col 4:10). Moses committed a violent crime when he killed an Egyptian in his rage over a mistreated Hebrew slave (Exod 2:12).

War Related Trauma

The Bible recounts many stories of warfare. War related trauma is the fourth category of the TEQ. Of the 23 personalities reviewed, only seven suffered traumatic events associated with war (see Table 3.1.) and of those, David and Moses had the most trauma caused by war.

David became a warrior at a very young age when he fought Goliath (1 Sam 17:32-50). He faced the traumas of war and fought the giant seasoned warriors feared to combat (1 Sam 17:8-11). The book of 1 Samuel records other battles David fought against the Philistines, Amalekites, and then against King Saul and Israel (1 Sam 21-30). As king of Judah, David had to fight a civil war against the house of Saul and Israel (2 Sam 2-3). Even in his

---

forbad trials on the Sabbath, they were probably forbidden on feast days" (Keener, *IVP Bible Background Commentary*, 177).

later years, the fighting continued when he had to battle a rebellion caused by his son Absalom, in which his son died (2 Sam 18).

Moses also had several war experiences. Pharaoh chased him and his followers into the Red Sea (Exod 14:9), the Amalekites attacked them at Rephidim (Exod 17:8), and he went to war with the Amorites (Num 21:21–24) and the Midianites (Num 31). Both David and Moses lived through many battles and they suffered both physically and emotionally the agony war creates.

Several other of the biblical personalities investigated survived war related traumatic events. Rahab hid the Israelite spies; then, helped them to escape Jericho, after which she witnessed the destruction of her city (Josh 2:2–22). Nebuchadnezzar besieged Jerusalem while Daniel resided there (Dan 1:1). Elisha suffered through the prolonged siege of Samaria by King Ben-Hadad that caused people to eat their children. The King blamed Elisha for this blockade and tried to kill him (2 Kgs 6:13–33). Gideon battled the Midianites, Amalekites, and other Eastern peoples (Judg 6:33). These ruthless tribes so frightened Gideon that the biblical account finds him threshing wheat in a wine press in his effort to hide from his attackers.[13] Jeremiah predicted and then witnessed the destruction of Jerusalem (Jer 6). These and many others not mentioned lived through the horrors of war and endured.

Hostage Event

The narrative of Scripture tells of times when people captured and held others against their will. Hostage events comprises the fifth category of the TEQ. Of the 23 characters investigated, seven endured the trauma of being taken prisoner (see Table 3.1.).

Sarai (Sarah) survived two hostage events. Interestingly, her husband Abram (Abraham) instigated both her captivities. The first happened in Egypt when Abram wanted to live there because of a famine in Negev (Gen 12:10). Abram feared Pharaoh would want beautiful Sarai and kill him for her. So, he told Sarai to tell people that she was his sister (Gen 12:11–13). Pharaoh took Sarai to make her his wife. Abram not only let Pharaoh seize her, he accepted dowry money for her (Gen 12:15–16). Only through God's intervention (i.e., inflicting serious diseases on Pharaoh and his household) did Sarai reunite with her family (Gen 12:17–20). Years later, the same thing happened again, only this time with King Abimelek of Gerar. Abraham told Sarah to again tell the king that she was his sister (Gen 20:1–2). Her beauty captured the King's heart and he took her into his palace to become his

---

13. Brensinger, *Believers ChurchBible Commentary*, 81.

wife. Through a dream, God told Abimelek of Abraham's deception and he gave Sarah back to Abraham along with sheep, cattle, slaves, and silver (Gen 20:3–17). Sarah must have been in Abimelek's household a long time because they realized that all the females (wife and slaves) could not conceive (Gen 20:17). The Bible does not elaborate on Sarah's feelings; yet, she probably felt abandonment by her husband, fear of being forced to be the wife of another, and distress over the thought of Abram being killed if the king found out. These emotionally traumatic events surely affected Sarah in her attitude towards her husband and God.

Other cases of hostage events include: Daniel seized and taken to Babylon to enter the king's service (Dan 1:2–5); David's wife and the wives and children of his army captured by the Amalekites (1 Sam 30:1–6); Abraham's enslavement of Hagar (Gen 16:1); Joseph sold into slavery by his brothers (Gen 37:25–27); Jeremiah and the remnant of Judah taken hostage to Egypt by Jonanah the son of Kareah (Jer 43:1–7); and Lot and his family taken hostage by the Kings of Elam, Goyim, Shinar, and Eilasar (Gen 14:12). Whether a person directly or vicariously (i.e., through family, friends) undergoes a hostage event it triggers a traumatic response. These men and women of the Bible understood the feelings of fear, anger, and hopelessness captivity produces.

Child/Adulthood Physical or Sexual Abuse

Child/adulthood physical or sexual abuse are the six and seventh categories of the TEQ. The Scripture does not speak much of childhood abuse. Nevertheless, of the 23 characters investigated, four survived adult sexual abuse (see Table 3.1.).

Joseph understood sexual harassment while living in Potiphar's house. He found favor with Potiphar and became the overseer of everything Potiphar owned (Gen 39:2–6). Potiphar's wife, who wanted the young and handsome Joseph, often tried to get him into her bed (Gen 39:7–10). Joseph continually refused until one day she caught him by the cloak, physically trying to get him to sleep with her. When he fled, leaving his cloak behind (Gen 39:12), Potiphar's wife accused him of trying to rape her (Gen 39:19–20). This accusation could have ended in execution, but Potiphar instead decided to throw him into prison.[14]

Lot lived in the city of Sodom and Gomorrah where sexual depravity abounded (Gen 18:20). It seems that this sexual corruption manifested in Lot and his family in two ways. First, Lot had no compulsion to protect his

14. Roop, *Believers ChurchBible Commentary: Genesis*, 257.

family from sexual harm. To keep his visitors from being abducted from his home and sexually molested by the men of his city, Lot offered his virgin daughters instead (Gen 19:8).[15] Second, Lot lost the respect of his daughters and, in their eyes, no sexual act was out of bounds.[16] Lot's daughters committed incest when they decided to sleep with him so that they could have children (Gen 19:35). It seems that sexual abuse began when Lot allowed his family to live in such a sexually immoral environment. This eventually eroded the natural human tendencies of family protection and parental respect, thereby, losing all human morality.[17]

Something, perhaps sexual, happened between Noah and his son Ham. The biblical account states that Ham "saw his father naked and told his two brothers outside" (Exod 9:22). Eugene Roop suggest that "saw his father naked" or "to uncover the nakedness" denotes a sexual event.[18] Thus, Noah cursed Ham and his descendants.

Prostitution can also be considered adult sexual abuse. Women, like Rahab[19] (Josh 2:1), most often do not have a choice in whether or not to

---

15. Eugene Roop sees Lot's offer of his virgin daughters to the mob to rape as Lot being willing to give his very best hospitality possible (Roop, *Believers Church Bible Commentary: Genesis*, 131–132). Danna Nolan Fewell and David Gunn find Lot's act of sacrificing his daughter's virginity for the sake of his guests "disgusting," showing the predominate values of "male over female, age over youth, with the father's power over the daughter epitomizing the social order. Lot is willing to sacrifice his daughters to uphold his honor as a provider of male hospitality" (Nolan Fewell and Gunn, *Gender, Power, and Promise*, 58).

16. Eugene Roop says that one could "condemn the daughters for arranging incest and belittling Lot for his drunken participation." He believes it is more the "action of very marginal people toward the future" (Roop, *Believers Church Bible Commentary: Genesis*, 132). Yet, Lusie Schottroff et al. state, "Israelite women consistently faced the threat of sexual assault. In addition to all her misery, a sexually assaulted woman must demonstrate her innocence and reckon with society's distain or be given as a wife to the man who assaulted her. If we read the explicit legal instructions of Leviticus 19 as an indication of a contrary reality, incest seems not to have been a rare occurrence. Behind the narrative of Lot's daughters there is possibly the recollection of daughters being sexually abused by their fathers" (Schottroff et al., *Feminist Interpretation*, 155).

17. Alice Ogden Bellis (*Helpmates, Harlots, and Heroes*, 66–67) agrees with the thought that having lived in the sexual perverse cities of Sodom and Gomorra, Lot's daughters lost their moral compass. She says, "Desperate to bear children, they commit incest with Lot by getting him drunk on two successive nights. To conceive children, they commit two sins: deception and incest. Ironically, they sexually manipulate the man who would have allowed a crowd to have their way with them."

18. Roop, *Believers ChurchBible Commentary: Genesis*, 76–77.

19. Some scholars state that Rahab was an innkeeper, not a harlot. Nevertheless, this cannot be justified in the Hebrew or Greek word translation, or its usage in Heb 11:31 or Jas 2:25. She may have engaged in both trades (Bible Hub, "Joshua 2:1").

use their bodies for survival.[20] The emotional trauma of both the sexual act and the psychosocial stigma overwhelms these women often to the point of hopelessness and despair.

Vicarious or Secondary Events

Traumatic events not only happen directly they can also happen vicariously. Vicarious (or secondary) events, the eighth category of the TEQ, happen when someone witnesses another person being mutilated, seriously injured, or violently killed. It can also occur when a person receives news of a family member or close friend being maimed, gravely hurt, or brutally murdered. Of the 23 characters investigated, over half suffered vicarious or secondary trauma (see Table 3.1.).

Secondary trauma affects a person most deeply when it involves family members. Many of the biblical characters studied had traumatic incidents within the family structure. Death of family members affected many of these people. Naomi lost her husband, Elimelech, and her two sons, Mahlon and Chilon, in a foreign land (Ruth 1:3, 5); a mighty wind killed all of Job's children (Job 1:18–19); and Lot's wife was turned to a pillar of salt (Gen 19:26). Jesus withdrew when he received the news that Herod had imprisoned (Matt 4:12) and, later, beheaded his cousin, John the Baptist (Matt 14:1–12; Mark 6:14–29). Mary, mother of Jesus, watched her son beaten and die on a cross (Matt 27:11–56; Mark 15:46) and later thought someone had stolen his body from the tomb (Mark 16:1; John 20:1–2). This trauma not only affected Mary but also her son's followers. Flora Keshgegian states,

> The cross was a crisis for Jesus' followers and those who came after. I would suggest that the crucifixion of Jesus was a traumatic event, for Jesus himself and for the community around him. It terrified and confused Jesus' friends. It left them bereft and abandoned. They did not know how to respond and deal with this loss and trauma, especially since they seemed more interested in sharing in Jesus' power than in his defeat.[21]

David suffered heartbreak when his son Absalom killed Amnon who raped Absalom's beautiful sister, Tamar (2 Sam 13).[22] He also anguished

---

20. Ogden-Bellis states that "In Hebrew society, harlots were outcasts who were tolerated but not held in honor . . . they wore different clothing, inhabited different parts of town, and did their business under the cover of night" (Ogden-Bellis, *Helpmates, Harlots, and Heroes*, 99).

21. Keshgegian, *Redeeming Memories*, 166.

22. The Bible does not say much about David's feelings about the rape of his

over the deaths of Absalom (2 Sam 18:33) and his newborn son with Bathsheba (2 Sam 12:15-18).

Biblical characters also endured vicarious trauma over the sufferings of friends and or acquaintances. Daniel might have observed the attempted killing of his friends Shadrach, Meshach, and Abednego when Nebuchadnezzar had them thrown into the blazing furnace (Dan 3:19–23).[23] David saw God kill Uzzah when he grabbed the falling Ark of the Covenant (1 Chron 13:10). Elijah lived with a widow and her son and witnessed the boy die (1 Kgs 17:18). King Jehoiakim killed the prophet Uriah, a compatriot of Jeremiah, for prophesying the same message of destruction (Jer 26:20–23). Jesus' friend Lazarus died (John 11) and it so affected Jesus that he wept (John 11:35).[24] Noah watched not only the people he lived with but also all the people of the earth die in the flood (Gen 7:6–16). Peter witnessed the arrest, trial, and possibly the crucifixion of his friend Jesus (Matt 26:47-67).

Secondary trauma can also affect people when they had a part to play in the event. Elijah called down fire from heaven and watched one hundred solders die (2 Kgs 1:9–14). God used Moses to free His people from Pharaoh. God employed Moses to turn water to blood (Exod 7:20) and sent plagues of frogs (Exod 8:5), gnats (Exod 8:17), flies (Exod 8:24), and locusts (Exod 10:13) against Egypt. God and Moses killed livestock (Exod 9:6), caused people to break out with boils (Exod 9:8-9), sent destructive hail (Exod 9:24), and plunged Egypt into darkness (Exod 10:22). Moses saw people he grew up with suffer under these plagues. Paul terrified and killed many in the early church before his conversion. In one vivid story, the people laid their coats at his feet before they stoned Steven, the first martyr (Acts 7:58). These vicarious traumatic events caused great suffering for these biblical characters.

---

daughter Tamar. Danna Nolan Fewell and David Gunn state, "When we read David's lament for Absalom we may mark the absence of such an outcry for Tamar. When he learns of the rape he is angry, but it is less clear that his anger is on behalf of Tamar more than it is frustration at the behavior of Amnon, 'for he loved him, for he was his firstborn son'" (Nolan Fewell and Gunn, *Gender, Power, and Promise*, 145).

23. The Bible does not record Daniel being present at this event, however, since he wrote about it in his book, one can conclude he knew what happened.

24. Some scholars believe that Jesus' compassion over the grief of Mary and Martha caused him to express emotional sadness. He "wept with those who wept" (Balswick and Balswick, *Family*, 203; Floyd, *Crisis Counseling*, loc. 1012; Macduff, *Mind of Jesus*, 42; Voorwinde, *Jesus' Emotions in the Gospels*, 172). Others claim that Jesus sobbed because "death was inevitable in a fallen world" (Allender and Longman, *Cry of the Soul*, loc. 1395) or that the "Divine Artificer mourning over His shattered handiwork; the Almighty Creator weeping over His ruined world; God, the God-man, 'grieving' over the Temple of the soul, a humiliating wreck of what once was made 'after His own image'" (Macduff, *Mind of Jesus*, 57).

Psychological/Physical Trauma

The last category of the TEQ, psychological or physical trauma, happens when someone perceives his or her immanent death or injury due to a traumatic event. A person can also have psychological/physical trauma with a traumatic conflict with another person or experiencing an incident that causes strong emotional reactions. Almost all the biblical characters studied experienced this trauma category (see Table 3.1.).

Psychological Trauma

Psychological trauma occurs when a person thinks he or she is in imminent danger or will be injured. Many of the biblical personas examined experienced this trauma in four ways. They received death threats, had conflict with others, experience spiritual terror, or suffered social related traumatic events.

DEATH THREATS

Throughout the Bible one observes death threats made on people by members of authority. When Nebuchadnezzar took Israel captive, Daniel often experienced death threats against him (Dan 2:12–13). The king even threw him in a den of lions because he would not change his devotional habits (Dan 6). God's prophets grew accustomed to the death threats of kings, queens, and the townsfolk. Jezebel wanted all prophets, including Elijah dead (1 Kgs 18:13—19:2). Not only did King Jehoiakim and Zedekiah covet Jeremiah's death (Jer 36:19—38:15), the people of Anathoth and Israel also desired his silence (Jer 11:18-23). Herod did not like what John the Baptist said about his relationship with his wife, Herodias, and planned to kill him (Matt 14:5; Mark 6:19). Paul received death threats in the towns where he preached the gospel: Antioch in Pisidian (Acts 13:50–51), Lconium (Acts 14:2, 5–6), Berea (Acts 17:13–14), Corinth (Acts 18:6), Achaia (Acts 18:12–17), Jerusalem (Acts 23:12–25), and Damascus (2 Cor 11:32–33).

The Bible also speaks about dysfunctional families. Moses faced a serious crisis when Pharaoh tried to kill him for murdering an Egyptian (Exod 2:15).[25] Gideon feared his family's anger so badly that he took down the family altar to Baal at night. Afterwards, the town's people tried to kill him (Judg 6:27, 30). Sarah mistreated her servant Hagar (Gen 16:6) and

---

25. Floyd, *Crisis Counseling*, loc. 273.

banished her and her son Ismael by sending them to die in the desert (Gen 21:8–10). Joseph's brothers hated him so much that they could not speak a kind word to him (Gen 37:4) and plotted to kill him (Gen 37:23). These life-threatening situations caused great fear and anxiety for the biblical men and women mentioned.

Conflict

Many Christians view conflict as sinful; nonetheless, many biblical characters had disagreements with others. Numbers of these clashes produced stress and probably became traumatic incidents. Abram and Lot encountered conflict between their families and servants causing a rift in the household (Gen 13:7–9). This dispute initiated a domestic split which eventually led Lot's family to a tragic turn of events in Sodom and Gomorrah.

Moses exemplifies leadership in conflict. He experienced the fear of rejection from the people God called him to lead.[26] The Israelites turned against him at the Red Sea (Exod 14:11), and they complained of having no water (Exod 15:23—17:3; Num 20:2) or food (Exod 16:3) in the desert. They did not want to follow Moses' commands (Exod 16:19–20). When the people revolted against God in Sinai, Moses had "whoever was on the Lord's side" slaughter their rebellious families, friends, and neighbors (Exod 32:25–29). The people mutinied at the entrance of the Promised Land and wanted to stone Moses (Num 14). Korah, Dathan, and Abiram, along with many others, revolted against Moses (Num 16:1–3) and the earth swallowed them alive. When the Children of Israel grumbled against him again later in their journey, God sent snakes to bite them (Num 21:4–8). Moses also had internal leadership conflict with Aaron and Miriam (Num 12:1).

Paul also experienced leadership difficulties. He had church conflict with the believers in Antioch (Acts 15:1–29), Corinth (1 and 2 Cor), Macedonia (2 Cor 7:5), Thessalonica (1 and 2 Thess), Galatia (Gal 3–6), and Philippi (Phil 1–3). He also exhibited personal conflict with Barnabas (Acts 15:2), and Peter (Gal 2:1–10).[27] Paul endured daily pressure with concern for all the churches in his care (2 Cor 11:23–28). These biblical stories related the difficulty of leadership and how it affects the emotions of the leader. Conflict produces anxiety and can at times be dangerous.

---

26. McNeal, *Work of Heart*, 7.
27. Meler, "Biblical Reflection," 472–75.

Spiritual Terror

Sometimes spiritual encounters can terrify a person thus becoming a traumatic experience. Nebuchadnezzar requested that Daniel interpret a dream, which caused the King to have terrifying thoughts (Dan 4:19). His vision of the four beasts frightened him so much that his face turned white (Dan 8:27). Daniel's vision of a man caused all those around him to flee in horror and left him on his knees with no strength, deathly pale, and trembling (Dan 10:7–8, 10, 12).

Satan tempted Jesus in the wilderness, which caused great emotional and physical stress (Matt 4:1–11; Mark 1:12, 13; Luke 4:1–13). He was "urged to use his power in his own service, rather than to depend on the Father's provision. He was given the chance to gain public notoriety short of serving others. He was offered kingship without personal sacrifice."[28] Jesus lived his life knowing he would die a horrible death on the cross, which for most human beings would have caused apprehension (Matt 16:21–28; Mark 8:31—9:1; Luke 9:22–27).

Used in the Septuagint version of Isaiah 53, the Greek word τραῦμα (trauma) describes how He [Jesus] was "wounded for our transgressions" (Isa 53:5). In this verse, Isaiah predicted that Christ would be traumatized so that humanity could be saved.[29]

John Macduff deems Jesus' life as one long martyrdom "[f]rom Bethlehem's manger to Calvary's cross, there was scarce one break in the clouds; these gathered more darkly and ominously around Him till they burst over His devoted head as He uttered His expiring cry."[30] Jesus went through deep emotional pain and spiritual trauma for the redemption of his people. This accounts for the basic emotional tenor of his life and ministry.[31]

Jesus also went through strong spiritual emotions at Gethsemane when sorrow overwhelmed him to the point of death as blood dripped from His pores (Matt 26:36–46; Mark 14:32–42; Luke 22:40–46).[32] Jesus' emotions completely unravel into a "state of extreme agitation."[33] Dan Allender and Temper Longman view these sufferings as dealing with pain, glory, and sight versus trust:

---

28. McNeal, *Work of Heart*, 58.
29. Floyd, *Crisis Counseling*, loc. 465.
30. Macduff, *Mind of Jesus*, 12.
31. Voorwinde, *Jesus' Emotions in the Gospels*, 217.
32. Allender and Longman, *Cry of the Soul*, loc. 1407; Casey, *Jesus of Nazareth*, 438.
33. Voorwinde, *Jesus' Emotions in the Gospels*, 47–48.

> Jesus began His earthly ministry with the temptation to fill His empty stomach (pain), regain the kingdoms of His creation (glory), and experience the tangible hand of God protecting Him (sight versus trust). At the end of His ministry, He was tempted again to avoid the agony of the cross (pain), demonstrate His power (glory), and be rescued by a legion of angels (sight versus trust).[34]

Three other biblical personalities confronted spiritual terror. Gideon had an encounter with the Angel of the Lord, which greatly alarmed him (Judg 6:22). Moses spoke face to face with God thus causing his face to shine so brilliantly that Moses covered it with a veil (Exod 34:29-35). Peter, along with the disciples, saw Jesus walking on the water and thought they saw a ghost, which frightened them (Matt 14:25). Peter asks Jesus if he can walk on water then becomes afraid and begins to sink (Matt 14:29-30). Meeting the all mighty God face to face can be a terrifying experience.

Social Related Traumatic Events

Trauma can also come through friends, family, or society. These types of events produce stress and trauma because people do not expect them. David did not envisage that King Saul would force his wife to marry another man during his exile (1 Sam 25:43-44). Betrayal abounds in the pages of Scripture: Joseph's brothers sold him into slavery (Gen 37:28) and the cup-bearer forgot his promise and left Joseph in prison (Gen 40:23). Judas betrayed Jesus for thirty pieces of silver (Matt 26:14-16; Mark 14:10-11; Luke 22:3-6). Peter disowned Jesus (Matt 26: 69-75; Mark 14:66-72; John 18:16-18, 25-27)[35] and people spoke falsely against Stephen which lead to his death (Acts 6:8-11).

Jesus suffered greatly from family, friends, and society. William O'Malley summarizes Jesus' traumatic last hours on earth:

> Jesus was betrayed by one of his own, humiliated and spat upon by ministers of his own religion, denied by his close friend, shunted from the Roman governor to the besotted puppet Herod and back again, rejected by the people who had cheered him through the streets the previous Sunday—for a convicted terrorist, scourged with leaded whips, mocked all night and beaten and crowned with thorns by solders with nothing better to do, booted throughout the streets, his raw back strewed on the stony ground as his wrists were nailed to the cross piece,

---

34. Allender and Longman, *Cry of the Soul*, loc. 1880.
35. Allender and Longman, *Cry of the Soul*, loc. 1411.

pulleyed upward to hang for at least three hours. Again, he was mocked by sadist priests shouting, "He saved others! He cannot save himself!" In mid-afternoon, he cried out in a loud voice... "My God! My God! Why have you deserted me?" (Ps. 22:1; Matt 27:47; Mark 15:34).[36]

Jesus anticipated rejection and violence from his disciples and society. However, his greatest anguish, and he may not have expected this, was when his Father turned his back on humanities sin placed on his son. Jesus for the first time felt abandoned and totally separated from God during his greatest time of need.[37]

Women often suffer because of societal rules. Sarah (Gen 11:30) and Hannah (1 Sam 1:5-7) experienced social and family taunting because of their barrenness. People in the Old Testament saw infertility as a sign of God's disfavor.[38] Mary might have still suffered "public disgrace" because of her pregnancy by the Holy Spirit even with Joseph trying to "divorce her quietly" (Matt 1:18-19). She also raised her child with a premonition of the violence her son would endure (Luke 2:34-35). Naomi (meaning pleasant) changed her name to Mara (meaning bitter) because of losing her husband and sons (Ruth 1:20). Psychological trauma causes havoc on the people who undergo it. As in contemporary society, biblical men and women suffered from death threats, traumatic conflict, spiritual terror, and unexpected traumatic social events.

Physical Trauma

Many of the biblical characters studied bore physical trauma. God gave Job painful sores from the soles of his feet to the crown of his head (Job 2:7). A large fish swallowed Jonah and he lived in the fish's stomach for three days (Jonah 1:17). Mary, eight months pregnant, traveled many miles to a strange city to give birth in a cave (Luke 2:4-7).[39] God blinded Paul at his conversion (Acts 9:8-9). Paul also claimed that for the ministry he often starved (2 Cor 11:27), worked too hard (2 Cor 11:27) and lived with what might have been a physical handicap (a thorn in the flesh) (2 Cor 12:7).[40]

36. O'Malley, *Redemptive Suffering*, 100-101.
37. Allender and Longman, *Cry of the Soul*, loc.1422.
38. Floyd, *Crisis Counseling*, loc. 768.
39. Craig Keener states that believers and pagans understood "that Jesus was born in a cave used as livestock shelter behind someone's home" (Keener, *IVP Bible Background Commentary*, 185).
40. Scholars have speculated that this thorn in the flesh could be epilepsy, depression, failing eyesight, or malaria (Stourton, *Paul of Tarsus*, 80).

Biblical men and women understood the traumatic forfeiture of property. Job lost all his livestock and wealth (Job 1:14–17). Naomi underwent physical and economic trauma being a resident alien in Moab (Ruth 1:1). As a widow with no sons or grandchildren, she had no way to make a living (Ruth 1:5).[41] Lot suffered the loss of his possessions when God destroyed Sodom and Gomorrah with fire (Gen 19:16–23). Moses forfeited the rights and comforts of royal living when Pharaoh banished him from Egypt (Exod 2:15).

Some biblical characters endured traumatic incidences because of hazardous locations. Lot lived a physically dangerous life in the sinful and treacherous city of Sodom and Gomorrah (Gen 18:20). Noah existed in a very violent world. He lived with the knowledge of God's future destruction of the world as he built a large ship in a place where it never rained (Gen 6:11–13). Physical trauma can happen to a person's body, to his or her property, or because of a precarious location. Psychological and physical traumatic experiences tend to wound both body and soul.

Table 3.1. Biblical Personalities TEQ Trauma

Trauma	Frequency	Percent
Danger of losing life/serious injury	20	87 percent
Vicarious trauma/ news of serious injury/ violent unexpected death of someone close	14	61 percent
Natural disaster	12	52 percent
Violent crime	11	48 percent
War Zone	7	30 percent
Taken Hostage	6	26 percent
Adult physical abuse	4	17 percent
Accident/fire/explosion	1	4 percent
Childhood physical or sexual abuse	0	0 percent

* In order of most trauma to least trauma.
(N = 23)

41. Roop, *Believers Church Bible Commentary: Ruth, Jonah, Esther*, 29–30.

The Bible does not paint an idealistic picture of the lives of those who follow God. The study of the traumatic incidents of these 23 biblical characters illustrates this point. People will eventually encounter loss and trauma at some point in their lives and God through His Word provides testimonies of those who lived through the same struggles. Stories of the traumatic accidents of Paul, the natural disasters Moses and Noah faced, the violent crimes Peter and Jeremiah endured, the trauma of war David and Elisha went through, the physical/sexual abuse borne by Joseph and Lot, the vicarious/secondary events Naomi and Mary the mother of Jesus witnessed, and the psychological/physical trauma experienced by Jeremiah and Lot show victims of trauma that they are not alone in their traumatic battles.

Trauma Types

Of the biblical characters studied, 11 experienced Type I traumas (i.e., single blow events).[42] Eight personalities experienced Type II trauma (e.g., war or sexual, physical, and emotional abuse, or if several Type 1 incidents happen repeatedly over a short time span in the past but then stopped).[43] Type III trauma (i.e., trauma that continues to happen such as racism or discrimination) happened to five of the people examined.[44] Interestingly, the five biblical characters that exhibited PTSD symptomatology suffered either Type II or III traumatic events.

Biblical Characters Presenting PTSD Symptomatology

Although most people have suffered at least one traumatic event during their lifetime, a small minority developed Post-Traumatic Stress Disorder (PTSD) (typically only 5 percent to 10 percent).[45] Yet, in this study five of 23 biblical characters (21.7 percent) displayed PTSD symptomatology (see Appendix C).

A diagnosis of (PTSD) must include seven symptoms found in the *Diagnostic and Statistical Manual of Mental Disorders, Fifth Edition* (DSM

---

42. These people include Elisha, Gideon, Hannah, John the Baptist, Jonah, Mary mother of Jesus, Noah, Peter, Sarah, and Stephen.

43. David, Elijah, Jesus, Job, Lot, Moses, Naomi, and Paul encountered repeated traumatic events.

44. Daniel, Hagar, Jeremiah, Joseph, and Rahab could be included in this group.

45. Bonanno et al., "What Predicts Psychological Resilience," 671; Bonanno et al., "Self-Enhancement Among High-Exposure Survivors," 984; Ibrahim et al., "Dynamics of Posttraumatic Growth," 121.

V).⁴⁶ For a person to develop PTSD, he or she must have exposure to a traumatic event and then exhibit a set of psychiatric indicators. According to the DSM-V, for a person to be diagnosed with PTSD, he or she must exhibit the following criterion: 1) For Criterion A, the person must have at least one stressor/trauma. 2) For Criterion B, the person must develop two intrusion symptoms (e.g., intrusive memories, nightmares, flashbacks, distress). 3) For Criterion C, the person must exhibit one avoidance symptom (e.g., avoiding trauma related thoughts, feelings, or external reminders such as people, places, etc.). 4) For Criterion D, the person must develop two or more negative alterations in cognitions and mood (e.g., cannot remember parts of the traumatic event, feelings of being bad, self-blame, not wanting to do pre-trauma activities, feelings of alienation, no positive emotions). 5) For Criterion E, the person must reveal two alterations in arousal (e.g., Irritable or aggressive and reckless behavior, hypervigilance, problems concentrating, cannot sleep). 6) For Criterion F, the person must exhibit these symptoms for at least a month.⁴⁷ With the difficulty of detecting these symptoms from the biblical account, some latitude must be allowed in assessing PTSD in the lives of Daniel, David, Elijah, Job, and Naomi.

Daniel

Daniel suffered from Type III trauma because he experienced traumatic events over a significant time period (Criterion A). He endured the horrors of war between Jerusalem and Babylon (Dan 1:1). King Nebuchadnezzar took him hostage and he remained in captivity the rest of his life (Dan 1:5). The king's officials wanted Daniel and all the wisemen dead (Dan 2:12–13). The other administrators tried to kill him by flattering the King to issue an edict that anyone who prayed to any other god except the King would be tossed into a den of lions (Dan 6). Daniel survived a night with hungry lions (Dan 6:1922). He also had terrifying prophetic dreams and interpretations (Dan 4:19; 7:28; 8:27; 10:7–8, 10, 12).

Daniel exhibited intrusive symptomatology (Criterion B) in several ways. The king asked Daniel to interpret his dream, which caused Daniel to be perplexed and terrified (Dan 4:19). The dream of the four beasts caused him to have deeply troubled thoughts and his face turned pale (Dan 7:28). The vision of the ram and goat wore out and exhausted Daniel for days (Dan 8:27). He had no strength and was left trembling after the

---

46. Bonanno et al., "Psychological Resilience after Disaster," 182.

47. American Psychiatric Association, *Diagnostic and Statistical Manual of Mental Disorders*, 271–80.

vision of the man (Dan 10:7-8). These prophetic encounters caused Daniel physical and emotional trauma.

One also sees avoidance and negative alterations in Daniel. He avoided interpreting Nebuchadnezzar's dream because it perplexed and terrified him (Criterion C) (Dan 4:19). The Bible vividly states the persistent negative emotions (Criterion D) of Daniel. He was terrified, deeply troubled, exhausted, overwhelmed with terror, and his face turned pale on several occasions (Dan 4:19; 7:28; 8:27; 10:7-8, 10, 12). He had feelings of alienation from others. His fellow wisemen feared him and government leaders wanted his death because of his dreams and visions (Dan 6—10). Daniel also had trouble sleeping (Criterion E) because of his disturbing dreams and visions (Dan 4, 7, 8, 10). With the symptomatology described in this section, one could diagnose Daniel as suffering from PTSD.

David

The Bible relates David's story in graphic detail. The Psalms recounts the emotional roller coaster of his life. The poetry of David's songs reaches beyond the words on the page and into the heart and soul of the reader.[48] David had many traumatic experiences (Criterion A) over his lifetime causing him to endure Type II trauma. In his youth, a lion and bear attacked him (1 Sam 17:37), he fought the giant Goliath (1 Sam 17:48-49), and he dodged many spears as King Saul tried repeatedly to kill him (1 Sam 18:10-11, 17; 19:11-14; 23:14-15). As an adult, David fought foreign wars with the Philistines and Amalekites (1 Sam), a civil war between Israel and Judah (2 Sam), and a rebellion with his son Absalom, which ended in Absalom's death (2 Sam 18). Family trauma also plagued David. King Saul forced David's wife to marry another man (1 Sam 25:43-44), the Amalekites captured David's wives and children (1 Sam 30:1-6), Amnon, David's son, rapes his daughter Tamar, which causes his other son Absalom to kill Amnon (2 Sam 13), and his infant son with Bathsheba dies because of David's sin (2 Sam 12:15-18). David also suffered vicarious trauma when he saw God kill Uzzah when he touched the Ark of the Covenant (1 Chron 13:10). With these accumulative traumatic events over David's lifetime, one could speculate that PTSD symptoms would follow.

The Psalms[49] graphically portray David's intrusive symptomatology (Criterion B). He writes about intense distress by saying, "I am poured out

---

48. Allender and Longman, *Cry of the Soul*, loc. 94.

49. Some scholars such as Nancy Declaisse-Walford, Rolf Jacobson, Beth Tanner, and Geoffrey Grogan do not believe David authored any of the Psalms (Declaisse-Walford

like water, and all my bones are out of joint. My heart has turned to wax; it has melted within me. My mouth is dried up like a potsherd, and my tongue sticks to the roof of my mouth; you lay me in the dust of death" (Ps 22:14–15). He felt great distress,

> "My eyes grow weak with sorrow, my soul and body with grief. My life is consumed by anguish and my years of groaning; my strength fails because of my affliction, and my bones grow weak. Because of my enemies I am the utter contempt of my neighbors and subject of dread to my closest friends-those who see me on the street flee from me. I am forgotten as though I were dead; I have become like broken pottery." (Ps 31:9–12)

David wrote about avoidance (Criterion C) by stating, "My thoughts trouble me and I am distraught because of what my enemy is saying, because of the threats of the wicked; or they bring down suffering on me and assail me in their anger . . . I said, 'Oh, that I had the wings of a dove! I would fly away and be at rest. I would flee far away and stay in the desert; I would hurry to my place of shelter, far from the tempest and storm'" (Ps 55:2–3, 6–8). He felt alienated from others (Criterion D) "But I am a worm and not a man, scorned by everyone, despised by the people. All who see me mock me; they hurl insults, shaking their heads" (Ps 22:6–7). David also exhibited persistent negative trauma related emotions, "My heart is in anguish within me; the terrors of death have fallen on me. Fear and trembling have beset me; horror has overwhelmed me" (Ps 55:4–5). He cannot sleep (Criterion E), "I am worn out from my groaning. All night long I flood my bed with weeping and drench my couch with tears. My eyes grow weak with sorrow; they fail because of all my foes" (Ps 6: 6–7). He had problems concentrating, "My thoughts trouble me and I am distraught because of what my enemy is saying, because of the threats of the wicked; for they bring down suffering on me and assail me in their anger" (Ps 55:2–3). David's traumatic events happened over a long period of time, "How long must I wrestle with my thoughts and day after day have sorrow in my life? How long will my enemy triumph over me?" (Ps 13:2). The overwhelming trauma David suffered left him feeling despised and alone (Ps 22:6–7). These symptoms seem to reveal a man suffering from PTSD.

---

et al., *Book of Psalms*, 11; Grogan, *Psalms,* 38). Nevertheless, other scholars deem that David wrote the seventy-three psalms superscripted *ledawid* reinforced by the facts of Old and New Testament support, the Jewish Talmud stating that David wrote all the psalms, and that the Dead Sea Scrolls claim that "David composed 3,000 psalms and 446 songs" (Holdcroft, *Psalms,* 12–13; Steveson, *Psalms,* xxv–xxvi). Therefore, this study will attribute to Davidic authorship the Psalms of 3–41, 51–72, and 138–145.

Elijah

The prophet Elijah survived Type II trauma by living through many traumatic events (Criterion A). Elijah suffered through a famine in Israel (1 Kgs 17:1, 7); while he lived at the house of a widow her son died (1 Kgs 17:18); he called down fire from heaven to kill one hundred solders (2 Kgs 1:10-12); and Queen Jezebel tried to kill him twice (1 Kgs 18:13—19:2). These situations combined to produce depression[50] and PTSD symptomatology in Elijah.

After the prolonged psychological distress of the traumas Elijah encountered (Criterion B), he came to a broom bush tree, sat down under it and prayed that he would die, "I have had enough, Lord," he said. 'Take my life; I am no better than my ancestors'" (1 Kgs 19:4-5). He suffered recurrent, involuntary, and intrusive memories when he told God, "The Israelites have rejected your covenant, torn down your altars, and put your prophets to death with the sword. I am the only one left, and now they are trying to kill me too" (1 Kgs 19:10). Avoidance (Criterion D) became evident when he ran for his life and while in the wilderness he prayed to die (1 Kgs 19:4-5). Elijah exhibited persistent, often distorted negative beliefs about himself and the world, "I am the only one left, and now they are trying to kill me too" (1 Kgs 19:10). He also blamed others (the Israelites) for causing the traumatic event (1 Kgs 19: 9). Elijah displayed self-destructive behavior (Criterion E) by not wanting to eat and desiring to die, and irritable behavior, when, after hearing from God, he "pulled his cloak over his face and went and stood at the mouth of the cave" (1 Kgs 19:13). With these symptoms, one could deduce a diagnosis of PTSD for Elijah.

Job

When a person thinks of biblical trauma, he or she often remembers Job. God allowed Satan to inflict Job with many traumatic events (Criterion A) causing him to suffer from Type II trauma. Fire came from heaven and killed all of Job's sheep and killed the shepherds watching them (Job 1:16). The Sabeans attacked and stole all of Job's oxen and donkeys and slayed all the servants guarding them (Job 1:15-16). The Chaldeans raided Job's camp, took all his camels and once again murdered all his servants (Job 1:17). A mighty windstorm slaughtered all of Job's children (Job 1:18-19) and then

---

50. Scholars have noted Elijah's depression (Baker, "Elijah," 2; Wohlgelernter, "Death Wish in the Bible," 135). Dwayne and Susan Howell state that Elijah's introversion and his maladaptive thought patterns may have factored into his depression (Howell and Howell, "Journey to Mount Horeb," 657-58).

he suffered from painful sores from the crown of his head to the soles of his feet (Job 2:7). These traumas happened in rapid succession leaving Job psychologically wounded, sitting in a pile of ashes.

Job presented intrusive symptomatology (Criterion B) when he declared that the "arrows of God" continued to poison him and the "terrors of God" assaulted him (Job 6:4). He felt God unjustly abusing him.[51] He displayed avoidance (Criterion C) by asking to be left alone (Job 13:13) and his reluctance to accept his friend's efforts at comforting him, "I have heard many things like these; you are miserable comforters, all of you!" (Job 16:2). He felt alienated from society because the text says that children despised him "Even the little boys scorn me: when I appear they ridicule me" (Job 19:18) and friends abhorred him, "All my intimate friends detest me; those I love have turned against me" (Job 19:19).

Job demonstrated negative alterations in mood (Criterion D) by cursing his birthday, "May the day of my birth perish, and the night that said, 'a boy is conceived!' That day-may it turn to darkness" (Job 3:3-4). By wishing he had never been born, "Why did I not perish at birth, and die as I came from the womb?" (Job 3:11). By giving up hope, "My days are swifter than a weaver's shuttle, and they come to an end without hope" (Job 7:6—19:10). By feeling anguish and bitterness of soul, "Therefore I will not keep silent; I will speak out in the anguish of my spirit, I will complain in the bitterness of my soul" (Job 7:11), and by hating his life, "I loathe my very life; therefore I will give free rein to my complaint and speak out in the bitterness of my soul" (Job 10:1). Job underwent "what John of the Cross called 'the dark night of the soul,' when everything in the soul, craves union but God is—or profoundly feels—silently distant."[52]

Job displayed irritable behavior (Criterion E) by tearing his clothes, shaving his head, and falling to the ground after hearing of his children's deaths (Job 1:20). He wept to the point of death, "My face is red with weeping, darks shadows ring my eyes" (Job 16:16). He could not sleep and had nightmares, "I have no peace, no quietness; I have no rest, but only turmoil" (Job 3:26). "When I lie down I think, 'How long before I get up?' The night drags on, and I toss and turn until dawn" (Job 7:4). "Even then, you frighten me with dreams and terrify me with visions" (Job 7:14). Job could not function occupationally or in society after his trauma because of his PTSD symptomatology.

---

51. Verbin, *Divinely Abused*, 2–3.
52. O'Malley, *Redemptive Suffering*, 74.

Naomi

Naomi's story starts with a natural traumatic event (Criterion A). Famine gripped the land of Israel. The scarcity of food caused Elimelech to leave Bethlehem with his wife, Naomi, and their two sons, Mahlon and Chilion, and settle in Moab (Ruth 1:1). Then, personal tragedy strikes, Elimelech dies (Ruth 1:3). This forces Naomi to fend for her sons in a foreign land. The sons marry two Moabite women named Orpah and Ruth (Ruth 1:4). Ten years later, Mahlon and Chilion die leaving their wives childless (Ruth 1:5). Once again, Naomi finds herself and her daughters-in-law in danger; they are women, without family, in a foreign land, deprived of a way to earn a living.[53] Grief stricken and hearing that the famine ended, Naomi decides to return to Judah. She starts the journey with both daughters-in-law but only Ruth stays with her to the end. These traumatic events caused Naomi to suffer Type II trauma.

Naomi exhibited irritable behavior (Criterion B) toward her daughters-in-law when she asked them to leave her (Ruth 1:11) and toward her neighbors when they tried to welcome her back to town (Ruth 1:19–20). She also displayed intense distress when she changed her name from Naomi (meaning pleasant, delightful, or happy) to Mara (meaning bitter) (Ruth 1:20). Naomi continually told her friends of her bitter circumstances (Criterion C) and blamed God for them (Ruth 1:21). She felt the persistent negative traumatic related emotion of shame (Criterion D).

Naomi demonstrated reckless behavior (Criterion E) by encouraging Ruth to be sexually seductive toward Boaz (Ruth 3:3–4).[54] The traumatic events caused Naomi to lose social status. She had become a widow, childless, and reduced to having her daughter-in-law glean fields. With the above symptomatology, Naomi could be diagnosed with PTSD.

God has filled the Bible with stories of people's lives and the traumatic events they survived. This study examined only 23 of them who endured traumatic accidents, natural disasters, violent crimes, war, hostage events, adult sexual abuse, vicarious, psychological, and physical trauma. These biblical characters withstood Types I through III trauma yet, as what can be seen in Scripture, only five exhibited PTSD symptomatology. This could be attributed to resiliency by the implementation of good coping skills.

---

53. Roop, *Believers Church Bible Commentary: Ruth, Jonah, Esther*, 30.
54. Roop, *Believers Church Bible Commentary: Ruth, Jonah, Esther*, 66.

Biblical Personalities and Coping

Most of the 23 biblical characters studied rebounded from their traumatic experiences and thrived. Even those who exhibited PTSD symptomatology seemed to cope with their misfortune and grew godlier in character. The coping mechanisms most common to all include: trusting God, asking assistance from God, praising and worshiping God, working with God, having a sense of call, expressing one's complaints to God (lamenting/venting), having a theology of suffering, and receiving help from family and society (see Appendix B). This section will review how the biblical personalities used these coping skills to undergo Post-Traumatic Growth.

Trusting in God

When times become traumatic, a person finds hope of survival in his or her trust in God.[55] This trust, nonetheless, does not mean that one does not experience doubt and fear. Ken Sande says,

> Trusting God does not mean that we will never have questions, doubts, or fears. We cannot simply turn off the natural thoughts and feelings that arise when we face difficult circumstances. Trusting God means that in spite of our questions, doubts, and fears we draw on His grace and continue to believe that He is loving, that He is in control, and that He is always working for our good. Such trust helps us to continue doing what is good and right, even in difficult circumstances.[56]

The highest coping skill used by the biblical characters examined is trusting in God. Of the 23 biblical characters, 16 trusted in God to help them survive the traumatic events they underwent. They realized that surrendering their perceived control to an all-powerful God would be the only way to endure the trauma they faced. These persons included Daniel, David, the prophets Elijah, Elisha, and Jeremiah, as well as other Old and New Testament characters.

Daniel

During his Babylon captivity, Daniel trusted God. He first showed this trust when, by not accepting the King's food, he declared his allegiance

---

55. Theodoret, *Theodoret of Cyrus Commentary on the Psalms*, 324.
56. Sande, *Peacemaker*, 65.

to God and trusted that God would keep him and his fellow Israelites healthier than the other captives.[57] Daniel trusted again when he heard that his friends Shadrach, Meshach, and Abednego professed their faith in the one true God causing the king to throw them into a blazing furnace. John Lederach deems that both narratives "are martyr stories in that Daniel and his three friends are ready to die rather than to deny their faith. In their faithfulness to God, Daniel and his companions are determined to follow their understanding of God's way whatever the cost."[58]

Under similar circumstances, the king threw Daniel into a den of lions because of his faith in God. When Daniel survives the night, "no wound was found on him, because he had trusted in his God" (Dan 6:23). Daniel illustrated the suffering servant in that he would serve the Lord even unto martyrdom.[59] He and his friends trusted in the God who shows mercy in all situations.[60] Daniel did not waver in his trust in the Lord.

David

The Psalm "of disorientation . . . captures the struggle of the heart" as it "attempts to grasp the goodness of God in light of heartache of life."[61] One of the major themes of David's Psalms is trust. James Waltner states, "Fear is the common reaction in the face of insecurity and whatever threatens life. However, the psalmist is not overcome by fear; instead, he overcomes his fear by trust in God. Trust in God robs fear of its quality of terror."[62]

When the Amalekites took the wives and children of David's army captive and his men wanted to kill him, David "strengthened himself with trust in his God" (1 Sam 30:6b, The Message). During David's enslavement by the Philistines, he put his trust in God (Ps 56:1–5). While he hid from King Saul, he trusted in the Lord and remained confident that God would deliver him (Ps 63:9–11). He trusted that the Lord would never let him down. In Psalm 34, he writes, "The Lord is close to the brokenhearted and saves those who are crushed in spirit. The righteous person may have many troubles, but the Lord delivers him from them all" (Ps 34:18–19).

In Psalms 142 one can sense David's desperation. The strain of being despised and pursued permeates every word. David saw no way out; he

---

57. Lederach, *Believers Church Bible Commentary: Daniel*, 39.
58. Lederach, *Believers Church Bible Commentary: Daniel*, 125.
59. Mathews, "When We Remember Zion." 115.
60. Lederach, *Believers Church Bible Commentary: Daniel*, 145.
61. Allender and Longman, *Cry of the Soul*, loc. 97.
62. Waltner, *Believers Church Bible Commentary: Psalms*, 280.

had no one to turn too except for the Lord. The Lord was his last chance, his only hope.[63] When King Saul's men waited outside David's house to kill him,[64] David proclaimed God's dependability stating that he could count on the Lord and because of this steadfast love he could sing in the midst of danger (Ps 59:10, 17).

David uses the Hebrew word בָּטַח (*batach*, trust) 17 times[65] and most of the time this trust in God relates to traumatic times. David writes: "To you they cried out and were saved; in you they trusted and were not put to shame" (Ps 22:5); "The Lord is my strength and my shield, my heart trusts in Him" (Ps 28:7); "the Lord's unfailing love surrounds the one who trusts in Him" (Ps 32:10); "When I was afraid, I put my trust in you" (Ps 56:3); "in God I trust and am not afraid" (Ps 56:4, 11). David learned that only in trusting in God could he survive the trauma in his life.

The sixteenth century theologian John Calvin views David as 1) accepting that God would be always present in his suffering. 2) David trusted God as a "powerful, open, accepting, and witnessing God" who would order all things. 3) From this sense of protection and trust the Psalms proclaim that God is in control and with His assistance "those who have felt helplessness in the face of violence can once again imagine themselves as agents whose actions in the world matter."[66] Trauma will cause fear. James Waltner sees David as not "overcome by fear; instead, he overcomes his fear by trust in God.[67] Trust in God robs fear of its quality of terror." The Psalms proclaim that David overcame his trauma because he suffered for the sake of God.[68] David wrote about his trust in God through his family's kidnapping, his capture and enslavement by the Philistines, and Saul hunting him. David knew to survive trauma, he had to trust in a God who had everything under control even in the face of chaos.

Elijah, Elisha, and Jeremiah

Prophets suffer many traumatic experiences because people do not like to be reminded of their sin or of how God will destroy them because of it. God often asked these men not only to speak His words, but also to

---

63. Waltner, *Believers Church Bible Commentary: Psalms*, 676.
64. Waltner, *Believers Church Bible Commentary: Psalms*, 289.
65. To trust in God: Ps 9:11; 21:8; 22:5, 6; 25:2; 26:1; 28:7; 32:10; 37:3; 40:4; 55:24; 56:5, 12; 62:9; 143:8. To trust or rely upon God: Ps 31:15; 37:5 (Bible Hub "982. Batach").
66. Jones, *Trauma and Grace*, 57.
67. Waltner, *Believers Church Bible Commentary: Psalms*, 280.
68. Mathews, "When We Remember Zion," 116.

live through the destruction they predicted. Elijah, Elisha, and Jeremiah trusted in the one true God and this faith helped them cope with the suffering they endured.

During a famine, Elijah trusted God to provide for him in the Kerith Ravine, east of Jordan. God sent ravens to supply him with food (1 Kgs 17:4). He later went to live with a widow and her son who had very little food. Elijah asked them to trust in God by first providing a meal for him, then themselves. He declared, "For this is what the Lord, the God of Israel says: 'The jar of flour will not be used up and the jug of oil will not run dry until the day the Lord sends rain on the land'" (1 Kgs 17:14).

When the Arameans surrounded Elisha's city, his frightened servant did not know what to do. Elisha trusted God to deliver them and said, "'Don't be afraid . . . Those who are with us are more than those who are with them' . . . the Lord opened the servant's eyes, and he looked and saw the hills full of horses and chariots of the fire all around Elisha" (2 Kgs 6:16–17).

Jeremiah trusted in God throughout his ministry. From the beginning, he had to hold on to this trust and proclaim the terrifying message of his people's annihilation. God told Jeremiah, "They will fight against you, but will not overcome you, for I am with you and will rescue you, declares the LORD" (Jer 1:19). Jeremiah had faith in God during Israel's drought and famine (Jer 14). Over and over, he proclaims the Lord's faithfulness as the hope of Israel and Savior in troubled times (Jer 14:8, 22). He continues by stating strength to endure trauma comes from the Lord alone (Jer 17:5–7) because he is a "refuge in the day of disaster" (Jer 17:17). God called Elijah, Elisha, and Jeremiah to speak the terrifying words of God and then live through the horror they just described. Yet, these prophets all trusted in the God they served to rescue them from the traumatic events they faced.

Other Old Testament Biblical Characters

Many other Old Testament characters coped with their trauma by trusting God. Gideon trusted that he would not die when he saw the Angel of God (Judg 6:23). In the midst of Job's suffering, he trusted in God's will for his life, "Shall we accept good from God, and not trouble?" (Job 2:10b). "Though he slay me, yet will I hope in him" (Job 13:15a). Job's coping style caused Soren Kirekegaard to denote him as the "prototype for humanity, who guarantees that there is a victory amidst the bitterest sorrow."[69] Susan Mathews sees Job's suffering as an illustration of what "a person of integrity

---

69. Kirekegaard, "The Lord Gave, and the Lord Took Away," 23.

does in the face of it: cling to God in faith and continue to serve God for nothing save that relationship."[70]

Jonah seemed to have complete trust in God. Even when running away from God's will, he slept through a violent storm (Jonah 1:5). However, a few scholars believe Jonah's deep sleep indicated a desire to die.[71] No matter how he felt in the boat, he trusted in God to rescue him from the fish's belly, "But you, Lord my God, brought my life up from the pit" (Jonah 2:6b).

Joseph trusted God in all his circumstances and later told his brothers, "Don't be afraid. Am I in the place of God? You intended to harm me, but God intended it for good to accomplish what is now being done, the saving of many lives" (Gen 50:19–20). He had the ability to view trials and suffering as God's way to help others, including his family[72] and to reveal God's glory.[73] Eugene Roop says that Joseph's story shows that "the presence of God brings life in the place of death, honor instead of humiliation, and fertility over sterility."[74]

Others also trusted God through in traumatic times. Moses trusted God when Pharaoh's army advanced toward the defenseless Israelites at the Red Sea. He stated, "Do not be afraid. Stand firm and you will see the deliverance the Lord will bring you today. The Egyptians you see today you will never see again. The Lord will fight for you; you need only to be still" (Exod 14:13–14). The Bible discloses that Noah trusted God and entered the Ark with his family (Gen 7). Rahab had faith in the foreign God of the Israelites. Since she hid and helped the Israelite spies escape, she and her family survived the destruction of Jericho (Josh 2–6). These people trusted in Jehovah to deliver them from whatever came their way.

New Testament Biblical Characters

Trusting in God continues in the lives of New Testament personalities. The most important person and model for all Christian coping is Jesus. At the beginning of his ministry, Satan tempted him in the wilderness. Jesus withstood the shame of temptation to model for all believers how they can withstand the shame often associated with trauma.[75] Jesus trusted his Father for food when

---

70. Mathews, "All for Not: My Servant Job," 68.

71. Bolin, *Freedom Beyond Forgiveness*, 30; Roop, *Believers Church Bible Commentary: Ruth, Jonah, Esther*, 116.

72. Floyd, *Crisis Counseling*, loc. 1347.

73. Kaiser, *Biblical Approach to Personal Suffering*, 126.

74. Roop, *Believers Church Bible Commentary: Genesis*, 261.

75. Allender and Longman, *Cry of the Soul*, loc. 1883.

he taught his disciples to pray, "Give us today our daily bread" (Matt 6:11); and for safety, "Deliver us from the evil one" (Matt 6:13).

As one reads the gospel story of Jesus, he or she witnesses examples of Jesus' trust in his Father. Jesus did not fear the violent storm, chiding his disciples by saying, "Why are you so afraid? Do you still have no faith?" (Mark 4:40; Luke 8:25). He believed that God would raise Lazarus from the dead, "Our friend Lazarus has fallen asleep; but I am going there to wake him up" (John 11:11). Jesus knew and trusted in God's will for his life, even to death on a cross. He tells Judas, "Get behind me Satan! You are a stumbling block to me; you do not have in mind the concerns of God, but merely human concerns" (Matt 16:23; Mark 8:33). In the Garden of Gethsemane while being arrested, he speaks to Peter, "Put your sword away! Shall I not drink the cup the Father has given me?" (John 18:11). Jesus communicates to the Sanhedrim at his trial, "You would have no power over me if it were not given to you from above" (John 19:11). Even His last words signified the trust he had in God, "Father, into your hands I commit my spirit" (Luke 23:46).

Jesus' mother, Mary, trusted in God throughout her traumatic life. When the angel appeared to tell her, she would conceive from the Holy Spirit, she replied in faith, "I am the Lord's servant . . . May your word to me be fulfilled" (Luke 1:38). From that moment on, Mary lived under the social stigma of conceiving a child out of wedlock and knowing that her son would suffer and die. The Bible says, "But Mary treasured up all these things and pondered them in her heart" (Luke 2:19) and by doing so, she expressed her hope and trust in God.

Stephen trusted God with his life. He preached the Word of God during violent times in Jerusalem. His words so infuriated the men in the synagogue that they took him outside the city and started stoning him. Through this traumatic event, one witnesses Stephen's faith when he or she reads his prayer, "'Lord Jesus, receive my spirit.' Then he fell on his knees and cried out, 'Lord, do not hold this sin against them'" (Acts 7:59–60).

When one hears Paul's story, he or she senses his strong trust in the Lord. He pens to the church in Corinth that through hard times, "Instead of trusting in our own strength or wits to get out of it, we are forced to trust God totally" (2 Cor 1:10, The Message). The prayers of believers assisted this trust as Paul writes, "As you help us by your prayers" (2 Cor 1:11). Paul knew that only through unreserved reliance on God and depending on the collective prayers of the church could he successfully cope with each traumatic experience.[76] Paul viewed everything that happened to him as

---

76. Tucker and Andrews, "Historical Notes on Missionary Care," 25.

the sovereign will of God (2 Cor 4:7–18). This does not mean that Paul did not have doubts or that he at no time asked God to relieve his suffering (2 Cor 12:7–8). But when the Lord's response did not match Paul's request, he consciously decided to believe that God had something better in mind (2 Cor 12:9–10). This was especially evident during Paul's many imprisonments, which he always considered to be part of God's plan for advancing his kingdom (Eph 4:1; Phil 1:12–14; Col 4:3).

Trust allowed Paul to express emotions paradoxical to what usually accompanies trauma. He declares with trust in Christ he could be "hard pressed on every side, but not crushed; perplexed, but not in despair; persecuted but not abandoned; struck down, but not destroyed" (2 Cor 4:8–9); "beaten, and yet not killed; sorrowful, yet always rejoicing poor, yet making many rich; having nothing, yet possessing everything" (2 Cor 6:9–10). As each traumatic event happened, Paul's trust in God grew.[77]

Paul also needed to trust God in his afflictions. He had to "trust God totally" (2 Cor 1:10, The Message) in a Corinthian jail. Even though he was "under great pressure, far beyond [his] ability to endure," "despaired of life," and felt he had received a death sentence, he knew it happened so that he would not rely on himself but on God "who raises the dead" (2 Cor 1:8–9). One can speculate that Paul writes to the various churches about what he has learned about trusting his Lord and Savior who helped him through being overworked, imprisoned, sleep deprived, starved, beaten, stoned, robbed, and shipwrecked. Despite all his traumatic experiences, he knew that only through trust in God could he find joy. He wrote to the Roman church, "May the God of hope fill you with all joy and peace as you trust in him, so that you may overflow with hope by the power of the Holy Spirit" (Rom 15:13).

Peter trusted God to help him do the impossible even when it led to traumatic events. He did not back away from crisis situations. Whether failing at walking on water or denying his Lord, Peter trusted that Jesus would forgive and restore him.[78] These biblical characters knew that to be resilient in traumatic times they had to put their trust in a God who had total control of their lives. They saw that hope and joy could only be realized through trust.

Asking Assistance from God

The second largest coping mechanism evidenced by the biblical personalities studied is asking God for help. This coping style works hand-in-hand

---

77. Sande, *Peacemaker*, 67–68.
78. Barclay, *Master's Men*, 23–24.

with trust because one must have faith in God to ask for His assistance. Jesus taught that like fathers on earth, the heavenly Father would listen and give good gifts to those who petition. "Ask and it will be given to you; seek and you will find; knock and the door will be opened to you. For everyone who asks receives; the one who seeks finds; and to the one who knocks, the door will be opened" (Luke 11:9–10). Of the 23 biblical personalities studied, 15 asked God for help in their trauma. The Bible records that David appears to talk to God more than the others.

David

David did not fear asking for God's assistance. While on the run from Saul, he cries for help in times of trouble and God hears him (Ps 18:6). When David calls out, God "saved him out of all his troubles" (Ps 34:6). David promises restful sleep for those who trust (Ps 3:5–6) and that He sends His angels to surround and protects those who ask (Ps 34:7). If one cries for assistance, "The Lord hears them; he delivers them from all their troubles" (Ps 34:17). God watches and listens attentively to every cry from the righteous (Ps 34:15). In Psalms 34, David once again calls out to God to rescue him from his enemies (v. 17). It is a fourfold cry for assistance to "deliver [v. 4], protect [v. 6], deliver [v. 17], save [v. 18]."[79] Martyrs through the ages have quoted Psalms 34, believing with David that God heard their prayers and, even in their darkest hours, they trusted in the Lord's liberation.[80]

David wrote Psalms 3 about his flight from his son Absalom.[81] During this traumatic event David turns to God stating, "With all my might I shout up to God, His answers thunder from the holy mountain. . . . Up, God! My God, help me! Slap their faces. . . . Real help comes from God. Your blessing clothes your people!" (Ps 3:3–8, The Message). David called for help when the Philistines captured him (Ps 56:9); he petitioned God for mercy while hiding in the caves from Saul (Ps 57:1–2; 142:5–6); and he appealed for deliverance when Saul tries to kill him in his home (Ps 59:1–2).

Throughout the Psalms, David pleads for God's help in times of trouble. He solicits for rescue (Ps 17:13; 22:21; 31:2), salvation (Ps 60:5—62:2), a quick remedy (Ps 70:5—71:12), and a listening ear (Ps 4:1; 17:6; 30:10). David cries out so much that he writes, "I am worn out calling for help; my throat is parched. My eyes fail, looking for my God" (Ps 69:3). Yet, through it all he knows that "The Lord is my strength and my shield; my heart trusts

79. Waltner, *Believers Church Bible Commentary: Psalms*, 291.
80. Waltner *Believers Church Bible Commentary: Psalms*, 183.
81. Theodoret, *Theodoret of Cyrus Commentary on the Psalms*, 60.

in him, and he helps me. My heart leaps for joy, and with my song I praise him" (Ps 28:7). David recognizes that to move from pain to hope one must allow God to minister to his or her wounded soul. Allender and Longman affirm, "Thus the psalmist's only recourse is to appeal to God for help and wait with confidence that He will turn sorrow into joy."[82]

John Calvin portrays the need for believers to directly petition God for provision and rescue.[83] This beseeching instills in the person the habits necessary for recovering from traumatic events. When everything seems to be going wrong, prayer begins with a cry for help. Then God answers the human call and goes into action to defend his people. As God stands by a person's side, he or she can face whatever comes.[84]

Old Testament Biblical Characters

Old Testament followers of God wanted to know how He would deliver them from trauma. During the destruction of Jerusalem, Jeremiah asked God to "pour out your wrath on the nations that do not acknowledge you, on the peoples who do not call on your name" (Jer 10:25). When the people of Anathoth plotted to kill him, Jeremiah requested to witness God's vengeance on them (Jer 11:20). While the drought and famine in Israel raged on, he pleaded, "Although our sins testify against us, do something, LORD, for the sake of your name. . . . You are among us, LORD; and we bear your name; do not forsake us!" (Jer 14:7, 9). Jeremiah requested that God rescue and avenge him as the Babylonians took him captive (Jer 15:15), when the people wanted to kill him (Jer 18:19–23), and after the guards beat and put him in stocks (Jer 20:11–12). God comforts Jeremiah when the King Zedekiah imprisoned him by saying, "Call to me and I will answer you and tell you great and unsearchable things you do not know" (Jer 33:3). The Old Testament followers of God wanted to know how he would deliver them from trauma.

Daniel knew that during hard times one had to pray and solicit God for assistance. When the wisemen of Babylon could not interpret the king's dream, the king decided to have them all put to death. Daniel urged his friends to "plead for mercy from God of heaven concerning this mystery" (Dan 2:18) and the Lord gave him the understanding for the vision. As the King threw Daniel into a den of lions, the King said, "May your God, whom you serve continually, rescue you!" (Dan 6:16). Daniel beseeched

---

82. Allender and Longman, *Cry of the Soul,* loc. 2284.
83. Jones, *Trauma and Grace,* 55–57.
84. Waltner, *Believers Church Bible Commentary: Psalms,* 42.

God over the desolation of Jerusalem, "Lord, listen! Lord, forgive! Lord, hear and act! For your sake, my God, do not delay, because your city and your people bear your name" (Dan 9:19). During the vision of a man dressed in linen, Daniel felt so weak that he could not communicate with the Lord and he begged God for strength. The man touched him and gave him the strength he needed (Dan 10:15-19).

These Old Testament people petitioned God for help in different traumatic situations. In times of war, people needed answers to their prayers of protection and victory. Elisha besought God to strike the Aram army with blindness so that he could lead them into Samaria where the city solders surrounded them (2 Kgs 6:18-22). Elisha also bids God to kill a contingent of fifty of Ahaziah's soldiers and their captain with fire from heaven (2 Kgs 1:12).

People call out to God during personal afflictions. God heard Ishmael's cry and led Hagar to a well of water (Gen 21:17-19). Hannah wept before the Lord pleading for a child (1 Sam 1:11-16). Her grief and crying out to God lasted for years, before she became pregnant because she "asked the Lord for him" (1 Sam 1:20).[85] After she gave her son to the temple, Eli blessed her and asked the Lord to bless her and give her more children (1 Sam 2:19-21). During his affliction of painful sores, Job solicited God for two things: to withdraw his hand and stop the trauma, and to call so that he could speak to God (Job 13:20-22). After being swallowed by a great fish, Jonah says, "In my distress I called to the Lord, and he answered me. From deep in the realm of the dead I called for help, and you listened to my cry" (Jonah 2:2).

God answers when asked to assist with conflict. Elisha did not like being teased about his bald head by a group of 42 boys. He "called down a curse on them in the name of the Lord" (2 Kgs 2:24) and as a result two bears mauled the boys. Rahab expected a *quid pro quo* from God. Since she showed kindness to the spies, she expected God to show her compassion and spare her family from the destruction of Jericho (Josh 2:11-13).

Moses appealed for help from the Lord many times during his 40-year journey in the wilderness. When the Israelites quarreled over not having water, Moses exclaimed, "What am I to do with these people? They are almost ready to stone me" (Exod 17:4-7) and the Lord told him what to do. When the people sinned against God, Moses interceded for them asking for God to show mercy (Exod 32:30-32). Moses entreated God to heal his sister Miriam of leprosy when she and her brother Aaron rebelled, wanting to lead the Israelites on their own (Num 12:10-13).

---

85. Floyd, *Crisis Counseling*, loc. 956.

Moses bargained with God to keep him from destroying the Israelites when they rebelled and would not enter the Promised Land (Num 14:13–19). When Korah, Dathan, and Abiram tried to take away Moses' leadership, he fell face down before the Lord to avert his wrath (Num 16: 4–15). No matter how rebellious the people of Israel became, Moses pleaded their case before God and the Lord relented and offered forgiveness (Num 21:7).

God answered prayers for healing and blessing. Elijah implored God to heal the widow's son (1 Kgs 17:20–21). Naomi requested that God bless Boaz so that he could become Ruth's kinsman redeemer (Ruth 2:20–22). When people lacked belief, God often sent a sign of his presence. Gideon tested God by asking him to have the morning dew only on the fleece and then the next day the dew would only be on the ground and not on the fleece (Judg 6:36–37). Testing God in the Old Testament usually was a sign of distain for God or attempting to force him to do the petitioner's will. God extends patience and mercy to Gideon because he needed assurance and was earnestly seeking God's will.[86] The Old Testament gives proof that when people in traumatic situations pleaded for help, *Yahweh* resolved their problems.

New Testament Biblical Characters

People in the New Testament continued to petition God for assistance in anxious times. Jesus consistently talked to the Father about all things, especially in traumatic situations. He comforted Martha, the sister of Lazarus, by saying "Your brother will rise again" (John 11:23). Then He called out at the tomb of Lazarus, "Father, I thank you that you have heard me. I knew that you always hear me, but I said this for the benefit of the people standing here, that they may believe you sent me" (John 11:41–42), and God answered him by raising Lazarus from the dead.

Jesus knew he would die, but as a human he did not want to go through the horrors this death would bring. So, he cries out, "Now my soul is troubled, and what shall I say? Father, save me from this hour? No, it was for this very reason I came to this hour. Father, glorify your name!" (John 12:27). Once again, in the garden of Gethsemane he pleads with his Father to take the "cup" away from him two times, but then he surrenders to the will of God (Matt 26:39, 42; Mark 14:35; Luke 22:42). Then, during His crucifixion, in the worst pain and anguish of His life, Jesus asks for the Father to "forgive them, for they do not know what they are doing" (Luke 23:33). Jesus knew the only way to withstand trauma was to call on God the Father for help and he would answer.

---

86. Brensinger, *Believers Church Bible Commentary: Judges*, 85.

The Apostle Paul also relied on praying for God's assistance during rough times in life. While in a Philippian jail, he writes, "Do not be anxious about anything, but in every situation, by prayer and petition, with thanksgiving, present your requests to God" (Phil 4:6). Paul pleaded with God three times to take away his "thorn in the flesh" (2 Cor 12:7–9). Nevertheless, God allowed Paul to suffer with this affliction, causing Paul to rely on God's strength to carry him through. He proclaims, "Therefore, I will boast all the more gladly about my weakness, so that Christ's power may rest on me. That is why, for Christ's sake, I delight in weakness, in insults, in hardships, in persecutions, in difficulties. For when I am weak, then I am strong" (2 Cor 12:9–10). Paul, along with the other biblical characters realized that to cope with trauma they had to ask God for help. These prayers gave strength and shifted their focus away from the traumatic event and onto the only one who could deliver them.

Praise and Worship to God

According to this study of biblical men and women, when one encounters horrific events, often praise and worship to God helps him or her to cope and move from suffering to joy. Of the 23 biblical characters studied, 12 used praise and worship as a coping devise. Throughout the Old and New Testament people raised their voices to God knowing that praising Him in hard times changed their attitude and focus. One witnesses this lavish praise and worship the most throughout the book of Psalms. Many of the songs David penned seemed to start with his frustration and pain over a traumatic situation but always ended in acclaim and adoration.[87] David and other biblical characters raised their voices in praise to the God, "an ever-present help in trouble" (Ps 46:1).

David

"The Psalter is a book of worship, driving us [believers] to God by insisting that we look to Him in the midst of our pain. When we do so, we find ourselves, and our problems absorbed into His bright glory."[88] The songs of David chronicle his long and painful struggle with the many traumas he

---

87. Many of the Psalms have a chiastic outline with the simplest form being A-B-B-A (Alden, "Chiastic Psalms (III)," 199).

88. Allender and Longman, *Cry of the Soul*, loc. 2390.

faced.[89] In times of trouble, David often starts his songs with accusations yet ends them with praise and worship to God. His Psalms teach others how "to wrestle with doubt" until their emotions erupt into praise and worship to God.[90]

After David witnessed God's deliverance from years of hiding from Saul, he praises the Lord, crying out his love for the God who saves (Ps 18:1–3).[91] He declares the importance of worship and seeks God in his temple amid danger (Ps 27:4). He sings of God's faithfulness to all who will listen (Ps 57:9–10).[92] For example, David fought valiantly in many battles. He even had to feign madness to keep from being captured by Abimelech. One again David opens his song with adoration, proclaiming that when a person worships God, it "opens the doors to all his goodness" (Ps 34:9 The Message).[93] He honors God, hungering and thirsting for more of him as he crosses the desert (Ps 63:1–8).[94] David calls out to God asking for mercy. He tells God all his complaints and troubles (Ps 142:1–2). Yet, he praised God for all the promises he fulfilled (Ps 56:12–13).

After the prophet Nathan told David that his infant son by Bathsheba would die because of his sin, David fasted and prayed desperately for mercy, sleeping on the floor and not leaving the palace. He was so distraught that his servants feared to tell him of the child's death. Yet, upon hearing the horrible news, David "got up from the ground. After he had washed, put on lotions and changed his clothes, he went into the house of the Lord and worshiped" (2 Sam 12:20).

David found strength in the Lord through adoration (Ps 21:13). Praise brought about joy even in suffering; "Praise be to the Lord, for he has heard my cry for mercy.... My heart leaps for joy, and with my song I praise him" (Ps 28:6–7). His wailing turned into dancing because God "removed [his] sackcloth and clothed [him] with joy" (Ps 30:11). He sang and played musical instruments proclaiming God's deliverance (Ps 71:22–23). He realized that only the Lord could endure his afflictions and bear his burdens (Ps 68:19). David understood the power of worship and praise in the face of adversity to raise his spirit and bring hope.

---

89. Allender and Longman, *Cry of the Soul*, loc. 1226.
90. Allender and Longman, *Cry of the Soul*, loc. 225.
91. Theodoret, *Theodoret of Cyrus Commentary on the Psalms*, 124; Waltner, *Believers Church Bible Commentary: Psalms*, 101.
92. Theodoret, *Theodoret of Cyrus Commentary on the Psalms*, 327.
93. Theodoret, *Theodoret of Cyrus Commentary on the Psalms*, 208.
94. Theodoret, *Theodoret of Cyrus Commentary on the Psalms*, 350.

Old Testament Biblical Characters

Many Old Testament biblical people offered up praise and worship during hard times. When King Nebuchadnezzar wanted to put all the wisemen including Daniel to death, Daniel praised the God who revealed "deep and hidden things" (Dan 2:22). The deliverance of Shadrach, Meshach, and Abednego from the fiery furnace caused Nebuchadnezzar to praise the God of these young men (Dan 3:28). "The prayer reflects the piety of the youths, while the narrative and the hymn provide a contrast between Nebuchadnezzar's limited power and majesty of God."[95] Even with a death threat over his head, Daniel continued to adore and thank his God three times a day (Dan 6:10). When he prayed about the desolation of Jerusalem, he praised the Lord for being a "great and awesome God, who keeps his covenant of love with those who love him and keep his commandments, we have sinned and done wrong" (Dan 9:4-5). Throughout Daniel's captivity, he continued to praise and to worship his God.

Others used praise and worship to God to cope with traumatic events. During the war with the Midianites, Amalekites, and Eastern people, Gideon worshiped God after learning about his part in winning the battle through the interpretation of a dream (Judg 7:13-15). As Hannah gave away her only beloved son to the temple she sings, "My heart rejoices in the LORD; in the LORD my horn is lifted high. My mouth boasts over my enemies for I delight in your deliverance" (1 Sam 2:1). Jeremiah declares that the Lord is his strength, fortress, and refuge in times of distress during the destruction of Jerusalem (Jer 16:19). While living through drought and famine he shouts, "Heal me, LORD, and I will be healed; save me and I will be saved for you are the one I praise" (Jer 17:14). After being beaten and put into stocks, Jeremiah sang to the Lord and praised him because "He rescues the life of the needy from the hands of the wicked" (Jer 20:13). Imprisoned by King Zedekiah, Jeremiah declared God's great power over the whole earth (Jer 32:17-19).

The man of suffering, Job also sang praises to the Lord. Upon hearing that raiders stole his livestock and a mighty wind killed his children, he fell to the ground and worshiped God proclaiming, "The Lord gave and the Lord has taken away; may the name of the Lord be praised" (Job 1:21b). After being affected with painful sores, Job praises God for his wisdom, power, counsel, and understanding (Job 12:13). Like Job, Jonah survived the trauma brought on by his disobedience by praising the Lord. During the violent storm at sea, he told the crewmembers that he worshiped "the

---

95. Lederach, *Believers Church Bible Commentary: Daniel*, 85.

Lord, the God of heaven, who made the sea and dry land" (Jonah 1:9). Even though premature, this song of thanksgiving allowed Jonah to hope in the Lord.[96] He shouted grateful praise to the Lord while in the stomach of the great fish (Jonah 2:9).

Moses also praised God during difficult times. Moses and his sister Miriam's song of praise (Exod 15:1–2) says that while walking through the Red Sea "I will sing to the Lord, for he is highly exalted. Both horse and driver he has hurled into the sea. The Lord is my strength and my defense he has become my salvation. He is my God, and I will praise him, my father's God, and I will exalt him."[97] Then, before his death Moses proclaims, "Oh, praise the greatness of our God! He is the Rock, his works are perfect, and all his ways are just. A faithful God who does no wrong, upright and just is he" (Deut 32:3–4). From birth to death and all the hardships in-between, God came near his people when they praised and worshiped him.

New Testament Biblical Characters

People living in New Testament times also realized the need to praise and worship God in traumatic times. When the angel told Mary that she would conceive a child by the Holy Spirit she praised the Lord God (Luke 1:46–49). Jesus constantly worshiped his Father. He proclaimed this to Satan during his temptation in the wilderness by saying, "Away from me Satan! For it is written: Worship the Lord your God, and serve him only" (Matt 4:10).

After Peter walked on water and almost drowned in the storm, he and the rest of the disciples worshiped the Son of God (Matt 13:32–33). Peter, along with the other apostles, continued to worship and praise the Lord, even when the Sanhedrin imprisoned and flogged them, proclaiming, "They had been counted worthy of suffering disgrace for the Name" (Acts 5:41).

While in a Philippian jail, Paul writes to the town's church: "Rejoice in the Lord always. I will say it again: Rejoice!" (Phil 4:4). Even when physically shackled, his spirit rejoiced unfettered.[98] In the same jail, Paul and Silas "were praying and singing hymns to God" (Acts 16:25) just before an earthquake set them free. Praise and worship to God does not change the traumatic circumstances a person suffers; nonetheless, these biblical characters realized that it did transform their attitude toward the suffering they endured.

---

96. McKenzie, *How to Read the Bible*, 8; Roop, *Believers Church Bible Commentary: Ruth, Jonah, Esther* 126, 149.

97. Janzen, *Believers Church Bible Commentary: Exodus*, 181.

98. Buechner, *Telling Secrets*, 102–3; Sande, *Peacemaker*, 67.

A Sense of Purpose/Call

In both the Old and New Testaments, God calls people to do a special work for him. This sense of call assisted 12 of the biblical characters studied to continue in the work no matter the trauma they experienced.

In the Old Testament, God called Abram to "go from your home country, your people and your father's household to the land I will show you" (Gen 12:1). This call moved Sarai into a nomadic lifestyle which probably affected her coping ability. From a burning bush, God called to Moses to go and deliver the Children of Israel from Pharaoh's cruelty (Exod 3:4-10). He did not turn away from his call even through traumatic times. An angel of the LORD called Gideon in his father's winepress saying, "Go in the strength you have and save Israel out of Midian's hand. Am I not sending you?" (Judg 6:14). Then Gideon tested this call by asking God for a sign (Judg 6:36-40). His call gave him assurance that God would be with him even when the odds were against him. Samuel anoints God's chosen king, David and "from that day on the Spirit of the Lord came powerfully upon David" (1 Sam 16:13). The Bible does not record Elijah's call, but God instructed Elijah to anoint Elisha as his successor (1 Kgs 19:16). Jeremiah also received a direct calling from God to be his prophet. Yahweh told him, "Before I formed you in the womb I knew you, before you were born I set you apart; I appointed you as a prophet to the nations" (Jer 1:5-10). Jonah ran from God's call to go to Nineveh and preach (Jonah 1:1).

God continued to call people in the New Testament. An angel called Mary to be the mother of Jesus (Luke 1:29-33). Jesus knew that he had to be about his Fathers business, which indicates a sense of calling (Luke 2:49). God called Jesus' cousin, John the Baptist before his conception (Luke 1:11-17). He leaned on his calling to be the messenger to prepare the way of the Lord while he waited for his death in prison (Matt 11:9-10). The Apostle Peter's calling came directly from Christ when he said, "Come follow me, . . . and I will send you out to fish for people" (Matt 4:18-20). Paul knew God called him on the road to Damascus to spread the gospel to both the Jews and Gentiles (Acts 9).

In times past, when people experienced trauma, they coped with these incidences by remaining hopeful and thinking positively with the help of the Holy Spirit (Phil 4:8). They understood living a Christian life meant one had to suffer like Christ and this suffering had meaning. They knew God would shape their characters through traumatic breaking and then rebuilding. The men and women studied had heard from God and this calling sustained them through the battles of life. Others, however, did not cope so well and did not recovered from the trauma they witnessed.

Working with God

When going through traumatic events, people cope better when they feel they have some power over the situation. Collaborating with God to solve traumatic problems gives the person a sense of control and lowers his or her anxiety level.[99] Of the 23 biblical personalities examined, eight of them used this coping technique. They worked with Jehovah in times of captivity, war, burdensome leadership, and traumatic circumstances. They found that through this collaboration, God built in them a godlier character.

Times of Captivity

Many biblical personalities experienced trauma because of captivity or because of living in exile. Nevertheless, as they worked with God, they not only survived their hostile environment, they thrived. In Babylon, Daniel decided not to defile himself by eating the royal food and wine. He asked permission from the chief official to allow the Hebrew young men to eat their Jewish diet. God blessed these young men and they became healthier than the other captives who dined on the royal food (Dan 1). The Lord helped Daniel interpret dreams for the Babylonian king (Dan 4:19–27).

Joseph worked together with God throughout his slavery in Egypt. Therefore, the Lord prospered everything he touched. He became the head of Potiphar's household (Gen 39:6). God granted him favor in prison and the warden gave him responsibility over all prisoners (Gen 39:20–21). After rising to power in Pharaoh's court, Joseph confronts his brothers and says, "I am your brother Joseph, the one you sold into Egypt! And now, do not be distressed and do not be angry with yourselves for selling me here, because it was to save lives that God sent me ahead of you" (Gen 45:4–5). Both Daniel and Joseph realized that even with the trauma of living in slavery, God had placed them in their situations for a reason and this understanding assisted them in the coping process. They also chose "faithfulness above desires and aspirations."[100]

Times of War

Men and women of the Bible collaborated with God to fight their enemies. Gideon worked with God by following His commands in thinning the army

---

99. Pargament, "Religious Methods of Coping," 220.
100. Lederach, *Believers Church Bible Commentary: Daniel*, 43.

to only three hundred men. God did this so that Israel would not believe they triumphed by their own strength (Judg 7:2-7).

David also cooperated with God in war. While running from King Saul, David proclaimed, "With your help I can advance against a troop; with my God I can scale a wall" (Ps 18:29). He declares his strength and training for battle included assistance from God, "It is God who arms me with strength and keeps my way secure. He makes my feet like the feet of the deer; he causes me to stand on the heights. He trains my hands for battle; my arms can bend a bow of bronze" (Ps 18:32-34). He worked with God when he slayed Goliath, "This day the Lord will deliver you into my hands, and I'll strike you down and cut off your head. All those gathered here will know that it is not by sword or spear that the Lord saves; for the battle is the Lord's, and he will give all of you into our hands" (1 Sam 17:46-47). Both Gideon and David learned to rely on God when they fought their enemy.

Times of Burdensome Leadership

Moses recognized his need to collaborate with God to lead the rebellious people of Israel. He pleaded with God to help his leadership skills, "You have been telling me, 'Lead these people,' but you have not let me know whom you will send with me. You have said, 'I know you by name and you have found favor with me.' If you are pleased with me, teach me your ways so I may know you and continue to find favor with you. Remember that this nation is your people" (Exod 33:1-13). God then responds to Moses' plea and promises, "My Presence will go with you, and I will give you rest" (Exod 33:14). Moses coped with very traumatic events during his 40-year desert wanderings by working with God. Many other biblical characters also had to learn to work with God to handle the traumatic circumstances they faced.

Times of Traumatic Circumstances

To survive life's circumstances people had to labor with God. Noah followed God's instructions to build an ark that would save him, his family, and the animals of the earth (Gen 6:11-21). Jesus raised Lazarus from the dead "for God's glory so that God's Son may be glorified through it." (John 11:4). Traumas happen throughout a person's lifetime, knowing that God works with humanity to bring about good, helps him or her to cope.

To Build Character

Paul preaches that working together with God through trauma produces a godly character. He states, "Therefore we do not lose heart. Through outwardly we are wasting away, yet inwardly we are being renewed day by day. For our light and momentary troubles are achieving for us an eternal glory that far outweighs them all" (2 Cor 4:16–17). Paul found strength through his trauma proclaiming, "That is why for Christ's sake, I delight in weaknesses, in insults, in hardships, in persecution, in difficulties. For when I am weak, then I am strong" (2 Cor 12:10). He told the Corinthian church that his sufferings would not only result in their "comfort and salvation" (2 Cor 1:6) but by watching God assist them through hard times they could turn around and help others (2 Cor 1:3–5). This character of service often comes through adversity.

To cope with traumatic situations, biblical characters understood that they served a God who wanted to be active in their day-to-day lives. As they learned to work with him they became more resilient. It did not matter if they lived in slavery, led people through a desert, fought in wars, or modeled suffering to wayward churches, these people grew in strength and character as they gave up control and worked with the Lord through whatever trauma they faced.

Expressing One's Complaints to God

The biblical personalities studied had no qualms complaining to God about their traumatic events. In many ways, this process allowed the person to vent his or her frustration and sort through the trauma to determine the best way to navigate toward a positive outcome. The God of the Bible does not seem bothered with being blamed for the traumatic situation. He created the human psyche to heal from trauma through expressing its fear and disappointments to someone who possibly can help.[101] Of the 23 biblical characters studied, eight expressed his or her complaints to God. These people included: David, Elijah, Jeremiah, Job, and other biblical characters.

David

David had no problem complaining about his trauma to God. The laments of Psalms encourage people "to risk the danger of speaking boldly and

---

101. Langberg, *Suffering and the Heart of God*, loc. 1357.

personally to the Lord of the universe."[102] While hiding from King Saul in a cave David writes, "I pour out before him [God] my complaint; before him I tell my trouble. . . . Look and see, there is no one at my right hand; no one is concerned for me. I have no refuge; no one cares for my life" (Ps 142:2, 4).[103] In Psalms 43:2, he cries, "You are God my stronghold. Why have you rejected me? Why must I go about mourning, oppressed by the enemy?" He also wonders at God's silence in trauma, "Lord, you have seen this; do not be silent. Do not be far from me, Lord" (Ps 35:22). Allender and Longman state, "In addition to mourning God's silence, in other places the psalmist takes an even more brazen, irreverent, mocking attitude in response to God's apparent inattention: he calls upon God to wake up. The biblical writers knew well that God does not sleep, as did the pagan gods. The psalmist's plea for God to wake up is a furious accusation" (Ps 44:23).[104] David even became angry with God when He killed Uzzah for trying to keep the Ark of the Covenant from falling from a cart (2 Sam 6:7). The Psalms of Lament scream from the innermost pain of the soul; when the person can no longer stand the onslaught of the waves of trauma. These cries accuse God of abandonment, injustice, and unfairness.[105] Yet, they also remember a faithful God who has helped them in the past.

Elijah

Elijah, in his fear of the queen Jezebel, ran into the wilderness, sat under a broom bush and complained "I have had enough, Lord . . . Take my life; I am no better than my ancestors" (1 Kgs 19:4). God sent an angel to feed him, had him sleep, and then asked why he had fled into the wilderness. Elijah responded, "I have been very zealous for the Lord God almighty. The Israelites have rejected your covenant, torn down your altars, and put your prophets to death with the sword. I am the only one left, and now they are trying to kill me too" (1 Kgs 19:10). Even after God responded to Elijah in the form of an earthquake, fire, and a gentle whisper he complained to God again over the same problem (1 Kgs 19:12-14). Nonetheless, God had patience with Elijah and reassured him that He had the situation under control.

---

102. Allender and Longman, *Cry of the Soul*, loc. 281.
103. Theodoret, *Theodoret of Cyrus Commentary on the Psalms*, 376.
104. Allender and Longman, *Cry of the Soul*, loc. 2101.
105. Waltner, *Believers Church Bible Commentary: Psalms*, 42–43.

Jeremiah

During the destruction of Jerusalem, Jeremiah questioned God about his idea of justice (Jer 12:1–4) complaining about his unfairness.[106] When a drought and famine ravished Israel he questioned, "Why have you afflicted us so that we cannot be healed?" (Jer 14:19). When Babylon took Jerusalem captive Jeremiah criticized, "Why is my pain unending and my wound grievous and incurable? You are to me like a deceptive brook, like a spring that fails" (Jer 15:18). Not only does Jeremiah feel the abandonment of his people, he believes God has not come through for him.[107] He again called God deceptive because even though he had done all God asked of him, God did not protect him from being beaten and put in stocks (Jer 20:7–10). However, even in his pain and anguish, Jeremiah could not stop proclaiming the word of God. "But if I say, 'I will not mention his word or speak anymore in his name,' his word is in my heart like a fire, a fire shut up in my bones. I am weary of holding it in; indeed, I cannot" (Jer 20:9). These feelings of frustration and pain lead the prophet to cursing the day God allowed him to be born (Jer 20:14–18).[108]

Job

Job not only cursed the day of his birth after his traumatic experience (Job 3:3–12; 10:8–9) he also asked for God to take his life (Job 6:8–10; 14:13). He would not keep silent in his complaints to God (Job 7:8). He cries,

> What is mankind that you make so much of them, that you give them so much attention, that you examine them every morning and test them every moment? Will you never look away from me, or let me alone even for an instant? If I have sinned, what have I done to you, you who see everything we do? Why have you made me your target? Have I become a burden to you? Why do you not pardon my offenses and forgive my sins? For I will soon lie down in the dust; you will search for me, but I will be no more. (Job 7:17–21)

He felt helpless trying to justify himself against God the righteous judge (Job 9:14–20; 23:2–5; 27:2–6). Job lamented about the God who he felt had turned against him (Job 16:7–9, 11–14; 17:6–7; 30:20–23).

---

106. Martens, *Believers Church Bible Commentary: Jeremiah*, 98.
107. Martens, *Believers Church Bible Commentary: Jeremiah*, 115.
108. Martens, *Believers Church Bible Commentary: Jeremiah*, 112–13.

Other Biblical Characters

Both the Old and New Testaments narrate the angry conversations people had with God. Jonah, after preaching to the Ninevites and their repentance, told the Lord "I'm so angry I wish I were dead" (Jonah 4:9).[109] He rails at God's seemingly injustice in saving the Ninevites.[110] Moses accused God of Pharaoh's response to the plagues, "Why Lord, why have you brought trouble on this people? Ever since I went to Pharaoh to speak in your name, he has brought trouble on this people, and you have not rescued your people at all" (Exod 5:22-23). It was this anger that kept Moses from seeing the Promised Land because he disobeyed God to get water to flow from a rock by striking it instead of using words (Num 20:9-12). Naomi had no problem complaining to her friends about the hardships the Lord sent her way. After the deaths of her husband and sons she responds "The Lord's hand has turned against me! . . . The Lord has brought me back empty . . . The Lord has afflicted me, the Almighty has brought misfortune upon me" (Ruth 1:13, 21).

Even the Son of God wept at Lazarus' tomb (John 11:35) and from the cross He cried, "My God, my God, why have you forsaken me?" (Matt 27:46). These outbursts of emotion proclaimed Jesus' incomprehensible suffering and despair. It "transforms all human sorrow from a horizontal loss to a vertical agony . . . The Lord's cry will never allow us to see human suffering as merely accidental or incidental to life. All loss is bound to God."[111]

These Old and New Testament personalities did not fear to vent to God their Father or lament over the trauma they endured. God turns critical confrontation into an act of worship that leaves the person "desperate and hungry for God."[112] Allender and Longman explain, "God invites and elicits the cold fury of our soul because it is in the midst of this struggle to express our heart to Him that we enter the passion of our desire and engage in relationship with Him. It appears that He blesses passion, even when it opposes Him, as long as we move toward Him to wrestle with who He is."[113] The expressions of frustration and helplessness voiced by these biblical people seemed to help them release their tension and emotions so they could cope with the reality of their shambled lives. Their cries to the Lord encourage current believers to express their rage, doubt, and terror

---

109. McKenzie, *How to Read the Bible*, 11.
110. Roop, *Believers Church Bible Commentary: Ruth, Jonah, Esther*, 151-52.
111. Allender and Longman, *Cry of the Soul*, loc. 1427.
112. Allender and Longman, *Cry of the Soul*, loc. 2120-22.
113. Allender and Longman, *Cry of the Soul*, loc. 2124.

to God and by doing so, grow in their understanding of Him and, thereby, their outrage becomes an act of worship.[114]

A Theology of Suffering

True followers of Christ understand life generates suffering and God utilizes this anguish to produce character.[115] Of the 23 biblical personalities examined, five demonstrated an understanding of the theology of suffering. Numerous Old Testament characters realized the suffering/character connection. For example, Joseph recognized suffering built his character so he could become the second-in-command of Egypt. The names he gave his children revealed his coping ability to exegete a theology of suffering. At the birth of Manasseh, he proclaimed, "It is because God has made me forget all my trouble and all my father's household" (Gen 41:51) and, with Ephraim, he stated, "It is because God has made me fruitful in the land of my suffering" (Gen 41:52). Job also had a theology of suffering when he stated, "Though he slay me, yet will I hope in him" (Job 13:15).

The New Testament reveals the way of the cross to be a road of suffering. Jesus said, "Whoever wants to be my disciple must deny themselves and take up their cross and follow me" (Mark 8:34). The Bible discloses a God who "overturns pain by experiencing it" and who expects his followers to do the same.[116] Stuart Devenish explains, "God suffers; Jesus suffers; the apostles suffer; and those subsequent disciples who are called to be leaders and exemplars in the church and world are likewise called to suffer."[117] Therefore, suffering becomes a vital part of discipleship.[118]

The Apostle Paul's love for Christ drove his life and ministry. He understood he shared in the sorrow of Christ with every traumatic event he endured.[119] He makes no distinction between the distressing events brought on by ministry or personal suffering (his thorn in the flesh).[120] He did not ask, "Why?" or try to find a reason for his travail. He just encourages the churches to identify with the suffering Christ, and by staying positive and trusting that in God's love they will find well-being.[121] For

---

114. Allender and Longman, *Cry of the Soul*, loc. 291–305.
115. Allender and Longman, *Cry of the Soul*, loc. 2259.
116. Allender and Longman, *Cry of the Soul*, loc. 2248.
117. Devenish, "Contribution of Spirituality," 58.
118. Dunn, *Theology of Paul the Apostle*, 496.
119. Barnett, *Paul Missionary of Jesus*, 165; Roetzel, *Paul*, 170.
120. Hooker, "Interchange and Suffering," 80.
121. Adewuya, "Sacrificial-Missiological Function," 97; Jervis, *At the Heart of the*

the Apostle states, "Who shall separate us from the love of Christ? Shall trouble or hardship or persecution or famine or nakedness or danger or sword? . . . No, in all these things we are more than conquerors through him who loved us" (Rom 8:35–37).

Paul writes to the New Testament church, "And we boast in the hope of the glory of God. Not only so, but we also glory in our sufferings, because we know that suffering produces perseverance; perseverance, character; and character, hope" (Rom 5:2–4). He learned how to face trauma with perseverance and power. He acknowledged that trauma could not be avoided so he needed to embrace it knowing that suffering would reveal God's glory and his character would be refined.[122] Paul saw his suffering as participating in the suffering of Christ (2 Cor 4:10–11) and, thereby, modeling Christ to the lost.[123] He believed this suffering to be part of his missionary calling.

Paul also realized the "thorn in the flesh" (2 Cor 12:7) he endured every day helped him keep in perspective God's ability to make feebleness resilient. He states,

> Three times I pleaded with the Lord to take it away from me. But he said to me, 'My grace is sufficient for you, for my power is made perfect in weakness.' Therefore I will boast all the more gladly about my weakness, so that Christ's power may rest on me. That is why, for Christ's sake, I delight in weakness, in insults, in hardships, in persecutions, in difficulties. For when I am weak, then I am strong. (2 Cor 12:8–10)

Many times, God does not heal and this can often throw a believer into despair. Paul recognized this and decided to view his infirmity as a character-building process because God's "grace is sufficient" and His "power is made perfect in weakness" (2 Cor 12:9).[124] Paul used this traumatic affliction to move the attention away from himself and onto Christ.[125]

Paul did not questioned God about the sorrows he went through but used his trials to encourage others in their trauma to endure for the sake of Christ. In his mind, suffering would become normative in the Christian walk as all conformed to the image of Christ.[126] With these warnings, the new Thessalonica church embraced suffering. Paul reminded the Thessalonians

---

Gospel, 65.

122. Clinton et al., *Caring for People God's Way*, 404.
123. Adewuya, "Sacrificial-Missiological Function," 89–90.
124. Opoku, "God's Grace, Healing, and Suffering," 125.
125. Fee, *God's Empowering Presence*, 354.
126. Adewuya, "Sacrificial-Missiological Function," 97; Allender and Longman, *Cry of the Soul*, loc. 2259.

that, "when we were with you, we kept telling you that we would be persecuted. And it turned out that way, as you well know" (1 Thess 3:4). He also encourages Timothy to "endure hardship with us like a good soldier of Christ Jesus" (2 Tim 2:3). According to Devenish Paul's idea of "weakness, suffering, and oppression were formidable tools for conveying the power of God, the truthfulness of the gospel, and the value of living the spiritual life to the minds and hearts of his human hearers."[127]

Paul would do whatever it took to convey the message of Jesus Christ to the lost. At the center of Paul's salvation message was the cross, the image of trauma, suffering, and death. With this imagery, he declares that only through pain and sorrow can the power and glory of God be discovered, and sanctification be achieved.[128] Paul also felt as non-believers witnessed how Christians dealt with trauma, they would be introduced to the Christ who assisted believers through each crisis.[129] Paul deemed trauma and anguish as a small price to pay for a life saved.[130] Therefore, he connected his missionary calling with suffering.

Peter also viewed suffering as a normal part of the Christian life. He tells believers "not [to] be surprised at the painful trial you are suffering, as though something strange were happening to you" (1 Pet 4:12). Suffering should never throw a person off balance.[131] Peter explains, "To this you were called, because Christ suffered for you, leaving you an example, that you should follow in his steps" (1 Pet 2:21). This shared suffering will lead to sanctification by taking up one's cross and following Christ's example (1 Pet 1:6–7).[132] James, along with Paul and Peter encourage followers to, "Consider it all joy, my brethren, when you encounter various trials" (Jas 1:2). These biblical characters realized that acceptance of suffering changed one's perspective of trauma he or she endured and allowed coping to happen.

Receiving Assistance from Family and Friends

People need people in traumatic times and the men and women studied showed the same inclination. When disaster strikes and it seems that God

---

127. Devenish, "Contribution of Spirituality," 57–58.

128. Grenz, *Theology for the Community of God*, 339; Hafemann, *Suffering and Ministry in the Spirit*, 226; Jervis, *At the Heart of the Gospel*, 119.

129. Grassi, *Informing the Future*, 106.

130. Adewuya, "Sacrificial-Missiological Function," 90.

131. Floyd, *Crisis Counseling*, loc. 253; McDonald, "View of Suffering," 180.

132. Grenz, *Theology for the Community of God*, 339; Hiebert et al., *Understanding Folk Religion*, 228; Sande, *Peacemaker*, 62.

is silent, the assistance of family, friends, and community helps the sufferer to endure.[133] Humanity often turns to family and friends; to not only assist them in finding solutions but to also help in physical and emotional ways. The Bible indicates that five of the 23 individuals studied turned to their friends and family in their time of need.

Naomi

When Naomi returned from Moab, her hometown community seemed to embrace her, not reject her (Ruth 1:18). Her extended family allowed her to send Ruth to glean the fields and even provided extra food for her table (Ruth 2:15–16). Ruth proclaimed, "Oh sir, such grace, such kindness—I don't deserve it. You've touched my heart and treated me like one of your own. And I don't even belong here" (Ruth 2:13, The Message). The community surrounds Naomi after the birth of her grandson. The women of Bethlehem give thanks to God on behalf of Naomi for his provision (Ruth 4:14–15). With this grandson, Naomi will not be hungry or childless again and this baby boy completes her joy (Ruth 4:14–16).[134]

Other Old and New Testament Characters

The Old Testament tells stories of people who aided others in traumatic situations. David found comfort in his friendship with Jonathan when King Saul tried to kill him in his home (1 Sam 18:1, 3–4). He also had a group of mighty men that became his trusted inner circle of comrades at arms. These men helped David through his exile and during the traumatic events he endured in his kingship (2 Sam 23:15–16). Elisha asks for assistance from the elders when the King of Samaria wants to kill him because of the famine in the besieged Samaria (2 Kgs 6:32). When the town's people wanted to execute Gideon, his family stood up for him and gave him their protection (Judg 6:31).

After they heard of the trauma Job underwent, friends left their homes to sympathize and comfort him. When they saw his condition, "they began to weep aloud, and they tore their robes and sprinkled dust on their heads. Then they sat on the ground with him for seven days and seven nights. No one said a word to him, because they saw how great his suffering was" (Job: 2:11–13). These friends empathized with Job, which

---

133. Roop, *Believers Church Bible Commentary: Ruth, Jonah, Esther*, 41.
134. Roop, *Believers Church Bible Commentary: Ruth, Jonah, Esther*, 83.

greatly help him in his affliction. Yet, when they later tried to figure out why God had sent this trauma, they caused added grief to Job's suffering. Peter realized the value in believers hearing the testimonies of others who undergo the same sufferings. These stories allow faith to grow and instill a stronger trust in God (1 Pet 5:9).

These biblical characters found that friends and family could aid them in coping with the trauma they faced. This community brought protection, encouragement, and physical relief to their distressed friends. They often stood in the gap when the victim had no strength to continue his or her fight. Besides the coping skills of trusting in God, asking for assistance from God, praise and worship to God, expressing one's complaints to God, and the assistance of friends and family, biblical personalities also used a variety of other coping mechanisms.

The trauma these 23 biblical characters encountered mirrors what people around the world currently go through. Humanity still faces natural traumas such as wild animal attacks, storms causing shipwrecks, earthquakes, and famine; man-made traumas like civil and foreign wars and robberies; prolonged and repeated trauma such as death threats, being beaten, imprisoned; and personal trauma like abuse, kidnapping, death of spouse and/or children, rape, hunger, sleep deprivation, physical impairments, and interpersonal conflicts. People, like these biblical men and women either cope effectively leading them to a life of well-being or poorly causing pain and despair.

A Biblical Theology of Well-Being

To develop a sound biblical theology of well-being, more biblical characters must be examined. However, a strong case can be made from the lives of the 23 characters studied. From these stories, a biblical pattern emerges which can assist humankind in developing a sense of well-being. A visualization of a flower symbolizes this theology because when a person copes well, he or she lives a beautifully growing life. Therefore, to follow the biblical design of coping, one must put their full trust in God no matter the circumstances. Trust is the center with all other biblical coping mechanisms moving in and out (trust causes the coping mechanism and the mechanism produces more trust) of the center forming pedals (see Figure 3.1.). Trust allows people to ask for assistance and to vent their anger and pain to God. Praise and worship instills and deepens this trust. Working with God builds trust. Watching how a caring God sends friends and family to help in times of need inspires trust. When one accepts the call of salvation or leadership, he or she understands that God uses suffering to refine one's character, trusting that God will see him or her through to a state of well-being.

Trusting in God

At the center of a biblical theology of well-being is trust. The Bible proclaims how trust builds hope, which research claims to be necessary to thwart PTSD symptomatology and produce PTG.[135] Paul prays, "May the God of hope fill you with all joy and peace as you trust in him, so that you may overflow with hope by the power of the Holy Spirit" (Rom 15:13). Yet, trauma attempts to drive out this hope trying to replace it with fear and confusion.

Trauma produces fear but trust relieves fear because the strong Lord will become one's defense and savior against all problems (Isa 12:2). Psalm 56 reveals when David grew fearful, he trusted God who "drives out all fear" (Ps 56:3–4, 11). No matter the traumatic experience "The Lord is good, a refuge in times of trouble. He cares for those who trust in him" (Nah 1:7). The Bible describes the one and only God as the place where trauma cannot penetrate: a fortress (Ps 91:2), a rock, a shield, a horn of salvation, and a stronghold (Ps 18:2; 1 Cor 10:4). Scripture also declares God to be a deliverer (Ps 18:2), a savior (Ps 62:2), and a redeemer (Ps 19:14). These descriptions of strength against adversity produce trust and hope. A person can rest in the consistency of the Lord because the God of the past will remain trustworthy in the present (Isa 25:9) and this steadfast trust in God will keep him or her in "perfect peace" (Isa 26:3).

In traumatic times one does not always understand why he or she must suffer but King Solomon explains that trust, not understanding, will make his or her "path straight" (Prov 3:5–6). One must trust the Lord in both good and bad times (Job 2:9–10) knowing that often he utilizes suffering to produce a better character (Phil 3:10). However, even in suffering, God's love "surrounds the people who trusts him" (Ps 32:10). "God is love" (1 John 4:8), therefore, love "always protects, always trusts, always hopes, always perseveres" (1 Cor 13:7). Whether watching friends or family going through their "fiery furnace" (Dan 3:17–18) or going through one's personal "lions' den," (Dan 6:21–22) only trusting God will bring about hope and peace.

Asking Assistance from God

In times of distress, people call on God to assist them. This cry for help comes from trust, believing the Lord will listen and produces trust when he answers. Christians should never be "anxious about anything, but in every

---

135. Calhoun and Tedeschi, "Posttraumatic Growth: Future Directions," 223–26.

situation, by prayer and petition, with thanksgiving, present your requests to God" (Phil 4:6). One can ask God to listen and reveal his mysteries (Dan 2:18-19; 9:19); he or she can even demand that he "rise up" and quickly come to rescue him or her from danger (Ps 44:26; 70:5; 71:12). People can petition the Lord for: deliverance (Ps 3:7; 59:1-2; 79:9; 108:6; Mark 14:35-36), refuge (Ps 57:1; 142:5-6), vindication (Ps 57:2), salvation (Ps 60:5), a sign (Judg 6:36-37), healing (Num 12:10-13; 1 Sam 1:17), mercy (Ps 6:9; 28:2), miracles (John 11:22-42), and forgiveness (Luke 23:34). In distress, they can be assured that God sees and hears and will deliver them from all their fears (Gen 21:17-19; Ps 18:6—34:4, 15) and troubles (Ps 34:6, 17). A believer can be certain when asked, God will defeat his or her enemies (1 Kgs 1:12; 2 Kgs 2:24; 6:18-22; Ps 36:9), heal (1 Kgs 17:20-21), answer (Jonah 2:2), and assist with conflict (Exod. 17:4-7). However, he or she must realize that God does not always answer prayers the way he or she prefers. Nevertheless, even then he or she must trust that God's will is best (Matt 26:42; 2 Cor 12:9-10).

The biblical narrative tells of a God who wants to be involved in each human being's life. He promises to listen for the smallest cry and answer by engaging in their struggles. This participation causes and fortifies trust.

Praise and Worship

When one trusts in God, he or she longs to sing praises and worship him. This praise and worship in turn instills more trust in the Lord. During times of trauma, praise and worship brings comfort and happiness (2 Cor 1:2-4; Jas 5:13). When the soul is downcast, praise brings about "hope in God" (Ps 42:5; 52:9; 71:14). It turns "wailing into dancing" and mourning into joy (Ps 30:11-12; 1 Sam 2:1-2). It changes one's focus from the problems faced, to the only one who can help and deliver (Ps 18:3; 56:10-11, 13; 63:7-8). It reveals the "wonders of his love" (Ps 31:21). It helps one remember how God delivered him or her in the past, and that his "faithfulness endures forever" (Exod 15:1; Ps 86:12-13; 117:1-2).

Praising the Lord encourages the suffering person (Acts 16:25). It satisfies the soul like "the richest of foods" (Ps 63:4-5). When he or she needs to work through a problematic situation, praise and worship gives him or her God's wisdom (Job 12:13-25; Dan 2:19-23). The nations watch as suffering Christians offer up praise and glory to the one true Lord (Ps 18:49). These believers proclaim the Lord's "wonderful deeds" (Ps 26:7) to a lost world. Praising and worshiping God when going through crisis enhances one's trust in God. Biblical men and women found hope and strength when they sang songs of God's faithfulness. Songs of praise and worship continue to uplift believers in troubled times.

A Sense of Purpose/Call

Having a firm sense of purpose or call helps people survive trauma.[136] This call can be a specific roll such as a pastor or missionary. It can also be generic in the call to salvation. God gives all believers a purpose: to proclaim his salvation story (Mark 16:15), to make disciples (Matt 28:19), and to touch the world with his love and grace (Mark 12:31). He warns his followers that by doing this, persecution and suffering will follow (Rev 2:10). Trust in God brings about one's call and knowing he or she has a sense of purpose produces trust.

A call starts a person on a journey with God (Gen 12:1). He sets this purpose and plan in place before birth (Jer 1:5–10; Luke 1:11–17, 29–33). A person's call can place him or her in a position of leadership (Exod 3:4–10) and ministry (Matt 4:18–20; Acts 9). At first, one feels inadequate for the responsibility the call requires (Exod. 3:11; Judg 6:36–40). Often call positions one into the midst of a spiritual or physical battle (Judg 6:14). Yet, it produces God's empowerment for victory (1 Sam 16:13). People can run from God's call (Jon 1:1) but the Lord continues to pursue them so that his will can be accomplished.

A sense of call and purpose gives humanity a reason to survive for each trial. It gives strength that helps Christians suffer for their faith. One's call must be grounded in trust and grow from trusting in God.

Working with God

Sometimes God wants total involvement in the traumatic situation to prove his power and preform a miracle. Other times a person needs to feel some sense of control in the crisis. Trusting that he or she co-labors with God through the suffering in turn builds trust that together they can do all things through his strength (Phil 4:13).

In hard times, one works with God by listening and speaking his words (Dan 4:18). He "arms and strengthens" a person as he or she fights through the trauma (Ps 18:29, 32–34) thus bringing about Gods deliverance (1 Sam 17:45–46). *Yahweh* knows the future and sometimes like Joseph, one must labor through many traumatic experiences over a long period of time before given respite and understanding (Gen 39:20–21; 45:5–8). Occasionally, the Lord asks a person to do, what in human thinking may seem irrational, things that can cause conflict, but also brings future deliverance (Gen 6:11–21). Often God wants to utilize one person to assist others in their suffering and produce healing (John 11:14). Leaders must remember that they cannot resolve the conflicts that working with people generates.

---

136. Carr, "Mobile Member Care Team," 80.

They must always toil together with God, learning from him how to lead with excellence (Exod 32:11–14).

Human beings need to feel useful especially during times of stress and trauma. Often the traumatic situation overwhelms them both emotionally and physically and only by working with God can they cope. Co-laboring with the one whom can do all things produces trust and hope for the future.

Lamenting/Venting

The Bible declares that God desires for humanity to release their anger and anxiety to him (Ps 142:2). Just being able to speak out loud one's emotions dissipates them.[137] Trusting the presence of a listening God allows a person to unburden him or herself of the weight of the trauma, which causes him or her to trust more.

Often during times of crisis, people feel abandoned by God (Ps 142:4; Matt 27:46). They want to die or wish they had never been born (1 Kgs 19:3–5; Job 3:3–26; Jon 4:9). Some believers can feel betrayed by God and yell at him for not caring for all the work they have done in his name (1 Kgs 19:9–10, 12–14). They can complain about the injustice of the wicked prospering when they do not (Jer 12:1–4). However, God allows people to blame him for their trauma (Jer 14:19–20; Job 7:17–21; 9:14–20; 10:2–22; 13:23–27; 16:7–14), unhappiness and bitterness (Job 7:7, 11—23:2–5; Ruth 1:13, 21), nightmares (Job 7:13–16), and not answering their cries (Job 30:20–23). This lamenting does not make God angry. He designed in humanity the need to air out their emotions so that healing from trauma can start.

A Theology of Suffering

Christians not only recognize a purpose for trauma in their call, they also realized that suffering builds character. God utilizes pain and sorrow to draw people to him. During a trauma, people must trust that God walks with them through the torment. At the end of the storm, they have more confidence in the Lord because he saw them through the trial.

God employs suffering in a variety of ways. Distress teaches one to become a better leader (Gen 41)—comprehending the torment of others. It is the key to discipleship (Mark 8:34). Suffering molds the character of a person (Rom 5:2–4). It instructs people to cope using positive thinking (Phil 4:8). Sorrow allows one to participate in the suffering of Christ (2 Cor 4:10–11). It also provokes people to surrender to God's will (2 Cor 12:9–10).

---

137. Joseph, *What Doesn't Kill Us*, loc. 2254.

Through suffering, a person realizes that God's "grace is sufficient" and his "power is made perfect in weakness" (2 Cor 12:8), thus molding him or her into Christ's image (1 Pet 1:6-7—2:21).

Suffering should bring joy, not sadness, (Jas 1:2) because through trials a person identifies with Christ and the church. This gives a meaning and reason for suffering which often helps a person cope. Reading the Bible or listening to the testimonies of other's journeys of suffering and surviving brings universality to the trials and hope that one can survive.

Assistance from Friends and Family

People should never endure trauma alone. They need to allow friends and family to walk beside them through the traumatic journey. Nevertheless, the traumatized need to trust that the people they open up too will not exacerbate the trauma. Then as these friends and family assist the victim with the healing process, he or she learns to trust in the God who brought these people into his or her life.

Friends and family will often help even placing themselves in danger (1 Sam 18:1, 3-4; Judg 6:30-32; Matt 26:51). They will fight when the wounded has no strength (2 Sam 23:15-16). They love when the victim feels worthless (1 Sam 1:5). Friends empathize by quietly standing with one through his or her suffering (Job 2:13). They praise the Lord on the surfer's behalf (Ruth 4:14). God instructs the church community to not only assist each other through trials (1 Cor 12: 26; Rom 16:2; Eph 4:29; Phil 4:3) but also those outside the community of faith (1 Thess 5:14).

From this study a biblical theology of well-being can be birthed. If one wants to grow post trauma, he or she must strive to do one thing, trust in God. Then the seven other identified coping mechanisms encircle this central key. One must trust in God, believing in his overarching reign. As he or she realizes that God has never failed in the past, he or she will find a sense of security and peace. From this center (see Figure 3.1.), the first petal (asking assistance from God) places control back into the hands of the one who has the power to fix the problem. The second petal (praise and worship to the Trinity) changes a person's perspective and takes his or her eyes off the situation and places them on the one who has the power to defeat the problem. Petal number three (a call) gives people a sense of purpose that will sustain them through whatever battle they face. The fourth petal (working with God) not only gives a person a sense of control, but also lightens the burden as he or she permits God to carry the load. Petal five (lamenting/venting) allows one to vent his or her emotions without fear to a God who not only created those feelings but experienced them himself. The sixth petal (a theology of suffering) recognizes that God intends to improve one's temperament. Just like the heat of a furnace refines gold, so too suffering perfects character. The last petal (assistance from friends and family) relieves stress and brings about healing. Only with God's aid can a person surmount the negative pathology resulting from trauma and move toward a life of well-being.

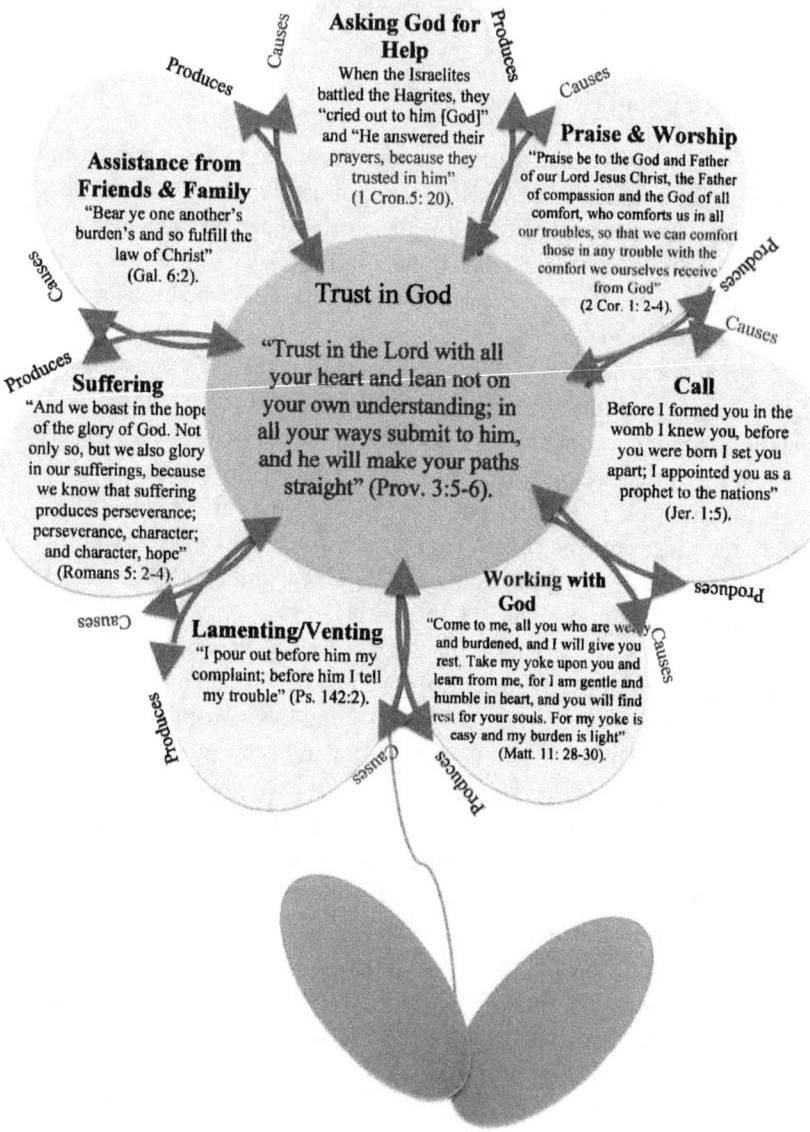

Figure 3.1. A Biblical Theology of Well-being Produces Post-Traumatic Growth

Conclusion

Trauma and suffering will eventually happen to everyone. This trauma can come in many forms, from a one-time holocaust to repeated blows. It can seem to originate from the hand of God or from humanity's evilness. Trauma can affect a person emotionally, physically, socially, and spiritually. How a person copes with these events will determine his or her emotional negative pathology or well-being.

The 23 biblical characters studied all lived through many traumatic experiences. They survived death threats, kidnappings, wars, deaths of spouses and children, famines, shipwrecks, beatings, imprisonment, and personal conflicts. Yet, most seemed to not only endure but also thrive. From their stories, the beginnings of a biblical theology of well-being can be deduced. The key component of this biblical theology is trust in God. From this center, seven other coping mechanisms emerge forming petals that begins in trust and also fosters trust. These seven petals include: asking God for help, praise and worship to God, working with God, a sense of call or purpose, the ability to lament or vent to God, an understanding of suffering, and assistance from friends and family. As people practice the components of this biblical theology of well-being, they will be better prepared to withstand the traumas life brings their way.

4

Contemporary Missionary Well-Being Regardless of Trauma

Introduction

TRAUMA TOUCHES THE LIVES of all humanity. Everyone will experience a death of someone close to them at some point in their lives. Some people live through more horrendous types of trauma, physical or sexual abuse, rape, war, genocide, terrorism, or natural disasters. Individuals who endure these out of control traumatic incidents fear for their lives. This trauma silences, isolates, and can "destroy love, dignity, and purpose."[1]

Studies have shown that missionaries endure more trauma than the average person.[2] With the added pressure of acculturation, feelings of isolation, and the loss of love, dignity, and purpose can be compounded for missionaries.[3] Yet, Bagley found that even with 94 percent of the missionaries he surveyed experiencing trauma, only 24 percent reported PTSD symptomatology.[4] Carr also witnessed that even though missionaries live in highly stressful locations and suffered multiple crises, the majority seem to "demonstrate a level of resilience and strength that is remarkable."[5] The question then arises as to how missionaries cope with the onslaught of traumatic experiences compounded with acculturation stress that living in a cross-cultural situation produces. To date, no formal study addressed this issue; therefore, this research examined the area of missionary coping

---

1. Langberg, *Suffering and the Heart of God*, loc. 2293.

2. Bagley, "Trauma and Traumatic Stress Among Missionaries," 104; Carr and Schaefer, "Trauma and Traumatic Stress," 279; Foyle, *Honorably Wounded*, 212; Gish, "Sources of Missionary Stress," 237; Grant, "Trauma in Missionary Life," 72; Irvine et al., "Traumatic Stress in a Missionary Population," 332; O'Donnell, "Member Care on the Field," 291; Schwandt and Moriarty, What Have the "Past 25 Years," 321–22.

3. Dodds and Dodds, "Love and Survival," 3–4.

4. Bagley, "Impact of Trauma," 151; Bagley, "Trauma and Traumatic Stress," 104–5.

5. Carr, "Mobile Member Care Team," 80.

skills by looking at the trauma AGWM missionaries endured and then determined what types of coping skills reduced PTSD symptoms and produced well-being.

Methodology

Research Design

The intention of this study was to determine the extent of trauma missionaries endure and to investigate how they cope with these traumatic incidences. The research employed both quantitative and qualitative methodology. A survey conducted with AGWM missionary participants with Qualtricsâ via the internet collected both quantitative and qualitative (with fill in sections) data. The key variables studied included perception of trauma, PTSD symptomatology, and coping skills utilized to bring about well-being.

The survey defined trauma as, "an emotional response to a terrible event."[6] It involves a painful, emotional experience or shock that overwhelms one's ability to cope.[7] Trauma can also be defined in terms of: physical (body injury), psychological (an incident that causes strong emotional reactions), social (oppressive social conditions e.g., war, poverty, discrimination, violence, conflict), historical (past personal or social violence), ongoing (daily violence), vicarious or secondary trauma (experienced when a trauma happens to a loved one). It can also be felt by disaster relief workers, or mental health helpers and called Compassion Fatigue (see Appendix D).[8] Participants responded to survey questions asking if they had been involved in traumatic events such as: serious accidents, natural disasters, violent crime, war, child or adult physical and/or sexual abuse, vicarious trauma, danger of losing his or her life, received news of a loved one's injury or death, serious conflict with another missionary or national church, any other incident the subject considered as traumatic, and an unspeakable trauma. The survey then asked about possible PTSD symptoms.

After determining the extent of trauma witnessed by AGWM missionaries and their potential PTSD symptomatology, the study examined the resiliency skills used by these missionaries. The coping section investigated the trauma managing areas of religious coping, resilience, calling, and satisfaction with life. Since the survey was sent only to missionaries on field, it

---

6. American Psychiatric Association, *Diagnostic and Statistical Manual*, 830.
7. Grant, "Trauma in Missionary Life," 72.
8. Wise, "Introduction," 3–4.

seems that their coping abilities have assisted them in overcoming difficult situations and maintain a state of well-being.

Selection of Participants

The participants of this study consisted of AGWM missionaries from the regions of Africa, Asia, Eurasia, Europe, International Ministries, and Latin America Caribbean. The sample was limited to fully appointed career missionaries and missionary associates (MA). For the quantitative research, the AGWM department provided 1,907 email address and each of these missionaries received a link to the Qualtricsâ website to participate in an online Trauma and Coping Survey.

Instruments

The survey (see Appendix E) combined several inventories available for public use on EBSCO Host PsycTESTS. This Trauma and Coping Survey utilized: the Trauma Event Questionnaire (TEQ) to survey the trauma AGWM missionaries experienced on and off field; the PTSD Checklist Civilian (PCT-C) to determine PTSD symptomatology; the Brief Religious Coping Scale (B-RCOPE) to establish religious coping skills; the Ego-Resiliency Scale (ERS) to assess adaptability; the Resilience Appraisal Scale (RAS) to ascertain social, emotional, and situational coping skills; the Resiliency Scale (RS) to look at general resiliency; a shortened Calling and Vocation Questionnaire (CVQ) to evaluate calling; and the Satisfaction with Life Scale (SWLS) to appraise the level of AGWM missionaries happiness with their life situations. An overview of these assessments follows.

The Trauma Event Questionnaire (TEQ)

Scott Vrana and Dean Lauterbach developed the TEQ to determine the eleven specific types of trauma reported in the DSM-III-R that usually produced PTSD symptomatology.[9] These traumatic events included:

> 1) Military combat, 2) large fires/explosions, 3) serious industrial/farm accidents, 4) sexual assault/rape, 5) natural disasters, 6) violent crimes, 7) adult abusive relationships, 8) physical/sexual child abuse, 9) witnessing someone mutilated, seriously injured,

---

9. Vrana and Lauterbach, "Trauma Events Questionnaire."

or violently killed, (10) other life-threatening situations, and (11) violent or very unexpected death of a loved one.[10]

Vrana and Lauterbach also included two additional categories labeled: "other event" (any other traumatic incident not listed) and "can't tell" (events so traumatic the individual cannot discuss them).[11] These last two classifications enabled assessment of trauma that did not fall clearly into one of the preceding event types.

Robert Bagley modified Vrana and Lauterbach's (1994a) TEQ to align it more closely with traumatic events missionaries might encounter. These changes comprised: 1) changing military combat to "combat, civil war, violent civil unrest, or evacuation due to any of these;" 2) shifting serious industrial/farm accident to "serious industrial/farm or car accidents;" and 3) defining violent crime as "assault, robbery, or holdup." He also asked if all event types happened while serving on field to distinguish between on and off field trauma.[12]

After being reviewed by the dissertation chairperson and AGWM leadership, they wanted Bagley's TEQ survey adjusted again to include a wider variety of traumatic events. The examples of violent crime comprised: rape, robbery, assault or a threat of violence such as pick-pocketing, burglary, intimidation, being put on a targeted list, or bugged. Traumatic events such as combat, civil war, violent civil unrest, or evacuation due to any of these changed to "living in a war zone (coup, uprising, revolt, gang violence, etc.) where you received friendly or hostile incoming fire from small arms, artillery, rockets, mortars, or bombs." Questions about witnessing an industrial, farm, or car accident, and seeing a large fire or explosion were combined. Additional questions include: Were you ever taken hostage? Have you ever had a traumatic conflict with a member(s) of the missionary fellowship? and Have you ever had a traumatic conflict with a member(s) of the national church? This study ran a reliability index and the TEQ received an acceptable Cronbach's Alpha = .763 ($n = 7$).

---

10. Vrana and Lauterbach, "Prevalence of Traumatic Events," 292.
11. Vrana and Lauterbach, "Prevalence of Traumatic Events," 292.
12. Bagley, "Impact of Trauma," 100–101; Vrana and Lauterbach, "Trauma Events Questionnaire."

The PTSD Checklist Civilian (PCL-C)

Frank Weathers et al. created the PCL-C to measure PTSD symptoms among non-combat personnel.[13] This 17-question checklist asks the respondent to reflect on a past trauma and determine how much it affected him or her at the time of the trauma and within the past month. The PCL-C uses a five-point Likert scale moving from "not at all" to "very much." The questions correspond to the three criteria (B, C, and D) needed to diagnose PTSD symptomatology as described in the DSM-IV. This survey used the PTSD Symptom Scale Interview (PSSI) which took the PCL-C questions and put them into a question format. When answering the question, the survey asked each participant to remember his or her most troubling traumatic event and respond for both the months right after the incident and their current reaction to the event. These answers will indicate the level of PTSD symptomatology at both the time of the trauma and at the time of the survey.

Weathers et al. allow for two potential ways to understand the PCL-C data.[14] First, one can use the categories and symptomatology needed of the DSM-IV such as: one re-experiencing symptom, three avoidance indications, and two increased arousal signs. The second way to interpret the data basically takes a collective score of fifty as the point between high and low PTSD. It seems that for research purposes the cluster method works very well in deducing the PCL-C scores.[15] Therefore, the cluster method will be used in this study to categorize respondents in either high or low categories based on their response on the PTSD scale. This study ran a reliability index and the PCL-C received an acceptable Cronbach's Alpha = .743 ($n = 35$).

The Brief Religious Coping Scale (B-RCOPE)

Kenneth Pargament and his associates first developed the Religious Coping Scale (RCOPE) to investigate 17 positive and negative coping factors that mirror the five purposes of religion (i.e., meaning, control, comfort/spirituality, intimacy, and life transformation).[16] Later, because of the considerable length of the RCOPE inventory, Pargament developed the Brief RCOPE (B-RCOPE) which has only 14 questions that determine positive and/or negative religious coping styles. It has become the most widely used

---

13. Weathers et al., "PTSD Checklist (PCL)."
14. Weathers et al., "PTSD Checklist (PCL)."
15. Bagley, "Impact of Trauma," 104–5.
16. Pargament et al., "Brief RCOPE."

measure of religious coping and has proven its predicative validity over the course of many studies.[17] The B-RCOPE cannot substitute for the more thorough RCOPE, however, for this study, the B-RCOPE should determine if AGWM missionaries use religious coping in a positive or negative way. The B-RCOPE uses a four-point Likert scale that moves from "not at all true" to "applies very strongly." This study ran a reliability index and the B-RCOPE received an acceptable Cronbach's Alpha = .798 ($n = 14$).

The Ego-Resiliency Scale (ERS)

Jack Block and Adam Kremen created the 14 item Ego-Resiliency Scale to measure the personality trait of "the inter and intra-individually adaptability capacity for building adequate adaption to the impacts of external and internal stressors."[18] This scale utilizes a four point Likert scale from "one—not at all true" to "four—applies very strongly." Participants can score a minimum of 14 showing a low tendency toward resiliency to a maximum score of 56 displaying a highly resilient personality. Sultana and associates used this scale successfully in various studies of how people respond to traumatic events.[19] This study ran a reliability index on the ERS and it obtained an excellent Cronbach's Alpha =.994 ($n = 14$).

The Resilience Appraisal Scale (RAS)

This 12-item inventory developed by J. Johnson and colleagues reveals a person's psychological resilience using social support, emotional regulation, skills, and problem solving capabilities.[20] It uses a five-point Likert scale that ranges from "one—strongly disagree" to "four—strongly agree."[21] This inventory will provide further insight into missionary resilience.

---

17. Pargament et al., "The Brief RCOPE," 72.
18. Block and Kremen, "IQ and Ego-Resiliency," Block and Block, "Role of Ego-control," 47–51.
19. Sultana et al., "Outcomes of Belief in Just World," 45.
20. Johnson et al., "Resilience Appraisal Scale."
21. Johnson et al., "Resilience as Positive Coping Appraisals," 179–86.

The Resiliency Scale (RS)

Lew Hardy et al. constructed the four item Resiliency Scale (RS) that measures a person's perception of his or her ability to rebound from trauma.[22] This inventory uses a five-point Likert scale from "one—strongly disagree" too "four—strongly agree."[23] The missionary's awareness of his or her capacity to withstand trauma will provide another layer of his or her coping aptitude. This study ran a reliability index on both the RAS and RS together and attained an excellent Cronbach's Alpha = .993 ($n = 16$).

The Calling and Vocation Questionnaire (CVQ)

The CVQ by Byron Dik et al. has 24 questions investigating the subscales of transcendent summons (searching/presence), purposeful work (searching/presence), and prosocial orientation (searching/presence).[24] It uses a four-point Likert scale moving from "one—not at all true of me" to "four—absolutely true of me."[25] This inventory had been given to the same group of missionaries a few months prior to this research. So, the AGWM leadership asked if this study could reduce the number of questions on calling. Therefore, this survey asked only 12 of the 24 CVQ questions, two from each subscale. This inventory will provide data concerning the importance of missionary call in the aftermath of trauma. This study ran a reliability index on the CVQ and it received an excellent Cronbach's Alpha = .980 ($n = 12$).

The Satisfaction with Life Scale (SWLS)

The SWLS designed by Ed Diener and associates assesses an adult's perception of his or her life satisfaction.[26] Diener et al. started with 48 items evaluating positive and negative affect. After using factor analyses, they rejected all affect items and factor loadings of less than 0.60. Of the remaining ten items, they selected five based semantic similarity. The participants use a seven-point Likert scale ranging from "one–strongly disagree" to

---

22. Hardy et al., "Resilience Scale."
23. Hardy et al., "Relationship Between Transformational," 22–23.
24. Dik et al., "Development and Validation of the Calling and Vocation Questionnaire."
25. Dik et al., "Development and Validation of the Calling and Vocation Questionnaire," 243.
26. Diener et al., "Satisfaction with Life Scale."

"seven–strongly agree."[27] This short self-report will determine the feelings of well-being among missionaries who have lived through traumatic events. This study preformed a reliability index and it achieved an excellent Cronbach's Alpha = .914 ($n = 5$).

Permission to Survey

An email asking for permission to survey AGWM missionaries along with a sample survey was sent to each AGWM regional director. Greg Beggs (Africa), Russ Turney (Asia), Omar Beiler (Eurasia), Paul Trementozzi (Europe), Dave Ellis (Latin America Caribbean), JoAnn Butrin (International Ministries), and Ron Maddux (North Asia). Beggs, Turney, Beiler, Trementozzi, Ellis, and Butrin gave approval to survey their missionaries; Maddux denied permission. Just before sending out this survey, the AGWM Executive Committee (EC) decided that because of a recent researcher causing problems amongst AGWM missionaries with his overabundance of reminders to fill out his survey, a ban would be instituted on all further research. After talking to each regional director who had earlier granted permission again, the EC gave permission for this survey to be sent out to AGWM missionaries in the regions of Africa, Asia, Eurasia, Europe, Latin America Caribbean, and International Ministries with the stipulation that only one reminder could be sent out.

Ethical Agreement and Practice

Each survey participant read the consent form (see Appendix F) that explained the purpose, description, method, and ethical conduct of the research. When the individual opened the survey, the first page informed him or her about selecting the sensitive country option for those living in a restricted access location. This second survey took out all references to religion, missionary, or missions. The consent page described the study and the procedure of the survey. It stated that the survey would take between 30 to 45 minutes to complete and that he or she could withdraw at any time for any reason including discomfort, anxiety, or stress describing traumatic events. The consent page also assured the participants of the confidentiality of their participation, the secureness of both the Qualtrics and Evangel University servers. Beginning the survey showed consent by each participant.

---

27. Diener et al., "Satisfaction with Life Scale," 71–72.

Research Procedure

After authorization by the dissertation chairperson, the leadership of AGWM received the survey for their approval. Every region except North Asia gave their consent to survey their missionaries. The survey gathered data in agreement with the study using human subjects and met all requisites of the Institutional Review Board (IRB). Each missionary read and gave informed consent and all data remained secure and only the researcher and statistics consultant had access to the survey data.

The survey asked demographical information from each participant. These questions requested information about his or her age, gender, marital status, education, region, years of missionary service, and if he or she had been trained in trauma or conflict management by AGWM or another school or organization. Before starting the Trauma and Coping Survey, the missionary read a definition of trauma, an explanation of how the survey would proceed, and the length of time he or she needed to finish.

Data Processing and Analyses

All inventories came from either EBSCO Host PsycTEST which stated that "test content may be reproduced and used for non-commercial research and educational purposes without seeking written permission" or internet public domain access.[28] The combination of these inventories produced a missionary trauma and coping inventory that was loaded into the Qualtrics Survey Softwareâ owned by Evangel University. The participating missionaries' data collected from Qualtricsâ was then downloaded into SPSS statistical software.

This study will look at the following three research questions and hypotheses: 1) How many AGWM missionaries live through traumatic events? Hypothesis 1, traumatic events will be prevalent in AGWM missionary population. 2) What types of trauma do AGWM missionaries endure? Hypothesis 1, the missionary population will show a wide variety of traumatic events along with multiple occurrences. 3) What coping skills minimize the negative impact of trauma in missionaries' lives and enhance AGWM missionary well-being? Hypothesis 1, missionaries with High Trauma and Low PTSD will have significantly higher positive coping skills than those in the other category. Hypothesis 2, missionaries with Low Trauma and High

---

28. Diener et al., "Satisfaction with Life Scale"; Dik et al., "Development and Validation of the Calling."; Foa et al., "Symptom Scale-Interview Version"; Hardy et al., "Resilience Scale"; Johnson et al., "Resilience Appraisal Scale"; Pargament et al., "Brief RCOPE"; Vrana and Lauterbach, "Trauma Events Questionnaire."

PTSD will have significantly lower positive coping skills than missionary in the other category.

Results

Preliminary Analysis

This research invited AGWM career and Missionary Associate (MA) missionaries to participate in a trauma and coping survey via the internet. The missionaries had access to the survey for thirty days between the dates of July 15, 2014 to August 15, 2014. For the quantitative research, the AGWM department provided 1,907 email address and each of these missionaries received a link to Qualtrics website to participate in an online Trauma and Coping Survey. Nevertheless, because of many emails being caught in the AGWM spam filter, missionaries only started 421 surveys. Of these 47 decided not to take the survey because of lack of interest, being too busy, poor internet, felt he or she had nothing to contribute, or a deficiency of experience. Of those who started the survey, 120 did not finish. Thus, this research used 254 complete surveys (N = 254). Their responses remained anonymous and only the principle researcher and statistics consultant viewed the data.

The survey added demographic questions such as age, gender, marital status, country of service, length of service, education level, and cross-cultural/conflict management training. At the beginning of the survey, missionaries serving in restricted access locations could select "Sensitive County" from the language drop down box where throughout the informed consent and survey words such as "missionary" and "AGWM" changed to "worker" and "agency."

Participant Characteristics

Table 4.1. shows the basic demographics of the survey sample. The missionaries who participated in the survey ranged in age from 23 to 79 with a mean age of 50. Males represented half of the population ($n = 127$) and females the other half ($n = 127$). More married individuals participated (80.7 percent) than singles (19.3 percent).

Table 4.1. Demographic Characteristics

Age Group	Frequency	Percent
23–30	15	6.0%
31–40	43	17.2%
41–50	56	22.0%
51–60	95	37.0%
61–70	41	16.2%
71–79	4	1.6%

Gender		
Male	127	50.0%
Female	127	50.0%

Marital Status		
Single	49	19.3%
Married	205	81.7%

(N = 254)

These missionaries serve in the following countries: 30.7 percent in Latin America Caribbean, 18.5 percent in Europe, 16.1 percent in Eurasia, 15.4 percent in Asia Pacific, 13 percent in Africa, 6.3 percent in International Ministries (see Table 4.2.). Their missionary experience ranges from one to 44 years (see Table 4.3.).

Table 4.2. Country of Service

Country	Frequency	Percent
Africa	33	13.0%
Asia Pacific	39	15.4%

Country	Frequency	Percent
Eurasia	41	16.1%
Europe	47	18.5%
International Ministries	16	6.3%
Latin America Caribbean	78	30.7%

(N = 254)

Table 4.3. Missionary Experience

Term	Frequency	Percent
First Term (1-4 years)	52	20.5%
Second Term (5-10 years)	48	18.8%
Third Term (11-16 years)	26	10.4%
Fourth Term (17-22 years)	46	18.0%
Fifth Term (23-28 years)	44	17.3%
Sixth Term (29-34 years)	28	11.0%
Seventh Term (35-40 years)	8	3.2%
Eight Term (41-44 years)	2	.8%

(N = 254)

The educational level of these missionaries ranged from high school to doctoral or professional degrees. Of these missionaries, 1.6 percent achieved a high school level degree, 12.6 percent attended some college, and percent graduated with an AA (two years of college) degree while the highest amount 36.6 percent finished their BA/BS degree. Just over a third (33.9 percent) of those surveyed earned a Masters, 1.2 percent Professional (JD, MD), or 8.3 percent a Doctoral degree (see Table 4.4.).

Table 4.4. Education

Grade Level	Frequency	Percent
High School/GED	4	1.6%
Some College	32	12.6%
2-Year College Degree (AA)	15	5.9%
4-Year College Degree (BA/BS)	93	36.6%
Masters Degree	86	33.8%
Doctoral Degree	21	8.3%
Professional Degree (JD, MD)	3	1.2%

($N = 254$)

As for cross-cultural training by AGWM, 80 percent of the missionaries ($N = 254$) stated that they received a good amount of training to help them in their field adjustment. Yet, when it came to the subject of trauma, stress, or conflict management, these missionaries did not receive adequate training. When asked if their training assisted them on field, the majority felt it did (see Figures 4.1–5.).

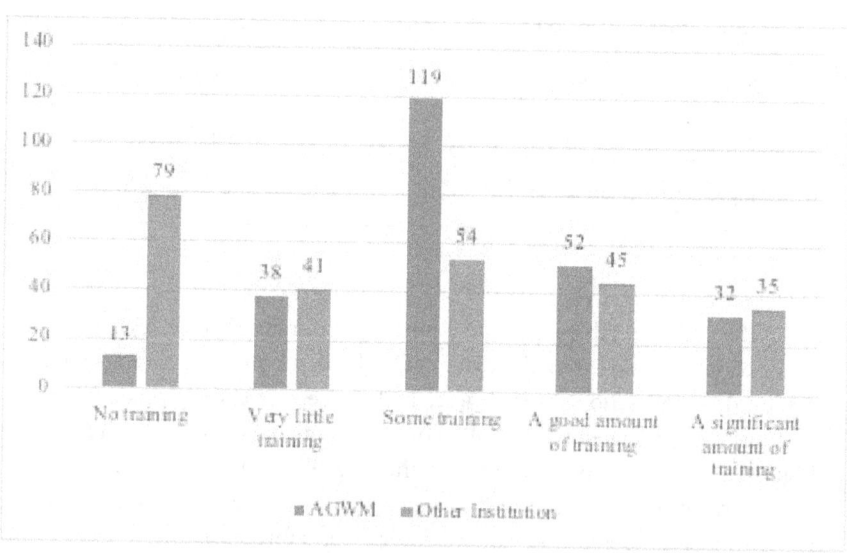

Figure 4.1. Missionary Training: Cross-cultural Training

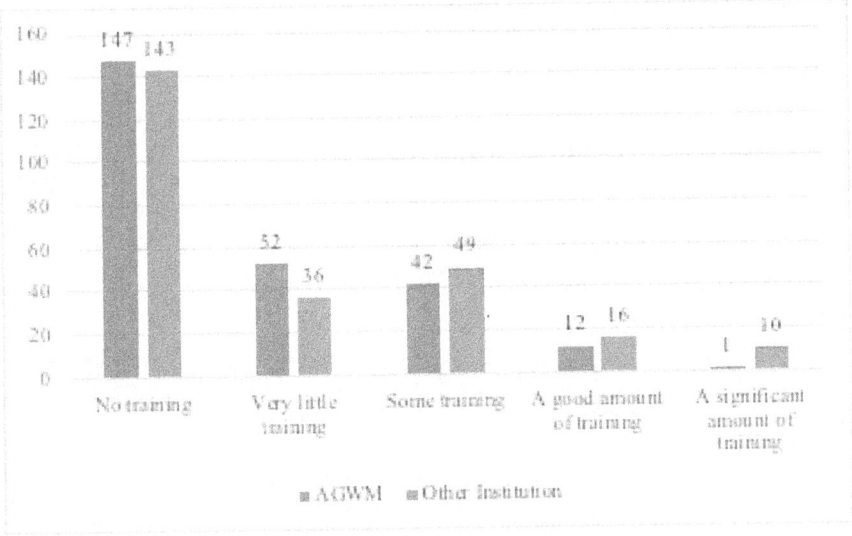

Figure 4.2. Missionary Training: Trauma Management

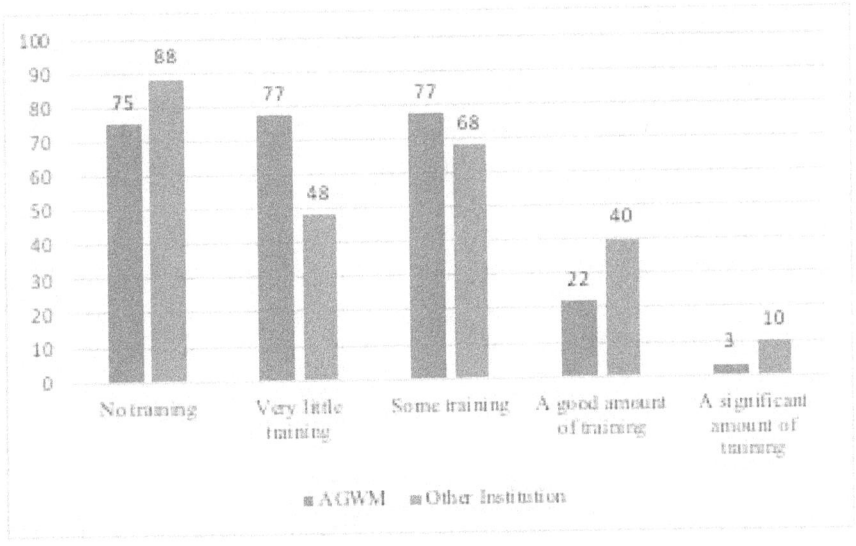

Figure 4.3. Missionary Training: Stress Management

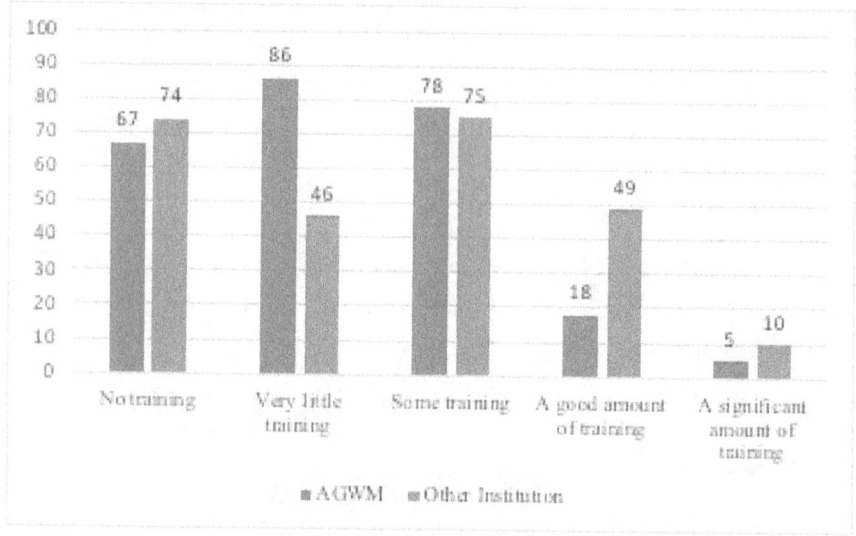

Figure 4.4. Missionary Training: Conflict Management

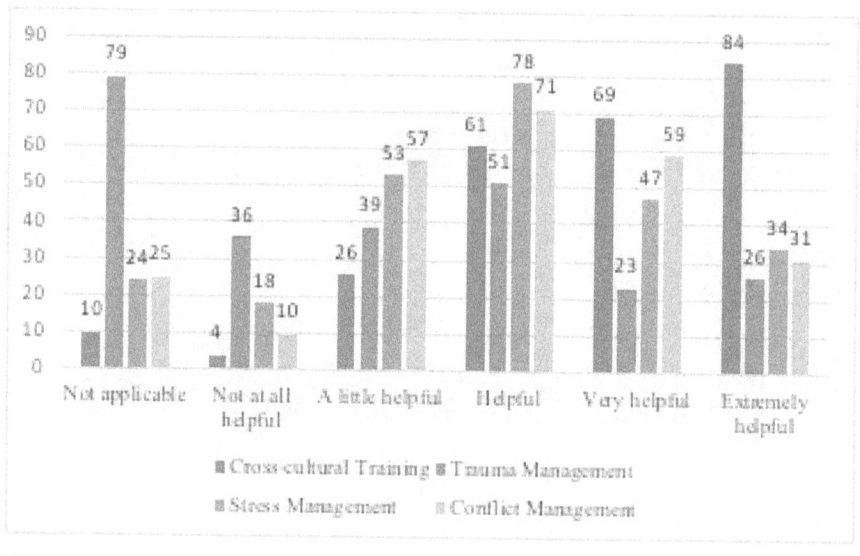

Figure 4.5. Missionary Training Helpfulness

How Many AGWM Missionaries Live Through Traumatic Events?

Missionaries, according to research, live through repeated traumatic events with the added stress of doing it in a cross-cultural setting.[29] Breslau et al. surveyed 1,007 young adults living in the United States and found that 39.1 percent experienced one or more traumatic incidences during their lives.[30] Of those, 32.7 percent (or 12.8 percent of total sample) underwent multiple traumas. Bagley's research reported that 94 percent of his 31 missionary participants conveyed that they had gone through at least one traumatic event and 65 percent of these missionaries went through trauma multiple times with 42 percent having these experiences within the survey year.[31] Candace Barbere-Stirling studied trauma suffered by Missionary Kids (MK). Of the 41 who participated in her study, 35 had endured a traumatic event prior to turning 25 years-old and of those 34 had faced multiple events.[32] Frauke Schaefer et al. studied 206 West African and 50 European missionaries from a variety of missions agencies. Of male European missionaries, 47 percent experienced one or more traumatic incidences and 30 percent of female missionaries underwent one or more traumatic occurrences. They found higher trauma exposure in West Africa with 71 percent male and 64 percent female missionaries encountering one or more traumatic episode.[33] Julie Irvine et al. studied 173 missionaries in which 80 percent reported having one or more traumatic stressors during their missionary career.[34]

This research hypothesizes that traumatic events will be prevalent in the AGWM missionary population. Per this survey, 100 percent of all 254 AGWM missionary participants had at least one traumatic event in his or her missionary career. This high number may be due to only missionaries who experienced trauma participated in the survey. Several emails from AGWM missionaries stated that they never had a traumatic event happen to them, so they did not fill out the survey. Therefore, this study divided the missionaries

---

29. Bagley, "Trauma and Traumatic Stress Among Missionaries," 104; Carr and Schaefer, "Trauma and Traumatic Stress," 279; Foyle, *Honorably Wounded*, 212; Gish, "Sources of Missionary Stress," 237; Grant, "Trauma in Missionary Life," 72; Irvine et al., "Traumatic Stress in a Missionary Population," 332; O'Donnell, "Member Care on the Field," 291; Schwandt and Moriarty, "What Have the Past 25 Years," 321–22.

30. Breslau et al., "Traumatic Events," 217.

31. Bagley, "Trauma and Traumatic Stress Among Missionaries," 104.

32. Barbere-Stirling, "Effects of Exposure," 131.

33. Schaefer et al., "Traumatic Events and Posttraumatic Stress," 529.

34. Irvine et al., "Traumatic Stress in a Missionary Population," 332–33.

into below average (= < .25), average (= 25.1 - 27.5) and above average (= > 27.5) responses to the question about trauma experiences. Based on the mean of a Trauma Sum Totals variable ($M = 26.3$, $SD = 2.4$).

What Types of Trauma Do AGWM Missionaries Endure?

Breslau et al. reported that North Americans most common traumatic events consisted of serious accidents, physical assaults, and news of sudden death of close friend or relative.[35] Bagley reported that missionaries endured even greater amounts of trauma than the average North American while on field.[36] Irvine et al. concurred with Bagley that missionaries live with traumatic stressors and endure catastrophic events during their missionary career (see Figure 4.6.).[37]

Barbere-Stirling states that her MK's reported that robbery of personal items or crime related trauma had the highest ranking. Other trauma suffered included: general disasters (e.g., political upheaval, third world poverty, living conditions), car accidents, and acts of nature.[38] Unlike Bagley's study,[39] 17 of the 35 MK's endured some form of sexual abuse (48.57 percent) with two happening in the family unit and several in the missionary fellowship. Physical assault happened to 15 MK's studied with three of these happening in the family unit.[40]

---

35. Breslau et al., "Traumatic Events," 217.
36. Bagley, "Impact of Trauma," 116–20.
37. Irvine et al., "Traumatic Stress in a Missionary Population," 330; Schaefer et al., "Traumatic Events and Posttraumatic Stress," 535.
38. Barbere-Stirling, "Effects of Exposure," 131.
39. Bagley, "Impact of Trauma," 116–20.
40. Barbere-Stirling, "Effects of Exposure," 131.

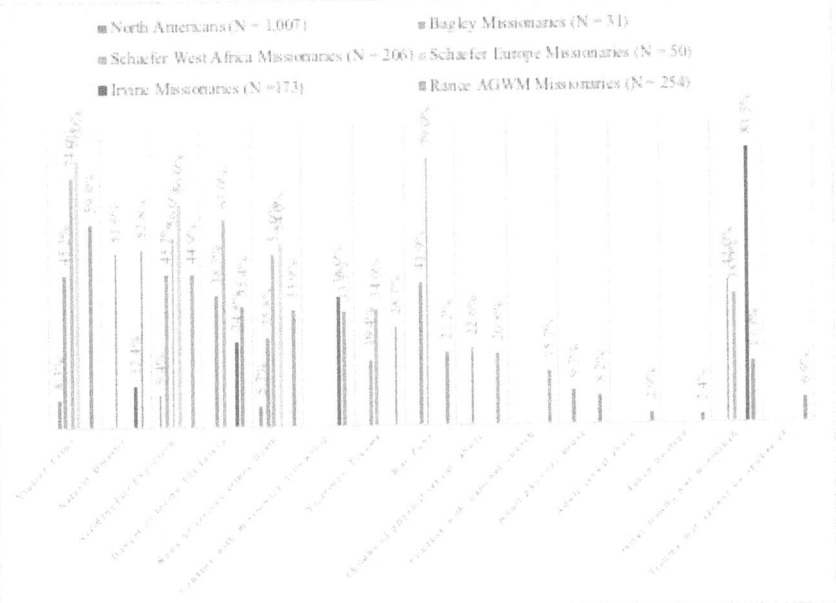

Figure 4.6. Comparison of Missionary Trauma Studies

This study hypothesized that the AGWM missionary population would also show a wide variety of traumatic events along with multiple occurrences. Table 4.5. shows that AGWM missionaries experienced various traumas multiple times, ranking these events from highest to lowest frequency.

Table 4.5. Percent of Missionaries Who Experienced Trauma by Category

Trauma	Frequency (Percent)	1 time	2 times	3+ times	On field	Declined
*Violent crime	152 (59.8%)	47 (30.9%)	34 (22.4%)	71 (46.7%)	131 (86.1%)	0
*Natural disaster	134 (52.8%)	38 (28.4%)	26 (19.4%)	70 (52.2%)	101 (75.4%)	0
*Accident/fire/ explosion	114 (44.9%)	28 (24.6%)	24 (21.1%)	62 (54.4%)	92 (80.7%)	0
*Danger of losing life/serious injury	90 (35.4%)	28 (31.1%)	24 (26.7%)	38 (42.2%)	60 (65.7%)	0

Trauma	Frequency (Percent)	1 time	2 times	3+ times	On field	Declined
News of serious injury/violent unexpected death of someone close	86 (33.9%)	41 (47.7%)	25 (29%)	26 (30.2%)	71 (82.6%)	0
*Conflict with missionary fellowship	85 (33.5%)	44 (51.8%)	31 (36.5%)	16 (18.8%)	85 (100%)	0
*Vicarious trauma	73 (28.7%)	31 (42.5%)	11 (15.1%)	31 (42.5%)	61 (83.6%)	0
*War Zone	52 (21.2%)	19 (36.5%)	8 (15.4%)	23 (44.2%)	46 (88.5%)	2 (3.8%)
*Childhood physical or sexual abuse	51 (20.8%)	–	–	–	–	0
*Other trauma not mentioned	45 (17.7%)	25 (47.2%)	15 (28.3%)	13 (24.5%)	36 (81.8%)	0
*Conflict with national church	40 (15.7%)	33 (71.7%)	9 (19.6%)	4 (8.7%)	40 (100%)	0
*Adult physical abuse	20 (8.2%)	14 (70%)	5 (25%)	1 (5%)	7 (35%)	0
*Trauma that cannot be spoken of	17 (6.9%)	9 (56.3%)	2 (12.5%)	5 (31.3%)	14 (82.4%)	1 (5.9 percent)
*Adult sexual abuse	7 (2.9%)	2 (28.6%)	1 (14.3%)	4 (57.1%)	3 (42.9%)	0
*Taken Hostage	6 (2.4%)	6 (100%)	0	0	6 (100%)	0

Sometimes the total of the times of trauma experience does not equal the frequency. This may be due to the possibility that some of the participants were confused with the question. (N = 254)

Violent Crime

The category with the highest number of AGWM missionary responses is violent crime. Some of these traumatic events included: rape, robbery assault, or a threat of violence such as pick-pocketing, burglary, intimidation, being put on a targeted list or electronically bugged. Of the 254 surveyed missionaries, 152 (59.8 percent) suffered one or more of these assaults. Most missionaries had a violent crime happen to them more than once (69.1 percent) and most of them happened on field (86.1 percent) (see Table 4.5.). The violent crimes did not injure the bulk of the missionaries (93.4 percent) nor did they feel their lives threatened (69.7 percent) (see Table 3.6.).[41] These missionaries also did not deem these violent crimes to be traumatic at the time of the event (56.6 percent) or at the time of the survey (93.4 percent).

Table 4.6. Violent Crimes

Question	Frequency	Percent
Were you injured during the violent crime(s)?		
1 Not at all	124	81.6%
2	7	4.6%
3	6	3.9%
4	5	3.3%
5	1	.7%
6	2	1.3%
7 Severely	3	2.0%
Declined to answer	4	2.6%
Did you feel your life was threatened by the violent crime(s)?		
1 Not at all	66	43.4%
2	14	9.2%
3	19	12.5%
4	7	4.6%

41. The statistics for all tables asking the questions: "Were you injured during the . . . ?", "Did you feel your life was threatened by the . . . ?", "How traumatic was the . . . ?", and "How traumatic is the . . . ?" were taken from the first trauma because all participants answered that question.

Question	Frequency	Percent
5	13	8.6%
6	10	6.6%
7 Severely	19	12.5%
Declined to answer	4	2.6%

How traumatic was the violent crime(s) for you at the time it happened?

	Frequency	Percent
1 Not at all	13	8.6%
2	33	21.7%
3	19	12.5%
4	21	13.8%
5	28	18.4%
6	17	11.2%
7 Severely	18	11.8%
Declined to answer	3	2.0%

How traumatic is the violent crime(s) for you now?

	Frequency	Percent
1 Not at all	96	63.2%
2	25	16.4%
3	17	11.2%
4	4	2.6%
5	4	2.6%
6	2	1.3%
7 Severely	1	.7%
Declined to answer	3	2.0%

*Totals for not at all to moderate include 1–4. Very to Severely 5–7. ($n = 152$)

Robberies, Pick-pockets, Burglary

AGWM missionaries endured more robberies (60.1 percent) than any other violent crime (see Table 4.5.). Missionaries have walked in on or been present during home robberies and survived muggings on the streets by gangs and thieves. Carjacking with weapons seems very traumatic for missionaries. One participant states, "My team mate and I experienced a car robbery at gunpoint. This caused her to have flashbacks and she ended up leaving the field prematurely. I was affected, but not traumatized."

Missionaries know that God may ask them to sacrifice their lives, nonetheless, they have higher anxiety when a violent crime involves their family. One respondent explained, "My wife and I were involved in a one car set up carjacking. I am not nearly concerned for my welfare as I am for that of my family. I realize that we go when it's our time to go. But somehow, we don't put our loved ones in the same frame of thought. We accept all the responsibility even when it is not ours to bear." Robberies cause great fear because of the feeling of helplessness as this missionary remembers, "I was held up at gunpoint with no option to run or fight back. I was completely out of control of the situation."

Pick-pocketing involves another form of robbery where the person is present during the event yet often unaware it happened until much later. Under a quarter (26.9 percent) of the 152 missionaries had this happen to them. Burglary usually happens in the home, office, or church without the presence of the victim. A little more than a quarter (35.4 percent) of the missionaries reporting being involved in a violent crime had this happen. These types of violent crime can make great missionary stories, yet the feelings of loss and invasion of personal space can be traumatic (see Table 4.7.).

Assault

Almost a quarter (23.6 percent) of the 152 AGWM missionaries reported being assaulted (see Table 4.7). Some suffered stoning like missionaries of the New Testament or physically attacked because of their work overseas. Threats of death often assail missionaries. After being affected by personal violence, two missionaries related, "The nationals threatened to burn down all foreigner's houses" or toward the church, "Men came to the door of our church on a religious holiday, describing in detail how they would firebomb the gathering . . . they had recently done this in another location." It can happen without warning as one missionary reported, "While walking home late at night, a gang of Gypsies surrounded me, shined lights in my face and started shouting at me. I did not know their dialect, and feared that I may be robbed, beaten, or worse. Fortunately, I was somehow able to pass through them and make it home without injury." Missionaries often put their lives in danger to preach the Word of Life to those who never heard. One such respondent explained, "A local chief threatened to have me killed in response to me entering his territory." One missionary describes how traumatic events are compounded when children are present during these assaults, "Road-blocks with protestors threatening to damage my vehicle. They stopped us and placed nails under our tires. I was alone with my ten-year-old daughter."

Intimidation, Targeted List, Bugged

Often because of their United States passports, governments regard missionaries as spies or rich. When they enter sensitive countries under a business, teaching, or education platform, they can raise suspicion as to their true reason for residing in the country. This can cause stress and anxiety in being intimidated, targeted, or having their homes or businesses bugged. A quarter (25.4 percent) of missionaries experiencing violent crime suffered from intimidation (see Table 3.7.). One missionary stated, "We were extorted by a government employee in [a sensitive country][42] and threatened with a large fine—unless we paid a large bribe."

Being put on a targeted list can also cause great anxiety which can last for months; a few (8.5 percent) of AGWM missionaries lived through this situation (see Table 4.7.). One recalls, "My wife and I are on a targeted list in the restricted access country where we live. We were told by a very reliable source that we are being watched for any signs of evangelistic activity. The government is not a threat—we would just be kicked out of the country. However, radical [religious groups] are more likely to injure or kill us."

Having one's privacy invaded over a long period can also be very traumatic. A few (9.7 percent) (see Table 4.7.) of these missionaries live with their homes or offices bugged by the governments where they live, "I was forced to leave the country I was serving in by the government. Over a period of about three to four months, we were watched, calls were listened to, vehicles were confiscated, questions were asked, threats were handed down, our homes were searched, personal items confiscated, and we were questioned." Missionaries say that the consistent and repeated mini-traumas

---

42. The researcher changed bracketed words to protect the anonymity of the participant.

by government officials and radical religious groups wear on their sense of stability and well-being,

> My experience in [a restricted country] was full of many mini-traumas: hiding items for other workers who were imprisoned for months, passports being taken, teammates being kicked out of the country on a day's notice, local believers being tortured/imprisoned for not recanting their faith, our school being drastically reduced in staff/admin[istration], our property being seized, our apartments being searched while we were questioned, and a forced emergency exit from the country.

Rape

During the act of many violent crimes, missionary women often feel that they could be raped in the process. One female missionary recounts, "We were robbed at knifepoint on a lonely road and one of the men said they were going to take me but the other said no. I know there was a spiritual element and that the Lord protected us." On this survey, 3.9 percent endured this violation (see Table 4.7.). One woman seems to put it as one of many things she went through on the field.

> Just to say here: we have had many traumatic situations, snakes, the plague, sickness—TB, malaria, typhoid, and even a very traumatic dentist situation in [sensitive country] when I realized they used reusable needles . . . not well cleaned in a very high HIV area . . . that was hard . . . What was the most traumatic . . . Perhaps being held up with my daughter in [sensitive country] with AKs and my hubby out of the country. It seems that and being raped were the only ones that had later triggers and Post Traumatic stress moments.

Other Violent Crime

A little over quarter (26.9 percent) of AGWM missionaries reported other violent crime other than rape, robbery, assault, pick-pocked, burglary, intimidation, being put on a target list, or being bugged (see Table 4.7.). Most of these events happened before going to the field as missionaries. One respondent recounted a story of a double homicide during his days as a police officer. Another told of rebuilding a black church in the south at the height of the civil rights movement and being shot at by the local town's people.

As a child, one missionary remembers living through gang violence in Los Angeles and witnessing a murder in front of his/her home. Pre-teen bulling also felt like a traumatic violent crime to some.

Violent crime, in whatever form it takes, leaves a traumatic impact on its victims. These AGWM missionaries encountered traumatic events both on and off field and as both adults and children. They often experienced them repeatedly and yet they still look at the experiences as insignificant. One missionary sums it up well: "During our time in the [sensitive country], there were many 'smaller' traumas. We were never injured, but there was an attempted car-jacking outside our home, we were put on a list by [religious] extremists, and I witnessed a mine being exploded just beyond where my husband was standing . . . perhaps nine burglaries in [sensitive country] helped numb us a bit. Lots of small stuff."

Table 4.7. Types of Violent Crimes

Crime	First Trauma Frequency	Percent	Second Trauma Frequency	Percent	Third Trauma Frequency	Percent
Robbery	42	27.6%	27	17.8%	23	14.7%
Burglary	20	13.2%	20	13.2%	14	9.0%
Pick Pocket	26	17.1%	12	7.9%	3	1.9%
Assault	15	9.9%	14	9.2%	7	4.5%
Intimidation	12	7.9%	14	9.2%	13	8.3%
Targeted List	5	3.3%	3	2.0%	5	3.2%
Bugged	3	2.0%	6	3.9%	6	3.8%
Rape	5	3.3%	0	0.0%	1	.6%
Other Types	22	14.5%	10	6.6%	9	5.8%
Did not answer	2	1.3%	46	30.3%	75	48.1%

($n = 152$)

Natural Disaster

Over half, 134 (52.8 percent) out of 252 AGWM missionaries witnessed natural disasters. This second most experienced traumatic event consisted of tornados, hurricanes, floods, major earthquakes, tsunamis, volcanic eruptions, typhoons, famine, or violent storms. Almost three quarters (71.6 percent) suffered more than one event and 75.4 percent of the missionaries went through these events while on field (see Table 4.5.). These natural disasters did not injure the missionaries (95.5 percent) nor did they feel their lives threatened (76 percent). Over half (65.7 percent) of the participants did not feel traumatized at the time of the event and 91.8 percent did not feel traumatized at the time they took the survey (see Table 4.8.).

Table 4.8. Traumatic Natural Disaster

Question	Frequency	Percent
Were you injured by the natural disaster?		
1 Not at all	123	91.8%
2	4	3.0%
3	0	0.0%
4	1	.7%
5	1	.7%
6	0	0.0%
7 Severely	1	.7%
Declined to answer	4	2.9%
Did you feel your life was threatened by the natural disaster?		
1 Not at all	46	34.3%
2	20	14.9%
3	16	11.9%
4	20	14.9%
5	13	9.7%
6	5	3.7%
7 Severely	10	7.5%
Declined to answer	4	3.0%

Question	Frequency	Percent
How traumatic was the natural disaster for you at the time it happened?		
1 Not at all	21	15.7%
2	26	19.4%
3	22	16.4%
4	19	14.2%
5	21	15.7%
6	9	6.7%
7 Severely	12	9.0%
Declined to answer	4	3.0%
How traumatic is the natural disaster for you now?		
1 Not at all	91	67.9%
2	21	15.7%
3	8	6.0%
4	3	2.2%
5	4	3.0%
6	3	2.2%
7 Severely	0	0.0%
Declined to answer	4	3.0%

*Totals for not at all to moderate include 1-4. Very to Severely 5-7. ($n = 134$)

The bulk of these missionaries suffered hurricanes (43.3 percent) with tornados (27.2 percent), major earthquakes (26.8 percent), and floods (17.3 percent). Disasters such as tornados and floods usually happened to missionaries while living in the United States, one respondent recalls, "In Missouri, I had to get under tables at SAMs as a tornado hit one block away." Another missionary recalls a traumatic experience in a flood, "I was driving with two of my children and an elderly lady and we were caught in torrential rains with flash flooding and we narrowly escaped a landslide and we had to crawl through it in the dark to get to safety not knowing exactly where we were."

Natural disasters also affect missionaries while on field. These events include multiple hurricanes in one year, or one very slow moving one like Hurricane Mitch in 1998 which wreaked havoc across the Caribbean and Central America. Earthquakes can also be traumatic like the 1986 and 2001 earthquakes in El Salvador. After experiencing volcanic eruptions, a missionary remembers, "We were trapped on disintegrating roads due to volcanic eruptions for three hours. The roads were extremely narrow, and the bridges were gone. [We] had to cross over makeshift wooden planks over deep ravines." These disasters can be difficult to overcome because missionaries not only live through them but also must start disaster relief work often before processing the trauma themselves.

Industrial, Farm, or Car Accident, Large Fire, Explosion

Of the 254 AGWM missionaries, 114 (44.9 percent) experienced the third most suffered trauma of industrial, farm, or car accidents, large fires, or explosions. Three quarters (75.5 percent) of these 114 missionaries experienced these traumatic incidents more than one time and 80.7 percent happened on field (see Table 4.5.). Many missionaries had involvements with car accidents (64.2 percent), then large fires (9.4 percent), explosions (6.8 percent), industrial accidents (3.9 percent), and farm accidents (3.9 percent). Most missionaries walked away with little to no injuries (85 percent) and did not sense their life threatened (69.3 percent). Only 51.5 percent felt moderate to no traumatic feelings at the time of the event and this number grew to 90.3 percent at the time of the survey (see Table 4.9.).

Table 4.9. Traumatic Accident

Question	Frequency	Percent
Were you injured at the time(s) of this/these event(s)?		
1 Not at all	73	64.0%
2	11	9.6%
3	8	7.0%
4	5	4.4%
5	6	5.3%
6	4	3.5%
7 Severely	2	1.8%
Declined to answer	5	4.4%

Question	Frequency	Percent
Did you feel your life was threatened at the time(s) of this/these event(s)?		
1 Not at all	50	43.9%
2	8	7.0%
3	9	7.9%
4	12	10.5%
5	9	7.9%
6	11	9.6%
7 Severely	11	9.6%
Declined to answer	4	3.5%
How traumatic was witnessing the serious traumatic accident?		
1 Not at all	12	10.3%
2	11	9.6%
3	17	14.9%
4	19	16.7%
5	20	17.5%
6	19	16.7%
7 Severely	10	8.8%
Declined to answer	6	5.3%
How traumatic is witnessing this serious traumatic accident for you now?		
1 Not at all	64	56.1%
2	26	22.8%
3	5	4.4%
4	8	7.0%
5	3	2.6%
6	2	1.8%
7 Severely	0	0.0%
Declined to answer	6	5.3%

*Totals for not at all to moderate include 1-4. Very to Severely 5-7. (n = 114)

Car Accidents

AGWM missionaries reported car accidents to be the most traumatic incident in this trauma type. These accidents happened both on and off field. They report not only being involved in car and motorcycle accidents but also seemingly regular head-on collisions that invariably seems to happen on busy foreign roads and highways.

Accidents that occur on field can be even more traumatic because of the lack of emergency response. They often must "drive on extremely dangerous roads where other missionaries lost their lives." Yet, in these situations, missionaries felt that God intervened. One respondent remembers, "Driving a tortuous road on a mountainside in Mexico in the rain, we lost control of the car and hydroplaned. It felt like God kept us from going over the precipice and put us back on the road." Another missionary writes, "[I was] in a car accident rolling down a hill—the car stopped inches from the front of a shack, that had we hit it, the house would have collapsed and the baby sleeping behind the front wall could have been injured." Still another says, "[I was in a] car accident at night in a hostile area—God's protection was very evident, but it was dangerous." These miracles also have helped missionaries in the United States, "while itinerating near Chicago. I had my CB on (yes, it was a long time ago) and I heard a trucker behind me describing my hydroplaning in a snowstorm yet being moved back onto the highway as 'a miracle.'"

Missionaries have also been hit by cars, "A car hit me (I was a pedestrian)." Another recalls, "At age six [I] was run over by a truck while riding my bike." When a car hurts a family member, it becomes traumatic for the missionary, "My daughter was hit by a car and seriously injured while on the mission field."

Missionaries must take other forms of transportation, so they reported other types of accidents they endured. Missionaries often spend much time on planes, and they do not always feel safe, "Thought a plane I was in was going down in a severe storm." Another remembers, "Being on an airplane when the pilot announced the landing gear was malfunctioning and being asked to take the position of a crash landing. My husband and small children were with me. The landing gear 'somehow' began functioning just before we landed." Missionaries often have to take boats to go to places where cars cannot go, and accidents or storms can make for a traumatic journey "The boat I was on sank about a mile from land. There were no life preservers."

Large Fires, Explosions, Industrial and Farm Accidents

This survey found AGWM missionaries also had involvement with large fires, explosions, and industrial and farm accidents both on and off field. From almost being "impaled on a pitchfork falling from a hayloft," to "experiencing a nuclear incident in the military" missionaries experienced many types of traumatic events. Several missionaries described trauma with out of control forest fires. One stated, "While working as a public safety officer and fighting a large woods fire, we had to respond to two other firefighters being trapped and surrounded by the fire. As we were responding, we were also trapped by the fire. The fire was cut off by a dozer just moments before reaching us." Then, another missionary who survived a house fire, described, "Entered a burning mobile home that was fully engulfed in fire due to the belief that a small child was still inside."

One missionary describes a bad explosion her husband experienced, "The trauma I experienced was when my husband was badly burned in an explosion. I was with him shortly after the explosion and when he told me a fuel tank was going to explode, all I could think was to cover his body with mine because he had already been burned enough. The tank did not explode, and if it had, I would have been burned or killed."

Danger of Losing Life or Serious Injury

Of the 254 AGWM missionaries, 90 (35.4 percent) felt that they had experienced the trauma of danger of losing their lives or having a serious injury. Over half (68.9 percent) of these missionaries experienced these traumas more than once and 65.7 percent experienced them on the mission field (see Table 4.5.). Even though they felt they were in danger of losing their life, the majority (60 percent) did not receive an injury yet they greatly feared for their lives (72.2 percent). At the time of the event 60 percent of the missionaries were very or severely traumatized but at the time of the survey, this number dropped to 4.4 percent (see Table 4.10.).

Table 4.10. Danger of Losing Life

Question	Frequency	Percent
Were you injured when you were in serious danger of losing your life?		
1 Not at all	54	60.0%
2	11	12.2%
3	4	4.4%
4	4	4.4%
5	6	6.7%
6	3	3.3%
7 Severely	5	5.6%
Declined to answer	3	3.3%
Did you feel your life was threatened when you were in serious danger?		
1 Not at all	4	4.4%
2	3	3.3%
3	7	7.8%
4	8	8.9%
5	13	14.4%
6	15	16.7%
7 Severely	37	41.1%
Declined to answer	3	3.3%
How traumatic was the serious danger of losing your life or being seriously injured for you at the time it happened?		
1 Not at all	4	4.4%
2	9	10.0%
3	9	10.0%
4	12	13.3%
5	13	14.4%
6	14	15.6%
7 Severely	27	30.0%
Declined to answer	2	2.2%

Question	Frequency	Percent
How traumatic is the serious danger of losing your life or being seriously injured for you now?		
1 Not at all	51	56.7%
2	19	21.1%
3	10	11.1%
4	4	4.4%
5	2	2.2%
6	1	1.1%
7 Severely	1	1.1%
Declined to answer	2	2.2%

*Totals for not at all to moderate include 1-4. Very to Severely 5-7. ($n = 90$)

The possibility of being injured or losing one's life can happen in any traumatic event. A female respondent detailed how it can happen in a car,

> I put my car into a swimming pool to avoid backing into a house at fast speed (the motor jammed in reverse FAST out of our driveway, crossed the road and was heading for the big house behind, when I maneuvered into the swimming pool). That was scary. We went to see a movie that night in which a man was trying to outrun a flood, and I had a mini PTSD reaction—"That was me TODAY!" Remembering the water rushing into the car while it was sinking in the pool and I couldn't get the doors open. Got out the windows after remembering I had to open them fast before the racing motor died.

One missionary sensed danger on a train,

> While waiting for a train late at night, a drug dealer approached me and asked what I wanted. After I refused, he spoke with two, large men in long trench coats. One reached inside his coat for what appeared to be a weapon, and the two started following me. They continued to chase me until I ducked into a train to flee. On the train, a man with a machine gun walked through, then, moments later a young woman burst into my compartment asking for someone who spoke English. She had been robbed by the conductor, and the other members of her compartment beat

him and returned her property; however, because nobody spoke English, she was frightened and came looking for help. All these events added up to a night, when I also feared for my safety.

A husband reveals how government conflict can also put his wife in danger,

> My wife had gone to the airport in [a sensitive country] during the civil war to pick up some supplies. On the way back to the compound, she was stopped at a check point and armed men approached the car with drawn weapons demanding that she get out of the car. She refused. The driver put the car in reverse and jammed his foot down on the accelerator. The gunmen did not shoot at the car and she escaped. I was not aware of this at the time. I only knew that she had not returned home, and I also knew that all of the other agencies that had sent cars to the airport that morning had returned long ago. She had a walkie-talkie radio with her, but she did not answer. I was very worried about her safety.

News of Mutilation, Serious Injury, or Violent Unexpected Death of Someone Close

About a third, 86 (33.9 percent) of the 254 of the missionaries surveyed felt traumatized by news of mutilation, serious injury, or the violent, unexpected death of someone close to them. The majority (59.2 percent) of these missionaries had to endure this traumatic event multiple times; however, 82.6 percent of them experienced it while on field (see Table 4.5.). Most (94.2 percent) of the missionaries did not suffer injury when they heard the news and 95.4 percent did not feel their lives threatened. Yet, 62.8 percent experienced traumatization at the time of the event but that dissipated to 10.5 percent at the time of the survey (see Table 4.11.).

Table 4.11. Received News of Mutilation, Serious Injury, or Violent/Unexpected Death of a Close Friend or Family Member

Question	Frequency	Percent
Were you injured when you received news of mutilation, serious injury, or violent/unexpected death of a close friend or family member?		
1 Not at all	80	93.0%
2	0	0.0%
3	1	1.2%
4	0	0.0%
5	0	0.0%
6	0	0.0%
7 Severely	1	1.2%
Declined to answer	4	4.7%
Did you feel your life was threatened when you received news of mutilation, serious injury, or violent/unexpected death of a close friend or family member?		
1 Not at all	78	90.7%
2	3	3.5%
3	1	1.2%
4	0	0.0%
5	1	1.2%
6	0	0.0%
7 Severely	0	0.0%
Declined to answer	3	3.5%
How traumatic was the news of the mutilation, serious injury, or violent/unexpected death of a close friend or family member at the time it happened?		
1 Not at all	2	2.3%
2	3	3.5%
3	10	11.6%
4	16	18.6%

Question	Frequency	Percent
5	10	11.6%
6	17	19.8%
7 Severely	27	31.4%
Declined to answer	1	1.2%

How traumatic is the event of the news of the mutilation, serious injury, or violent/unexpected death of a friend or family member for you now?

1 Not at all	31	36.0%
2	31	36.0%
3	8	9.3%
4	6	7.0%
5	2	2.3%
6	3	3.5%
7 Severely	4	4.7%
Declined to answer	1	1.2%

*Totals for not at all to moderate include 1-4. Very to Severely 5-7. (n = 86)

Missionaries had difficulty hearing news of close friends or family members being hurt or dying mostly because of the obstacle of getting to that person or family member, "My father died while on the field of a drug related illness. It took three days before I could get permission to leave country due to country regulations on the missionaries at the time. By the time, I reached my father all I got was his personal belongings. I did not get to say goodbye or that I loved him despite his addiction to drugs." Even being in the United States when danger threatens one's family can be traumatic,

> During 9/11, I am from NJ and two of my brothers who live in NYC were in danger. Both were protected but we couldn't find out how they were for two days. My folks were ok in NJ. People from my home church were killed (many spared as well) I was just back in USA from [sensitive country] and my husband was stuck in [sensitive country]. My family was very unsettled . . . I actually vomited when the second tower was hit . . . My brother

usually gets the subway under the twin towers—but God spared his life. Friends of family were killed as well.

Hearing about friends going through trauma can also cause powerful traumatic emotions, "My daughter in [sensitive country] and the mall where all the [school] kids go was held by [a religious group]. Although my daughter was safe, it was traumatic for us to see what happened and to hear the reports of fellow [school mates] who lost family . . . it was just too close to home . . . kids away from home in a country where Christian are targets . . . there is still unrest . . . still danger." It seems even harder with converts being killed for their faith.

> When I was working in [sensitive country], there was a [national] woman who had come to the Lord. She came to our house often for Bible studies and ate at our table. Unfortunately, she was mentally unstable. For long periods she would be perfectly normal, but from time to time she would have spells when she lost her normal reasoning and wandered the streets, babbling. Finally, her family was so shamed by her Christianity and her mental instability that they locked her in her bedroom and let her starve to death.

Another missionary recalls,

> I had a [national] friend who was a refugee in [sensitive country] when I worked in [sensitive city]. He was a Christian with a very powerful testimony of being saved after he was delivered from demon possession which had caused him to be chained up because he was so violent. He had also been delivered from a [national] gunman in a miraculous way when the man tried to shoot him at point blank range, but the weapon would not fire. But when he pointed the gun elsewhere, it did fire. We were very close. He was extremely gentle and sweet tempered. Although he had been miraculously delivered once, on another occasion he encountered a [national] gunman and the Lord did not keep the gun from firing, and he was killed.

Conflict with Missionary Fellowship

Even though conflict with fellow missionaries was one of the top five reasons why missionaries leave the field,[43] it came in as the sixth most experienced trauma in this survey with only 85 (33.5 percent) of the 254 AGWM

43. Blocher, "ReMAP I," 13.

missionaries. Most of the missionaries (51.8 percent) had only one traumatic conflict with fellow missionaries (see Table 4.5.). It seems that the longer a missionary remained on field, the less conflict occurred. A missionary's first four years held the most missionary conflict (69.4 percent). The conflict seemed to take a few months to five years to resolve (68.5 percent) with one conflict lasting 20 plus years; 20 people declined to answer, this may mean that they continue to wait for the conflict to end (see Table 4.12.).

Table 4.12. Traumatic Missionary Conflict

Term	Frequency	Percent
What term were you in at the time of your traumatic conflict with the member(s) of your missionary fellowship?		
1st Term (1–4 years)	59	69.4%
2nd Term (5–10 years)	13	15.3%
3rd Term (11–16 years)	10	11.8%
4th Term (17–22 years)	2	2.4%
Declined to answer	1	1.2%
If the traumatic conflict with the member(s) of the missionary fellowship is resolved, how long did it take?		
1 to 6 months	19	22.4%
6 months to 1 year	18	21.4%
1–5 years	21	24.7%
5–10 years	6	7.1%
20+ years	1	1.2%
Declined to answer	20	23.5%
($n = 85$)		

Missionaries do not expect to have conflict with fellow missionaries and therefore the suffering from the people they should get along with makes the event even more traumatic. Most of the missionaries did not feel their lives were threatened (91.8 percent). Over half (65.8 percent) of these missionaries underwent severe traumatization at the time of the incident but by the time of the survey their trauma had resided to 11.8 percent (see Table 4.13.).

Table 4.13. Traumatic Missionary Conflict

Question	Frequency	Percent
Did you feel your life was threatened when you had the traumatic conflict with the member(s) of the missionary fellowship?		
1 Not at all	75	88.2%
2	1	1.2%
3	1	1.2%
4	1	1.2%
5	2	2.4%
6	0	0.0%
7 Severely	0	0.0%
Not Applicable	5	5.9%
How traumatic was this conflict with the member(s) of the missionary fellowship for you at the time of the event?		
1 Not at all	2	2.4%
2	4	4.7%
3	13	15.3%
4	9	10.6%
5	16	18.8%
6	15	17.6%
7 Severely	25	29.4%
Not Applicable	1	1.2%
How Traumatic is the conflict event with the member(s) of the missionary fellowship for you at the time of the event?		
1 Not at all	33	38.8%
2	28	32.9%
3	11	12.9%
4	0	0.0%
5	3	3.5%

Question	Frequency	Percent
6	5	5.9%
7 Severely	2	2.4%
Not Applicable	3	3.5%

*Totals for not at all to moderate include 1-4. Very to Severely 5-7.
(n = 85)

Some people had undergone church conflict before becoming missionaries, "Conflict with a pastor and his wife over a situation that was out of our hands. The ultimate decision did not lie within our power to make monetary decisions. [The] conflict [was] over money." Missionaries who pastored a church before going on field understood having conflicts with board members, or church members not liking the way they pastored. These conflicts felt like betrayal and had severe consequences, "I was told to stop doing theatre or leave the church. SO, I left the church. It took seventeen years to come back to Christ and trust anyone in the church. God has healed." Yet, conflict on field compounded with the added stress of acculturation often pushed missionaries over the edge. Some new missionaries felt they were emotionally and psychologically abused by their host missionary,

> I was being told how to walk, talk, act, [and] breathe . . . what to wear and basically that everything I did was not right and needed to be changed. The first six months on the field [were] HORRIFIC . . . the missionary was trying to make me fit into a churchified box of her making and I have REFUSED to ever be treated or spoken to like that. We basically had a massive conflict that lead to mutual respect and resolve to better communicate. SO, in the end, it was good.

Another new field worker states, "When our mentor missionary verbally attacked my daughter for writing her name in the dust on his car. He has PTSD and was shaking, and he was screaming at her, [my daughter] was thirteen years old and she was and still is scared of him. As her dad I want to protect my little girl, but I was in shock that this was someone that I showed complete loyalty and trust."

Mentor missionaries also felt stress when the new missionaries made them look bad, "Missionaries in training sent to be under our supervision. Had addictions and vices, including violent temper and overt hostility. Yet, we were looked on as the bad missionaries if they failed . . . They did." Another older missionary writes, "I was coaching a missionary associate and he reacted violently toward me. He is a trained fighter and I thought he was going to seriously hurt me. The pain of this event was compounded when my field leadership told me that they did not believe he was capable of doing what I said he did. I had to continue working with him for another three months until he was reassigned to another ministry."

Many missionaries view missionary conflict as the most traumatic event they ever went through, "Each event affected me in a different way. Conflict with [a] missionary caused the most pain/depression. It is also the only event that lingered for a longer period and caused me to consider quitting." Another states, "Between a house fire and conflict with fellow workers, the conflict with fellow workers felt much more traumatic on a personal and emotional level." Some missionaries still carry the scares of unresolved conflict, "The most traumatic would be the event with my fellow missionary on the field. All the other events have been dealt with and healed by the power of Jesus and his restoration."

Conflict also happens between the missionary and AGWM leadership. To keep the participants anonymous, their stories will not be shared. Nevertheless, missionaries have felt that their leadership have not kept confidences, "misheard, misinterpreted, and miscommunicated information," played favoritism, refused to discuss problems, and threatened termination. Of course, these stories are one-sided, yet the impression of not having an ally or that their leadership did not facilitate their success causing some of these missionaries anxiety, depression, and career uncertainty.

Vicarious Trauma

Of the 254 AGWM missionaries, 73 (28.7 percent) encountered vicarious trauma. This type of trauma happens when a person witnesses a trauma or becomes engulfed in the trauma of others through relief or medical work and counseling. A little over half (57.6 percent) of these missionaries lived through vicarious trauma more than one time. Most (83.6 percent) bore this trauma on field (see Table 4.5.). The majority (95.7 percent) received little to no injury and did not believe the trauma threatened their lives (84.9 percent). These missionaries felt extremely traumatize at the time of the event (60.3 percent) yet at the time of the survey, this number dropped to 9.5 percent (see Table 4.14.).

Table 4.14. Vicarious Trauma

Question	Frequency	Percent
Were you injured when you witnessed someone who was mutilated, seriously injured, or violently killed?		
1 Not at all	69	94.3%
2	0	0.0%
3	1	1.4%
4	0	0.0%
5	1	1.4%
6	0	0.0%
7 Severely	2	2.7%
Declined to answer	0	0.0%
Did you feel your life was threatened when you witnessed someone who was mutilated, seriously injured, or violently killed?		
1 Not at all	54	74.0%
2	2	2.7%
3	2	2.7%
4	4	5.5%
5	3	4.1%
6	5	6.8%
7 Severely	3	4.1%
Declined to answer	0	0.0%
How traumatic was witnessing someone who was mutilated, seriously injured, or violently killed at the time it happened?		
1 Not at all	3	4.1%
2	5	6.8%
3	14	19.2%
4	7	9.6%
5	17	23.3%
6	13	17.8%
7 Severely	14	19.2%
Declined to answer	0	0.0%

Question	Frequency	Percent
How traumatic is witnessing someone who was mutilated, seriously injured, or violently killed for you now?		
1 Not at all	29	39.7%
2	19	26.0%
3	12	16.4%
4	6	8.2%
5	2	2.7%
6	3	4.1%
7 Severely	2	2.7%
Declined to answer	0	0.0%

*Totals for not at all to moderate include 1-4. Very to Severely 5-7. (n = 73)

Witnessing death of any kind can be very traumatic, "Finding the parents of my best friend murdered is the only traumatic event I have experienced in my life. It was traumatic, but was dealt with by counseling, prayer, support, and time." While encountering this type of trauma, another missionary reports, "watching the car in front of me (which had just passed me at high speed in a pitch-dark situation) hit a pedestrian that I would have hit had he not passed me. The young pedestrian went through his windshield and was dying as I helped put him in the car to be driven to the hospital. My pants and hands were full of blood."

Working in places where people suffer can cause trauma to infiltrate the helper's soul. Many missionaries work in sex trafficking. One missionary writes, "My ministry involves entering brothels/nightclubs and things that are seen inside really affects me emotionally and stay with me for quite some time. I've had some teens die from our at-risk youth group in very violent ways. This has affected me emotionally." Another missionary explains, "Entering the brothels/nightclubs really affects me emotionally and I always need to take some time to recover with the Lord."

Relief work can also take its toll on the emotions of a missionary, "During the refugee crisis in [sensitive country], we were involved in health ministry. The town of [sensitive city] was flooded with refugees and soldiers. Cholera was killing hundreds each day. Dead bodies and the dying were everywhere. There was no 'trustworthy' security for us or anyone. Gunshots were frequently heard. It seemed that hell was pouring into that place to me."

A disaster at a place where one frequents, can cause feelings of fear,

> A suicide bomber blew up a restaurant we planned to be at for lunch. We changed our mind just before lunch and went to another restaurant. While eating we heard the sirens. After lunch, we drove to the restaurant that was destroyed by the bomb. That scene was shocking and horrifying. Most of the people inside died. People we knew. A safe and fun place for us became a place of death in the matter of seconds. Even though we did not see the explosion as it happened, we heard the sirens immediately after it happened and knew something was very wrong. We were on the scene within thirty minutes. Truly it is the closest I have felt to death—even more than when rockets fell on our city.

Living in a War Zone

Of the 254 missionaries surveyed, 52 (21.2 percent) lived in a war zone at some point in their lives. Over half (59.6 percent) of these missionaries experienced war type trauma more than once in their lives and 88.5 percent lived in a war zone during their missionary career (see Table 3.5.). Miraculously, 96.1 percent of these missionaries never received an injury and 55.8 percent did not feel their lives threatened. A little over half (57.7 percent) did not deem living in a war zone as traumatic and they felt less so at the time of the survey (96.2 percent) (see Table 4.15.).

Table 4.15. Living in a War Zone

Question	Frequency	Percent
Were you injured when you received friendly or hostile incoming fire from small arms or artillery?		
1 Not at all	49	94.2%
2	1	1.9%
3	0	0.0%
4	0	0.0%
5	1	1.9%
6	0	0.0%
7 Severely	0	0.0%
Declined to answer	1	1.9%

Question	Frequency	Percent
Did you feel your life was threatened while in a war zone?		
1 Not at all	8	15.4%
2	8	15.4%
3	6	11.5%
4	7	13.5%
5	5	9.6%
6	11	21.2%
7 Severely	6	11.5%
Declined to answer	1	1.9%
How traumatic was living in a war zone for you?		
1 Not at all	3	5.8%
2	8	15.4%
3	10	19.2%
4	9	17.3%
5	8	15.4%
6	6	11.5%
7 Severely	8	15.4%
Declined to answer	0	0.0%
How traumatic is having lived in a war zone for you now?		
1 Not at all	26	50.0%
2	16	30.8%
3	4	7.7%
4	4	7.7%
5	1	1.9%
6	0	0.0%
7 Severely	1	1.9%
Declined to answer	0	0.0%

*Totals for not at all to moderate include 1-4. Very to Severely 5-7. ($n = 52$)

A few missionaries mentioned being in the military, witnessing war, and being wounded in Vietnam. Sometimes God calls missionaries to live and work in countries at war. The sounds of gun fire and exploding bombs can become common place; however, when active fighting affects the missionary's home and family, war can become traumatic,

> Eight soldiers stopped my van and told me to take them to a spot down the road, they were armed, the country was in civil war. We were sitting in the car talking with the dome light on, it was night, when we heard a shoot-out two houses away from us. We drove from [country] to [country] with our children, hearing shots, seeing dead bodies on the road and had a flat tire in the middle of a dangerous area.

Another missionary recalls,

> Being alone in [a country] during a coup with shelling a couple blocks from our house toward the end of the Civil War. [My husband] was in a neighboring country for eleven days. I was pregnant and home with our two-year-old. The phone lines and electricity were cut. I sought help from the embassy, and they refused to help me. We had no team, so I had nowhere to go for help. I hunkered down at home and waited it out.

A few missionaries had to be evacuated from their countries, "[Sensitive country] evacuation—it was a very unsettling time in [sensitive country] at that time . . . I liken it to living on the lip of a volcano. STRESS was very high. I lived by a soldier camp. I was pregnant, how to get out of country and when to get out were all very stressful questions. It was then that I learned that when I am under extreme stress, I forget names of people, places, etc. . . . "

A missionary described having to "scrounge for food while protestors blocked the roadways. I was in an escape mode the entire time" during the national strikes. Missionaries have had terrorists attack their churches, been surrounded by Special Forces with assault weapons drawn, been caught in crossfire, walked through land mines, had rockets land near their house, but not detonate, and been separated from their children during a military coup. One missionary spoke of a narrow escape from an airport,

> My husband and I were passing through an airport in a war zone and about to get on a plane when a sniper opened fire. We lay down on the pavement. When the gunfire ceased, we proceeded and boarded the plane. The plane taxied to a spot between shipping containers on the runway to hide when the gunfire started

again. The pilot revved up the plane's engine and we took off in a rain of gunfire and flew to our home place.

Childhood Physical or Sexual Abuse

About a fifth, 51 (20.8 percent) of the 254 AGWM missionaries experienced childhood physical or sexual abuse (see Table 3.5.). Eight (15.7 percent) missionaries suffered physical abuse, while 42 (82.4 percent) experienced sexual abuse. This exploitation happened between the ages of three to 11 with the majority (78.4 percent) of the abuse happening between five to ten years of age with the abuse lasting from one time to 16 years (see Table 4.16.).

Table 4.16. Ages of Childhood Physical/Sexual Abuse

Question	Frequency	Percent
How old were you when the physical or sexual abuse began?		
3 years	3	5.9%
4	4	7.8%
5	7	13.7%
6	6	11.8%
7	9	17.6%
8	8	15.7%
9	4	7.8%
10	6	11.8%
11	1	2.0%
12	1	2.0%
13	1	2.0%
Declined to answer	1	2.0%
How old were you when the physical or sexual abuse ended?		
4 years	2	3.9%
5	3	5.9%
6	4	7.8%
7	6	11.8%

Question	Frequency	Percent
8	2	3.9%
9	3	5.9%
10	4	7.8%
11	7	13.7%
12	4	7.8%
13	2	3.9%
14	2	3.9%
15	5	9.8%
16	2	3.9%
17	3	5.9%
20	2	3.9%
Declined to answer	0	0.0%

Duration of Abuse		
1 time	20	
1 year	3	
2	4	
3	4	
4	2	
5	2	
6	2	
7	2	
8	4	
9	3	
11	1	
13	1	
14	1	
16	1	
Declined to answer	1	

($n = 51$)

Nearly all (84.2 percent) of the missionaries experienced moderate to no injury by the abuse nor did they feel their lives threatened (86.3 percent). Yet, 56.6 percent believed themselves to be traumatized at the time of the event, whereas their sense of trauma over childhood sexual abuse at time of survey receded to 7.9 percent (see Table 4.17.).

Table 4.17. Childhood Physical or Sexual Abuse

Question	Frequency	Percent
Were you injured by the physical or sexual abuse?		
1 Not at all	22	43.1%
2	7	13.7%
3	9	17.6%
4	5	9.8%
5	2	3.9%
6	3	9.8%
7 Severely	1	2.0%
Declined to answer	0	0.0%
Did you feel your life was threatened by the physical or sexual abuse?		
1 Not at all	30	58.8%
2	6	11.8%
3	3	5.9%
4	5	9.8%
5	2	3.9%
6	1	2.0%
7 Severely	4	7.8%
Declined to answer	0	0.0%
How traumatic was the physical or sexual abuse for you at the time it happened?		
1 Not at all	2	3.9%
2	7	13.7%
3	9	17.6%

Question	Frequency	Percent
4	4	7.8%
5	10	19.6%
6	7	13.7%
7 Severely	12	23.3%
Declined to answer	0	0.0%

How traumatic is the physical or sexual abuse event for you now?

1 Not at all	17	33.3%
2	16	31.4%
3	10	19.6%
4	4	7.8%
5	2	3.9%
6	1	2.0%
7 Severely	1	2.0%
Declined to answer	0	0.0%

*Totals for not at all to moderate include 1-4. Very to Severely 5-7.
(n = 51)

As children, many AGWM missionaries suffered verbal, physical, and sexual abuse mostly from family members, "I have a history of verbal abuse from my father, using the Bible as a tool against me with multiple accusations of lying and being a rebellious (as in the sin of witchcraft) youth and never being believed by my father that I was telling the truth, when, in fact, I never lied to him." Another recounts, "I witnessed my father verbally and physically abuse my mother. Although I knew he abused her in private—that was the first time I actually witnessed it. Moreover, he forced me and my siblings to watch and would not allow us to leave the room." Another stated that he/she endured "Continual physical abuse (beatings) and deprivation as a child."

Missionaries also remember sexual traumatic events. Ones that they felt vicariously, "Finding out my father had been molesting my older half-sisters (same mother different dad)," or ones they endured themselves. One missionary was gang raped at ten years of age. Another comments, "sexual abuse at the age of four—it profoundly affected the way I perceived and responded to life following the abuse." Another writes,

> When I was seven years old a family member (uncle's brother) had made me touch/rub his penis over his clothes and he proceeded to touch me. Because I was so young, I knew it was wrong, but I never remembered if I told my parents about this event. Years later when I worked up the courage to say something, my mother told me that I did say something to her at the time. I felt empowered that as a young girl I knew the right thing to say. And if I was in a situation that was not right, I would not keep my mouth shut. To this day I have never seen that man again, and I have never been assaulted again.

Other Trauma Not Mentioned

Less than a fifth, 45 (17.7 percent) of the 254 missionaries felt they had gone through traumatic events not mentioned in the survey. A little over half (52.8 percent) of these missionaries went through these events more than once and 81.8 percent of these events happened on field (see Table 4.5.). Almost all (95.5 percent) of these missionaries did not receive injury nor did they feel their lives threatened (93.4 percent). Nevertheless, 66.7 percent felt tremendously traumatized at the time of the event, yet currently only 4.4 percent still feel traumatized (see Table 4.18.).

Table 4.18. Other Traumatic Events

Question	Frequency	Percent
Were you injured during any of these other very traumatic event(s)?		
1 Not at all	37	82.2%
2	3	6.7%
3	2	4.4%
4	1	2.2%
5	1	2.2%
6	0	0.0%
7 Severely	1	2.2%
Declined to answer	0	0.0%

Question	Frequency	Percent
Did you feel your life was threatened during any of these other very traumatic events?		
1 Not at all	35	77.8%
2	1	2.2%
3	3	6.7%
4	3	6.7%
5	1	2.2%
6	1	2.2%
7 Severely	1	2.2%
Declined to answer	0	0.0%
How traumatic was this other very traumatic event for you at the time it happened?		
1 Not at all	1	2.2%
2	1	2.2%
3	3	6.7%
4	8	17.8%
5	3	6.7%
6	9	20.0%
7 Severely	18	40.0%
Declined to answer	2	4.4%
How traumatic is this other very traumatic event for you now?		
1 Not at all	12	26.0%
2	18	40.0%
3	8	17.8%
4	4	8.9%
5	0	0.0%
6	2	4.4%
7 Severely	0	0.0%
Declined to answer	1	2.2%

*Totals for not at all to moderate include 1-4. Very to Severely 5-7.
($n = 45$)

These AGWM missionaries felt traumatized by incidents such as health problems, physical trauma, near drowning, sickness or death of children, childhood fears, spiritual warfare, and living cross-culturally. These events, along with the ones listed by the TEQ caused great anxiety and grief for these missionaries.

Health Problems

Health concerns can be very problematic especially when countries of service have sub-par medical presence,

> Unless I missed it you didn't mention serious illness as a source of trauma. In my life a serious illness for my twelve-year-old son and myself on a field where there is no medical care to speak of has been the most traumatic thing that has happened to me. The stress caused by these illnesses has been the longest lasting source of stress in our missionary career.

Another missionary recounts a similar story,

> We had just moved to a small town six weeks earlier and were preparing for our first event in our new church plant when my husband complained of sickness. Within a few days he was very ill. We didn't know hardly anyone or the healthcare system and after calling our landlord who helped us find a clinic my husband was diagnosed with appendicitis. I had the responsibility of getting him out of the town which had very substandard healthcare to a larger town four hours away but the only way there was through dangerous Andes mountains. We found when we arrived that his appendix had ruptured, and he had peritonitis. I had to care for him in the clinic because it was over the Christmas and New Year's holidays.

Missionaries have suffered asthma attacks and surgeries gone wrong: "Had massive reconstructive back surgery, contracted a staph infection that went systemic, doctors said they had done all that could be done, but feared I might die. All we could do was wait and pray; I was terrified; our son was only two-years old." Even mosquito bites can be traumatic. "I was bitten by a mosquito during a training seminar in [a country] and the bite turned into a bad infection which spread into my lung infecting it and limiting my breathing. I was rushed to the hospital and spent five days there."

Physical Trauma

Missionaries have had physical trauma both as children and adults. They have fallen off cliffs, been thrown off horses, and wiped out on skis and snowboards. To children, physical trauma can be very terrifying. The following childhood trauma remains one of the most profound of this missionary's life:

> When I was six years old, I accompanied my older brothers for a night of Trick-or-Treating. As we walked down the street, a pickup truck with boys in back drove by throwing liquid filled balloons at cars and people. The balloons contained a very corrosive and acidic mixture, and one of the balloons struck me in the face. The liquid injured my left eye and burned my face. I almost lost my eye due to the injury.

Another missionary describes his/her childhood trauma:

> It happened on Christmas morning [when I was eight years old] when I fell on a broken pop bottle. My left hand was sliced open in two places, parallel from the top of my hand down my wrist. My thumb was hanging completely off, and the left side of my hand was filleted open. Arteries, muscle, tendons, bone, etc., were exposed. It was gruesome. I received about seventy stitches in my hand, and tendons were just millimeters from being sliced. I was about an eighth of a mile from my house and I had to run all the way home holding my hand together as it poured out blood, which added to my trauma.

Near Drowning

AGWM missionaries found that near drowning both on and off field to be very traumatic experiences. Many talked about being pulled out into the ocean while swimming or snorkeling. One missionary recalls a surfing incident that happened in the United States,

> I was surfing in Galveston, TX, and was pulled out by a rip tide. I swam to the end of the jetty and lost my surfboard. I struggled to stay afloat as the waves continued to pull me under and carry me out farther. I saw a young lady sunbathing on the jetty and called for help; she looked at me and laid back down. My heart sank. I felt so helpless and abandoned. The current at the end of the jetty created a whirlpool and I was pulled completely under

water. I reached a point of blacking out and was about to drown when suddenly, I recovered my board (by pulling on the leash attached to the board). It popped me out of the whirlpool directly in front on the jetty. I was able to climb onto the jetty and walk to the beach. I did suffer cuts and bruises on my body, and no, I did not punch the girl as I walked past her on the jetty!

Another missionary remembers a surfing accident while on field:

In 1988, I was surfing along the coast of [a country], and almost drowned. I was surfing some huge and powerful waves when I was knocked off my board and struck in the face by the fin, while inside the wave. I was pinned down on the bottom of twenty feet of water, semi unconscious. Miraculously, I was able to awaken, retrieve my board by pulling the leash attached to the board, and it pulled me to the surface. My face/jaw was severely cut open, requiring twenty stitches. It was definitely a God-moment!

Many times, missionaries must ride in boats on the ocean or rivers to get to places of service. Sometimes these journeys can be terrifying, "I was with my son and three others in a small boat to go to a part of the [country's] coast that was difficult to reach by land and a storm had passed by earlier but we didn't realize that the ocean was still very rough and we had to travel 1 ½ hours in these conditions and I was in fear the entire time that we would capsize and I am a very poor swimmer."

Sickness or Death of Spouses or Children

Missionaries wrote about traumatic events such as the sexual assault of their child, a child's attempted suicide, or a child almost dying due to doctor error as being crises moments. Many women missionaries commented that often people do not think of miscarriage as traumatic. Nonetheless, to them, this was a death of a child and caused great pain and turmoil. Several missionaries stated that having their children or spouses sick with terminal illnesses, and then having them die caused horrific trauma. Watching one's child suffer caused the worst traumatic experience for this missionary, "The medical crisis of my son when he had an arterial venous malformation that burst in his brain and had less than a 2 percent chance of surviving. This occurred in our third year of our first term on the field."

Childhood Fears

Children can be scared by things they do not understand. These fears can be compounded when the parents or adults the child trusts do not calm the child's fears. One missionary wrote about an incident that happened in his/her childhood that caused trauma remembered to this day.

> Viewing a rapture movie when I was seven. I was terrified for a number of years after that. I was going to Hell and at any moment all that I loved or needed would be removed from me. The church I attended did not have the maturity to explain to me that I was just a child and had nothing to fear if I loved God. My parents were not spiritually mature enough to explain this to me either. The threat very real and I lived in dread for many years. I slept on the floor of my brother's bedroom until I was ten.

Spiritual Warfare

When missionaries live and work in areas where spiritual darkness abides, they will encounter spiritual oppression and warfare. These incidents can cause great fear but also great rejoicing when one sees how God protected them. One missionary wrote about how a dream helped her and her husband escape a possible traumatic situation:

> My husband and I pulled over at a rest stop after driving thirteen hours to get a little nap in the evening and I woke up startled from a vision of this man and woman breaking our windows, beating us severely, and robbing us. I quickly woke up my husband and we rushed out of there and were immediately followed by a car with this same man and woman I had seen in my vision—they followed us for over twenty minutes speeding on the interstate.

Dreams can also be traumatic especially when missionaries encounter satanic creatures, "Demonic manifestation in a dream. I was wrestling with a wolf-like creature in the dream. When I awoke, blood was coming through my skin, but there were no puncture wounds." When missionaries cast out demons, they can encounter problematic situations,

> After praying with a young man for deliverance from demonic possession, a three to four-foot-tall creature appeared in my room and told my roommates he had come to destroy me. The next week after visiting an elderly couple from my church they

called and said that a three to four-foot-tall creature walked into their room and asked where I was. He said he had come to destroy me. I personally never saw the creature, but only heard from those who had.

Missionaries encounter witch doctors and demons who do not want them in their territories,

> A shaman wanted to meet with me to demonstrate his powers (laying hands on a person, breaking their leg, laying hands again having it be healed, etc.) I also had a woman walk by me on the street, and hiss. As she did her eyes rolled back and became solid black. Then blood started pouring out of her mouth. After she passed me, she returned to normal and kept walking. During this time, there were several times when small, demonic creatures physically manifested themselves near or around our house (our dog also barked at them). It was during this time that I kept having a vision/dream of a ruler sitting on a throne in our city, surrounded by these small creatures. He kept saying he ruled here, and we were not welcome (several others had the same dream or similar experiences).

Sometimes what can seem like coincidence, missionaries know to be spiritual warfare. "On a walk home on a clear, windless day, a green, healthy tree suddenly snapped in two and fell across my path, grazing me. About fifty meters later, a car came across a sidewalk nearly hitting me. At the time I had already been sensing spiritual attack and unease, so the incidents seemed connected."

Cross-cultural Living

Just moving from the familiarity of home to a new country and having to adapt to a new culture can be traumatic. Missionaries must learn a new language, new cultural rules, and witness things they have never seen before. This can wear on a missionary's psyche and cause anxiety and depression, "Frankly, the trauma I have experienced is the day-to-day grind of corruption along with the sickness and death endemic with poverty. So, I would not say that I have experience a single traumatic event as much as an accumulation of medium-sized events." These small stressors can magnify the normal incidents of life and cause them to have traumatic effects, "Probably the most traumatic thing was an injury that happened on the field. Though it was 'normal' it was at a time when I was vulnerable, and the enemy used it to set me back in the strides I was taking in cultural adjustment."

Traumatic National Church Conflict

Of the 254 missionaries, 40 (15.7 percent) reported having experienced a traumatic conflict with the national church. The bulk of the participants (71.7 percent) had only one conflict with the national church during their time on field (see Table 3.5.). A little over a quarter (35 percent) of the conflict happened in the missionaries first term (1-4 years) of service with 27.5 percent occurring in the second term (5-10 years) and 25 percent transpiring in the third term (11-16 years). Interestingly, 19.4 percent declined to answer which may indicate that the conflict continues to the time of the survey (see Table 4.19.).

Table 4.19. Traumatic National Church Conflict

Term	Frequency	Percent
What term were you in at the time of your traumatic conflict with member(s) of the national church?		
1st Term (1–4 years)	14	35.0%
2nd Term (5–10 years)	11	27.5%
3rd Term (11–16 years)	10	25.0%
4th Term (17–22 years)	3	7.5%
5th Term (23–28 years)	2	5.0%
Declined to answer	0	
If the traumatic conflict with the member(s) of the national church is resolved, how long did it take?		
1 to 6 months	12	30.0%
6 months to 1 year	9	22.3%
1-5 years	7	20.0%
5-10 years	6	7.1%
20+ years	1	1.2%
Declined to answer	5	19.4%

*Sometimes the total number of participants of this chart differs from Table 4:7. This may be due to the possibility that some of the participants were confused with the question. (n = 40)

The majority (82.5 percent) of the missionaries did not feel a profound threat to their lives from the conflict. A little over half (55 percent) of the missionaries claimed that the conflict felt exceedingly traumatic at the time of the event, which dropped to 7.7 percent at the time of the survey (see Table 4.20.).

Table 4.20. Traumatic National Church Conflict

Question	Frequency	Percent
Did you feel your life was threatened when you had the traumatic conflict with members of the national church?		
1 Not at all	28	70.0%
2	3	7.5%
3	2	5.0%
5	1	2.5%
7 Severely	2	5.0%
Declined to answer	4	10.0%
How traumatic was this conflict with the member(s) of the national church for you at the time of the event?		
1 Not at all	2	5.0%
2	3	7.5%
3	2	5.0%
4	8	20.0%
5	8	20.0%
6	3	7.5%
7 Severely	11	27.5%
Declined to answer	3	7.5%
How traumatic is this conflict with the member(s) of the national church for you now?		
1 Not at all	21	52.5%
2	9	22.5%
3	4	10.0%
4	1	2.5%

Question	Frequency	Percent
5	1	2.5%
6	1	2.5%
7 Severely	0	0.0%
Declined to answer	3	7.5%

*Totals for not at all to moderate include 1-4. Very to Severely 5-7.
($n = 40$)

AGWM missionaries work hand-in-hand with the national Assemblies of God church (if one exists) in the country where they serve. This gives an added layer of leadership by which missionaries must abide. Sometimes this can become difficult because of differences in cultural mores and thus conflicts can occur. These conflicts can become very traumatic when it also involves feelings of betrayal from the missionary fellowship or agency,

> The most traumatic thing that has ever happened to me was the scandal we endured with the national exposer. My husband was taped secretly, and it aired nationally eight months after arriving on the field. We endured five years of court cases, cover ups from the national church, including an assembly in which we were made to appear guilty and never mentioned the person who caused the problem and lied about us to cover it up (under oath). Two veteran couples on the field took the side of the national church and called for our removal from the post we held (not from the field) because we would not apologize to the guilty national leader for removing [his/her] project (done after it was clear [he/she] planned to frame us). In short, it was horrible.

Another missionary recalls an event that started outside the church but affected his or her ministry with the church,

> Animal rights group in [my country] made false accusations and fabricated outright lies about me, regarding injuries to a stray animal. They took their falsehoods to the media. It was all over the local and national news... I was arrested, put in a holding cell. At that time, I had no idea how long I would be there. I was taken away from my wife, my attorney and my missionary colleagues, and I had no knowledge of legal terms in the local language. After nearly a year of trial hearings, the court found

me "Not Guilty." This only angered the animal rights people more. They harassed me and my family for nearly two years; calling and hanging up at all times of day and night; making threatening calls. Several times, people threatened my life via email and phone calls. They terrified my daughters (ages sixteen and ten years at that time). A few neighbors who really knew us (quietly) stood by us and supported us, but in secret for fear of the media and the animal rights group. For the most part, I felt abandoned by the national church. The AGWM missionaries . . . prayed with and for us and affirmed their love and support, but they had to keep their public image unspotted, so even their support felt a bit less than authentic. However, I can appreciate the very difficult position they were in with the national church, the community at large, and the media. Several of the national pastors firmly supported us, but one of the executive committee members had had it in for us from our first year . . . On two occasions, he verbally attacked me in front of the whole committee and made false accusations. In the end, he prevented me and my family from returning . . . to continue ministry.

Adult Physical Abuse

Less than a tenth, 20 (8.2 percent) of the 254 missionaries surveyed said they had been physically abused as an adult. A good amount (70 percent) reported the event only happening one time and only 35 percent said it occurred on field (see Table 4.5.). Even though the missionaries spoke of physical abuse, 65 percent stated they suffered no injury. The majority 90 percent felt no threat to their lives felt their lives. The bulk (70 percent) underwent intense traumatization at the time of the abuse, yet this number went down to 0 percent at the time of the survey (see Table 4.21.).

Table 4.21 Adult Physical Abuse

Question	Frequency	Percent
Were you injured during the adult physical or other abuse?		
1 Not at all	13	65.0%
2	0	0.0%
3	1	5.0%
4	3	15.0%

Question	Frequency	Percent
5	1	5.0%
6	0	0.0%
7 Severely	0	0.0%
Declined to answer	2	10.0%

Did you feel your life was threatened during the adult physical or other abuse?

	Frequency	Percent
1 Not at all	12	60.0%
2	2	10.0%
3	0	20.0%
4	0	0.0%
5	4	5.0%
6	1	0.0%
7 Severely	0	0.0%
Declined to answer	1	5.0%

How traumatic was the adult physical or other abuse at the time it happened?

	Frequency	Percent
1 Not at all	0	0.0%
2	2	10.0%
3	0	0.0%
4	3	15.0%
5	6	30.0%
6	4	20.0%
7 Severely	4	20.0%
Declined to answer	1	5.0%

How traumatic is the adult physical or other abuse for you now?

	Frequency	Percent
1 Not at all	10	50.0%
2	2	10.0%
3	5	25.0%
4	3	15.0%

Question	Frequency	Percent
5	0	0.0%
6	0	0.0%
7 Severely	0	0.0%
Declined to answer	0	0.0%

*Totals for not at all to moderate include 1-4. Very to Severely 5-7. (n = 20)

AGWM missionaries did not seem to want to speak about physical abuse. A few talked about verbal abuse which in many cases can hurt as much as a physical hit, "After I was married, the verbal abuse from my father continued while he tried to control my married life and I was threatened with things like 'never becoming a mother' and other things that I wanted to be and do that I was told would never happen because I was 'doing things against the will of God in my life.'" Another missionary remembers, "Spiritual and verbal abuse from controlling leadership at a Teen Challenge center, stateside. I was miscarrying and didn't even want to tell my boss for fear of her—I preferred to work an overnight shift (at first, then I had to tell her because I could not work)."

Trauma That Cannot Be Spoken

Many times, people cannot speak of a traumatic event in their lives. Of the 254 AGWM missionaries, 17 (6.9 percent) reported this level of trauma. Over half (56.3 percent) of these missionaries had this terrible event happen only once and the majority (82.4 percent) of the events happened on field (see Table 3.5.). None of the missionaries sustained serious injury nor did they believe their lives were threatened during these incidents. Yet 64.7 percent bore enormous traumatization at the time of the event with only 23.5 percent feeling the same at the time of the survey (see Table 4.22.).

Table 4.22. Traumatic Events that Cannot be Spoken

Question	Frequency	Percent
Were you injured during any of these experiences that you feel you can speak about?		
1 Not at all	14	82.4%
2	1	5.9%

Question	Frequency	Percent
3	1	5.9%
4	1	5.9%
5	0	0.0%
6	0	0.0%
7 Severely	0	0.0%
Declined to answer	0	0.0%

Did you feel your life was threatened during any of these experiences that you feel you cannot speak about?

1 Not at all	13	76.5%
2	2	11.8%
3	1	5.9%
4	0	0.0%
5	0	0.0%
6	0	0.0%
7 Severely	0	0.0%
Declined to answer	1	5.9%

How traumatic was/were any of these experiences that you feel you cannot speak about at the time it happened?

1 Not at all	0	0.0%
2	1	5.9%
3	3	17.6%
4	1	5.9%
5	4	23.5%
6	6	35.3%
7 Severely	1	5.9%
Declined to answer	1	5.9%

How traumatic is/are the events that you feel you cannot speak about for you now?

1 Not at all	2	11.8%
2	7	41.2%

Question	Frequency	Percent
3	2	11.8%
4	1	5.9%
5	3	17.6%
6	1	5.9%
7 Severely	0	0.0%
Declined to answer	1	5.9%

*Totals for not at all to moderate include 1-4. Very to Severely 5-7.
(n = 17)

Adult Sexual Abuse

Only seven (2.9 percent) of the 254 missionaries experienced adult sexual abuse. A little more than half (57.1 percent) experienced this abuse three or more times with 42.9 percent of the events happening on field (see Table 4:5.). The majority (71.5 percent) did not receive much injury nor felt their lives very threatened (71.6 percent). Under half (42.9 percent) believed themselves tremendously traumatized at the time of the incident and this number fell to 0 percent at the time of the survey (see Table 4.23.).

Table 4.23. Adult Sexual Abuse

Question	Frequency	Percent
Were you injured when you had the unwanted sexual experience?		
1 Not at all	3	42.9%
2	0	0.0%
3	1	14.3%
4	1	14.3%
5	0	0.0%
6	0	0.0%
7 Severely	0	0.0%
Declined to answer	2	28.6%

Question	Frequency	Percent
Did you feel your life was threatened when you had the unwanted sexual experience?		
1 Not at all	4	57.1%
2	1	14.3%
3	0	0.0%
4	0	0.0%
5	0	0.0%
6	0	0.0%
7 Severely	0	0.0%
Declined to answer	2	28.6%
How traumatic was the unwanted sexual experience for you at the time it happened?		
1 Not at all	0	0.0%
2	0	0.0%
3	1	14.3%
4	1	14.3%
5	1	14.3%
6	2	28.6%
7 Severely	0	0.0%
Declined to answer	2	28.6%
How traumatic is the unwanted sexual experience for you now?		
1 Not at all	3	41.9%
2	1	14.3%
3	1	14.3%
4	0	0.0%
5	0	0.0%
6	0	0.0%
7 Severely	0	0.0%
Declined to answer	2	28.6%

*Totals for not at all to moderate include 1-4. Very to Severely 5-7.
($n = 7$)

Attempted Kidnaping or Taken Hostage

The lowest percentage of AGWM missionaries encountered being kidnapped or taken hostage. Just six (2.4 percent) of the 254 missionaries endured an attempted kidnaping or taken hostage situation. This happened only once to all six missionaries and all these incidents happened on field (see Table 4.5.). None of the missionaries received injury, yet all (except one who declined to answer) felt their lives threatened. Almost all (83.4 percent) felt enormously traumatized at the time of the event and of these, only 16.7 percent feel somewhat traumatized at the time of the survey (see Table 4.24.).

Table 4.24. Taken Hostage

Question	Frequency	Percent
Were you injured when you were taken hostage?		
1 Not at all	3	50.0%
2	2	33.3%
3	1	16.7%
4	0	0.0%
5	0	0.0%
6	0	0.0%
7 Severely	0	0.0%
Declined to answer	0	0.0%
Did you feel your life was threatened when you were taken hostage?		
1 Not at all	0	0.0%
2	0	0.0%
3	0	0.0%
4	0	0.0%
5	0	0.0%
6	0	0.0%
7 Severely	6	100.0%
Declined to answer	0	0.0%

Question	Frequency	Percent
How traumatic was being taken hostage for you at the time it happened?		
1 Not at all	1	16.7%
2	0	0.0%
3	0	0.0%
4	0	0.0%
5	0	0.0%
6	1	16.7%
7 Severely	4	66.7%
Declined to answer	0	0.0%
How traumatic is having been taken hostage for you now?		
1 Not at all	2	33.3%
2	2	33.3%
3	1	16.7%
4	0	0.0%
5	1	16.7%
6	0	0.0%
7 Severely	0	0.0%
Declined to answer	0	0.0%

*Totals for not at all to moderate include 1-4. Very to Severely 5-7.
($n = 6$)

Being taken hostage means being in situation where one does not have the freedom to leave when he or she desires.[44] Therefore, missionaries encounter hostage situations every time they cross country boarders. Border guards can detain, question, intimidate, deport, or incarcerate a missionary, consequently, these crossings can be traumatic. Missionaries also wrote about attempted kidnappings during robberies and abductions during carjackings on field. These hostage events can be even more terrifying when the situation involves the missionaries' families.

44. Fort Sherman Academy, "B+ Security Training."

This survey has conveyed, both in numbers and in personal testimony, the amount of trauma AGWM missionaries have suffered. They have endured most these traumatic events while serving in countries far away from home. Unlike Bagley's survey, AGWM missionaries experienced each category of the TEQ.[45] Yet, these battle-worn men and women have survived and remained on field. The second part of this survey looks at the coping mechanisms these missionaries utilized that helped with maintaining resiliency and hopefully produce Post-Traumatic Growth.

What Coping Skills Minimize the Negative Impact of Trauma in Missionaries' Lives and Enhance AGWM Missionary Well-being?

Many researchers have studied the resiliency of missionaries who survive the stress that traumatic field experiences bring. Lois and Lawrence Dodds indicate that for missionaries, "coping ability gradually increases to meet the demand of the stressors. They learn to use more resources for growth."[46] Carr and Schaefer denote missionaries cope with trauma by using spiritual and emotional support factors, training and education, and psychological interventions.[47] One might deduce that missionaries would rely on religious coping over other types when they encounter stressful incidences. Yet, coping research has largely overlooked this occupational demographic.[48]

This study sought to determine what types of coping skills minimize the negative impact of trauma in missionaries' lives and enhance AGWM missionary well-being. To resolve this, it used two hypotheses: Hypothesis one—Missionaries with High Trauma and Low PTSD will demonstrate through their responses statistically significant higher positive coping skills than those with Low Trauma and High PTSD. To establish High and Low Trauma, a participant could have three or more trauma events per the 17 TEQ questions. Therefore, a mean score of 26 would indicate a score of 0 to 26 as Low Trauma and a score of 27 and higher as High Trauma. Of the 240 participants who completed this section of the survey, 45.9 percent ($n = 110$) had Low Trauma scores and 54.2 percent ($n = 130$) received High Trauma scores.

---

45. Bagley, "Impact of Trauma," 147–50.
46. Dodds and Dodds, "How People Get Sick," 15.
47. Carr and Schaefer, "Trauma and Traumatic Stress," para. 11.
48. Bjorck and Kim, "Religious Coping," 612–13.

Only 242 missionaries answered the PTC-C checklist, of those 85.1 percent ($n = 206$) did not indicate PTSD symptomatology, while 14.9 percent ($n = 36$) had PTSD indicators. Thus, this study determined one independent variable (IV) of PTSD with two categories High and Low. The seven dependent variables (DV's) consisted of the coping styles tested which included: Adventurousness (ERS), Social Resiliency (RAS), Resiliency (RS), Call (CVQ), Satisfaction with Life (SWLS), and Spirituality with both positive and negative Religious Coping (B-RCOPE).

This researcher then created a new IV based on recoding the High and Low PTSD variables into another with four categories as: High PTSD-Low Trauma, Low PTSD-High Trauma, High PTSD-High Trauma, and Low PTSD-Low Trauma. An ANOVA[49] was calculated comparing the means scores of these groups on the DV's but focused primarily on the outcome between the two extremes: High PTSD–Low Trauma, determining these as High Functioning, and Low PTSD–High Trauma, labeling these as Low Functioning. The research question proposed to investigate only these two groups thus, the study only reported the statistically significant differences in means scores between these two categories on the dependent variables.

Adventurousness (ERS)

This study tabulated a correlation coefficient (Pearson r) to determine the relationship between the predictor variable PTSD Sum Total and the Ego-Resiliency Scale criterion or outcome variables. When analyzing the relationship between the PTSD means scores and the ERS as a whole, no statistically significant relationship was indicated ($r = -.04$, $n = 245$, $p > .05$). So, respondent's PTSD score could not predict scores on the ERS composite variable (see Table 3.25.). However, 98 percent of the participants ($n = 249$) responded to the ERS with "Applies somewhat or Applies very strongly" and 2 percent ($n = 5$) answered "Applies slightly if at all or Not at all true" (see Table 4.26.).

Social Resiliency (RAS)

This study tabulated a correlation coefficient (Pearson r) to determine the relationship between the predictor variable PTSD Sum Total and the Resilience Appraisal Scale criterion or outcome variables. When analyzing

49. ANOVA or analysis of variance "is a technique from statistical interference that allows [for one] to deal with several populations. Comparison of Means" (Taylor, "What is ANOVA?").

the relationship between the PTSD means scores and the RAS divided into three areas: Social, Emotional, and Situational Resiliency. No statistically significant relationship was indicated in any of these divisions: Social ($r = -.02$, $n = 245$, $p > .05$), Emotional ($r = -.03$, $n = 245$, $p > .05$), and Situational ($r = -.03$, $n = 245$, $p > .05$). So, respondent's PTSD score would not reliably predict scores on the RAS composite variable (see Table 4.25.). Yet, 94.1 percent of the participants responded "Agree or Agree strongly" with the questions related to Social Resiliency ($n = 229$), 87 percent replied "Agree or Agree strongly" with the questions related to Emotional Resiliency ($n = 221$), and 97.6 percent answered "Agree or Agree strongly" to Situational Resiliency ($n = 248$). Whereas, 5.9 percent of the missionaries replied "Disagree or Strongly disagree" to Social Resiliency ($n = 15$), 13 percent responded "Disagree or Strongly disagree" to Emotional Resiliency ($n = 33$), and 2.4 percent answered "Disagree or Strongly disagree" to Situational Resiliency ($n = 6$) (see Table 4.26.).

General Resiliency (RS)

This study tabulated a correlation coefficient (Pearson r) to determine the relationship between the predictor variable PTSD Sum Total and the General Resiliency Scale criterion or outcome variables. When analyzing the relationship between the PTSD means scores and the RS as a whole, no statistically significant relationship was indicated ($r = -.05$, $n = 245$, $p > .05$). So, respondent's PTSD score would not reliably predict scores on the RS composite variable (see Table 3.25.). Nevertheless, 93.3 percent of the participants ($n = 237$) responded with the questions related to the ERS with "Agree or Agree strongly" while only 6.7 percent ($n = 17$) answered "Disagree or Strongly disagree" (see Table 4.26.).

Call (CVQ)

This study tabulated a correlation coefficient (Pearson r) to determine the relationship between the predictor variable PTSD Sum Total and the Call/Vocation Questionnaire criterion or outcome variables. When analyzing the relationship between the PTSD means scores and the CVQ divided into positive and negative, no statistically significant relationship was indicated: positive ($r = -.022$, $n = 245$, $p > .05$) and negative ($r = -.018$, $n = 245$, $p > .05$). So, respondent's PTSD score would not reliably predict scores on the CVQ composite variable (see Table 4.25.). Nonetheless, 95.7 percent of the participants ($n = 243$) responded to the CVQ with "Mostly true of me or

Absolutely true of me" while 4.3 percent replied, "Somewhat true of me or Not at all true of me" (see Table 4.26.).

Table 4.25. Pearson Correlation

		PTSD Sum Total
Ego Resiliency Scale	Pearson Correlation	-.039
	Sig. (2-tailed)	.547
	N	245
Resilience Appraisal Scale: Social Support	Pearson Correlation	-.021
	Sig. (2-tailed)	.738
	N	245
RAS: Emotional Coping	Pearson Correlation	-.032
	Sig. (2-tailed)	.614
	N	245
RAS: Situational Coping	Pearson Correlation	-.025
	Sig. (2-tailed)	.699
	N	245
General Resiliency Scale	Pearson Correlation	-.047
	Sig. (2-tailed)	.468
	N	245
Calling/Vocational Questionnaire—Positive	Pearson Correlation	-.022
	Sig. (2-tailed)	.735
	N	245
Calling/Vocational Questionnaire—Negative	Pearson Correlation	.018
	Sig. (2-tailed)	.783
	N	245
Satisfaction with Life Scale	Pearson Correlation	-.007
	Sig. (2-tailed)	.908
	N	245

		PTSD Sum Total
Brief Religious Coping—Positive	Pearson Correlation	.131
	Sig. (2-tailed)	.059
	N	209

Table 4.26. Coping Scales Frequency

	Number	Mean	SD	High	Percent	Low	Percent
Ego Resiliency Scale	254	38.83	90.181	249	98.0%	5	2.0%
Resilience Appraisal Scale—Support	254	15.99	26.093	239	94.1%	15	5.9%
RAS: Emotional Coping	254	13.62	26.712	221	87.0%	33	13.0%
RAS: Situational Coping	254	15.40	25.996	248	97.6%	6	2.4%
Resiliency Scale	254	13.56	26.687	237	93.3%	17	6.7%
Calling/Vocational Questionnaire—Positive	254	21.82	45.167	243	95.7%	11	4.3%
Satisfaction with Life Scale	254	24.16	33.402	200	78.7%	54	21.3%
Brief Religious Coping—Positive	254	22.09	4.831	188	74.0%	66	26.0%
Brief Religious Cooping—Negative	254	10.98	4.236	29	11.4%	225	88.6%

Satisfaction with Life (SWLS)

This study tabulated a correlation coefficient (Pearson *r*) to determine the relationship between the predictor variable PTSD Sum Total and certain

Satisfaction in Life Scale criterion or outcome variables. While 21.3 percent of the missionaries ($n = 54$) responded to the SWLS questions as indicated in the composite score for these variables with "Strongly disagree, Moderately disagree, or Disagree," 78.7 percent ($n = 200$) replied "Agree, Moderately agree, or Strongly agree" (see Table 4.26.). When analyzing the relationship between the sum of PTSD means scores and the individual SWLS questions the data indicated a nearly negligible, yet statistically significant negative relationship for those particular variables: "In most ways my life is close to my ideal," ($r = -.20$, $n = 242$, $p < .001$), "The conditions of my life are excellent" ($r = -.30$, $n = 241$, $p < .001$), "I am satisfied with my life" ($r = -.27$, $n = 241$, $p < .001$), "If I could live my life over, I would change almost nothing" ($r = -.21$, $n = 241$, $p < .001$), and "So far I have gotten the important things I want in life" ($r = -.15$, $n = 241$, $p < .05$). So, the higher the respondents rated the PTSD score the lower they ranked their answers to these statements. In fact, the proportion of variance accounted for indicates that when researchers utilize the question "The conditions in life are excellent," they would be 9 percent more accurate than r-squared ($r = -.30$, $n = 253$, $r^2 = .09$) (see Table 4.27.). Since the relationships were mostly negligible, researchers using this data would only be able to predict with between 2 percent and 9 percent more accuracy the scores on these SWLS variables if the PTSD scores were known.

Table 4.27. SWLS Pearson Correlation

Question		Number	Mean	SD	PTSD Sum Total
In most ways my life is close to my ideal.		242	5.17	1.601	
	Pearson Correlation				-.201
	Sig. (2-tailed)				.002
	N				241
The conditions of my life are excellent.		253	5.32	1.407	
	Pearson Correlation				-.301
	Sig. (2-tailed)				.000
	N				241

Question		Number	Mean	SD	PTSD Sum Total
I am satisfied with my life.		253	5.62	1.514	
	Pearson Correlation				-.265
	Sig. (2-tailed)				.000
	N				241
If I could live my life over, I would change almost nothing.		253	4.60	1.824	
	Pearson Correlation				-.211
	Sig. (2-tailed)				.001
	N				241
So far I have gotten the important things I want in life		253	5.51	1.513	
	Pearson Correlation				-.153
	Sig. (2-tailed)				.017
	N				241

Positive Religious Coping (B-RCOPE-P)

This study tabulated a correlation coefficient (Pearson r) to determine the relationship between the predictor variable PTSD Sum Total and Positive Religious Coping (B-RCOPE-P) criterion or outcome variables. When analyzing the relationship between the PTSD means scores and the B-RCOPE-P as a whole, no statistically significant relationship was indicated ($r = .13$, $n = 209$, $p > .05$). So, respondent's PTSD score would not reliably predict scores on the B-RCOPE-P composite variable (see Table 4.25.). Yet, 74 percent of the participants ($n = 188$) responded to the B-RCOPE-P questions with "Agree or Agree strongly" while only 26 percent ($n = 66$) answered "Disagree or Strongly disagree" (see Table 4.26.).

Negative Religious Coping (B-RCOPE-N)

This study tabulated a correlation coefficient (Pearson r) to determine the relationship between the predictor variable PTSD Sum Total and certain Negative Religious Coping (B-RCOPE-N) criterion or outcome variables. When analyzing the relationship between the PTSD mean scores and the following questions the data did indicate a statistically significant negative relationship. "When I went through a traumatic event, I felt punished by God for my lack of devotion" had a weak but statistically significant link to high PTSD ($r = .29$, $n = 229$, $r^2 = .08$, $p < .001$). As a result, when the researcher uses this data, he or she is 8 percent more accurate in predicting the scores on the criterion "I felt punished by God for my lack of devotion" when he or she knows the PTSD scores.

"When I went through a traumatic event, I wondered whether God had abandoned me" had a very strong correlation with high PTSD ($r = .46$, $n = 21$, $r^2 = .21$, $p < .001$). As a result, when the researcher uses this data, he or she is 21 percent more accurate in predicting the scores on the criterion "I wondered whether God had abandoned me" when he or she knows the PTSD scores.

"When I went through a traumatic event, I wondered what I did for God to punish me" had a moderately strong association with high PTSD ($r = .33$, $n = 233$, $r^2 = .11$, $p < .001$). As a result, when the researcher uses this data, he or she is 11 percent more accurate in predicting the scores on the criterion "I wondered what I did for God to punish me" when he or she knows the PTSD scores.

"When I went through a traumatic event I questioned God's love for me" had a strong relationship with high PTSD ($r = .39$, $n = 232$, $r^2 = .15$, $p < .001$). As a result, when the researcher uses this data, he or she is 15 percent more accurate in predicting the scores on the criterion "I questioned God's love for me" when he or she knows the PTSD scores.

"When I went through a traumatic event, I wondered whether my (missionary fellowship/national church/AGWM) had abandoned me" produced a strong relationship with high PTSD ($r = .35$, $n = 217$, $r^2 = .12$, $p < .001$). As a result, when the researcher uses this data, he or she is 12 percent more accurate in predicting the scores on the criterion "I wondered whether my (missionary fellowship/national church/AGWM) had abandoned me" when he or she knows the PTSD scores.

"When I went through a traumatic event, I decided the devil made this happen" had a weak but statistically significant correlation to high PTSD ($r = .22$, $n = 230$, $r^2 = .05$, $p < .001$). As a result, when the researcher uses this data, he or she is 5 percent more accurate in predicting the scores on the criterion "I decided the devil made this happen" when he or she knows the PTSD scores.

"When I went through a traumatic event, I questioned the power of God" had a strong association with high PTSD ($r = .33$, $n = 231$, $r^2 = .11$, $p < .001$). As a result, when the researcher uses this data, he or she is 11 percent more accurate in predicting the scores on the criterion "I questioned the power of God" when he or she knows the PTSD scores. (see Table 4.28.). Therefore, the higher the missionaries rated their tendency to apply a Negative Religious Coping mechanism the higher their PTSD score. When this research tabulated the correlation coefficient (Pearson r) on the negative B-RCOPE variables, a very strong predictive relationship, trending toward significance was indicated so that based on this data; the researcher is 23 percent more accurate in predicting responses on Negative Religious Coping variables when he or she knows the PTSD scores. (see Table 4.29.).

Table 4.28. B-RCOPE-N Pearson Correlation

Question	Number	Mean	SD	PTSD Sum Total
When I went through a traumatic event, I felt punished by God for my lack of devotion.	242	51.34	.737	
Pearson Correlation				.285
Sig. (2-tailed)				.000
N				229
When I went through a traumatic event, I wondered whether God had abandoned me.	242	1.64	.984	
Pearson Correlation				.456
Sig. (2-tailed)				.000
N				230
When I went through a traumatic event, I wondered what I did for God to punish me.	245	1.41	.777	
Pearson Correlation				.328
Sig. (2-tailed)				.000
N				232

Question	Number	Mean	SD	PTSD Sum Total
When I went through a traumatic event, I questioned God's love for me.	244	1.50	.933	
Pearson Correlation				.386
Sig. (2-tailed)				.000
N				232
When I went through a traumatic event, I wondered whether my (missionary fellowship/national church/AGWM) had abandoned me.	229	1.83	1.112	
Pearson Correlation				.353
Sig. (2-tailed)				.000
N				217
When I went through a traumatic event, I decided the devil made this happen.	242	1.85	.987	
Pearson Correlation				.220
Sig. (2-tailed)				.001
N				230
When I went through a traumatic event, I questioned the power of God.	243	1.56	.931	
Pearson Correlation				.331
Sig. (2-tailed)				.000
N				231

Table 4.29. B-RCOPE-P and B-RCOPE-N Pearson Correlation

PTSD Sum Total	B-RCOPE-P Sum Total	B-RCOPE-N Sum Total
Pearson Correlation	1.130	.481
Sig. (2-tailed)	.059	.000
N	209	212

The study calculated a one-way, between subject's ANOVA comparing four categories of a PTSD and Trauma Grouping Variable as the dependent variable, and the means scores on Negative Religious Coping variables as the dependent variables. This research focuses primarily on statistically significant differences between the High Trauma—Low PTSD and the Low Trauma—High PTSD groups.

When the study compared the means scores between these two groups it revealed a statistically significant difference between those two groups ratings on the following statements: "When I went through a traumatic event, I felt punished by God for my lack of devotion," those in the High Trauma—Low PTSD group scored significantly lower ($M = 1.3$, $SD = .65$, $n = 107$) than those in the Low Trauma—High PTSD group ($M = 1.5$, $SD = .90$, $n = 23$), $F(3, 223) = 5.65$, $p < .001$; "When I went through a traumatic event, I wondered whether God had abandoned me," those in the High Trauma—Low PTSD group scored significantly lower ($M = 1.5$, $SD = .83$, $n = 106$) than those in the Low Trauma—High PTSD group ($M = 2.2$, $SD = 1.3$, $n = 106$), $F(3, 224) = 16.46$, $p < .001$; "When I went through a traumatic event, I wondered what I did for God to punish me," those in the High Trauma—Low PTSD group scored significantly lower ($M = 1.3$, $SD = .70$, $n = 109$) than those in the Low Trauma—High PTSD group ($M = 1.6$, $SD = .89$, $n = 23$), $F(3, 227) = 15.83$, $p < .001$; "When I went through a traumatic event, I questioned God's love for me," those in the High Trauma—Low PTSD group scored significantly lower ($M = 1.3$, $SD = .73$, $n = 108$) than those in the Low Trauma—High PTSD group ($M = 2.0$, $SD = .73$, $n = 23$), $F(3, 226) = 8.10$, $p < .001$; "When I went through a traumatic event I wondered whether my (missionary fellowship/national church/AGWM) had abandoned me," those in the High Trauma—Low PTSD group scored significantly lower ($M = 1.6$, $SD = .98$, $n = 98$) than those in the Low Trauma—High PTSD group ($M = 2.7$, $SD = 1.3$, $n = 22$), $F(3, 211) = 9.49$, $p < .001$; and "When I went through a traumatic event, I questioned the power of God," those in the High Trauma—Low PTSD group scored significantly lower ($M = 1.5$, $SD = .92$, $n = 108$) than those in the Low Trauma—High PTSD group ($M = 2.1$, $SD = 1.4$, $n = 23$), $F(3, 225) = 4.85$, $p < .05$. Only the statement, "When I went through a traumatic event, I decided the devil made this happen," indicated no statistically significant difference. Those in the High Trauma—Low PTSD group scored slightly lower ($M = 1.8$, $SD = 1.0$, $n = 106$) than those in the Low Trauma—High PTSD group ($M = 2.0$, $SD = 1.0$, $n = 23$), $F(3, 224) = 1.53$, $p > .01$ (see Table 4.30. and Table 4.31.).

Table 4.30. PTSD Groupings and B-RCOPE-N ANOVA

Question		Sum of Squares	df	Mean Square	F	Sig.
When I went through a traumatic event, I felt punished by God for my lack of devotion.	Between Groups	7.347	3	2.449	5.649	.001
	Within Groups	96.679	223	.434		
	Total	104.026	226			
When I went through a traumatic event, I wondered whether God had abandoned me.	Between Groups	38.130	3	12.710	16.464	.000
	Within Groups	172.923	225	.772		
	Total	211.053	227			
When I went through a traumatic event, I wondered what I did for God to punish me.	Between Groups	22.618	3	7.539	15.483	.000
	Within Groups	110.533	227	.487		
	Total	133.152	230			
When I went through a traumatic event, I questioned God's love for me.	Between Groups	24.298	3	8.099	11.221	.000
	Within Groups	163.133	226	.722		
	Total	187.430	229			
When I went through a traumatic event, I wondered whether my (missionary fellowship/ national church/AGWM) had abandoned me.	Between Groups	31.287	3	10.429	9.485	.000
	Within Groups	231.997	211	1.100		
	Total	263.284	214			

Question		Sum of Squares	df	Mean Square	F	Sig.
When I went through a traumatic event, I decided the devil made this happen.	Between Groups	4.370	3	1.457	1.525	.209
	Within Groups	213.946	224	.955		
	Total	218.316	227			
When I went through a traumatic event, I questioned the power of God.	Between Groups	12.399	3	4.133	4.848	.003
	Within Groups	191.802	225	.852		
	Total	204.201	226			

Table 4.31. PTSD and Trauma Groupings and B-COPE-N One-way Descriptives

Question	Trauma/ PTSD	N	Mean	SD	Std. Error	95 percent Confidence interval for Mean		Min.
						Lower Bound	Upper Bound	
When I went through a traumatic event, I felt punished by God for my lack of devotion.	Low Trauma—Low PTSD	85	1.22	.564	.061	1.10	1.35	1
	Low Trauma—High PTSD	23	1.48	.898	.187	1.09	1.87	1
	High Trauma—Low PTSD	107	1.25	.646	.062	1.13	1.38	1
	High Trauma—High PTSD	12	2.0	.853	.246	1.46	2.54	1
	Total	227	1.30	.678	.058	1.22	1.39	1

Question	Trauma/PTSD	N	Mean	SD	Std. Error	95 percent Confidence interval for Mean		Min.
						Lower Bound	Upper Bound	
When I went through a traumatic event, I wondered whether God had abandoned me.	Low Trauma—Low PTSD	87	1.47	.819	.088	1.30	1.65	1
	Low Trauma—High PTSD	23	2.22	1.278	.266	1.66	2.77	1
	High Trauma—Low PTSD	106	1.47	.803	.081	1.31	1.63	1
	High Trauma—High PTSD	12	3.08	.793	.229	2.58	3.59	1
	Total	228	1.63	.964	.064	1.51	1.76	1
When I went through a traumatic event, I wondered what I did for God to punish me.	Low Trauma—Low PTSD	87	1.28	.543	.058	1.16	1.39	1
	Low Trauma—High PTSD	23	1.61	.891	.186	1.22	1.99	1
	High Trauma—Low PTSD	109	1.30	.701	.067	1.17	1.44	1
	High Trauma—High PTSD	12	2.67	1.155	.333	1.93	3.40	1
	Total	231	1.39	.761	.050	1.30	1.49	1
When I went through a traumatic event, I questioned God's love for me.	Low Trauma—Low PTSD	87	1.40	.814	.087	1.23	1.58	1
	Low Trauma—High PTSD	23	2.00	1.206	.251	1.48	2.52	1
	High Trauma—Low PTSD	108	1.31	.732	.070	1.18	1.45	1
	High Trauma—High PTSD	12	2.58	1.240	.358	1.80	3.37	1
	Total	230	1.48	.905	.060	1.37	1.60	1

Question	Trauma/ PTSD	N	Mean	SD	Std. Error	95 percent Confidence interval for Mean		Min.
						Lower Bound	Upper Bound	
When I went through a traumatic event, I wondered whether my (missionary fellowship/ national church/ AGWM) had abandoned me.	Low Trauma— Low PTSD	85	1.81	1.041	.113	1.59	2.04	1
	Low Trauma— High PTSD	22	2.73	1.279	.273	2.16	3.29	1
	High Trauma— Low PTSD	98	1.55	.975	.099	1.36	1.75	1
	High Trauma— High PTSD	10	2.60	1.265	.400	1.70	3.50	1
	Total	215	1.82	1.109	.076	1.67	1.97	1
When I went through a traumatic event, I decided the devil made this happen.	Low Trauma— Low PTSD	87	1.84	.963	.103	1.63	2.04	1
	Low Trauma— High PTSD	23	2.09	1.041	.217	1.64	2.54	1
	High Trauma— Low PTSD	106	1.75	.996	.097	1.55	1.94	1
	High Trauma— High PTSD	12	2.25	1.754	.218	1.77	2.73	1
	Total	228	1.84	.981	.065	1.71	1.97	1
When I went through a traumatic event, I questioned the power of God.	Low Trauma— Low PTSD	86	1.45	.730	.079	1.30	1.61	1
	Low Trauma— High PTSD	23	2.13	1.359	.283	1.54	2.72	1
	High Trauma— Low PTSD	108	1.48	.922	.089	1.31	1.66	1
	High Trauma— High PTSD	12	2.08	1.165	.336	1.35	2.82	1
	Total	229	1.57	.946	.063	1.44	1.69	1

Respondent Demographic and Training Factors

This study looked at several other factors pertaining to the Trauma Sum and PTSD Sum variables. There was no statistically significant relationship detected between the actual age of the missionary at the time of the survey and his or her scores on the PTSD Sum Total variable. Nevertheless, from this data it appears that the older the missionary is the lower his or her score on the Trauma Sum Total variable ($r = -.218$, $n = 245$, $p < .001$). When using this data, researchers would be 5 percent more accurate in predicting the score on the Trauma Sum Total variable if the age of the missionary is known ($r^2 = .047$). So, the age of the person can be a predictor of the way he or she perceives trauma (see Table 4.32.).

The research showed no statistically significant relationship indicated between the respondent's time of missionary service and the PTSD Sum Total variable when analyzing the relationship between the Trauma Sum Total means scores and the number of years on field, produced a statistically significant negative relationship ($r = .245$, $n = 245$, $p < .001$). So, the data indicates that the longer a person remains on the field, the lower he or she will likely score on the Trauma Sum Total variable. In fact, in using this data, researchers would be 6 percent more accurate in predicting Trauma Sum Total scores if time on the field is known ($r^2 = .06$) (see Table 4.32).

When analyzing the relationship between the Trauma Sum Total and the PTSD Sum Total mean scores and the highest level of education, the data indicated no statistically significant relationship (see Table 4.31.). So, a person's education level was not an accurate predictor of his or her perception of trauma or PTSD levels.

When investigating the relationship between missionary training of the respondents and their Trauma Sum and PTSD Sum variable scores, several types of training showed a statistically significant relationship. When regarding the Trauma Sum Total and "Have you ever received training from another school or organization in Trauma Management," the more training respondents received from another school or organization in Trauma Management the lower their Trauma Sum Total scores ($r = -.23$, $n = 245$, $p < .001$), so researchers would be 5 percent more accurate in predicting the Trauma Sum Total scores if the amount of training is known ($r^2 = .05$).

When asked "Have you ever received training from AGWM in Trauma Management," the more training respondents received from AGWM in Trauma Management the lower their Trauma Sum Total scores ($r = -.20$, $n = 242$, $p < .05$), thus researchers would be 4 percent more accurate in predicting the Trauma Sum Total scores if the amount of training is known ($r^2 = .04$).

When looking at the question, "Have you ever received training from another school or organization in Cross-cultural Training," the more training respondents received from another school or organization in Cross-cultural understanding the lower their Trauma Sum Total scores ($r = -.19$, $n = 245$, $p < .05$), hence, researchers would be 4 percent more accurate in predicting the Trauma Sum Total scores if the amount of training is known ($r^2 = .04$) (see Table 4.32.).

Table 4.32. Respondent Demographic and Training Factors in Relationship to PTSD Sum and Trauma Sum Variables Pearson Correlation

Question		PTSD Sum Total	Trauma Sum Total
What is your age?	Pearson Correlation	-.028	-.218
	Sig. (2-tailed)	.660	.001
	N	242	245
How long have you served as a missionary?	Pearson Correlation	-.003	-.245
	Sig. (2-tailed)	.968	.000
	N	245	245
Have you ever received training from AGWM in Trauma Management?	Pearson Correlation	-.053	-.126
	Sig. (2-tailed)	.411	.048
	N	242	245
Trauma Management training from another school / organization?	Pearson Correlation	.198	-.229
	Sig. (2-tailed)	.002	.000
	N	242	245
Have you ever received training from AGWM in Conflict Management?	Pearson Correlation	-.004	-.013
	Sig. (2-tailed)	.955	.834
	N	242	245
Conflict Management training from another school/ organization?	Pearson Correlation	.058	-.088
	Sig. (2-tailed)	.369	.171
	N	242	245

Question		PTSD Sum Total	Trauma Sum Total
Have you ever received training from AGWM in Stress Management?	Pearson Correlation	.058	-.098
	Sig. (2-tailed)	.365	.127
	N	242	245
Stress Management training from another school/organization?	Pearson Correlation	.152	-.134
	Sig. (2-tailed)	.018	.037
	N	242	245
Have you ever received training from AGWM in Cross-cultural training?	Pearson Correlation	.015	-.026
	Sig. (2-tailed)	.819	.687
	N	242	245
Cross-cultural training from another school/organization?	Pearson Correlation	.044	-.187
	Sig. (2-tailed)	.496	.003
	N	242	245

Discussion

This study researched three major questions: How many AGWM missionaries live through traumatic events? (RQ1); what types of trauma do AGWM missionaries endure? (RQ2); and what coping skills minimize the negative impact of trauma in missionaries' lives and enhance AGWM missionary well-being? (RQ3). The answer revealed in this research to the first question matched other studies, AGWM missionaries suffered an abundance of traumatic incidences.[50] Every AGWM participant (100 percent) reported experiencing at least one traumatic incident during their lifetime. Nonetheless, unlike other studies, AGWM missionaries experienced each of the Trauma Event Questionnaire categories including childhood and adult physical/sexual abuse and being taken hostage. The top five experienced traumas include: violent crimes, natural disasters, accidents, attempts on their lives, and news

---

50. Bagley, "Impact of Trauma"; Barber-Stirling, "Effects of Exposure to Traumatic Events"; Irvine et al., "Traumatic Stress in a Missionary Population"; Schaefer et al., "Traumatic Events."

of a serious injury of violent death or friends and relatives. Despite the high amount and types of trauma, only 14.9 percent showed PTSD symptomatology and all the participants remained on field.

To determine how AGWM missionaries cope with the stress and trauma they inevitably face, the survey included several coping inventories. The Ego Resiliency Survey considered the person's adventurous spirit which has been found to assist with missionary resilience.[51] The Resiliency Appraisal Scale determined the missionary's use of social support during high stress times.[52] The Resiliency Scale tested the missionary's basic resilience.[53] Several researchers concluded that call affected a missionary's ability to cope with trauma, therefore, AGWM missionaries took the Calling and Vocation Questionnaire.[54] The Satisfaction with Life Scale reveals a person's optimism in the face of adversity. Studies have shown that optimistic people display a better coping style.[55] With the general population utilizing religious coping during times of suffering, one could speculate that missionaries would turn to religious coping quite naturally.[56] Thus, the survey used the Brief Religious Coping Scale to determine the religious coping skills of the AGWM missionary participants.

This study hypothesized that missionaries who suffered high amounts of trauma and showed low PTSD symptomatology would be utilizing good coping techniques and those who underwent lower amounts of trauma yet displayed high PTSD symptoms would be employing poor or negative coping skills. The results of survey found no statistical difference between Low Trauma—High PTSD and High Trauma—Low PTSD participants and their coping ability in the areas of Adventurousness, Social Support, Resiliency, Calling, or Positive Religious Coping. The majority possessed and implemented these skills while dealing with trauma. However, the survey did

---

51. Carr, "Mobile Member Care Team," 80; Carr, "Resources for Effective Support: Personal Resilience," loc. 2067.

52. Bjorck and Kim, "Religious Coping," 613; Carr, "Resources for Effective Support: Effective Community Support," loc. 1639; Smith, "Buffering Role of Social Support," 17–18.

53. Carr, "Mobile Member Care Team," 80; Chen, "Literature Review on Missionary Functioning," 33–34; Schaefer et al., "Traumatic Events," 536; Whiteman, "Integral Training Today," 9–10.

54. Carr, "Mobile Member Care Team," 80; Carr, "Resources for Effective Support: Personal Resilience," loc. 2050; Stills, *Missionary Call*, loc. 2080.

55. Abu-Raiya and Pargament, "Religious Coping," 30; Kebza and Solcova, "Trends in Resilience Theory," 16; Keckler, "Comprehensive Missionary Wellness," 88–89.

56. Bjorck and Kim, "Religious Coping," 612–13; Pargament et al., "God Help Me!," 509; Pargament and Park, "In Times of Stress," 46.

reveal statistical differences in the development of PTSD and the missionaries' satisfaction with life (optimism) and negative religious coping.

Per this survey's results, AGWM missionaries who had an optimistic and satisfied view on life had a less likely chance of developing PTSD. Other studies had similar findings. Raheela Sultana et al. established that belief in a just world had a negative effect on PTSD with victims of natural or human-made disasters.[57] Therefore, the more optimism/satisfaction with life a person had, the less likely he or she would develop PTSD. Bjorck and Kim discovered that the more missionaries combined positive religious coping and feelings that God supported their actions, the higher their life satisfaction.[58] Yet, when missionaries used positive religious coping alone, their life satisfaction dropped.[59] Thus, trust in a supportive God and positive religious coping, raises the person's satisfaction with life which in turn, lowers potential for PTSD.

This study also exposed significant correlation between negative religious coping and PTSD. AGWM missionaries who utilized negative religious coping had higher PTSD symptomatology. The strongest indicator for increased PTSD occurred when AGWM missionaries felt abandoned by God. A moderately strong predictor of PTSD happened when they thought their suffering happened because God wanted to punish them. Strong indicators of PTSD occurred when AGWM missionaries questioned God's love; when they felt abandoned by coworkers, the national church, or AGWM; or when they questioned God's power. The weakest contributor to PTSD symptomatology ensued when AGWM missionaries felt punishment for lack of devotion or believing the devil had his hand in the incident. This correlates with other studies where negative religious coping during trauma predicted negative psychological and health related issues.[60]

Other factors that seemed to help missionaries with trauma perception and PTSD levels were the age of the missionary and his or her time on field. Just as in the Patricia Miersma study, the more life experiences a person has, the less traumatic events produce negative effects.[61] He or she has more tools to negotiate new traumatic incidents. With more time on field, the missionary understands and can navigate in the host culture, thereby, limiting the stress of new trauma. A person's education level did not factor

---

57. Raheela Sultana et al., "Outcomes of Belief in Just World," 53–54.
58. Bjorck and Kim, "Religious Coping," 623.
59. Bjorck and Kim, "Religious Coping," 623.
60. Gerber et al., "Unique Contributions," 299; Kuile and Ehring, "Predictors of Changes in Religiosity," 358; Werdel et al., "Unique Role of Spirituality," 67.
61. Miersma, "Understanding Missionary Stress," 98.

into predicting either trauma perception or PTSD levels; yet, certain types of training were significant predictors. Trauma management training was a positive predictor of both a missionary's trauma perception and PTSD level because the more trauma management training a missionary had, the lower the amount of trauma perceived, and PTSD indicated. It seems that knowing about trauma, its symptomatology, and having tools to assist in its management help the missionary cope well. Cross-cultural training can also be considered a positive predictor of missionary trauma perception. When a missionary cannot comprehend the cultural norms of his or her host country, the perception of trauma heightens. Thus, the more a missionary knows the culture's language and societal rules, the easier he or she can navigate crisis and trauma.

AGWM missionaries tend to experience catastrophic amounts of trauma, yet the majority of them cope well and they do not develop PTSD. They believe themselves to be in God's will and they have a purpose in that calling giving them a satisfaction with life that sustains them through whatever life throws at them. A few, on the other hand, sense little or no control over the traumatic event they are facing and cope negatively sensing God's displeasure, abandonment, or punishment.[62] This can often lead to higher PTSD and possible attrition. To minimize the negative impact of trauma in AGWM missionaries' lives and enhance their well-being continued Trauma Management training must be given, moving them away from a negative view of God and teaching them positive coping skills which will enhance their satisfaction with life and well-being.

Study Limitations

As with all research, this study also had several limitations. The number of AGWM participants ($N = 254$) was small compared to the 1,907 surveys sent out. Hence, while the results of the study cannot be a confident representation of all AGWM or Evangelical missionaries living in cross-cultural situations, it may be indicative of how appointed AGWM missionaries would respond. The participation size was influenced by certain limiting factors. First, the internet-based survey became caught in the AGWM email spam filter and many missionaries did not receive the survey invitation. This situation worsened because of the limitation by AGWM of only sending one survey reminder, which also got trapped in the AGWM

---

62. Pargament et al., "Patterns of Positive and Negative Religious Coping," 720–21; Schottenbauer et al., "Religious Coping Research and Contemporary Personality Theory," 514; Smith et al., "Noah Revisited," 182.

email spam filter. Second, the web-based survey reduced participation by not allowing missionaries with restricted or limited internet access to take the survey. Third, according to emails, many missionaries did not take the survey feeling they never had a traumatic experience on field and therefore had nothing to say in the survey.

The survey may have been perceived as too lengthy for some and thus some may have not completed it due to question fatigue. Incomplete surveys were not used in the research. On the TEQ, the separate questions on multiple traumas may have become confusing for the participants. They may have had problems keeping straight which trauma they were rating. Finally, the delivery method of the survey (online) did not allow the respondents to go back to cross-check previous questions or answers.

Future Research Suggestions

With the uniqueness of missionary life, more research needs to be directed to this people group. This survey only looked at United States missionaries from one denomination. With the vast influx of missionaries being sent from third world nations in Latin America, Africa, Europe, and Asia, research should be done to find out how trauma affects these missionaries and their coping mechanisms. These studies could determine how a person's cultural background affects his or her perception of trauma and coping. This study also just observed missionaries who remained on field. Future studies need to examine missionaries who have left the field to establish if trauma occurred and how their lack of coping abilities caused their attrition.

Conclusion

This research resolved that AGWM missionaries ($N = 254$), like missionaries previously studied, experience multiple traumatic events on and off field. The largest number, 59.8 percent ($n = 152$) experienced violent crimes. The list continues: 52.8 percent ($n = 134$) faced natural disasters, 44.9 percent ($n = 114$) suffered accidents, 35.4 percent ($n = 90$) felt they were in danger of losing their life or having a serious injury, 33.9 percent ($n = 86$) heard news of the death or injury of a close friend or family member, 33.5 percent ($n = 85$) had conflict with a member of the field fellowship, 28.7 percent ($n = 73$) experienced vicarious trauma, 21.2 percent ($n = 52$) lived in a war zone, 20.8 percent ($n = 51$) suffered childhood physical or sexual abuse, 17.7 percent ($n = 45$) underwent trauma not mentioned on the questionnaire, 15.7 percent ($n = 40$) had conflict with the national church, 8.2 percent ($n = 20$)

lived through adult physical abuse, 6.9 percent ($n = 17$) suffered such severe trauma they could not speak of it, 2.9 percent ($n = 7$) endured adult sexual abuse, and 2.4 percent ($n = 6$) underwent being taken hostage.

Even with the great amount of trauma that all the AGMW missionaries suffered, only 14.9 percent ($n = 36$) indicated PTSD symptomatology. Most AGWM missionaries use positive coping skills and remain emotionally and physically healthy. Yet, the strongest finding of this study revealed a significant correlation between negative religious coping and PTSD. The more missionaries felt abandoned or punished by God, questioned His love or power, or felt abandoned by coworkers, the national church, or AGWM personnel reported higher PTSD symptoms. One AGWM missionary told of her multi-layered trauma story which lasted years. After the unexpected death of her grandfather, she miscarried. With the stress of doing all the funeral arrangements, she did not grieve properly for these two deaths. She, later, became pregnant again, but the baby died in utero at 12 weeks.

> Alone at the appointment, I watched the ultrasound screen anxiously looking for the heartbeat with the doctor that would never be within this perfectly formed fetus. I was told that surgery would be required since my body did not naturally abort the fetus. At this news, I could feel my body going numb and completely shutting down emotionally. I became very angry with God and had a serious faith crisis.

She became pregnant again and had a son. Outwardly, she rejoiced; inwardly, she struggled.

> Now, I believe that hormonal imbalances and unresolved heart issues toward God contributed to my postpartum issues. I am grateful that I am a high-functioning depressed person, although in retrospect, I should have sought counseling, etc. My Southern religious culture has a stigma against mental health sometimes that makes a person (especially involved in ministry) as if they prayed enough, they would be okay. Throughout that year (we had also moved into a new town as we entered full-time ministry) God continued to show me through his word that his unfailing love for me had never been removed, even though I had at times withdrawn my love from him. He really used some verses in Lamentations to give me hope that I could climb out of my depression and return to him—not the same as before, but a new creation, stronger and now able to share with others about my struggles. Also, if I had not gone through this time and came to the realization that there is nothing wrong with seeking professional help when needed,

> I don't know if we would have survived our first year on the field. My daughter exhibited severe culture-shock and transitional disorder. After 1.5 years and a lot of conflict with some on-field leadership, we came home for help to discover that she has an anxiety disorder that explained a lot about her behavior through the years. Even though life hasn't always been easy, I am glad that God uses our experiences to help us grow in the areas where he knows we will need to be stronger so that we will not break when hard times come in the future.

This missionary coped negatively by "becoming angry with God and having a faith crisis." These unresolved "heart issues" (Negative Religious Coping) lead to depression. Nonetheless, as she started to employ positive coping, finding "hope that I could climb out of my depression and return to him [God]," caused Post-Traumatic Growth. She realized that her suffering caused her to become a stronger person so that she would "not break when hard times come in the future."

To assist AGWM missionaries in overcoming trauma and living a life of well-being, pre-field and on-field training must occur. This study found that Trauma Management and Cross-cultural training had a significant impact on how missionaries perceive trauma and PTSD impact levels. Therefore, missions agencies must increase training in these two areas so that their missionaries can overcome the trauma they will endure.

5

Conclusion

A Biblical Theory of Well-being

THIS STUDY REVIEWED THE psychological understanding of trauma and its theories of how people cope with its effects. It examined the negative outcomes of traumatic experiences such as stress, anxiety, burnout, depression, and PTSD. It explored positive internal coping resources like resilience, hardiness, and optimism; and external coping skills such as problem solving, the support of friends and family, finding meaning or purpose in the event, and giving the problem to God. People can also cope negatively by feeling a lack of control, self-blame, and or believing God has abandoned them. Yet, through it all, most individuals journey through suffering and, in the end, achieve Post-Traumatic Growth.

When missionaries follow the call of Christ to go to other cultures to spread the gospel, they often do not realize the cultural stress and trauma they will endure. They must go through the process of application and then raise their support. They leave friends and family and move to a country where they do not know the language or the cultural rules. They often suffer through added traumas of violent crime, accidents, war, and natural disasters. Nonetheless, most missionaries remain on field and grow stronger through these trials. Thus, the question arises: How do missionaries cope with trauma? This chapter will take the results of the Trauma and Coping Survey and the biblical theology of well-being model developed in this study and endeavor to develop a Biblical Theory of Well-being

Overview of Trauma and Coping Survey

All the AGWM missionaries surveyed stated they had suffered at least one traumatic event during their missionary career. Many of these missionaries experienced multiple or repeated traumatic events. Yet, these missionaries remained on field with few experiencing PTSD symptomatology. Even though there was no statistically significant relationship between the missionaries' PTSD symptoms and most of their coping skills, the majority scored high on Adventurousness (ERS), Social Resiliency (RAS), General Resiliency (RS), Call (CVQ), and Positive Religious Coping (B-RCOPE-P) (see Table 4.26.). Hence, one can speculate that these missionaries managed their trauma through good coping ability.

The significantly significant factors that emerged in this study were Optimism (SWLS) and Negative Religious Coping (B-RCOPE-N). Missionaries who scored low in their satisfaction with life or who had high scores in feeling God had abandoned them had higher PTSD scores. Therefore, missionaries who had High—Trauma and High—PTSD tended to blame God and had a pessimistic view of life.

Overview of Biblical Theology of Well-being

This research examined Scripture through the lens of trauma and coping to determine if patterns of trauma management could be identified. After investigating 23 biblical characters, a biblical theology of well-being emerged. This examination revealed that to cope well in times of stress and trauma a person must utilize the central spiritual coping factor of trusting in God; then, from this trust, employ seven biblical coping skills: asking God for help, praise and worship, a sense of call, working with God, lamenting/venting, a theology of suffering, and assistance from friends and family. These seven coping mechanisms come from trust in God and when applied, cause that trust to grow. These cyclical patterns continue through life's traumas causing the person to strengthen his or her coping ability.

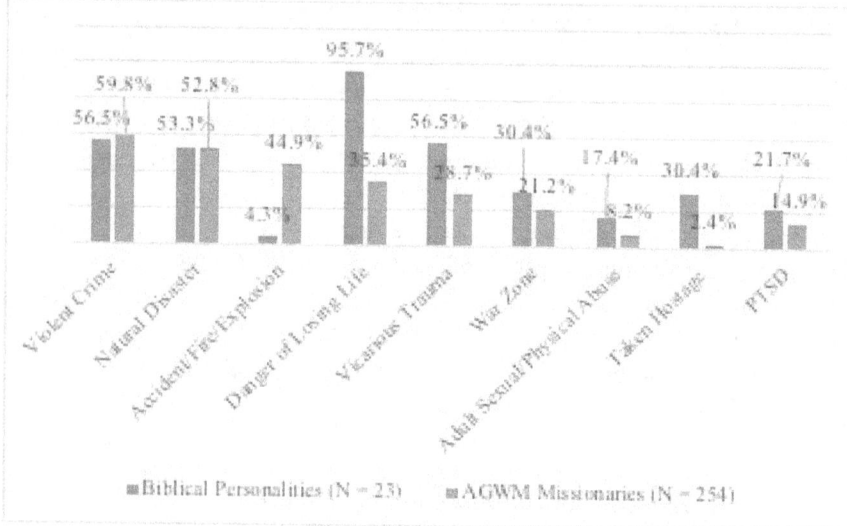

Figure 5.1. Trauma Comparison of Biblical Personalities and AGWM Missionaries

A Biblical Theory of Well-being

One could assume when a person decides to go into pastoral ministry, he or she would be an expert on spiritual matters. Yet, missionaries must learn increasingly higher levels of discipleship through "trials and testings" (Jas 1:3). Missionaries, more than others, withstand vast amounts of "trials and testings" often in the form of traumatic events. These missionaries need to apply a theory of missionary well-being to survive.

This research realized that the AGWM survey results fortified the biblical theology of well-being and thereby, turned this model (See Figure 3.1.) into the Biblical Theory of Well-being. When a missionary utilizes this model, he or she will be able to cope with trauma and remain on field with a sense of well-being. This section will reinforce this theory by showing how coping theories, the biblical text, and the AGWM missionary surveys strengthen each of the model's segments.

Trust in God

This study found trust in God to be the most important coping skill used by 69.6 percent of the biblical personalities and 79.2 percent of AGWM missionaries (See Figure 5.1.). All monotheistic traditions communicate the importance of trusting in God, however, the idea started in conventional Jewish thought.¹ Proverbs 3:5-6 teaches, "Trust in the Lord with all your heart and lean not on your own understanding; in all your ways submit to him, and he will make your paths straight." The Psalms declare to "trust in the Lord" and He will be one's "strength and shield" (28:7), "refuge" and "fortress" (91:2), and "help" (115:10, 11). If one trusts in the Lord, He will "surround" him or her with His "unfailing love" (Ps 32:10), He will "put a new song," a "hymn of praise" in his or her "mouth" (Ps 40:3), and He will make him or her "like Mount Zion, which cannot be shaken but endures forever" (Ps 125:1). The writer of Hebrews confirms, "The fundamental fact of existence is that this trust in God, this faith, is the firm foundation under everything that makes life worth living" (Heb 11:1, The Message).

Many of the Bible characters studied knew when they had come to the end of their human strength they had to lean completely on the Lord. Daniel could do nothing but give his life into God's hands when the king threw him into the den of lions (Dan 6). David knew he could only survive if God showed up to fight his battles (Ps 18:32-34). *Yahweh* thinned Gideon's army so that Gideon and Israel knew He won the war (Judg 7:2-7). Only God could give barren women like Sarah and Hannah a child (Gen 16:1; 21:6-7; 1 Sam 1:17-19). Moses comprehended only God could cause: the plagues that destroyed Egypt (Exod 7-11), the parting of the Red Sea (Exod 14), manna (Exod 16), and water from rocks (Exod 17:5-6; Num 20:9-11). Paul understood his physical limitations and, only with God's help, could he preach the gospel (2 Cor 12:9-10).

According to Carr and Schaefer, missionaries cope by trusting God.² Pargament et al. states that people can cope effectively using a deferring style where they give the situation to God and trust him for its outcome.³ Denney, Aten, and Leavel observed that trusting in God brought about well-being.⁴ Missionaries, as well as the biblical personalities mentioned must recognize their boundaries and exercise the deferring coping style by giving their problems entirely to God. They must trust God and know that he alone will make them stand firm and not be "shaken" (Ps 125: 1).

Trusting in God takes time to learn and comprehend and one can express his or her feelings of anger and hurt to God and still trust him.⁵

1. Rosmarin et al.," Incorporating Spiritual Beliefs," 692.

2. Carr and Schaefer, "Trauma and Traumatic Stress," 281; Carr and Schaefer, "Coping with Stress and Trauma," para. 11.

3. Pargament et al., "Patterns of Positive," 720-21.

4. Denney et al., "Post Traumatic Spiritual Growth," 378.

5. Floyd, *Crisis Counseling,* loc. 2697; Schaefer and Schaefer, "Resources for Effective Support," loc. 3431.

Some scholars, such as Jervis and Rosmarin et al., view not trusting God as sin. "Sin's goal is to separate humanity from God's love by causing the sufferer to question God's character. When a suffer allows her trust in God to be defeated by the terrifying power of suffering, sin has had its way."[6] This trust/mistrust in God affects one's emotional attitudes of worry, depression, and anxiety.[7]

Several of the biblical personalities studied did not trust God. Lot did not seem to have the same trust in God as his uncle Abraham. Yet, Lot's inability to trust and follow God's direction led him to Sodom and Gomorrah where he chose to put his children in harm's way for the sake of two strangers (Gen 19:14). This lack of trust caused Lot's life to degenerate into living in a cave and being raped by his daughters so that they could have children (Gen 19:30). Sarah, after many years of not being able to conceive, started to lose her trust in God and tried to find alternative ways to have a child (Gen 16:1). One can hear her resentment and agony as she reveals her plan to Abraham.[8] Her scheme, however, did not make her happy. Hagar became pregnant and Sarah started to despise her servant, which caused her greater suffering than she had before (Gen 16:4–5). Naomi did not appear to trust God to meet her needs either. She takes matters into her own hands and secures a husband for Ruth and when a baby is born, only the women around her praise and give thanks to God (Ruth 4:14–15). It seems that Naomi felt abandoned by God and, therefore, could not find joy in being a grandmother. As with these biblical personalities, this study's survey also disclosed that missionaries who did not trust but felt abandoned by God, had the highest probability of having PTSD symptomatology. They also coped poorly when they felt that God wanted to punish them, questioned God's love for them, or questioned God's power.

Missionaries must trust in God to survive the trauma involved in living in precarious places. Their trust will grow stronger as they meet and endure each crisis. Therefore, trust in God is the foundation for the Biblical Theory of Well-being.

Asking God for Help

One of the most powerful survival tools a missionary has is prayer.[9] Of the biblical personalities, 65.2 percent and 77.2 percent of the AGWM

---

6. Jervis, *At the Heart of the Gospel*, 131–32.
7. Rosmarin et al., "Incorporating Spiritual Beliefs," 692.
8. Roop, *Believers Church Bible Commentary: Genesis*, 118–19.
9. Carr, "Crisis Intervention for Missionaries," para. 17; Flemming, *Contextual-*

missionaries cope with trauma by asking God's help through prayer (see Figure 5.1.); nevertheless, when they cannot pray, the prayers of others can sustain them.[10] The Apostle Paul communicates that the prayers of the early church assisted him when he stated, "He has delivered us from such a deadly peril, and he will deliver us again. On him we have set our hope that he will continue to deliver us, as you help us by your prayers. Then many will give thanks on our behalf for the gracious favor granted us in answer to the prayers of many" (2 Cor 1:10–11).

The second major coping skill amongst the 23 biblical characters, asking God for help, would seem to be the first logical step in trauma management. David often invites God's assistance often in the Psalms. He knew the source of his strength and with each rescue his trust in God grew (Ps 34:6–7). When their whole worlds changed because of the besiegement of their cities, Jeremiah, and Elisha cried to God for help (Jer 15:5; 2 Kgs 6:18–22). Daniel requested that God aid him in interpreting dreams (Dan 2:18). Moses petitioned for assistance in the leadership of his people (Exod 17:4–7; 32:30–31).

Post-Traumatic Growth occurs when a person asks God for help and, then, sees his answer, enhancing his or her relationship with God.[11] Prayer offers hope, and when the individual comes out the other side of the struggle, he or she can look back and see how God walked with him or her each step of the way.[12] This produces not only PTG but also deeper trust in the Lord. When missionaries intentionally ask for God's help, they will keep negative coping at bay, decrease their probability of developing PTSD, and triggering a sense of well-being.

Praise and Worship

The third coping mechanism in the Biblical Theory of Well-being causes the missionary to reframe his or her problem through praise and worship of God. Of the biblical characters, 52.2 percent coped with trauma with praise and worship and 87.4 percent of AGWM missionaries used positive religious coping which included praise and worship (see Figure 5.1.). Optimism grows through praise by causing the realization that an

---

ization in the New Testament, 243.

10. Foyle, *Honorably Wounded*, loc. 1241.

11. Barnett, "How Christian Trauma Survivors," 196; Khechuashvili, "Comparative Study of Psychological Well-Being," 54.

12. Werdel et al., "Unique Role of Spirituality," 58, 67.

all-powerful God is in control. Worship centers the emotions and causes feelings of peace, joy, and well-being.

Coping researchers comprehend that for people to cope well they must have the internal resource of optimism which helps with one's sense of identity and purpose.[13] Laughter, humor, cheerfulness, and other positive emotions lower feelings of distress.[14] A positive attitude assists people in times of trauma and suffering.[15] This research also showed the positive outcome satisfaction with life (optimism) had on PTSD scores.

Many biblical characters seemed to have positive dispositions toward the trauma they faced. Daniel worshiped his God during dangerous times (Dan 2:19–23). David sang songs of praise and adoration to God when he faced times of difficulty (Psalms). Mary, mother of Jesus, maintained a positive attitude when she learned of her pregnancy out of wedlock (Luke 1:46–49). Paul instructed the church that the positive attitudes needed to assure human well-being were the fruit of the Spirit: "love, joy, peace, forbearance, kindness, goodness, faithfulness, gentleness and self-control" (Gal 5:22–23).[16] He lived his words as he faced each crisis.

As proven in the Psalms, music is central to praise and worship to God. The Bible says to, "be filled with the Spirit, speaking to one another with psalms, hymns, and songs from the Spirit. Sing and make music from your heart to the Lord" (Eph 5:18–19). Music, more than any other medium, can change one's mood and emotions.

Music expresses a moment in time.[17] "More than any other art form, music works through a flexible relationship between actual and perceived time, where present and past might meet and move towards an as yet unknown future."[18] Music captures the emotions one feels during traumatic experiences and counselors have noted how it restores health to trauma victims.[19]

People praise and worship through music to foster trust in times of trouble. One just needs to look through the pages of a hymnbook or listen to Christian music on the radio to understand the importance of singing about suffering and putting one's trust in God for deliverance. These hymns

13. Pulley and Wakefield, *Building Resiliency*, 10–21; Taylor, "How Psychosocial Resources," 66.

14. Papousek and Genullter, "Don't Take an X for a U," 14.

15. Frankl, *Man's Search for Meaning*, 160.

16. Ellsworth and Ellsworth, "Church that Enhance Spiritually," 135.

17. Moffitt, "Improvisation," 15.

18. Sutton, "Flash of the Obvious," 66.

19. Bendikesen, "PTSD and Religious Coping," 60–61; Bowland et al., "Evaluation of a Spiritually Focused Intervention," 74–75; Joseph, *What Doesn't Kill Us*, loc. 169; Langberg, *Suffering and the Heart of God*, loc. 1338.

and songs encourage believers to, "be not dismayed what'er betide, God will take care of you; beneath his wings of love abide, God will take care of you."[20] They remind one that, "great is Thy faithfulness, O God my Father; there is no shadow of turning with Thee. Thou changest not, Thy compassions they fail not, as Thou has been, Thou forever will be. Great is Thy faithfulness! Great is Thy faithfulness! Morning by morning new mercies I see. All I have needed Thy hand hath provided, great is Thy faithfulness, Lord unto me!"[21] Through these songs believers learn that "tis so sweet to trust in Jesus, just to take Him at His Word: just to rest upon His promise, and to know, 'Thus says the Lord!' Jesus, Jesus, how I trust Him! How I've proved Him o'er and o'er. Jesus, Jesus, precious Jesus! O for grace to trust Him more!"[22] Believers can only be content when they "Trust and obey, for there no other way to be happy in Jesus, but to trust and obey"[23]

These songs will help keep missionaries' hearts and minds from negative thoughts about God's power and ability to help. Praise and worship will keep missionaries focused on trusting God through each and every traumatic experience, leading them toward a sense of peace and well-being.

Sense of Purpose/Call

A sense of call had the same number of biblical characters as praise and worship, thus becoming the fourth coping mechanism of the Theory of Biblical Missionary Well-being. Of the biblical personalities, 52.2 percent felt called by God and 95.7 percent of the AGWM missionaries sensed the same (see Figure 5.1.). God continues to call men and women into his service like he did in biblical days. He calls some like Jeremiah before birth (Jer 1:5–8). Others hear an audible voice like Moses (Exod 3:4–10), Peter (Matt 4:18–20), and Paul (Acts 9: 3–6).

Missionaries realize their life is not a game; it is a war where the spiritual battle becomes reality.[24] Choosing this exceptionally physical, emotional, and psychological existence requires significant mental and spiritual stability.[25] One does not just decide to become a missionary like other vocations. A person must know God called him or her for this task. This clear calling to mission work from God most often will be the only thing that

20. Martin, *God Will Take Care of You*.
21. Chisholm, *Great is Thy Faithfulness*.
22. Stead, *Tis So Sweet To Trust in Jesus*.
23. Sammis, *Trust and Obey*.
24. Taylor, "Challenging the Missions Stakeholders," 358–59.
25. Grant, "Trauma in Missionary Life," 72.

keeps a missionary from leaving the field after a crisis or traumatic event. Ruth Tucker indicates that missionaries historically had to have the "nebulous and indefinable 'missionary call' that impelled them to move out. If ministries in the homeland could be pursued without 'call,' foreign missions could not. The stakes were too high, and it was that sense of calling, more than anything else that was the staying power."[26]

Of the AGWM missionaries surveyed, 95.7 percent had a clear missions calling. God called them, thus they accept risk and suffering as part of their committed purpose.[27] However, this sense of call must be built on trust in God so these missionaries can withstand with a sense of well-being the spiritual warfare, stress, crisis, and trauma they will encounter.

Working with God

The fifth coping skill missionaries need to master is working with God. Of the biblical personalities, 34.8 percent used this coping skill and 79.2 percent of the AGWM missionaries also sensed they worked with God. To cope well, a person needs to have a sense of control over the situation.[28] Missionaries must turn control over to God; Yet, they still have a part to play in the outcome.

Pargament et al. calls working with God in the problem-solving process the collaborative coping style.[29] The biblical men and women who handled trauma well often utilized this type of coping style. Noah labored with God to build a large ship to protect his family and the animals of earth (Gen 6:11–21). Joseph and Daniel, usually under the threat of death, labored with God to interpret dreams and visions (Gen 40; Dan 4:18). Moses led the rebellious Israelites with guidance from *Yahweh* (Exod 13:21–22). David often applied this collaborative style, knowing that God worked with him through traumatic events (i.e., slaying of Goliath—1 Sam 17:45–46; killing wild animals—1 Sam 17:37; help in battle—1 Sam– 2 Sam). Jesus always labored hand-in-hand with his Father. He states this collaboration when he raised Lazarus from the dead by saying, "Father, I thank you that you have heard me. I knew that you always hear me, but I said this for the benefit of the people standing here, that they may believe that you sent me" (John 11:41–42).

26. Tucker, *From Jerusalem to Irian Jaya*, 487.

27. Schaefer et al., "Traumatic Events," 538.

28. Lazarus and Folkman, *Stress, Appraisal, and Coping*, 179; Pargament et al., "God Help Me!," 505; Schottenbauer et al., "Religious Coping Research," 500.

29. Pargament et al., "Patterns of Positive and Negative Religious Coping," 720–21.

One must be careful to work in collaboration with God and not without him. Pargament et al. calls this coping style, self-directing, that involves the person exposed to a trauma actively trying to solve the problem on his or her own.[30] The difficulty with this coping mechanism is that it usually leads to a poor outcome. Sarah tried to solve her barrenness by having her husband impregnate her slave (Gen 16:1–5). Lot attempted to save his houseguests from the lust-crazed townsmen by offering up his virgin daughters (Gen 19:68). Moses, because of his anger at the people of Israel, forgot God's instructions and struck the rock instead of speaking to it. This act of taking things into his own hands kept him from entering the Promised Land (Num 20:1–13). Naomi utilized this self-directing style when she went against social norms and asked Ruth to seduce Boaz (Ruth 3).[31] David endeavored to fix his sin of adultery with Bathsheba by trying to entice her husband Uriah to sleep with her and when that did not work he had him killed by sending him into the most dangerous part of the battle (2 Sam 11). Jonah tried to run from God because he did not want a nation to be saved (Jon 1:3). These Old Testament men and women did not seek God's guidance with their problems, but actively tried to solve them in their flawed, human abilities.

Taylor considers problem-solving as one of the three most important psychosocial resources.[32] Though not statistically significant, the survey did show that most of the missionaries were actively coping with the trauma they faced. They put their "plans into action together with God" (B-RCOPE), they problem solved (RAS), and they found others to help (RAS). These are just a few of the ways missionaries work with God. They learn to hear and obey the voice of God during times of suffering. This co-laboring with God builds upon the foundation of trust causing a sense of well-being.

Lamenting/Venting

In counseling, venting can be seen as a negative emotion-focused coping strategy.[33] Nevertheless, others comprehend the benefits of a person venting his or her emotions.[34] For the sixth coping skill, the biblical characters utilized

---

30. Pargament et al., "Religion and the Problem-Solving Process," 90–104.
31. Roop, *Believers Church Bible Commentary: Ruth, Jonah, Esther*, 66.
32. Taylor, "How Psychosocial Resources," 66.
33. Connor-Smith and Flachsbart, "Relations Between Personality and Coping," 1082–83; Schottenbauer et al., "Religious Coping Research," 450.
34. Joseph, *What Doesn't Kill Us*, loc. 2254; Maltby et al., "Cognitive Nature of Forgiveness," 557.

both good (30.4 percent) and poor (4.3 percent) coping through venting and AGWM missionaries also employed this coping skill both positively (77.2 percent) and negatively (11.4 percent) (see Figure 5.1.). This research found the difference between beneficial lamenting/venting and negative religious coping to be the core of trust in God.

David often complained to God. He grumbles that he has been rejected (Ps 44:9) and that God is ignoring him (Ps 35:22). He even has the audacity to tell God to wake up (Ps 44:23). Elijah felt God betrayed him (1 Kgs 19:9–10), Jeremiah and Job blamed God for their trauma (Jer 14:19–20; Job 7:17–21), yet in the end, they trusted that God would see them through. They determined in their hearts that they would place their hope in him no matter the circumstances and with Job declare, "Though he slay me, yet will I hope in him" (Job 13:15).

Lamenting/venting becomes destructive when the person believes in God's supposed betrayal, abandoning, or lack of power and he or she becomes bitter and loses hope (e.g., Naomi, Lot, Sarah). This research revealed how negative lamenting/venting can predict PTSD. Missionaries must be able to vent their frustrations to God, but they must always return to trusting in the One who can do all things. As they release their negative emotions and trust, they will discover a sense of well-being amid their pain.

Theology of Suffering

Positive belief structures and a well-formed understanding of the theology of suffering can assist missionaries in any type of crisis.[35] Of the biblical characters examined, 21.7 percent understood this concept and of the AGWM missionaries, 76.1 percent comprehended this seventh coping mechanism (see Figure 5.1.). Spirituality concerns itself with deep culturally relevant religious feelings and beliefs that reorient the crisis into a meaning-making situation.[36] Pargament states that, "people seek significance" and when trauma happens they want to see their significance in the event and grow from it.[37] Other coping researchers also contend that individuals need to find meaning in the sorrow they live through to survive.[38] A theology of suffering does just that.

---

35. Balswick and Balswick, *Families In Pain*, 33; Bowland et al., "Evaluation of a Spiritually Focused Intervention," 73–75; Ross et al., "Relationship Between Religion," 46.

36. Gerber et al., "Unique Contributions of Positive," 298.

37. Pargament, *Psychology of Religion and Coping*, 91–106.

38. Davis et al., "Making Sense of Loss," 572; Frankl, *Man's Search for Meaning*,

CONCLUSION

The Bible chronicles the suffering of God and humanity. All of the 23 biblical characters studied suffered multiple tragedies. Nonetheless, the Old and New Testament writers give purpose to the suffering—taking up one's cross and following Jesus (Mark 8:34). The Apostle Paul did not deal with trauma with rest or professional counseling, but with a deep comprehension of suffering for Christ and religious coping, which included dependence on God and collective prayer (2 Cor 1:9–11).[39]

Stressful experiences frequently reinforce serving God because the missionary perceives this suffering to be of divine purpose for personal growth.[40] Being religious does not diminish the threat or harm in a situation, it does however, frame life's problems in positive and constructive terms.[41] This viewpoint prolongs positive psychological adjustment and health amid the crisis. No matter one's age or religious affiliation, his or her understanding of suffering and application of this theology of well-being in times of stress and trauma enhances his or her spiritual maturity.[42]

The AGWM missionaries studied also experienced tremendous trauma (100 percent suffered one or more traumatic events). For the missionary, it seems biblical coping would be the first line of defense to crisis and trauma. Yet, this study revealed some missionaries feel abandoned by God and a perceived lack of God support which caused an increase of PTSD symptoms. Thus, a theology of suffering becomes a vital part of biblical coping. To be able to manage the stress and trauma associated with missionary life with a sense of well-being, the foreign worker must trust in a God who suffered, thereby realizing that he or she does not suffer alone or in vain. Taking to heart the verse that says, "In all things God works for the good of those who love him, who have been called according to his purpose" (Rom 8:28).

Assistance from Friends and Family

When hard times come, missionaries rely on co-workers, national friendships, and family to help them survive.[43] The missionary agency also has a

---

98–99; Riley and Park, "Problem-Focused," 587–88; Thompson, "Finding Positive Meaning," 280.

39. Tucker and Andrews, "Historical Notes on Missionary Care," 25.
40. Pargament et al., "Red Flags and Religious Coping," 1337.
41. Pargament et al., "God Help Me!," 509.
42. Bjorck and Kim, "Religious Coping," 612–13; Bjorck et al., "Adolescent Religious Coping Scale," 357.
43. Bagley, "Impact of Trauma," 127–37; Bjorck and Kim, "Religious Coping," 612–13.

responsibility to lend emotional support.[44] Of the biblical personalities examined, 21.7 percent coped with the assistance of friends and family and 94.1 percent of AGWM missionaries utilized this eighth means of coping (see Figure 5.1.). Therefore, for missionaries to endure they must be able to receive emotional, physical, and spiritual support from these networks.

Assistance from One's Friends

To survive trauma, people need to be able to reach out to others for help.[45] Assistance from friends (co-workers or nationals) happens when they help with physical needs and listen to the stories of trauma. To relieve stress and tension, a missionary must be able to share his or her story with others. Just as Yalom and Leszcz realized that groups underwent several therapeutic experiences that helped the individual process his or her emotional distress, the religious community can use testimony to bring about the same results.[46]

Friends of many of the biblical characters studied gave them positive support. Even in captivity, Daniel had his friends Shadrach, Meshach, and Abendnego with him (Dan 1:6–7). They faced many traumatic experiences together in which surely, they gave each other support and guidance. David had a wonderful friendship with Jonathan (1 Sam 18:1), assistance from his mighty men (2 Sam 23:8–39), and from the prophets Samuel (1 Sam 19:18) and Nathan (2 Sam 7, 12). Naomi received care from her hometown community (Ruth 1:19). They helped her and Ruth with food (Ruth 2), comfort, and celebration at the birth of her grandson (Ruth 4:14–15). Jesus found friendship not only with his twelve disciples, but also with women who "car[ed] for his needs" (Matt 27:55; Luke 10:38–42). Paul knew he could not survive his many tragedies without the prayers of the church and the encouragement of Barnabas, Silas, Timothy, Apollos, Aquila, Priscilla and a host of others who sustained him physically and emotionally (2 Cor 1:3–11).

Missionaries also need the support of friends to survive. The social support of the missionary fellowship positively affects the way a missionary manages stressful events. This encouragement enhances the feeling of being loved, esteemed, and valued. It also reduces the effects of stress and speeds

---

44. Blocher and Lewis, "Further Findings in the Research Data," 111; Camp et al., "Missionary Perspectives," 365–66.

45. Balswick and Balswick, *Families In Pain*, 201; Benight, "Understanding Human Adaptation," 4; Janoff-Bulman, *Shattered Assumptions*, 95.

46. Yalom and Leszcz, *Theory and Practice of Group Psychotherapy*, 82–85.

the recovery of health and well-being.[47] Not finding a community who listens and authenticates negative experiences directs one toward social seclusion and despair, creating emotions of inferiority and inadequacy.[48]

A person under stress needs emotional and spiritual support not only from his or her missionary family, but also from the national church members and pastors.[49] These relationships will assist in the missionary's understanding of culture and language if he or she will do the hard work of overcoming these barriers. Yet, as this study disclosed, many AGWM missionaries suffered from traumatic conflict with members from their missionary fellowships and national church. Some felt these personal conflicts to be their worst traumatic experience on field. Care needs to be taken to help missionaries navigate these conflicts so that health and well-being can be restored to these needed relationships.

Assistance from One's Family

Some of the biblical personalities studied received help from their families. Gideon's family stood up for him when the town wanted to kill him (Judg 6:31). Loving husbands supported Sarah and Hannah through their years of barrenness (Gen 16; 1 Sam 1:5).

Family members may be the missionary's only confidants. This can be beneficial, especially if the family is tight-knit and has the maturity to assist one another through tough times. Yet, many times the family as a whole experience the same traumatic event and as this study revealed, the parents' trauma intensifies with the involvement of their children. When the family can adapt to crisis as a functional unit they have "family resilience" and how a child copes with trauma is contingent on how the parents react.[50] As missionary parents learn and implement this Biblical Theory of Well-being, they will be able to adapt to and manage each traumatic event and, thereby, teach their children to trust and rely on God.

---

47. Carr, "Mobile Member Care Team," 80; O'Donnell, "Member Care on the Field," 294.

48. Grant, "Trauma in Missionary Life," 80.

49. Krause et al., "Church-Based Social Support," 652.

50. Parker and Zakour, "Triumph Over Tragedy," 282; Pulley and Wakefield, *Building Resiliency*, 15.

Assistance from One's Mission Agency

Often, missionaries do not want to deal with their sending agencies because of its perceived bureaucracy. Most missionaries do not like being told "no" or made to work through all the paperwork and reporting most agencies require. Some leave the field because they believe their agency does not provide spiritual or financial support, have policy discrepancies, and/or theological disagreements.[51] Nevertheless, in times of crisis, good communication between the agency and the missionary may lower unnecessary attrition.[52]

Something as simple as supplying information helps a missionary understand stressful events and gives relevant resources to ascertain coping strategies.[53] Agencies must also provide a healing environment, which restores safety, support, justice, understanding, and hope with counselors who listen intently to the victim's stories and assist in making sense of the trauma.[54] To do this, missions agencies must produce competent leaders and counselors who watch for early warning signs of missionary stress, can assist in restoring the missionary to health, and set up beneficial member care structure with training and counseling. Good agencies must be sensitive to the Spirit so that they will know when not to allow a missionary to stay on field.[55]

This study showed with statistical significance that when missionaries deemed their missionary fellowship, the national church, or AGWM had abandoned them, they had higher PTSD symptoms. During stress and trauma, missionaries must cope by seeking help from their missionary community, national church, family, and/or sending agency. They must tell their story to people who want to listen and empathize with them. These traumatized fieldworkers need guidance from well-trained, Spirit filled leaders and counselors. As they find this support, their sense of well-being will increase.

---

51. Blocher, "ReMAP I," 13.
52. Blocher and Lewis, "Further Findings in the Research Data," 111.
53. Taylor et al., "Culture and Social Support," 355.
54. Grant, "Trauma in Missionary Life," 72.
55. Taylor, "Revisiting a Provocative Theme," 70.

CONCLUSION

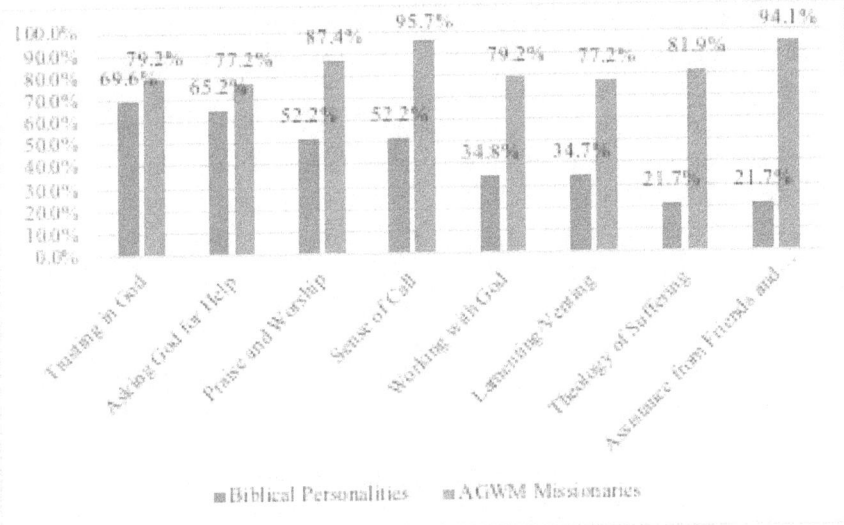

Figure 5.2. Biblical Personalities and AGWM Missionaries
Biblical Theory of Well-being

Education/Training

AGWM Missionary leaders down through the years clearly understood the need for missionary training. In 1922, J. Roswell Flower sent out a call for prayer that a missionary training center would be created. He announced the greatest problem of fulfilling the Macedonian cry to "come over and help us" was not a lack of volunteers, but to "secure workers who have been properly trained to make them effective workers when they reach the field."[56]

History proves a direct link between education and ministry because people can only live out what they learn.[57] Yet presently, churches and agencies seem to be sending out missionaries with less and less training. Eugene Nida once commented to Darrell Whiteman, "There are perhaps more missionaries today than ever before, but they are more poorly trained and prepared than at any other period in mission history."[58] Whiteman went on to survey 60 North American Protestant missions' agencies and requested they list the eleven most important areas of missionary training, and then solicited

---

56. Flower, "Pray, Pray, Pray," 12.
57. Brewer, "Lifelong Learning Link," 190.
58. Whiteman, "Integral Training Today," 5.

what percent of time each received in their missionary training.[59] The agencies listed Mission Team Dynamics as the number one training needed for missionaries, yet the subject only received 11 percent of the training time. Policies and Procedures received the most amount of time (14 percent), yet only ranked number six in importance. Interestingly, Spiritual Warfare ranked number five in significance, but only received 5 percent of educational time.[60] Whiteman further revealed 3.5 weeks to be the average amount of time devoted to missionary training, and agencies only spent 12 percent of their annual budget towards missionary education.[61]

Missions training in Bible institutes increased during the early 1900s, yet research revealed that even with this push for missionary education, by the late 1900s missionaries continued to go to the foreign field without significant study in methods of contextualization of the gospel. It seems the old method of "trial and error" on field remained the training method of choice.[62] It seems more and more people who apply for missionary appointment come from professions other than pastoral, and do not have biblical or missiological education. Moreover, many did not attend Sunday school, so even a rudimentary Bible foundation does not exist.[63] Educators view missionary training in many ways, but most deem it should occur at three important times during the missionary career: pre-field, on-field, and during furloughs.[64]

Pre-field Education

Good pre-field education can be accomplished in Bible schools, seminaries, or missionary training schools. Whatever the venue, a well-trained missionary needs a blend of cognitive and experiential education. A biblical education is foundational in a missionary's training process, so he or she

---

59. Whiteman, "Integral Training Today," 7–8.

60. Missions agencies listed the top eleven subjects for missionary training and the percentages of time given to each as: 1. Mission Team Dynamics (11 percent), 2. Cross-Cultural Communication (13 percent), 3. Understanding Cultural Differences (12 percent), 4. Discipleship (9 percent), 5. Spiritual Warfare (5 percent), 6. Policies and Procedures (14 percent), 7. Theology of Missions (8 percent), 8. Culture Shock (6 percent), 9. Understanding World Religions (6 percent), 10. Psychology Testing and Personality Assessment (4 percent), Church Planting (7 percent) (Whiteman, "Integral Training Today," 7–8).

61. Whiteman, "Integral Training Today," 7–8.

62. Henderson, "Historical Review of Missions," 215.

63. Whiteman, "Integral Training Today," 8–9.

64. Hubble, "Reasons for Missionary Training," 258.

can proclaim the gospel with confidence. Understanding the *missio Dei* (mission of God) will fortify the missionary's call and vocation.[65] Classes such as Hermeneutics, Homiletics, Contextualization, Cross-Cultural Communication, and Bible Survey will give the missionary candidate a firm foundation on which to build a successful missionary career.

Missionary training must also focus on giving missionaries the tools to discover and comprehend the deeper differences between their home culture and the host culture, thereby fortifying adaptation.[66] Cross-cultural workers must adjust not only to the host culture but also to the missionary community. Robert Brynjolfson and Jonathan Lewis state an effective missionary has skills in "cultural adaption, language acquisition, interpersonal relationships and communication skills, conflict resolution, and transference of gifting ministry skills into the new cultural context."[67] Training should also focus on the missionary's call and his or her role with the national church.[68] Most educational institutions focus curriculum on cross-cultural communication, biblical knowledge, and anthropology, all necessary, yet, as Brynijolfson and Lewis and Gupta and Lingenfelter suggest, insight into interpersonal skills and conflict resolution must also round out a missionary's education.

Field Training

One must know that cross-cultural knowledge does not always lead to cultural competence.[69] The first on-field training most missionaries' encounter is language school. Therefore, these schools should be more than a place to learn language. They must also help the student put into practice the intercultural knowledge he or she hopefully acquired in pre-field education.[70] Other field training should include mentoring from veteran missionaries and the national church and continued formal education through Bible school or seminary extension sites.

---

65. Whiteman, "Integral Training Today," 9–10.

66. Gupta and Lingenfelter, *Breaking Tradition to Accomplish Vision*, 96–97; Whiteman, "Integral Training Today," 9–10.

67. Brynjolfson and Lewis, *Integral Ministry Training Design*, 29.

68. Gupta and Lingenfelter, *Breaking Tradition to Accomplish Vision*, 63.

69. Bennett, "On Becoming a Global Soul," 13.

70. Wittenbach, "Training of a Missionary," 407.

Furlough Education

When missionaries return to their home country, they should continue their education, especially in areas of recognized need on field.[71] Even with its proven worth, many missions agencies discourage continuing education, focusing instead on fundraising. Whiteman argues that agencies must make ongoing training and education a priority if they want to maintain missionary resilience.[72] Aspects of culture become easier to understand with experience, and as a missionary hones his or her skills through continuing education, he or she will become a more effective cross-cultural worker. National churches all over the world can be greatly impacted by educated Western missionaries, willing to serve, equip, and mentor national workers, and by doing so, can increase their impact on a nation one hundred-fold.[73]

This study asked AGWM missionaries about their training in the areas of cross-cultural training, trauma, stress, and conflict management. Of the 254 missionaries surveyed, 179 (70.5 percent) received "none, very little, or some" AGWM cross-cultural training (See Figure 4.1.); 241 (94.9 percent) had "none, very little, or some" AGWM trauma management training (see Figure 4.2.); 229 (90.2 percent) took "none, very little, or some" AGWM stress management training (see Figure 4.3.); and 231 (90.1 percent) studied "none, very little, or some" AGWM conflict management training (see Figure 4.4.). Nonetheless, 84 percent of the missionaries who had cross-cultural training felt it extremely helpful, 51 percent considered trauma management training to be helpful, 78 percent deemed stress management training to be helpful, and 71 percent believed conflict management to be helpful (see Figure 4.5.). The survey showed statistical significance in both length of time on field and trauma management training on predicting PTSD. Experience of dealing with trauma assists with future traumatic events. The Biblical Theory of Well-being, with its circular nature, helps missionaries grow in his or her capability to better cope with future trauma. This theory also needs to be part of missionary trauma training so that missionaries can use this tool when they face the trauma that will occur on field.

Missionaries must utilize this Biblical Theory of Well-being to enhance their survival on field. They need to always trust in God no matter the circumstances or difficulties they face. Then from this core of trust, they need to engage in the seven spiritual support coping mechanisms. Missionaries must be prepared to ask for help from God and then listen and obey what He

---

71. Wittenbach, "Training of a Missionary," 410.
72. Whiteman, "Integral Training Today," 9–10.
73. Gupta and Lingenfelter, *Breaking Tradition to Accomplish Vision*, 182.

asks them to do. They must continually be in a state of praise and worship to God, so that when hard times come their hearts and minds will be ready. Missionaries must co-labor with God, making sure they do not try to solve the problems on their own. They can vent to God without fear; however, they must not allow their pain to turn into hard-hearted bitterness. They also need support from friends, family, and their mission sending agency so that they can have their physical needs met and have a safe and empathic place to tell their trauma narratives. Missionaries need to have a theology of suffering so that they can "rejoice" as they "participate in the sufferings of Christ, so that" they "may be overjoyed when his glory is revealed" (1 Pet 4:13). They must constantly remember their calling which will give them the sense of purpose they need when stress and trauma come their way. As missionaries need to be trained in this Biblical Theory of Well-being so that they will continue to grow through each crisis and remain on field as vibrant, emotionally, and spiritually healthy men and women of God.

Conclusion

Beneficial coping allows a person to overcome emotional pitfalls and live a life of well-being despite trauma. Good use of the internal coping resources of personality, emotions, and external coping assets facilitate a thriving mentality. When individuals cope negatively, they will not only increase their fear and anxiety but also their PTSD symptomatology. Finding meaning in one's pain and suffering can move him or her from just surviving traumatic incidents to growing from them. Post-Traumatic Growth incorporates the scars and life change that trauma brings and produces a person with wisdom and a refined character. As people tell their survival narratives of God's intervention and assistance, they can live a life of well-being during the traumatic storms of life.

This research showed that despite all the stress and trauma life in foreign countries entail, missionaries adapt. Yet, their coping can be enhanced with the use of the Biblical Theory of Well-being. This trauma management tool can assist missionaries in moving deeper into their trust of God by using the coping skills of asking God for help, praise and worship, a sense of call, working with God, lamenting/venting, a theology of suffering, and assistance from friends and family. The theory can keep missionaries from the ravages of PTSD by keeping them away from negative religious coping and encouraging them to think optimistically so that they will have a better outlook on life.

Stress and trauma will happen to people who leave the comfort of home and acculturate in the land of their calling. These men and women have the God given resilience to adapt and cope with the demands of missionary life. Yet, they also need education and training so that they have understanding and resources such as the Biblical Theory of Well-being available when needed. Agencies need to provide this education and good member care, encouraging their workers to go to professional counselors they may need in the aftermath of traumatic events. With these things in place, future missionary preventable attrition may be a thing of the past.

Appendix A
Biblical Character Trauma Overview

Name	TA*	NT*	VC*	WR*	HE*	CPSA*	APSA*	VT*	PPT*	TI*	TII*	TIII*	TIV*	PTSD*
Daniel			1	1				1	5		x			x
David		1	1	4	1			4	1	x				x
Elijah		1						2	2	x				x
Elisha		1		2						x				
Gideon				1				2		x				
Hagar					1				3		x			
Hannah								2		x				
Jeremiah		1	4	1	1			1	4		x			
Jesus		1	4					2	4	x				
Job		1	2					1	2	x				x
John the Baptist		2						1		x				
Jonah		2							4	x				
Joseph			2		1		1		3		x			
Lot		1	2		1		2	2	3			x		
Mary Mother of Jesus			1					2	3	x				
Moses	3	1		4				9	14	x				
Naomi		1						2	4	x				x

243

APPENDIX A: BIBLICAL CHARACTER TRAUMA OVERVIEW

Name	TA*	NT*	VC*	WR*	HE*	CPSA*	APSA*	VT*	PPT*	TI*	TII*	TIII*	TIV*	PTSD*
Noah		1						1	1	2	X			
Paul	3	1	3					1	14		X			
Peter			5					1	3		X			
Rehab				2			1					X		
Sarah					2				1		X			
Stephen									1		X			
Totals	1	12	11	7	7	0	4	13	21	10	8	5	0	5

*TA—Traumatic Accident: Car accidents, fires, explosion (TEQ 1).

*NT—Natural Trauma: Earthquakes, tornadoes, avalanches, floods, fires, hurricanes, and volcanic eruptions (TEQ 2).

*VC—Violent Crime: Rape, robbery, assault (TEQ 3)

*WR—War Related Trauma: (TEQ 4)

*HE—Hostage Event: (TEQ 5)

*CPSA—Childhood Physical or Sexual Abuse: (TEQ 6).

*APSA—Adult Physical or Sexual Abuse (TEQ 7,8).

*VT—Vicarious or secondary trauma: Witnessing someone being mutilated, seriously injured, or violently killed. Receiving news of some close being mutilated, seriously injured or his or her violent or unexpected death (TEQ 9, 11).

*PPT—Psychological/Physical Trauma: Serious danger of losing one's life or being seriously injured. A traumatic conflict with another person. An incident that causes strong emotional reactions. (TEQ 10, 12, 13).

*TI—Type I Trauma—single-blow events.

*TII—Type II Trauma—war, or sexual, physical, and emotional abuse, or if several Type 1 incidents happen repeatedly over a short time span in the past but then stopped.

*TIII—trauma that continues to happen such as racism or discrimination.

*TIV—The cumulative effects of traumatic victimization over a life span.

*PTSD—PTSD criteria met per the DSM-V.

Appendix B
Biblical Character Coping Overview

Name	PW*	S*	AAG*	WG*	TG*	VL*	S*	F*	*C	*TS
Daniel	4		3	2	1					
David	16		12	2	2	3	2		1	
Dinah										
Elijah			2	•	1	3				
Elisha			2		1		1		1	
Gideon	1		1	1	1			1	1	
Hagar			1							
Hannah	1		2							
Jeremiah	4		7		2	7			1	
Jesus	1		5	1	7	2			1	3
Job	2		1		1	5	1			1
John the Baptist									1	
Jonah	2		1		2	1			1	
Joseph				2	1					1
Lot										
Mary Mother of Jesus	1				1				1	
Moses	2		3	2	1	1			1	1
Naomi			1			1	1			

APPENDIX B: BIBLICAL CHARACTER COPING OVERVIEW

Name	PW*	S*	AAG*	WG*	TG*	VL*	S*	F*	*C	*TS
Noah					1	1				
Paul	3	1	2	2	2				1	4
Peter	4	1							1	1
Rehab			1		1					
Sarah		1							1	
Stephen					1					
Totals	12	3	15	8	16	8	4	1	12	5

*PW—Praise and Worship to God

*S—Singing

*AAG—Asking Assistance from God

*WG—Working with God

*VL—Venting/Lamenting

*S—Social

*F—Family

*C—Sense of Call

*TG—Trusting in God

*TS—Theology of Suffering

Appendix C

PTSD Diagnoses for Biblical Characters Using the DSM-V Criteria

Daniel

Criterion A Stressor* (1 required)	1. War with Nebuchadnezzar (Dan 1:1) 2. Taken Hostage (Dan 1:34) 3. Friends thrown into blazing furnace. (Dan 3) 4. Thrown into den of lions. (Dan 6) 5. Death threats. (Dan 2:13) 6. Prophetic dreams (Dan 4,7, 8)
Criterion B Intrusion Symptoms* (1 required)	1. Intense destress: King wanted him to interpret a dream which perplexed and terrified Daniel (Dan 4:19). 2. Dream of four beasts: deeply troubled by thoughts (Dan 7:28). 3. Vision of Ram and Goat: worn out and exhausted for days (Dan. 8:27). 4. Vision of man: no strength, trembling (Dan 10:7–8).
Criterion C Avoidance* (1 required)	1. Did not want to interpret the king's dream because it perplexed and terrified him. (Dan 4:19).
Criterion D Negative Alterations* (2 required)	1. **Persistent negative emotions**: He was terrified, deeply troubled, exhausted, overwhelmed with terror, face turned pale (Dan 4:19—7:28—8:27—10:7–8, 10, 12). 2. **Feeling alienated from others**: other wisemen were afraid of him and leaders wanted his death because of his dreams and visions (Dan 6—10).

Daniel

Criterion E Alterations in Arousal* (2 required)	1. The dreams and visions disturbed his sleep (Dan. 4—7—8—10). 2. Bible does not specify.
Criterion F Duration* (more than 1 month)	Not sure, but the Bible says he was perplexed for a time (Dan 4:19).
Criterion G Functional Significance*	Daniel seemed to continue the King's business in the midst of the trauma.
Criterion H Exclusion*	Not due to drug abuse or illness.

David

Criterion A Stressor* (1 required)	1. Attacked by lion and bear (1 Sam 17:34-35). 2. King Saul tries to kill him repeatedly (1 Sam 19). 3. Fights the giant Goliath (1 Sam 17). 4. Foreign wars with Philistines, Amalekites (1 Sam 14; 2 Sam 5). 5. Civil war between Israel and Judah. Rebellion and death of son Absalom (2 Sam 13). 6. Capture of wives and children by Amalekites (1 Sam 30). 7. Son Amnon rapes his daughter Tamar (2 Sam 13). 8. Infant son dies because of David's sin (2 Sam 12). 9. Son kills son Amnon because of rape of Tamar (2 Sam 13). 10. Uzzah killed by God when he grabs the Ark (2 Sam 6:3-8).
Criterion B Intrusion Symptoms* (1 required)	1. **Intense destress:** King wanted him to interpret a dream which perplexed and terrified Daniel (Dan 4:19). 2. Dream of four beasts: deeply troubled by thoughts (Dan 7:28). 3. Vision of Ram and Goat: worn out and exhausted for days (Dan. 8:27). 4. Vision of man: no strength, trembling (Dan 10:7–8).

APPENDIX C: PTSD DIAGNOSES FOR BIBLICAL CHARACTERS   249

David

Criterion C Avoidance* (1 required)	1. **Wanting to flee:** "My thoughts trouble me and I am distraught because of what my enemy is saying, because of the threats of the wicked; or They bring down suffering on me and assail me in their anger . . . I said, "Oh, that I had the wings of a dove! I would fly away and be at rest. I would flee far away and stay in the desert; I would hurry to my place of shelter, far from the tempest and storm" (Ps 55:2-3, 6-8).
Criterion D Negative Alterations* (2 required)	1. **Feeling alienated from others:** "But I am a worm and not a man, scorned by everyone, despised by the people. All who see me mock me; they hurl insults, shaking their heads" (Ps 22:6-7). 2. **Persistent negative trauma-related emotions:** "My heart is in anguish within me; the terrors of death have fallen on me. Fear and trembling have beset me; horror has overwhelmed me" (Ps 55:4-5).
Criterion E Alterations in Arousal* (2 required	1. **Sleep disturbance:** "I am worn out from my groaning. All night long I flood my bed with weeping and drench my ouch with tears. My eyes grow weak with sorrow; they fail because of all my foes" (Ps 6: 6-7). 2. **Cognitive problems:** ". . . My thoughts trouble me and I am distraught because of what my enemy is saying, because of the threats of the wicked; for they bring me down suffering on me and assail me in their anger" (Ps 55:2-3).
Criterion F Duration* (more than 1 month	1. **He has had reoccurring trauma all his life:** "How long must I wrestle with my thoughts and day after day have sorrow in my life? How long will my enemy triumph over me?" (Ps 13:2).
Criterion G Functional Significance*	1. **Feels he has no friends:** "Look and see, there is no one at my right hand; no one is concerned for me. I have no refuge; no one cares for my life" (Ps 142:4).
Criterion H Exclusion*	Not due to drug abuse or illness.

Elijah

Criterion A Stressor* (1 required)	1. Famine in Israel. No water or food (1 Kgs 18). 2. At the widow's house where he was staying, her son dies (1 Kgs 17). 3. He calls down fire from heaven to kill 100 solders (2 Kgs 1). 4. Jezebel tries to kill him twice (1 Kgs 18—19).
Criterion B Intrusion Symptoms* (1 required)	1. **Intense, prolonged psychological distress:** "He came to a broom bush sat down under it and prayed that he might die. 'I have had enough, Lord,' he said. 'Take my life; I am no better than my ancestors'" (1 Kgs 19:4–5). 2. **Recurrent, involuntary, and intrusive memories:** "The Israelites have rejected your covenant, torn down your alters, and put your prophets to death with the sword. I am the only one left, and now they are trying to kill me too" (1 Kgs 19:10).
Criterion C Avoidance* (1 required)	1. **Trauma-related external reminders:** "Elijah was afraid and ran for his life. When he came to Beersheba in Judah, he left his servant there, while he himself went a day's journey into the wilderness. He came to a broom bush sat down under it and prayed that he might die" (1 Kgs 19:1–3).
Criterion D Negative Alterations* (2 required)	1. **Persistent and often distorted negative beliefs and expectations about oneself or the world:** "I have been very zealous for the Lord God almighty. The Israelites have rejected your covenant, torn down your alters, and put your prophets to death with the sword. I am the only one left, and now they are trying to kill me too" (1 Kgs 19:10). 2. **Persistent distorted blame of self or others for causing the traumatic event or for resulting consequences:** "I have been very zealous for the Lord God Almighty. The Israelites have rejected your covenant, torn down your altars, and put your prophets to death with the sword. I am the only one left, and now they are going to kill me too" (1 Kgs 19:10).
Criterion E Alterations in Arousal* (2 required	1. **Self-destructive or reckless behavior:** Not eating and wanting to die. (1 Kgs 19) 2. **Irritable or aggressive behavior:** "And after the fire came a gentle whisper. When Elijah heard it, he pulled his cloak over his face and went and stood at the mouth of the cave" (1 Kgs 19:13).
Criterion F Duration* (more than 1 month)	Not sure how long Elijah was in the cave in the wilderness (1 Kgs 19).

Elijah

Criterion G Functional Significance*	Elijah ran away from being a prophet (1 Kgs 19).
Criterion H Exclusion*	Not due to drug abuse or illness.

Job

Criterion A Stressor* (1 required)	1. All possessions stolen from him (Job 1). 2. All his children were killed (Job 1). 3. He became ill with terrible sores all over his body (Job 2).
Criterion B Intrusion Symptoms* (1 required)	1. Traumatic nightmares: "When I think my bed will comfort me and my couch will ease my complaint, even then you frighten me with dreams and terrify me with visions, so that I prefer strangling and death, rather than this body of mine." (Job 7:14).
Criterion C Avoidance* (1 required)	1. Trauma-related thoughts or feelings: Job wants to be left alone (Job 13:13). 2. Trauma-related external reminders: Job is not happy with his friend's comfort (Job 16:2); Children despise him (Job 19:18); Friends abhorred him (Job 19:19).
Criterion D Negative Alterations* (2 required)	1. Persistent and often distorted negative beliefs and expectations about oneself or the world: Job curses the day he was born (Job 3:1-10); Job wished he had died before he was born (Job 3:11); Job hates his life (Job 10:1). 2. Persistent negative trauma-related emotions: Job has no hope (Job 7:6—19:10); Job speaks of anguish and bitterness of soul (Job 7:11).

Job

Criterion E Alterations in Arousal* (2 required	1. **Irritable or aggressive behavior:** Job tore his clothes, shaved his head, and fell to the ground after hearing of his children's deaths and loss of possessions (Job 1:20). 2. **Sleep disturbance:** Job could not sleep. He has nightmares (Job 3:26— 7:4, 14). 3. **Self-destructive or reckless behavior:** Job weeps to the point of death (Job 16:16).
Criterion F Duration* (more than 1 month	Not sure the length of time Job was in this state.
Criterion G Functional Significance*	All he could do was sit in a pile of ashes and scrape his sores.
Criterion H Exclusion*	Not due to drug abuse or illness.

* Criterion A: stressor

The person was exposed to: death, threatened death, actual or threatened serious injury, or actual or threatened sexual violence, as follows: (one required)

1. Direct exposure.

2. Witnessing, in person.

3. Indirectly, by learning that a close relative or close friend was exposed to trauma. If the event involved actual or threatened death, it must have been violent or accidental.

4. Repeated or extreme indirect exposure to aversive details of the event(s), usually in the course of professional duties (e.g., first responders, collecting body parts; professionals repeatedly exposed to details of child abuse). This does not include indirect non-professional exposure through electronic media, television, movies, or pictures.

* Criterion B: intrusion symptoms

The traumatic event is persistently re-experienced in the following way(s): (one required)

1. Recurrent, involuntary, and intrusive memories. Note: Children older than six may express this symptom in repetitive play.
2. Traumatic nightmares. Note: Children may have frightening dreams without content related to the trauma(s).
3. Dissociative reactions (e.g., flashbacks) which may occur on a continuum from brief episodes to complete loss of consciousness. Note: Children may reenact the event in play.
4. Intense or prolonged distress after exposure to traumatic reminders.
5. Marked physiologic reactivity after exposure to trauma-related stimuli.

* Criterion C: avoidance

Persistent effortful avoidance of distressing trauma-related stimuli after the event: (one required)

1. Trauma-related thoughts or feelings.
2. Trauma-related external reminders (e.g., people, places, conversations, activities, objects, or situations).

* Criterion D: negative alterations in cognitions and mood

Negative alterations in cognitions and mood that began or worsened after the traumatic event: (two required)

1. Inability to recall key features of the traumatic event (usually dissociative amnesia; not due to head injury, alcohol, or drugs).
2. Persistent (and often distorted) negative beliefs and expectations about oneself or the world (e.g., "I am bad," "The world is completely dangerous").
3. Persistent distorted blame of self or others for causing the traumatic event or for resulting consequences.
4. Persistent negative trauma-related emotions (e.g., fear, horror, anger, guilt, or shame).
5. Markedly diminished interest in (pre-traumatic) significant activities.

6. Feeling alienated from others (e.g., detachment or estrangement).

7. Constricted affect: persistent inability to experience positive emotions.

* **Criterion E: alterations in arousal and reactivity**

Trauma-related alterations in arousal and reactivity that began or worsened after the traumatic event: (two required)

1. Irritable or aggressive behavior
2. Self-destructive or reckless behavior
3. Hypervigilance
4. Exaggerated startle response
5. Problems in concentration
6. Sleep disturbance

* **Criterion F: duration**

Persistence of symptoms (in Criteria B, C, D, and E) for more than one month.

* **Criterion G: functional significance**

Significant symptom-related distress or functional impairment (e.g., social, occupational).

* **Criterion H: exclusion**

Disturbance is not due to medication, substance use, or other illness (American Psychiatric Association 2013, 280-190

Appendix D
Survey Trauma Explanation

Trauma is an emotional response to a terrible event.[1] It involves a painful, emotional experience or shock that overwhelms one's ability to cope.[2] Trauma can also be defined in terms of:

- Physical (body injury)
- Psychological (an incident that causes strong emotional reactions)
- Social (oppressive social conditions e.g.: war, poverty, discrimination, violence, conflict)
- Historical (past personal or social violence)
- Ongoing (daily violence)
- Vicarious or secondary trauma (experienced when a trauma happens to a loved one. Also can be felt by disaster relief workers, or mental health helpers called Compassion Fatigue).[3]

Each person experiences trauma uniquely; what is traumatic for one may not be for another. Thus, this survey seeks to determine what types of trauma AGWM missionaries have experienced, how they reacted to the trauma(s), and how they coped with those trauma(s). The survey has three sections:

- Section one (18 questions) will ask you if you experienced different types of trauma. If you answer no, you will be taken to the next type of trauma. If you answer yes, you will be asked a series of 6-8 questions about that trauma.

    1. American Psychological Association. 2014 "Definition of Trauma" http://www.apa.org/topics/truam (accessed June 4, 2014).

    2. Grant, Robert. 1995. "Trauma in Missionary Life" Missiology: An International Review 23(1): 71—83. 71.

    3. Wise, Judith. 2007. "Introduction: Empowerment as a Response to Trauma" in Trauma Transformed: An Empowerment Response ed. Marian Bussey and Judith Wise. 3-12. New York: Columbia University Press. 3-4.

APPENDIX D: SURVEY TRAUMA EXPLANATION

- Section two (17 questions) seeks to see how you reacted at the time of your most severe trauma, and your reactions today.
- Section three (60 questions) looks at how you cope with the trauma you experienced.
- This survey should only take you between 30 to 40 minutes to finish. Thank you again for your participation.

Appendix E
Trauma and Coping Survey

Demographics

1. What is your age? Slide to your age:
2. What is your gender?
   - Male
   - Female
3. What is your marital status?
   - Single
   - Married
4. What is the highest level of education you have completed?
   - A. Less than High School
   - High School / GED
   - Some College
   - 2-year College Degree
   - 4-year College Degree
   - Masters Degree
   - Doctoral Degree
   - Professional Degree (JD, MD)
5. What region you are currently serving in?
   - Africa
   - Asia Pacific
   - Eurasia

- Europe
- International Ministries
- Latin America/ Caribbean

6. How long have you served as a missionary? (Please include years with other organizations, also.)

7. Have you ever received training from AGWM in any of the following areas? (No training, Very little training, Some training, A good amount of training, A significant amount of training):

   - Trauma Management
   - Stress Management
   - Conflict Management
   - Cross-cultural Training

8. Have you ever received training from another school or organization in any of the following areas?

   - Trauma Management
   - Stress Management
   - Conflict Management
   - Cross-cultural Training

9. How helpful has your training in the following areas been to you during your missionary career? (Not at all helpful, A little helpful, Helpful, Very helpful, Extremely helpful, Not Applicable):

   - Trauma Management
   - Stress Management
   - Conflict Management
   - Cross-cultural Training

Main Trauma questions 1-15:

Section one (18 questions) will ask you if you experienced different types of trauma. If you answer no, you will be taken to the next type of trauma. If you answer yes, you will be asked a series of 6-8 questions about that trauma.

Section two (17 questions) seeks to see how you reacted at the time of your most severe trauma, and your reactions today.

APPENDIX E: TRAUMA AND COPING SURVEY

Section three (60 questions) looks at how you cope with the trauma you experienced.

This survey should only take you between 30 to 40 minutes to finish. Thank you again for your participation.

The following 18 questions ask you about traumatic events that may have affected you sometime during your life. You will be asked later if this event happened while you worked on field. You can answer each major question in the following ways:

- A Yes answer will lead you to answer additional questions about that specific trauma.
- A No answer will move you on to the next major question.
- A decline to answer means that you lived through this traumatic event but do not want to talk about it. If you click this answer you will be lead to the next major question.

1. Have you been in or witnessed a serious industrial, farm, or car accident, or large fire or explosion?

    - Yes
    - No
    - Decline to answer

    a. How many times have you been in or witnessed a serious industrial, farm, or car accident, or large fire or explosion? [BL 1-3]

       - One time
       - Two times
       - Three or more times

    b. How many times *on the field* have you been in or witnessed a serious industrial, farm, or car accident, or large fire or explosion?

       - One time
       - Two times
       - Three or more times

    c. How old were you at the time(s) of this/these event(s)? (a serious industrial, farm, or car accident, or large fire or explosion) (If you have more than three events, list the three most traumatic. If you only experienced one or two events, click *Not Applicable* on the other events.) (Child (0-10), Teen (11-19), Adult (20+), Not Applicable)

- First Event
- Second Event
- Third Event

d. Were you Injured at the time(s) of this/these event(s)? (a serious industrial, farm, or car accident, or large fire or explosion) (If you have more than three events, list the three most traumatic. If you only experienced one or two events, click *Not Applicable* on the other events.) (1Not at All, 2-3-4-5-6-7 severely, Not Applicable)

- First Event
- Second Event
- Third Event

e. Did you feel your life was threatened at the time(s) of this/these events? (a serious industrial, farm, or car accident, or large fire or explosion) (If you have more than three events, list the three most traumatic. If you only experienced one or two events, click *Not Applicable* on the other events.) (1Not at All, 2-3-4-5-6-7 severely, Not Applicable)

- First Event
- Second Event
- Third Event

f. How traumatic was witnessing the serious industrial, farm, or car accident, or large fire or explosion for you *at the time it happened*? (If you have more than three events, list the three most traumatic. If you only experienced one or two events, click *Not Applicable* on the other events.) (1Not at All, 2-3-4-5-6-7 severely, Not Applicable)

- First Event
- Second Event
- Third Event

g. How traumatic is witnessing this serious industrial, farm, or car accident, or large fire or explosion *for you now*? (If you have more than three events, list the three most traumatic. If you only

APPENDIX E: TRAUMA AND COPING SURVEY   261

experienced one or two events, click Not Applicable on the other events.) (1Not at All, 2–3–4–5–6–7 severely, Not Applicable)

- First Event
- Second Event
- Third Event

h. Which of the following terms best describes the *first event* you experienced? (If you have more than three events, list the three most traumatic.)

- Industrial Accident
- Farm Accident
- Car Accident
- Large Fire
- Explosion
- Other (please describe)

i. Which of the following terms best describes the *second event* you experienced? (If you have more than three events, list the three most traumatic. If you only experienced one or two events, click *Not Applicable* on the other events.)

- Industrial Accident
- Farm Accident
- Car Accident
- Large Fire
- Explosion
- Other (please describe)

j. Which of the following terms best describes the *third event* you experienced? (If you have more than three events, list the three most traumatic. If you only experienced one or two events, click *Not Applicable* on the other events.)

- Industrial Accident
- Farm Accident
- Car Accident
- Large Fire
- Explosion

- Other (please describe)

2. Have you been in a natural disaster such as a tornado, hurricane, flood, or major earthquake?

    - Yes
    - No
    - Decline to answer

    a. How many times have you been in a natural disaster such as a tornado, hurricane, flood, or major earthquake?

        - One time
        - Two times
        - Three or more times

    b. How many times *on the field* have you been in a natural disaster such as a tornado, hurricane, flood, or major earthquake?

        - One time
        - Two times
        - Three or more times

    c. How old were you at the time(s) of the natural disaster? (e.g., tornado, hurricane, flood, or major earthquake) (If you have more than three events, list the three most traumatic. If you only experienced one or two events, click *Not Applicable* on the other events.) (Child (0-10), Teen (11-19), Adult (20+), Not Applicable)

        - First Event
        - Second Event
        - Third Event

    d. Were you Injured by the natural disaster? (e.g., tornado, hurricane, flood, or major earthquake) (If you have more than three events, list the three most traumatic. If you only experienced one or two events, click *Not Applicable* on the other events.) (1Not at All, 2-3-4-5-6-7 severely, Not Applicable)

        - First Event
        - Second Event
        - Third Event

APPENDIX E: TRAUMA AND COPING SURVEY 263

e. Did you feel your life was threatened by the natural disaster? (e.g., tornado, hurricane, flood, or major earthquake) (If you have more than three events, list the three most traumatic. If you only experienced one or two events, click *Not Applicable* on the other events.) (1Not at All, 2–3–4–5–6–7 severely, Not Applicable)

- First Event
- Second Event
- Third Event

f. How traumatic was the natural disaster for you *at the time it happened*? (e.g., tornado, hurricane, flood, or major earthquake) (If you have more than three events, list the three most traumatic. If you only experienced one or two events, click *Not Applicable* on the other events.) (1Not at All, 2–3–4–5–6–7 severely, Not Applicable)

- First Event
- Second Event
- Third Event

g. How traumatic is the natural disaster *for you now*? (e.g., tornado, hurricane, flood, or major earthquake) (If you have more than three events, list the three most traumatic. If you only experienced one or two events, click Not Applicable on the other events.) (1Not at All, 2–3–4–5–6–7 severely, Not Applicable)

- First Event
- Second Event
- Third Event

h. Which of the following terms best describes the *first natural disaster* you experienced? (If you have more than three events, list the three most traumatic.)

- Tornado
- Hurricane
- Flood
- Major earthquake
- Other (please describe)

i. Which of the following terms best describes the *second natural disaster* you experienced? (If you have more than three events, list the three most traumatic. If you only experienced one or two events, click *Not Applicable* on the other events.)

- Tornado
- Hurricane
- Flood
- Major earthquake
- Other (please describe)

j. Which of the following terms best describes the *third natural disaster* you experienced? (If you have more than three events, list the three most traumatic. If you only experienced one or two events, click *Not Applicable* on the other events.)

- Tornado
- Hurricane
- Flood
- Major earthquake
- Other (please describe)

3. Have you been a victim of a violent crime such as rape, robbery, assault or a threat of violence such as pick-pocketing, burglary, intimidation, being put on a targeted list, or bugged?

- Yes
- No
- Decline to answer

a. How many times were you a victim of a violent crime? (e.g., rape, robbery, assault, pickpocketing, burglary, intimidation, being put on a targeted list, or bugged)

- One time
- Two times
- Three or more times

b. How many times *on field* were you a victim of a violent crime? (e.g., rape, robbery, assault, pick-pocketing, burglary, intimidation, being put on a targeted list, or bugged)?

- One time

- Two times
- Three or more times

c. How old were you at the time(s) of this/these violent crime(s)? (e.g., rape, robbery, assault, pick-pocketing, burglary, intimidation, being put on a targeted list, or bugged) (If you only experienced one or two events, click *Not Applicable* on the other events.) (Child (0-10), Teen (11-19), Adult (20+), Not Applicable)

- First Event
- Second Event
- Third Event

d. Were you Injured during the violent crime(s)? (e.g. rape, robbery, assault, pick-pocketing, burglary, intimidation, being put on a targeted list, or bugged) (If you have more than three events, list the three most traumatic. If you only experienced one or two events, click *Not Applicable* on the other events.) (1Not at All, 2-3-4-5-6-7 severely, Not Applicable)

- First Event
- Second Event
- Third Event

e. Did you feel your life was threatened by the violent crime(s)? (e.g., rape, robbery, assault, pickpocketing, burglary, intimidation, being put on a targeted list, or bugged) (If you have more than three events, list the three most traumatic. If you only experienced one or two events, click *Not Applicable* on the other events.) (1Not at All, 2-3-4-5-6-7 severely, Not Applicable)

- First Event
- Second Event
- Third Event

f. How traumatic was the violent crime(s) for you *at the time it happened*? (e.g., rape, robbery, assault, pick-pocketing, burglary, intimidation, being put on a targeted list, or bugged) (If you have more than three events, list the three most traumatic. If you only experienced one or two events, click *Not Applicable* on the other events.) (1Not at All, 2-3-4-5-6-7 severely, Not Applicable)

- First Event

- Second Event
- Third Event

g. How traumatic is the violent crime(s) *for you now*? (e.g., rape, robbery, assault, pickpocketing, burglary, intimidation, being put on a targeted list, or bugged) (If you have more than three events, list the three most traumatic. If you only experienced one or two events, click Not Applicable on the other events.) (1Not at All, 2–3–4–5–6–7 severely, Not Applicable)

- First Event
- Second Event
- Third Event

h. Which of the following terms best describes *the first violent crime* you experienced? (If you have more than three events, list the three most traumatic.)

- Rape
- Robbery
- Assault
- Pick-pocketed
- Burglary
- Intimidation
- On a targeted list
- Bugged
- Other (please describe)

i. Which of the following terms best describes *the second violent crime* you experienced? (If you have more than three events, list the three most traumatic. If you only experienced one or two events, click *Not Applicable* on the other events.)

- Rape
- Robbery
- Assault
- Pick-pocketed
- Burglary
- Intimidation

APPENDIX E: TRAUMA AND COPING SURVEY

- On a targeted list
- Bugged
- Other (please describe)

j. Which of the following terms best describes *the third violent crime* you experienced? (If you have more than three events, list the three most traumatic. If you only experienced one or two events, click *Not Applicable* on the other events.)

- Rape
- Robbery
- Assault
- Pick-pocketed
- Burglary
- Intimidation
- On a targeted list
- Bugged
- Other (please describe)

4. Did you ever live in a war zone where you received friendly or hostile incoming fire from small arms, artillery, rockets, mortars, or bombs?

- Yes
- No
- Decline to answer

   a. How many times while living in a war zone did you received friendly or hostile incoming fire from small arms, artillery, rockets, mortars, or bombs?

   - One time
   - Two times
   - Three or more times

   b. How many times while serving as a missionary have you lived in a war zone where you received friendly or hostile incoming fire from small arms, artillery, rockets, mortars, or bombs?

   - One time
   - Two times

- Three or more times

c. How old were you at the time(s) you received friendly or hostile incoming fire from small arms, artillery, rockets, mortars, or bombs? (If you only experienced one or two events, click *Not Applicable* on the other events.) (Child (0-10), Teen (11-19), Adult (20+), Not Applicable)

- First Event
- Second Event
- Third Event

d. Were you Injured when you received friendly or hostile incoming fire from small arms, artillery, rockets, mortars, or bombs? (1Not at All, 2–3–4–5–6–7 severely, Not Applicable)

- First Event
- Second Event
- Third Event

e. Did you feel your life was threatened while in a war zone where you received friendly or hostile incoming fire from small arms, artillery, rockets, mortars, or bombs? (1Not at All, 2–3–4–5–6–7 severely, Not Applicable)

- First Event
- Second Event
- Third Event

f. How traumatic was living in a war zone for you *at the time*? (where you received friendly or hostile incoming fire from small arms, artillery, rockets, mortars, or bombs) (1Not at All, 2–3–4–5–6–7 severely, Not Applicable)

- First Event
- Second Event
- Third Event

g. How traumatic is having lived in a war zone *for you now*? (where you received friendly or hostile incoming fire from small arms, artillery, rockets, mortars, or bombs) (1Not at All, 2–3–4–5–6–7 severely, Not Applicable)

- First Event

APPENDIX E: TRAUMA AND COPING SURVEY

- Second Event
- Third Event

5. Were you ever taken hostage?

   - Yes
   - No
   - Decline to answer

   a. How many times were you taken hostage?
      - One time
      - Two times
      - Three or more times

   b. How many times were you taken hostage on field?
      - One time
      - Two times
      - Three or more times

   c. How old were you at the time(s) you were taken hostage? (If you only experienced one or two events, click *Not Applicable* on the other events.) (Child (0-10), Teen (11-19), Adult (20+), Not Applicable)
      - First Event
      - Second Event
      - Third Event

   d. Were you Injured when you were taken hostage? (1Not at All, 2-3-4-5-6-7 severely, Not Applicable)
      - First Event
      - Second Event
      - Third Event

   e. Did you feel your life was threatened when you were taken hostage? (1Not at All, 2-3-4-5-6-7 severely, Not Applicable)
      - First Event
      - Second Event
      - Third Event

f. How traumatic was being taken hostage for you *at the time it happened*? (1Not at All, 2-3-4-5-6-7 severely, Not Applicable)

- First Event
- Second Event
- Third Event

g. How traumatic is having been taken hostage *for you now*? (1Not at All, 2-3-4-5-6-7 severely, Not Applicable)

- First Event
- Second Event
- Third Event

6. As a child, were you the victim of either physical or sexual abuse?

- Yes
- No
- Decline to answer

a. How old were you when the physical or sexual abuse began?

- One time
- Two times
- Three or more times

b. How old were you when the physical or sexual abuse ended?

- One time
- Two times
- Three or more times

c. Were you Injured by the physical or sexual abuse? (1Not at All, 2-3-4-5-6-7 severely, Not Applicable)

- First Event
- Second Event
- Third Event

d. Did you feel your life was threatened by the physical or sexual abuse? (1Not at All, 2-3-4-5-6-7 severely, Not Applicable)

- First Event

- Second Event
- Third Event

e. How traumatic was the physical or sexual abuse for you *at the time it happened*? (1Not at All, 2-3-4-5-6-7 severely, Not Applicable)

- First Event
- Second Event
- Third Event

f. How traumatic is the physical or sexual abuse event *for you now*? (1Not at All, 2-3-4-5-6-7 severely, Not Applicable)

- First Event
- Second Event
- Third Event

7. As an adult, have you had any unwanted sexual experiences that involved the threat or use of force?

- Yes
- No
- Decline to answer

a. How many times as an adult have you had any unwanted sexual experiences that involved the threat or use of force?

- One time
- Two times
- Three or more times

b. How many times on field, as an adult, have you had any unwanted sexual experiences that involved the threat or use of force?

- One time
- Two times
- Three or more times

c. How old were you at the time(s) you had an unwanted sexual experience that involved the threat or use of force? (If you only experienced one or two events, click *Not Applicable* on the other events.) (Child (0-10), Teen (11-19), Adult (20+), Not Applicable)

- First Event
- Second Event
- Third Event

d. Were you Injured when you had the unwanted sexual experience that involved the threat or use of force? (1Not at All, 2–3–4–5–6–7 severely, Not Applicable)

- First Event
- Second Event
- Third Event

e. Did you feel your life was threatened when you had the unwanted sexual experience that involved the threat or use of force? (1Not at All, 2–3–4–5–6–7 severely, Not Applicable)

- First Event
- Second Event
- Third Event

f. How traumatic was the unwanted sexual experience that involved the treat or use of force for you *at the time it happened*? (1Not at All, 2–3–4–5–6–7 severely, Not Applicable)

- First Event
- Second Event
- Third Event

g. How traumatic is the unwanted sexual experience that involved the threat or use of force *for you now*? (1Not at All, 2–3–4–5–6–7 severely, Not Applicable)

- First Event
- Second Event
- Third Event

8. As an adult have you ever been in a relationship in which you were abused either physically or otherwise?

- Yes
- No
- Decline to answer

APPENDIX E: TRAUMA AND COPING SURVEY 273

a. How many times as an adult have you been in a relationship in which you were abused either physically or otherwise?

- One time
- Two times
- Three or more times

b. How many times on field as an adult have you been in a relationship in which you were abused either physically or otherwise?

- One time
- Two times
- Three or more times

c. How old were you when the adult physical or other abuse began? (If you only experienced one or two events, click *Not Applicable* on the other events.) (Child (0-10), Teen (11-19), Adult (20+), Not Applicable)

- First Event
- Second Event
- Third Event

d. How old were you when the physical or other abuse ended? (0= Not Applicable)

- First Event
- Second Event
- Third Event

e. Were you Injured during the adult physical or other abuse? (1 Not at All, 2-3-4-5-6-7 severely, Not Applicable)

- First Event
- Second Event
- Third Event

f. Did you feel your life was threatened during the adult physical or other abuse? (1 Not at All, 2-3-4-5-6-7 severely, Not Applicable)

- First Event
- Second Event
- Third Event

g. How traumatic was the adult physical or other abuse *at the time it happened*? (1Not at All, 2-3-4-5-6-7 severely, Not Applicable)

- First Event
- Second Event
- Third Event

h. How traumatic is the adult physical or other abuse *for you now*? (1Not at All, 2-3-4-5-6-7 severely, Not Applicable)

- First Event
- Second Event
- Third Event

9. Have you witnessed someone who was mutilated, seriously injured, or violently killed?

- Yes
- No
- Decline to answer

a. How many times did you witness someone who was mutilated, seriously injured, or violently killed?

- One time
- Two times
- Three or more times

b. How many times on field did you witness someone who was mutilated, seriously injured, or violently killed?

- One time
- Two times
- Three or more times

c. How old were you at the time(s) you witnessed someone who was mutilated, seriously injured, or violently killed? (If you only experienced one or two events, click *Not Applicable* on the other events.) (Child (0-10), Teen (11-19), Adult (20+), Not Applicable)

- First Event
- Second Event
- Third Event

APPENDIX E: TRAUMA AND COPING SURVEY 275

   d. Were you Injured when you witnessed someone who was militated, seriously injured, or violently killed? (1Not at All, 2-3-4-5-6-7 severely, Not Applicable)

   - First Event
   - Second Event
   - Third Event

   e. Did you feel your life was threatened when you witnessed someone who was militated, seriously injured, or violently killed? (1Not at All, 2-3-4-5-6-7 severely, Not Applicable)

   - First Event
   - Second Event
   - Third Event

   f. How traumatic was witnessing someone who was militated, seriously injured, or violently killed for you *at the time of the event*? (1Not at All, 2-3-4-5-6-7 severely, Not Applicable)

   - First Event
   - Second Event
   - Third Event

   g. How traumatic is witnessing someone who was militated, seriously injured, or killed *for you now*? (1Not at All, 2-3-4-5-6-7 severely, Not Applicable)

   - First Event
   - Second Event
   - Third Event

10. Have you been in serious danger of losing your life or of being seriously injured?

    - Yes
    - No
    - Decline to answer

    a. How many times have you been in serious danger of losing your life or of being seriously injured?

       - One time

- Two times
- Three or more times

b. How many times on field have you been in serious danger of losing your life or of being seriously injured?

- One time
- Two times
- Three or more times

c. How old were you at the time(s) you were in serious danger of losing your life or of being seriously injured? (If you only experienced one or two events, click *Not Applicable* on the other events.) (Child (0-10), Teen (11-19), Adult (20+), Not Applicable)

- First Event
- Second Event
- Third Event

d. Were you Injured when you were in serious danger of losing your life? (1Not at All, 2-3-4-5-6-7 severely, Not Applicable)

- First Event
- Second Event
- Third Event

e. Did you feel your life was threatened when you were in serious danger? (1Not at All, 2-3-4-5-6-7 severely, Not Applicable)

- First Event
- Second Event
- Third Event

f. How traumatic was the serious danger of losing your life or of being seriously injured for you *at the time it happened*? (1Not at All, 2-3-4-5-6-7 severely, Not Applicable)

- First Event
- Second Event
- Third Event

g. How traumatic is the serious danger of losing your life or of being seriously injure event *for you now*? (1Not at All, 2-3-4-5-6-7 severely, Not Applicable)

APPENDIX E: TRAUMA AND COPING SURVEY

- First Event
- Second Event
- Third Event

h. What was the first serious danger of losing your life or being seriously injured event?

- Fill in the blank

i. What was the second serious danger of losing your life or being seriously injured event?

- Fill in the blank

j. What was the third serious danger of losing your life or being seriously injured event?

- Fill in the blank

11. Have you received news of the mutilation, serious injury, or violent/unexpected death of someone close to you?

- Yes
- No
- Decline to answer

a. How many times have you received news of the mutilation, serious injury, or
   - violent/unexpected death of someone close to you?
   - One time
   - Two times
   - Three or more times

b. How many times on field have you received news of the mutilation, serious injury, or violent/unexpected death of someone close to you?
   - One time
   - Two times
   - Three or more times

c. How old were you at the time(s) you received news of the mutilation, serious injury, or violent/unexpected death of someone close to you? (If you only experienced one or two events, click *Not*

Applicable on the other events.) (Child (0-10), Teen (11-19), Adult (20+), Not Applicable)

- First Event
- Second Event
- Third Event

d. Were you Injured when you received news of the mutilation, serious injury, or violent/unexpected death of someone close to you? (1Not at All, 2-3-4-5-6-7 severely, Not Applicable)

- First Event
- Second Event
- Third Event

e. Did you feel your life was threatened when you received news of the mutilation, serious injury, or violent/unexpected death of someone close to you? (1Not at All, 2-3-4-5-6-7 severely, Not Applicable)

- First Event
- Second Event
- Third Event

f. How traumatic was the news of the mutilation, serious injury, or violent/unexpected death of someone close to you *at the time it happened*? (1Not at All, 2-3-4-5-6-7 severely, Not Applicable)

- First Event
- Second Event
- Third Event

g. How traumatic is the event of the news of the mutilation, serious injury, or violent/unexpected death of someone close *to you now*? (1Not at All, 2-3-4-5-6-7 severely, Not Applicable)

- First Event
- Second Event
- Third Event

12. Have you ever had a traumatic conflict with a member(s) of the missionary fellowship?

- Yes
- No
- Decline to answer

a. How many times have you had a traumatic conflict with a member(s) of the missionary fellowship?

- One time
- Two times
- Three or more times

b. What term were you in at the time(s) of your traumatic conflict with the member(s) of the missionary fellowship? (1st Term through 10th Term, Not Applicable)

- First Event
- Second Event
- Third Event

c. If the traumatic conflict with the member(s) of the missionary fellowship is resolved, how long did it take? (1-6 months, 6 months to 1 year, 1-5 years, 5-10 years, 10-15 years, 15-20 years, 20+ years, Not Applicable)

- First Event
- Second Event
- Third Event

d. Did you feel your life was threatened when you had the traumatic conflict with the member(s) of the missionary fellowship? (1 Not at All, 2-3-4-5-6-7 severely, Not Applicable)

- First Event
- Second Event
- Third Event

e. How traumatic was this conflict with the member(s) of the missionary fellowship for you *at the time it happened*? (1 Not at All, 2-3-4-5-6-7 severely, Not Applicable)

- First Event
- Second Event
- Third Event

f. How traumatic is the conflict event with the member(s) of the missionary fellowship for you now? (1Not at All, 2-3-4-5-6-7 severely, Not Applicable)

- First Event
- Second Event
- Third Event

13. Have you ever had a traumatic conflict with a member(s) of the national church?

    - Yes
    - No
    - Decline to answer

    a. How many times have you had a traumatic conflict with a member(s) of the national church?

    - One time
    - Two times
    - Three or more times

    b. What term were you in at the time(s) of your traumatic conflict with the member(s) of the national church? (1st Term through 10th Term, Not Applicable)

    - First Event
    - Second Event
    - Third Event

    c. If the traumatic conflict with the member(s) of the national church is resolved, how long did it take? (1-6 months, 6 months to 1 year, 1-5 years, 5-10 years, 10-15 years, 15-20 years, 20+ years, Not Applicable)

    - First Event
    - Second Event
    - Third Event

    d. Did you feel your life was threatened when you had the traumatic conflict with the member(s) of the national church? (1Not at All, 2-3-4-5-6-7 severely, Not Applicable)

APPENDIX E: TRAUMA AND COPING SURVEY

- First Event
- Second Event
- Third Event

e. How traumatic was this conflict with the member(s) of the national church for you *at the time it happened*? (1Not at All, 2-3-4-5-6-7 severely, Not Applicable)

- First Event
- Second Event
- Third Event

f. How traumatic is the conflict event with the member(s) of the national church *for you now*? (1Not at All, 2-3-4-5-6-7 severely, Not Applicable)

- First Event
- Second Event
- Third Event

14. Have you ever had any other very traumatic event like these?

- Yes
- No
- Decline to answer

a. How many times have you had any other very traumatic event like these?

- One time
- Two times
- Three or more times

b. How old were you at the time(s) of this/these other traumatic event(s)? (If you only experienced one or two events, click *Not Applicable* on the other events.) (Child (0-10), Teen (11-19), Adult (20+), Not Applicable)

- First Event
- Second Event
- Third Event

c. Were you Injured during any of these other very traumatic event(s)? (1Not at All, 2-3-4-5-6-7 severely, Not Applicable)

- First Event
- Second Event
- Third Event

d. Did you feel your life was threatened during any of these other very traumatic event(s)? (1Not at All, 2-3-4-5-6-7 severely, Not Applicable)

- First Event
- Second Event
- Third Event

e. How traumatic was this other very traumatic event for you *at the time it happened*? (1Not at All, 2-3-4-5-6-7 severely, Not Applicable)

- First Event
- Second Event
- Third Event

f. How traumatic is this other very traumatic event *for you now*? (1Not at All, 2-3-4-5-6-7 severely, Not Applicable)

- First Event
- Second Event
- Third Event

g. What was the first traumatic event?

- Fill in the blank

h. What was the second traumatic event?

- Fill in the blank

i. What was the third traumatic event?

- Fill in the blank

15. Have you had any experience(s) like these that you feel you cannot speak about (note: you do not have to describe the event)?

- Yes

- No
- Decline to answer

a. How many times have you had any experience(s) like these that you feel you cannot speak about?

  - One time
  - Two times
  - Three or more times

b. How many times on field have you had any experience(s) like these that you feel you cannot speak about?

  - One time
  - Two times
  - Three or more times

c. How old were you at the time(s) of this/these event(s) that you feel you cannot speak about? (If you only experienced one or two events, click *Not Applicable* on the other events.) (Child (0-10), Teen (11-19), Adult (20+), Not Applicable)

  - First Event
  - Second Event
  - Third Event

d. Were you Injured during any of these experiences that you feel you cannot speak about? (1Not at All, 2-3-4-5-6-7 severely, Not Applicable)

  - First Event
  - Second Event
  - Third Event

e. Did you feel your life was threatened during any of these experiences that you feel you cannot speak about? (1Not at All, 2-3-4-5-6-7 severely, Not Applicable)

  - First Event
  - Second Event
  - Third Event

f. How traumatic was/were any of these experiences that you feel you cannot speak about *at the time it/they happened*? (1Not at All, 2-3-4-5-6-7 severely, Not Applicable)

- First Event
- Second Event
- Third Event

g. How traumatic is/are the event(s) that you feel you cannot speak about *for you now*? (1Not at All, 2-3-4-5-6-7 severely, Not Applicable)

- First Event
- Second Event
- Third Event

16. If you answered "yes" to one or more of the questions above, which was the most traumatic thing to have happen to you?

    - Fill in the blank

17. Did you answer "yes" to more than one question above while referring to the same event? If you did what was the event?

    - Fill in the blank

18. If you answered "no" to all questions, describe briefly the most traumatic thing that has happened to you. (My most traumatic event is:)

    - Fill in the blank

    a. How many times did this traumatic event happen to you?
       - One time
       - Two times
       - Three or more times

    b. How many times did this traumatic event happen to you on field?
       - One time
       - Two times
       - Three or more times

c. How old were you at the time(s) of this/these traumatic event(s)? (If you only experienced one or two events, click *Not Applicable* on the other events.) (Child (0-10), Teen (11-19), Adult (20+), Not Applicable)

- First Event
- Second Event
- Third Event

d. Were you Injured during this traumatic event? (1Not at All, 2-3-4-5-6-7 severely, Not Applicable)

- First Event
- Second Event
- Third Event

e. Did you feel your life was threatened during this traumatic event? (1Not at All, 2-3-4-5-6-7 severely, Not Applicable)

- First Event
- Second Event
- Third Event

f. How traumatic was this event for you *at the time it happened*? (1Not at All, 2-3-4-5-6-7 severely, Not Applicable)

- First Event
- Second Event
- Third Event

g. How traumatic is this event *for you now*? (1Not at All, 2-3-4-5-6-7 severely, Not Applicable)

- First Event
- Second Event
- Third Event

PTSD Check List:

Great job getting to this point!

The next 18 questions will look at the Post Traumatic Stress you had at the time of the trauma and within the past month. Think about the most

APPENDIX E: TRAUMA AND COPING SURVEY

traumatic event you have ever had and then answer each question based on how you felt then (at the most difficult period of adjustment) and how you feel now (during the past month).

Not at all, Once per week or less/a little, 2 to 4 times per week/somewhat, 5 or more times per week/very much.

- During the most difficult time of adjustment.
- During the past month.
- 1 Not at All, 2–3–4–5–6–7 severely, Not Applicable.

1. Have you had recurrent or intrusive distressing thoughts or recollections about the trauma?
2. Have you been having recurrent bad dreams or nightmares about the trauma?
3. Have you had the experience of suddenly reliving the trauma, flashbacks of it, acting or feeling as if it were re-occurring?
4. Have you been intensely EMOTIONALLY upset when reminded of the trauma (includes anniversary reactions)?
5. Have you been having intense PHYSICAL reactions (e.g. sweaty palms, heart palpitations) when reminded of the trauma?
6. Have you persistently been making efforts to avoid thoughts or feelings associated with the trauma?
7. Have you persistently been making efforts to avoid activities, situations, or places that remind you of the trauma?
8. Are there any important aspects about the trauma that you still cannot recall?
9. Have you markedly lost interest in free time activities since the trauma?
10. Have you felt detached or cut off from others around you since the trauma?
11. Have you felt that your ability to experience the whole range of emotions is impaired (e.g. unable to have loving feelings)?
12. Have you felt that any future plans or hopes have changed because of the trauma (e.g. no career, marriage, children, or long life)?
13. Have you had persistent difficulty falling or staying asleep?
14. Have you been continuously irritable or have outbursts of anger?
15. Have you had persistent difficulty concentrating?

APPENDIX E: TRAUMA AND COPING SURVEY

16. Are you overly alert (e.g. check to see who is around you, etc.) since the trauma?
17. Have you been jumpier, more easily startled since the trauma?
18. How traumatic was this event for you at the time?

Coping Section:

You are almost done! Thanks for hanging in there for me!

This last section is looking at how you cope with traumatic events. There are 60 questions looking at different types of coping mechanisms. This may seem like a lot but if you do not over think the question and go with your first response you will be able to get through them very quickly. Answering these questions will help me determine how missionaries stay on field after going through traumatic events.

Satisfaction with life Scale (SWLS)

Choose one: Strongly disagree, Moderately disagree, Disagree, Neither agree or disagree, Agree, Moderately agree, Strongly Agree

1. In most ways my life is close to my ideal.
2. The conditions of my life are excellent.
3. I am satisfied with my life.
4. So far I have gotten the important things I want in life.
5. If I could live my life over, I would change almost nothing.

Brief Religious Coping Scale (B-RCOPE)

Choose One: Not at all true, Applies slightly, if at all, Applies somewhat, Applies very Strongly, Not Applicable. (Choose *Not Applicable* if you *never* went through a traumatic event.)

1. When I went through a traumatic event I looked for a stronger connection with God.
2. When I went through a traumatic event I sought God's love and care.
3. When I went through a traumatic event I sought help from God in letting go of my anger.
4. When I went through a traumatic event I tried to put my plans into action together with God.

5. When I went through a traumatic event I tried to see how God might be trying to strengthen me in this situation.

6. When I went through a traumatic event I asked forgiveness for my sins.

7. When I went through a traumatic event I focused on religion to stop worrying about my problems.

8. When I went through a traumatic event I felt punished by God for my lack of devotion.

9. When I went through a traumatic event I wondered whether God had abandoned me.

10. When I went through a traumatic event I wondered what I did for God to punish me.

11. When I went through a traumatic event I questioned God's love for me.

12. When I went through a traumatic event I wondered whether my (missionary fellowship/ national church/ AGWM) had abandoned me.

13. When I went through a traumatic event I decided the devil made this happen.

14. When I went through a traumatic event I questioned the power of God.

Ego-Resiliency Scale (ESC)

Choose One: Not at all true, Applies slightly, if at all, Applies somewhat, Applies very Strongly, Not Applicable.

1. I am generous with my friends.
2. I quickly get over and recover from being startled.
3. I enjoy dealing with new and unusual situations.
4. I usually succeed in making a favorable impression on people.
5. I enjoy trying new foods I have never tasted before.
6. I am regarded as a very energetic person.
7. I like to take different paths to familiar places.
8. I am more curious than most people.
9. Most of the people I meet are likable.
10. I usually think carefully about something before acting.

11. I like to do new and different things.
12. My daily life is full of things that keep me interested.
13. I would be willing to describe myself as a pretty "strong" personality.
14. I get over my anger at someone reasonably quickly.

Resiliency Appraisal Scale (RAS)

Choose one: Strongly disagree, Disagree, Neither agree or disagree, Agree, Strongly Agree

1. If I were to have problems, I have people I could turn to.
2. My family or friends are very supportive of me.
3. In difficult situations, I can manage my emotions.
4. I can put up with my negative emotions.
5. When faced with a problem I can usually find a solution.
6. If I were in trouble, I know of others who would be able to help me.
7. I can generally solve problems that occur.
8. I can control my emotions.
9. I can usually find a way of overcoming problems.
10. I could find family or friends who listen to me if I needed them to.
11. If faced with a setback, I could probably find a way around the problem.
12. I can handle my emotions.

Resiliency Scale (RS)

Choose one: Strongly disagree, Disagree, Neither agree or disagree, Agree, Strongly Agree

1. I bounce back from performing poorly and succeed.
2. I bounce back from a major injury and succeed.
3. I am able to adapt to different training situations and be successful.
4. I am consistently successful week after week.

Development and Validation of Calling and Vocation Questionnaire (CVQ)

Choose one: Not at all true of me, Somewhat true of me, Mostly true of me, Absolutely true of me.

1. I believe that I have been called to my current missionary career.
2. I am searching for my calling in my missionary career.
3. My missionary career helps me live out my life's purpose.
4. I do not believe that God has helped guide me to my missionary career.
5. I was drawn by God to pursue my current missionary career.
6. I yearn for a sense of calling in my career.
7. I see my missionary career as a path to purpose in life.
8. I am trying to figure out what my calling is in the context of my missionary career.
9. I am trying to identify the area of work I was meant to pursue.
10. My missionary career is an important part of my life's meaning.
11. I am pursuing my missionary career because I believe I have been called to do so.
12. I try to live out my life purpose when I am working.

Appendix F
Informed Consent

Risks or Discomforts:

Participating in this survey could have minimal physical and/or psychological risk. The survey asks about traumatic episodes and material of a personal nature. The participant can at any time refuse, without explanation, to answer any question or discuss any topic that could cause distress, emotional discomfort, anxiety, stress, or seems too private.

Benefits:

Participants may not benefit directly from their involvement in this research; however, the potential benefits of participation include the possibility that their responses may result in enhancement in missionary trauma education and improved member care.

Confidentiality:

All survey responses and other research materials are confidential, and only the investigator and her professors will have access to the information, which will be stored in a locked facility at Evangel University. Electronic files will be stored digitally on the servers of Evangel University in Springfield, Missouri or on the secure servers administered by QualtricsÒ.[1] No personnel without an expressed right to access the materials will be granted access. Every effort will be made to ensure data security and respondent confidentiality. Participants' names will not be used in any published reports of this research, and individual cases will not be reported, even anonymously.

Procedures for Withdrawal of Participants:

Participation in this study is voluntary. Withdrawal or refusal to contribute will not incur any penalty or loss of benefits. Participants may discontinue

---

1. See http://www.qualtrics.com/university/researchsuite

involvement at any time by notifying the investigator in writing of their desire to withdraw from the study.

New Findings:

Following the conclusion of this study, participants may contact Valerie A. Rance for results of this study and for information on follow-up studies.

Research-Related Injuries:

Injuries resulting from participation in this study are the sole responsibility of the participant. The Assemblies of God Theological Seminary maintains no responsibility for any injuries resulting from, or related to, this research. In the event of injury, the cost of health care services is the responsibility of the participant.

Questions:

If you have any questions about this research project, please call Valerie A. Rance at [number blocked for privacy reasons] or email her at rancev@evangel.edu. If you have any questions or concerns about your rights as a research participant in this study, please direct them to Dr. Johan Mostert, the Institutional Review Board Manager at the Assemblies of God Theological Seminary, Counseling Office at (417) 268-1073.

I AM 18 YEARS OR OLDER AND HAVE READ AND UNDERSTAND THE INFORMATION IN THIS FORM. I HAVE BEEN ENCOURAGED TO ASK QUESTIONS AND ALL OF MY QUESTIONS HAVE BEEN ANSWERED TO MY SATISFACTION. BY CLICKING BELOW, I AGREE VOLUNTARY TO PARTICIPATE IN THE SURVEY RESEARCH DESCRIBED ABOVE. I UNDERSTAND THAT ALL SURVEY RESPONSES PROVIDED TO VALERIE A. RANCE WILL BE KEPT CONFIDENTIAL AND THAT I MAY PRINT A COPY OF THIS CONSENT FOR MY OWN RECORDS.

Begin the Survey

No, I do not want to participate (please indicate why below).

Bibliography

Abbassi, Amir, and James Stacks. "Culture and Anxiety: A Cross-Cultural Study Among College Students." *Journal of Professional Counseling: Practice, Theory, and Research* 35 (2007) 26–37.
Abu-Raiya, Hisham, and Kenneth I. Pargament. "Religious Coping Among Diverse Religions: Commonalities and Divergences." *Psychology of Religion and Spirituality* 7 (2015) 24–33.
Adejunmo, Adebayo O. "The Need for Cultural Contextualization in Establishing Psychological Wellness or Illness." In *Psychological Well-being*, edited by Ingrid E. Wells, 213–21. New York: Nova Science, 2010.
Adewuya, J. Ayodeji. "The Sacrificial-Missiological Function of Paul's Sufferings in the Context of 2 Corinthians." In *Paul as Missionary: Identity, Activity, Theology, and Practice*, edited by Trevor Burke and Brian Rosner, 88–98. New York: T. & T. Clark, 2011.
AGWM. "Assemblies of God World Missions." www.worldmissions.ag.org.
Alden, Robert L. "Chiastic Psalms (III): A Study in the Mechanics of Semitic Poetry in Psalms 101–150." *JETS* 21 (1978) 199–210.
Aldwin, Carolyn M. "Stress and Coping Across the Lifespan." In *The Oxford Handbook of Stress, Health, and Coping*, edited by Susan Folkman, 15–34. New York: Oxford University Press, 2011.
———. *Stress, Coping, and Development: An Integrative Perspective.* New York: Guilford, 1994.
Allen, Frank. "Why Do They Leave? Reflections on Attrition." In *Helping Missionaries Grow: Readings in Mental Health and Missions*, edited by Kelly O'Donnell and Michele O'Donnell, 421–31. Pasadena: William Carey Library, 1988.
Allen, Jon. *Coping with Trauma: A Guide to Self-Understanding.* Washington, DC: American Psychiatric, 1995.
Allender, Dan B., and Tempelton Longman. *The Cry of the Soul: How Our Emotions Reveal Our Deepest Questions About God.* Colorado Springs: Navpress, 1994.
American Psychiatric Association. "Definition of Trauma." http://www.apa.org/topics/trauma.
———. *Diagnostic and Statistical Manual of Mental Disorders (DSM-5).* Washington, DC: American Psychiatric, 2013.
Appley, Motimer H., and Richard Trumbull. "On the Concept of Psychological Stress." In *Stress and Coping: An Anthology*, edited by Alan Monat and Richard S. Lazarus, 58–66. New York: Columbia University Press, 1977.

Arndersson-Arnten, Ann-Christine, et al. "Influence of Affective Personality Type and Gender Upon Coping Behavior, Mood, and Stress." *Individual Differences Research* 6 (2008) 139–68.

Aten, Jamie D. "Disaster Spiritual and Emotional Care in Professional Psychology: A Christian Integrative Approach." *Journal of Psychology and Theology* 40 (2012) 131–35.

Bagley, Robert. "The Impact of Trauma and Traumatic Stress on Missionaries of the Wesleyan Church." PhD diss., Trinity International University, 2000.

———. "Trauma and Traumatic Stress Among Missionaries." *Journal of Psychology and Theology* 31 (2003) 97–112.

Baker, Tony. "Elijah—A God Just Like His." *Evangel* 20 (2002) 2–4.

Balswick, Jack, and Judith Balswick. *Families In Pain: Working Through the Hurts.* Grand Rapids: Fleming H. Revell, 1997.

———. *The Family: A Christian Perspective on the Contemporary Home.* Grand Rapids: Baker Academic, 1998.

Banziger, Sarah, et al. "Praying and Coping: The Relation Between Varieties of Praying and Religious Coping Styles." *Mental Health, Religion and Culture* 11 (2008) 101–18.

Barber-Stirling, Candace Mary. "The Effects of Exposure to Traumatic Events in Missionary Children Upon Their Spirituality as Adult Missionary Kids Living in Their Country of Passport." PhD diss., Acadia Divinity College, 2008.

Barclay, William. *The Master's Men.* Nashville: Abingdon, 1959.

Barnett, Becca. "How Christian Trauma Survivors Construct Models of God and Solutions to the Problem of Evil." PhD diss., Alliant International University, 2003.

Barnett, Keri L., et al. "Psychological and Spiritual Predictors of Domains of Functioning and Effectiveness of Short-term Missionaries." *Journal of Psychology and Theology* 33 (2005) 27–40.

Barnett, Paul. *Paul Missionary of Jesus.* Grand Rapids: Eerdmans, 2008.

Bendikesen, Brittany Anne. "PTSD and Religious Coping: Clinical Implications for Missionaries and Relief Workers." PhD diss., Biola University, 2015.

Benight, Charles. "Understanding Human Adaptation to Traumatic Stress Exposure: Beyond the Medical Model." *Psychological Trauma: Theory, Research, Practice, and Policy* 4 (2012) 1–8.

Bennett, Janet M. "On Becoming a Global Soul: A Path to Engagement During Study Abroad." In *Developing Intercultural Competence and Transformation: Theory, Research, and Application in International Education,* edited by Victor Savicki, 13–31. Sterling, VA: Stylus, 2008.

Beste, Jennifer. *God and the Victim: Traumatic Intrusions on Grace and Freedom.* New York: Oxford University Press, 2007.

Bible Hub. "982. Batch." http://biblehub.com/hebrew/982.htm.

———. "Joshua 2:1." http://biblehub.com/commentaries/joshua/2-1.htm.

Bjorck, Jeferey P., et al. "The Adolescent Religious Coping Scale: Development, Validation, and Cross-validation." *Journal of Child Family Study* 19 (2010) 343–59.

Bjorck, Jeferey P., and Jean-Woo Kim. "Religious Coping, Religious Support, and Psychological Functioning Among Short-term Missionaries." *Mental Health, Religion and Culture* 12 (2009) 611–26.

Blaikie, Norman, and Paul Kelsen. "Locating Self and Giving Meaning to Existence: A Typology of Paths to Spiritual Well-being Based on New Religious Movements in Australia." In *Spiritual Well-being: Sociological Perspectives*, edited by David Moberg, 133–51. Washington, DC: University Press of America, 1979.

Blocher, Detlef. "ReMAP I (Reducing Missionary Attrition Project)." In *Worth Keeping: Global Perspectives on Best Practice in Missionary Retention*, edited by Rob Hay et al., 9–22. Pasadena: William Carey Library, 2007.

Blocher, Detlef, and Jonathan Lewis. "Further Findings in the Research Data." In *Too Valuable to Lose: Exploring the Causes and Cures of Missionary Attrition*, edited by William Taylor, 105–26. Pasadena: William Carey Library, 1997.

Block, Jack, and Adam M. Kremen. "IQ and Ego-Resiliency: Conceptual and Empirical Connections and Separateness." *Journal of Personality and Social Psychology* 70 (1996) 349–61.

Block, Jeanne H., and Jack Block. "The Role of Ego-control and Ego-resiliency in the Origination of Behavior." In *The Minnesota Symposia on Child Psychology*, edited by W. Andrew Collins, 39–101. Hillsdale, NJ: Erlbaum, 1978.

Blomquist, Martys. "P =Parental Support; Caring for Children During Times of War." In *Healing the Children of War: A Handbook for Ministry to Children Who have Suffered Deep Traumas*, edited by Phyllis Kilbourn, 197–214. Monrovia: Marc, 1995.

Bolin, Thomas. *Freedom Beyond Forgiveness: The Book of Jonah Re-Examined*. Sheffield, England: Sheffield Academic, 1997.

Bonanno, George A. "Grief, Trauma, and Resilience." In *Violent Death: Resilience and Intervention Beyond the Crisis*, edited by E. K. Rynearson, 31–46. New York: Routledge, 2006.

———. "Loss, Trauma, and Human Resilience: Have We Underestimated the Human Capacity to Thrive after Extremely Aversive Events?" *Psychological Trauma: Theory, Research, Practice, and Policy* 1 (2008) 101–13.

———. "Resilience in the Face of Potential Trauma." *Current Directions in Psychological Science* 14 (2005) 135–38.

Bonanno, George A., and Anthony D. Mancini. "Bereavement-Related Depression and PTSD: Evaluating Interventions." In *Psychological Interventions in Times of Crisis*, edited by Laura Barbanel, and Robert Sternberb, 37–55. New York: Springer, 2006.

Bonanno, George A., and Stacey Kaltman. "Toward an Integrative Perspective on Bereavement." *Psychological Bulletin* 125 (1999) 760–76.

Bonanno, George. A., et al. "Coping Flexibility and Trauma: The Perceived Ability to Cope with Trauma (PACT) Scale." *Psychological Trauma: Theory, Research, Practice, and Policy* 3 (2011) 117–29.

———. "Psychological Resilience after Disaster: New York City in the Aftermath of the September 11th Terrorist Attack." *Psychological Science* 17 (2006) 181–86.

———. "Resilience to Loss and Chronic Grief: A Prospective Study from Pre-Loss to 18 Month Post-Loss." *Journal of Personality and Social Psychology* 83 (2002) 1150–64.

———. "Self-Enhancement Among High-Exposure Survivors of the September 11th Terrorist Attack: Resilience or Social Maladjustment?" *Journal of Personality and Social Psychology* 88 (2005) 984–98.

———. "What Predicts Psychological Resilience After Disaster? The Role of Demographics, Resources, and Life Stress." *Journal of Consulting and Clinical Psychology* 75 (2007) 671–82.

Bormann, Jill E., et al. "Spiritual Wellbeing Mediates PTSD Change in Veterans with Military-Related PTSD." *International Society of Behavioral Medicine* 19 (2012) 496–502.

Bowland, Sharon, et al. "Evaluation of a Spiritually Focused Intervention with Older Trauma Survivors." *Social Work* 57 (2012) 73–82.

Brensinger, Terry. *Believers Church Bible Commentary: Judges*. Scottdale, PA: Herald, 1999.

Breslau, Joshua. "Cultures of Trauma: Anthropological Views of Posttraumatic Stress Disorder in International Health." *Culture, Medicine, and Psychiatry* 28 (2004) 113–26.

Breslau, Naomi, et al. "Traumatic Events and Post Traumatic Stress Disorder in an Urban Population of Young Adults." *Archives of General Psychiatry* 48 (1991) 216–22.

Brewer, Monroe. "The Lifelong Learning Link: Twelve Reasons for Continuous Education for Missionaries." *Missiology: An International Review* 19 (1991) 185–202.

Brison, Susan. *Aftermath: Violence and the Remaking of Self*. Princeton: Princeton University Press, 2002.

Bromiley, Geoffrey. *The International Standard Bible Encyclopedia*. Grand Rapids: Eerdmans, 1982.

Brueggemann, Walter. "Epilogue." In *The Bible on Suffering: Social and Political Implications*, edited by Anthony Tambasco, 211–20. New York: Paulist, 2001.

Brunet, Alain, et al. "The Effects of Initial Trauma Exposure on the Symptomatic Response to a Subsequent Trauma." *Canadian Journal of Philosophy* 32 (2001) 97–102.

Bryant-Davis, Thema, and Eunice Wong. "Faith to Move Mountains: Religious Coping, Spirituality, and Interpersonal Trauma Recovery." *American Psychologist* 68 (2013) 657–84.

Bryant-Davis, Thema, et al. "Religiosity, Spirituality, and Trauma Recovery in the Lives of Children and Adolescents." *Professional Psychology: Research and Practice* 43 (2012) 306–14.

Bryant, Richard A. "Acute Stress Disorder: Course, Epidemiology, Assessment, and Treatment." In *Early Intervention for Trauma and Traumatic Loss*, edited by Brett T. Litz, 15–33. New York: Guilford, 2004.

Brynjolfson, Robert, and Jonathan Lewis. *Integral Ministry Training Design and Evaluation*. Pasadena: William Carey Library, 2006.

Buechner, Frederick. *Telling Secrets*. New York: HarperCollins, 1991.

Calhoun, Lawrence G., and Richard C. Tedeschi. "Early Posttraumatic Interventions: Facilitating Possibilities for Growth." In *Posttraumatic Stress Intervention: Challenges, Issues, and Perspectives*, edited by John M. Volanti, et al., 135–52. Springfield, IL: Charles C. Thomas, 2000.

Calhoun, Lawrence G., and Richard G. Tedeschi. *Facilitating Posttraumatic Growth: A Clinician's Guide*. Mahwah, NJ: Erlbaum, 1999.

———. "Posttraumatic Growth: Future Directions." In *Posttraumatic Growth: Positive Changes in the Aftermath of Crisis*, edited by Richard G. et al., 215–38. Mahwah, NJ: Erlbaum, 1998.

Camp, Clair A., et al. "Missionary Perspectives on the Effectiveness of Current Member Care Practices." *Journal of Psychology and Theology* 42 (2014) 359–68.

Carlson, Bonnie E. "A Stress and Coping Approach to Intervention with Abused Women." *Family Relations* 46 (1997) 291–98.
Carr, Karen. "Crisis Intervention for Missionaries." *Evangelical Missions Quarterly*. 33 no. 4 (October 1997) 450–58.
———. "Critical Incident Stress Debriefings for Cross-Cultural Workers: Harmful or Helpful?" www.mmct.org.
———. "The Mobile Member Care Team as a Means of Responding to Crisis: West Africa." In *Psychological Interventions in Times of Crisis*, edited by Bob Sternberg and Laura Barbanel, 75–97. New York: Springer, 2006.
———. "Resources for Effective Support: Effective Community Support." In *Trauma and Resilience: A Handbook*, edited by Frauke C. Schaefer, and Charles A. Schaefer, 1637–2030. Fresno, CA: Corderopress, 2012.
———. "Resources for Effective Support: Normal Reactions after Trauma." In *Trauma and Resilience: A Handbook*, edited by Frauke C. Schaefer and Charles A. Schaefer, 1022–626. Fresno, CA: Corderopress, 2012.
———. "Resources for Effective Support: Personal Resilience." In *Trauma and Resilience: A Handbook*, edited by Frauke C. Schaefer, and Charles A. Schaefer, 2042–2280. Fresno, CA: Corderopress, 2012.
———. "Trauma and Post-Traumatic Stress Disorder among Missionaries: How to Recognize, Prevent, and Treat it." *Evangelical Missions Quarterly* 30 (1994) 246–55.
Carr, Karen, and Frauke Schaefer. "Coping with Stress and Trauma in Crisis Cultural Missions: A Brief Summary for Missionaries in West Africa." http:// www.mmct.org.
———. "Trauma and Traumatic Stress in Cross-Cultural Missions: How to Promote Resilience." *Evangelical Missiological Society* 46 (2010) 278–85.
Casey, Maurice. *Jesus of Nazareth: An Independent Historian's Account of His Life and Teaching*. New York: T. & T. Clark, 2010.
Center for Disease Control and Prevention. "Health-Related Quality of Life: Well-being Concepts." www.cdc.gov/hrqol/wellbeing.htm.
Chatard, Armand, et al. "Extent of Trauma Exposure and PTSD Symptom Severity as Predictors of Anxiety-Buffer Functioning." *Psychologieal Trauma: Theory, Research, Practice, and Policy* 4 (2012) 47–55.
Chen, Joanne. "A Literature Review on Missionary Functioning: An Ecological Perspective." PhD diss., Azusa Pacific University, 2016.
Chisholm, Thomas. "Great is Thy Faithfulness." Carol Stream, IL: Hope, 1923.
Clinton, Timothy, et al. *Caring for People God's Way: Personal and Emotional Issues, Addictions, Grief, and Trauma*. Nashville: Thomas Nelson, 2005.
Collins, S., and A. Long. "Too Tired to Care? The Psychological Effects of Working with Trauma." *Journal of Psychiatric and Mental Health Nursing* 10 (2003) 17–27.
Connor-Smith, Jennifer, and Celeste Flachsbart. "Relations Between Personality and Coping: A Meta-Analysis." *Journal of Personality and Social Psychology* 93 (2007) 1080–107.
Corey, Gerald, et al. *Issues and Ethics in the Helping Professions*. Stanford, CT: Cengage Learning, 2015.
Craig, C. D., and G. Sprang. "Compassion Satisfaction, Compassion Fatigue, and Burnout in a National Sample of Trauma Treatment Therapists." *Anxiety, Stress, and Coping* 23 (2010) 319–39.

Crawford, Nancy, and Helen M. DeVries. "Relationship Between Role Perception and Well-Being in Married Female Missionaries." *Journal of Psychology and Theology* 33 (2005) 187–98.

Creamer, Mark. "A Cognitive Processing Formulation of Posttrauma Reactions." In *Beyond Trauma: Cultural and Societal Dynamics*, edited by Rolf J. Kleber et al., 55–74. New York: Plenum, 1995.

Crenshaw, David. "Neuroscience and Trauma Treatment: Implications for Creative Arts Therapists." In *Expressive and Creative Arts Methods for Trauma Survivors*, edited by Lois Carey, 21–40. London: Jessica Kengsley, 2006.

Davis, Christopher G., et al. "Making Sense of Loss and Benefiting from the Experience: Two Construals of Meaning." *Journal of Personality and Social Psychology* 75 (1998) 561–74.

Declaisse-Walford, Nancy, et al. *The Book of Psalms*. Grand Rapids: Eerdmans, 2014.

Deighton, Russell, et al. "Factors Affecting Burnout and Compassion Fatigue in Psychotherapists Treating Torture Survivors: Is the Therapist's Attitude to Working Through Trauma Relevant?" *Journal of Traumatic Stress* 20 (2007) 63–75.

Denney, Ryan M., et al. "Post Traumatic Spiritual Growth: A Phenomenological Study of Cancer Survivors." *Mental Health, Religion and Culture* 14 (2011) 371–91.

Devenish, Stuart. "The Contribution of Spirituality to our Understanding of Human Flourishing: The Perspective of Christian Theology." In *Beyond Well-Being: Spirituality and Human Flourishing*, edited by Maurcon Miner, et al., 49–64. Charlotte, NC: Information Age, 2012.

Devilly, Grant, et al. "Vicarious Trauma, Secondary Traumatic Stress or Simply Burnout? Effect of Trauma Therapy on Mental Health Professionals." *The Royal Australian and New Zealand College of Psychiatrists* 43 (2009) 373–85.

Diener, Ed, et al. "The Satisfaction with Life Scale." *Journal of Personality Assessments*. 49 (1985) 71–75.

———. "The Satisfaction with Life Scale." http://www.abiebr.com/set/17-assessment-outcomes-following-acquiredtraumatic-brain-injury/1719-satisfaction-life-scale.

Dik, Byron J., et al. "Development and Validation of the Calling and Vocation Questionnaire (CVQ) and Brief Calling Scale (BCS)." *Journal of Career Assessment* 20 (2012) 242–63.

———. "Development and Validation of the Calling and Vocation Questionnaire (CVQ) and Brief Calling Scale (BCS)." https://www.researchgate.net/publication/254111004_Development_and_Validation_of_the_Calling_and_Vocation_Questionnaire_CVQ_and_Brief_Calling_Scale_BCS.

Dodds, Lois, and Lawrence Dodds. "How People Get Sick and Wounded: Levels of Prevention and Intervention." Mental Health and Missions Conference. Angola, Indiana, November 19–21, 1993.

———. "Love and Survival: In Life, in Missions." Mental Health and Missions Conference. Angola, Indiana, November 16–20, 1999.

Donovan, Kathy, and Ruth Myors. "Reflections on Attrition in Career Missionaries: A Generational Perspective into the Future." In *Too Valuable to Lose: Exploring the Causes and Cures of Missionary Attrition*, edited by William Taylor, 41–74. Pasadena: William Carey Library, 1997.

Drake, David. "The Art of Thinking Narratively: Implications for Coaching Psychology and Practice." *Australian Psychologist* 42 (2007) 283–94.

Dulin, Patrick, and Teesha Passmore. "Avoidance of Potentially Traumatic Stimuli Mediate the Relationship Between Accumulated Lifetime Trauma and Late-Life Depression and Anxiety." *Journal of Traumatic Stress* 23 (2010) 296–99.

Dunn, James. *Theology of Paul the Apostle.* New York: T. & T. Clark, 1998.

Dybdahl, Ragnhild. "Psychosocial Assistance to Civilians in War: The Bosnian Experience." In *Psychological Interventions in Times of Crisis,* edited by Laura Barbanel, and Robert Sternberb, 133–49. New York: Springer, 2006.

Ehring, Thomas, et al. "The Role of Rumination and Reduced Concreteness in the Maintenance of Posttraumatic Stress Disorder and Depression Following Trauma." *Cognitive Theory Research* 32 (2008) 488–506.

Ellison, Christopher G., et al. "Religious Resources, Spiritual Struggles, and Mental Health in a Nationwide Sample of PCUSA Clergy." *Pastoral Psychology* 59 (2010) 287–304.

Ellsworth, Robert B., and Janet B. Ellsworth. "Church that Enhance Spiritually and Wellbeing." *International Journal of Applied Psychoanalytic Studies* 7 (2010) 131–42.

Elmer, Duane. *Cross-Cultural Servanthood: Serving the World in Christlike Humility.* Downers Grove, IL: InterVarsity, 2006.

Eschleman, Kevin, et al. "A Meta-Analytic Examination of Hardiness." *International Journal of Stress Management* 17 (2010) 277–307.

Farmer, Paul. *Pathologies of Power: Health, Human Rights, and the New War on the Poor.* Berkeley: University of California Press, 2005.

Fassin, Didier, and Richard Rechtman. *The Empire of Trauma: An Inquiry into the Condition of Victim Hood.* Translated by Rachel Gomme. New Jersey: Princeton University Press, 2009.

Fazio, Robert J., and Lauren M. Fazio. "Growth Through Loss: Promoting Healing and Growth in the Face of Trauma, Crisis, and Loss." *Journal of Loss and Trauma* 10 (2005) 221–52.

Fee, Gordon. *God's Empowering Presence: The Holy Spirit in the Letters of Paul.* Peabody, MA: Hendrickson, 1994.

Feldman, David B., and Lee Daniel Cravat. *Supersurvivors: The Surprising Link Between Suffering and Success.* Sydney, Australia: HarperCollins, 2014.

Figley, Charles. *Helping Traumatized Families.* San Francisco: Oxford, 1989.

Figley, Charles, and Kathleen Figley. "Stemming the Tide of Trauma Systemically: The Role of Family Therapy." *The Australian and New Zealand and Journal of Family Therapy* 30 (2009) 173–83.

Fischer, Peter, et al. "Relationship Between Religious Identity and Preferred Coping Strategies: An Examination of the Relative Importance of Interpersonal and Intrapersonal Coping in Muslim and Christian Faiths." *Review of General Psychology* 14 (2012) 365–81.

Flach, Frederic. "The Resilience Hypothesis and Post Traumatic Stress Disorder." In *Post Traumatic Stress Disorder: Etiology, Phenomenology, and Treatment,* edited by Marion E. Wolf and Aron D. Mosnaim, 40–65. Washington, DC: American Psychiatric Association, 1990.

Flaskerud, J., and G. Uman. "Acculturation and its Effect on Self-Esteem Among Immigrant Latina Women." *Behavioral Medicine* 22 (1996) 123–33.

Flemming, Dean. *Contextualization in the New Testament: Patterns for Theology and Mission.* Downers Grove, IL: IVP Academic, 2005.

Flower, J. Roswell. "Pray, Pray, Pray: Missionary Training School Needed." *The Pentecostal Evangel* (January 1922) 7.

Floyd, Scott. *Crisis Counseling: A Guide for Pastors and Professionals*. Grand Rapids: Kregel, 2008.

Foa, E. B., et al. "Symptom Scale-Interview Version." http://web.a.ebscohost.com/ehost/search.

Folger-Dye Sally. "Decreasing Fatigue and Illness in Field-Work." *Missiology: An International Review* 2 (1973) 79–109.

Forde, Gerhard. *On Being a Theologian of the Cross: Reflections on Luther's Heidelberg Disputation, 1518*. Grand Rapids: Eerdmans, 1997.

Fort Sherman Academy. "B+ Security Training." Springfield, MO. June 8–10, 2016.

Foy, David W., and Kent D. Drescher. "Faith and Honor in Trauma Treatment for Military Personnel and Their Families." In *Spiritually Oriented Psychotherapy for Trauma*, edited by Donald F. Walker, et al., 233–52. Washington, DC: American Psychological Association, 2015.

Foyle, Marjory. *Honorably Wounded: Stress Among Christian Workers*. London: Monarch, 2001.

Frankl, Viktor. *Man's Search for Meaning*. Boston: Beacon, 2006.

Freedman, Jill, and Gene Combs. *Narrative Therapy: The Social Construction of Preferred Realities*. New York: W. W. Norton and Company, 1996.

Freudenberger, Herbert. *Burnout: The High Cost of High Achievement*. Garden City, NY: Doubleday, 1980.

Friedman, Matthew, et al. "Classification of Trauma and Stressor-Related Disorders in DSM-5." *Depression and Anxiety* 28 (2011) 737–49.

Furnham, Adrian, and Stephen Bochner. *Culture Shock: Psychological Reactions to Unfamiliar Environments*. New York: Methuen, 1986.

Gardner, Brenda, et al. "Cognitive Therapy and Behavioral Coping in the Management of Work-Related Stress: An Intervention Study." *Work and Stress* 19 (2005) 137–52.

Gardner, Kathryn, et al. "Developmental Correlates of Emotional Intelligence: Temperament, Family Environment, and Childhood Trauma." *Australian Journal of Psychology* 63 (2011) 75–82.

Gardner, Laura Mae. "Proactive Care of Missionary Personnel." In *Helping Missionaries Grow: Readings in Mental Health and Missions*, edited by Kelly O'Donnell and Michele O'Donnell, 432–46. Pasadena: William Carey Library, 1988.

Garfin, Dana Rose, et al. "Children's Reactions to the 2010 Chilean Earthquake: The Role of Trauma Exposure, Family Context, and School-Based Mental Health Programming." *Psychological Trauma: Theory, Research, Practice, and Policy* 6 (2014) 563–73.

Gaudiano, B. A., and M. Zimmerman. "The Relationship Between Childhood Trauma History and the Psychotic Subtype of Major Depression." *Acta Psychiatrica Scandinavica* 121 (2010) 462–70.

Geisler, Fay, et al. "What Coping Tells about Personality." *European Journal of Personality* 23 (2009) 289–306.

Gerber, Monica, et al. "The Unique Contributions of Positive and Negative Religious Coping to Posttraumatic Growth and PTSD." *Psychology of Religion and Spirituality* 3 (2011) 298–307.

Gerstenberger, Erhard, and Wolfgang Schrage. *Suffering*. Nashville: Abingdon, 1977.

Gigliotti, Marcus A. "Qoheleth: Portrait of an Artist in Pain." In *The Bible on Suffering: Social and Political Implications*, edited by Anthony Tambasco, 72–92. New York: Paulist, 2001.

Gilbar, Ora, et al. "Coping, Mastery, Stress Appraisals, Mental Preparation, and Unit Cohesion Predicting Distress and Performance: A Longitudinal Study of Soldiers Undertaking Evacuation Tasks." *Anxiety, Stress, and Coping* 23 (2010) 547–62.

Gish, Dorothy. "Sources of Missionary Stress." *Journal of Psychology and Theology* 11 (1983) 238–42.

Gow, Kathryn, et al. "Religious Orientation and its Relationship to Well Being and Open-Close Mindedness and Religious Groups." In *Wayfinding Through Life's Challenges: Coping and Survival*, edited by Kathryn M. Gow and Marek J. Celinski, 141–61. New York: Nova Science, 2011.

Grant, Robert. "Trauma in Missionary Life." *Missiology: An International Review* 23 (1995) 71–83.

Grassi, Joseph. "Informing the Future: Social Justice in the New Testament." New York: Paulist, 2003.

Greeff, Abraham, and Ayesha Wentworth. "Resilience in Families that Have Experienced Heart-related Trauma." *Curr Psychol* 28 (2009) 302–14.

Grenz, Stanley. *Theology for the Community of God*. Grand Rapids: Eerdmans, 2000.

Grogan, Geoffrey W. *Psalms*. Grand Rapids: Eerdmans, 2008.

Grunlan, Stephen A., and Marvin K. Mayers. *Cultural Anthropology: A Christian Perspective*. Grand Rapids: Zondervan Academic, 1979.

Gupta, Paul, and Sherwood Lingenfelter. *Breaking Tradition to Accomplish Vision: Training Leaders for a Church-Planting Movement*. Winona Lake, IN: BMH, 2006.

Gus, Licette, et al. "Emotion Coaching: A Universal Strategy for Supporting and Promoting Sustainable Emotional and Behavioural Well-Being." *Educational and Child Psychology* 32 (2015) 31–41.

Hafemann, Scott J. *Suffering and Ministry in the Spirit: Paul's Defense of His Ministry in II Corinthians 2:14–3:3*. Grand Rapids: Eerdmans, 1990.

Hahn, Roger L. *Matthew: A Commentary for Bible Students*. Indianapolis: Wesleyan, 2007.

Hambrick, Erin, and David McCord. "Proactive Coping and its Relation to the Five-Factor Model of Personality." *Individual Differences Research* 8 (2010) 67–77.

Hardy, Lew, et al. "The Relationship Between Transformational Leadership Behaviors, Psychological, and Training Outcomes in the Elite Military Recruits." *The Leadership Quarterly* 21 (2010) 20–32.

———. "Resilience Scale." http://web.a.ebscohost.com/ehost/search.

Harney, Patricia. "Resilience Processes in Context: Contributions and Implications of Bronfenbrennenr's Person-Process-Context Model." *Journal of Aggressions, Maltreatment and Trauma* 14 (2007) 73–81.

Hay, Rob, et al. "Organizational Values–Work/Life Balance." In *Worth Keeping: Global Perspectives on Best Practice in Missionary Retention*, edited by Rob Hay et al., 213–22. Pasadena: William Carey Library, 2007.

———. "Selection." In *Worth Keeping: Global Perspectives on Best Practice in Missionary Retention*, edited by Rob Hay, et al., 69–80. Pasadena: William Carey Library, 2007.

Heard, Mickie. "O = Organized Play: A Necessary Method for Helping and Healing." In *Healing the Children of War: A Handbook for Ministry to Children Who have Suffered Deep Traumas*, edited by Phyllis Kilbourn, 175–96. Monrovia: Marc, 1995.

Henderson, Alan. "A Historical Review of Missions and Missionary Training in the Churches of Christ." *Restoration Quarterly* 35 (1993) 203–17.

Hess, Cynthia. *Sites of Violence, Sites of Grace: Christian Nonviolence and the Traumatized Self.* New York: Lexington, 2009.

Heubach, Paul. *The Problem of Human Suffering: Comforting Answers to a Difficult Question.* Nashville: Southern Publisher Association, 1980.

Hiebert, Paul. "The Missionary as Mediator of Global Theologizing." In *Globalizing Theology: Belief and Practice in an Era of World Christianity*, edited by Craig Ott and Harold Netland, 288–308. Grand Rapids: Baker Academic, 2006.

Hiebert, Paul, et al. *Understanding Folk Religion: A Christian Response to Popular Beliefs and Practices.* Grand Rapids: Baker, 1999.

Ho, Samuel M. Y. "Resilience, Growth, and Distress After a Traumatic Experience." In *Healing Trauma: Professional Guide*, edited by Kitty K. Wu et al., 89–95. Aberdeen, Hong Kong: Hong Kong University Press, 2011.

Hobfoll, Stevan E. "The Influence of Culture, Community, and the Nested-Self in the Stress Process: Advancing Conservation of Resources Theory." *Applied Psychology: An International Review* 50 (2001) 337–421.

———. *Stress, Culture, and Community: The Psychology and Philosophy of Stress.* New York: Plenum, 1998.

Hofstede, Geert, and Gert Hofstede. *Cultures and Organizations Software of the Mind: Intercultural Cooperation and its Importance for Survival.* New York: McGraw-Hill, 2005.

Holdcroft, Thomas L. *Psalms: The Bible's Heartbeat.* Abbotsford, Canada: CeeTeC, 2006.

Hooker, Morna. "Interchange and Suffering." In *Suffering and Martyrdom in the New Testament*, edited by William Horbury and Brian McNeil, 70–83. Cambridge: Cambridge University Press, 1981.

Howell, Dwayne J., and Susan H. Howell. "Journey to Mount Horeb: Cognitive Theory and 1 Kings 19:1–18." *Mental Health, Religion and Culture* 11 (2008) 655–60.

Hubble, Gwyneth. "Reasons for Missionary Training." *The International Review of Missions* 52 (1963) 257–65.

Hwang, Wei-Chin, and Julia Y. Ting. "Disaggregating the Effects of Acculturation and Acculturative Stress on the Mental Health of Asian Americans." *Cultural Diversity and Ethnic Minority Psychology* 14 (2008) 147–54.

Ibrahim, Kira A., et al. "The Dynamics of Posttraumatic Growth Across Different Trauma Types in a Palestinian Sample." *Journal of Loss and Trauma* 18 (2013) 120–39.

Irvine, Julie, et al. "Traumatic Stress in a Missionary Population: Dimension and Impact." *Journal of Psychology and Theology* 34 (2006) 27–336.

James, Richard K., and Burl E. Gilliland. *Crisis Intervention Strategies.* Belmont, CA: Brooks/Cole, 2013.

Janoff-Bulman, Ronnie. *Shattered Assumptions: Towards a New Psychology of Trauma.* New York: Free, 1992.

Janzen, Waldemar. *Believers Church Bible Commentary: Exodus.* Scottdale, PA: Herald, 1989.

Jeffery, Renee. *Evil and International Relations: Human Suffering in an Age of Terror.* New York: Palgrave Macmillan, 2008.

Jensma, Jeanne L. "Critical Incident Intervention with Missionaries: A Comprehensive Approach." *Journal of Psychology and Theology* 27 (1999) 130–38.

Jervis, L. Ann. *At the Heart of the Gospel: Suffering in the Earliest Christian Message.* Grand Rapids: Eerdmans, 2007.
Jobson, Laura, and Richard O'Kearney. "Cultural Differences in Personal Identity in Post-Traumatic Stress Disorder." *British Journal of Clinical Psychology* 47 (2008) 95–109.
Johnson, J., et al. "Resilience Appraisal Scale." http://web.a. ebscohost.com/ehost/search.
———. "Resilience as Positive Coping Appraisals: Testing the Schematic Appraisals Model of Suicide (SAMS)." *Behavioral Research and Therapy* 49 (2010) 179–86.
Jones, Edgar, and Simon Wesley. "Psychological Trauma: A Historical Perspective." *Psychistry* 5 (2006) 217–20.
Jones, Marge. *Psychology of Missionary Adjustment.* Springfield, MO: Logion, 1995.
Jones, Serene. *Trauma and Grace: Theology in a Ruptured World.* Louisville, KY: Westminster John Knox, 2009.
Joseph, Stephen. *What Doesn't Kill Us: The New Psychology of Posttraumatic Growth.* New York: Basic, 2011.
Kaiser, Walter. *A Biblical Approach to Personal Suffering.* Chicago: Moody, 1982.
Kaltman, Stacey, et al. "Trauma, Depression, and Comorbid PTSD/Depression in a Community Sample of Latina Immigrants." *Psychological Trauma: Theory, Research, Practice, and Policy* 2 (2010) 31–39.
Kastenmuller, Andreas, et al. "Posttraumatic Growth: Why Do People Grow From Their Trauma?" *Anxiety, Stress, and Coping* 25 (2012) 477–89.
Kebza, Vladimir, and Iva Solcova. "Trends in Resilience Theory and Research." In *Wayfinding Through Life's Challenges: Coping and Survival,* edited by Kathryn M. Gow, and Marek J. Celinski, 13–30. New York: Nova Science, 2011.
Keckler, Wade. "Comprehensive Missionary Wellness as Described by Mental Health/Member Care Professionals." PhD diss., Regent University, 2007.
Keener, Craig S. *The IVP Bible Background Commentary: New Testament.* Downers Grove, IL: InterVarsity, 1993.
Kelley, Thomas. "Natural Resilience and Innate Mental Health." *American Psychologist* (2005) 265.
Keshgegian, Flora. *Redeeming Memories: A Theology of Healing and Transformation.* Nashville: Abingdon, 2000.
Khechuashvili, Lili. "Comparative Study of Psychological Well-Being and Posttraumatic Growth Indicators in IDP and Non-IDP Citizens of Georgia." *GESJ: Education Science and Psychology* 6 (2014) 52–58.
Kierkegaard, Soren. "The Lord Gave, and the Lord Took Away. Blessed be the Name of the Lord." In *Eighteen Upbuilding Discourses,* edited by Howard V Hong and Edna H. Hong, Princeton: Princeton University Press, 1990.
Kilbourn, Phyllis. "An Introduction to the STOP Sign Model." In *Healing the Children of War: A Handbook for Ministry to Children Who Have Suffered Deep Traumas,* edited by Phyllis Kilbourn, 133–46. Monrovia: Marc, 1995.
———. "S = Structure." *Healing the Children of War: A Handbook for Ministry to Children Who have Suffered Deep Traumas,* edited by Phyllis Kilbourn, 147–56. Monrovia: Marc, 1995.
Kobasa, Suzanne C. "Stressful Life Events, Personality, and Health: An Inquiry into Hardiness." *Journal of Personality and Social Psychology* 37 (1979) 1–11.
Kraft, Charles H. *Communication Theory for Christian Witness.* Maryknoll: Orbis, 1991.

Krause, Neal, et al. "Church-Based Social Support and Religious Coping." *Journal for the Scientific Study of Religion* 40 (2001) 637–56.

Kuile, Hagar, and Thomas Ehring. "Predictors of Changes in Religiosity After Trauma: Trauma, Religiosity and Posttraumatic Stress Disorder." *Psychological Trauma, Theory, Research, Practice, and Policy* 6 (2014) 353–60.

Kumpter, Karol L., et al. "Engendering Resilience in Families Facing Chronic Adversity Through Family Strengthening Programs." In *Wayfinding Through Life's Challenges: Coping and Survival*, edited by Kathryn M. Gow and Marek J. Celinski, 461–83. New York: Nova Science, 2011.

Kusner, Katherine, and Kenneth I. Pargament. "Shaken to the Core: Understanding and Addressing the Spiritual Dimension of Trauma." In *Trauma Therapy in Context: The Science and Craft of Evidence-Based Practice*, edited by Robert A. McMackin et al., 211–30. Washington, DC: American Psychological Association, 2012.

Ladd, George. *A Theology of the New Testament*. Grand Rapids: Eerdmans, 1993.

Lahad, Mooli, and Dmitry Leykin. "Introduction: The Integrative Model of Resiliency—The 'Basic Ph' Model, or What Do We Know about Survival?" In *The "Basic Ph" Model of Coping and Resiliency: Theory, Research, and Cross-Cultural Application*, edited by Mooli Lahad, et al., 9–30. London: Jessica Kengsley, 2013.

Langberg, Diane. *Suffering and the Heart of God: How Trauma Destroys and Christ Restores*. Greensboro, NC: New Growth, 2015.

Larsson, Magnus, et al. "The Interaction Between Baseline Trait Anxiety and Trauma Exposure as Predictor of Post-Trauma Symptoms of Anxiety and Insomnia." *Scandinavian Journal of Psychology* 49 (2008) 447–50.

Lazarus, Richard S. *Psychological Stress and the Coping Process*. New York: McGraw-Hill, 1966.

Lazarus, Richard S., and Susan Folkman. *Stress, Appraisal, and Coping*. New York: Springer, 1984.

Lederach, John. "Missionaries Facing Conflict and Violence: Problems and Prospects." *Missiology: An International Review* 20 (1992) 11–19.

Lederach, Paul. *Believers Church Bible Commentary: Daniel*. Scottdale, PA: Herald, 1994.

Lewis-Hall, M. Elizabeth, and Nancy S. Duvall. "Married Women in Missions: The Effects of Cross-Cultural and Self Gender-Role Expectations on Well-Being, Stress, and Self-Esteem." *Journal of Psychology and Theology* 31 (2003) 303–14.

Lewis, C. S. *The Problem of Pain*. New York: Collier, Macmillan, 1940.

Li, Xu, and Xue Zheng. "Adult Attachment Orientations and Subjective Well-Being: Emotional Intelligence and Self-Esteem as Moderators." *Social Behavior and Personality* 42 (2014) 1257–66.

Linahan, Jane E. "The Grieving Spirit: The Holy Spirit as Bearer of the Suffering of the World in Moltmann's Pneumatology." In *The Spirit in the Church and the World*, edited by Bradford Hinze, 41–64. Maryknoll: Orbis, 2003.

Lindquist, Brent. "Mission Agency Screening and Orientation: A Personal Journey." In *Too Valuable to Lose: Exploring the Causes and Cures of Missionary Attrition*, edited by William Taylor, 241–50. Pasadena: William Carey Library, 1997.

Lindquist, Stanley E. "Prediction of Success in Overseas Adjustment." *Journal of Psychology and Christianity* 1 (1982) 22–25.

Lingenfelter, Judith, and Sherwood Lingenfelter. *Teaching Cross-Culturally: An Incarnational Model for Learning and Teaching*. Grand Rapids: Baker Academic, 2003.

Livingston, James, et al. *Modern Christian Thought: The Twentieth Century*. Minneapolis: First Fortress, 2006.

Love, Rick. *Muslims, Magic and the Kingdom of God: Church Planting Among Folk Muslims*. Pasadena: William Carey Library, 2000.

Lowe, Walter. *Theology and Difference: The Wound of Reason*. N.d.: The Association of American University Presses' Resolution, 1993.

Maas, Heike, and Frank Spinath. "Personality and Coping with Professional Demands: A Behavioral Genetics Analysis." *Journal of Occupational Health Psychology* 17 (2012) 376–85.

Macduff, John. *The Mind of Jesus*. New York: Floating, 2009.

Maloney, Carrie. "Critical Incident Stress Debriefing and Pediatric Nurses: An Approach to Support the Work Environment and Mitigate Negative Consequences." *Pediatric Nursing* 38 (2012) 110–13.

Maltby, John, et al. "The Cognitive Nature of Forgiveness: Using Cognitive Strategies of Primary Appraisal and Coping to Describe the Process of Forgiving." *Journal of Clinical Psychology* 63 (2007) 555–66.

Mancini, Anthony D., and George A. Bonanno. "Resilience in the Face of Potential Trauma: Clinical Practices and Illustrations." *Journal of Clinical Psychology in Session* 62 (2006) 971–85.

Martens, Elmer. *Believers Church Bible Commentary: Jeremiah*. Scottdale, PA: Herald, 1980.

Martin, Civilla D. "God Will Take Care of You." 1904. http://library.timelesstruths.org/music/God_Will_Take_Care_of_You_Martin/.

Martinez-Marti, Maria L., and Willibald Ruch. "Character Strengths and Well-Being Across the Life Span: Data from a Representative Sample of German-Speaking Adults Living in Switzerland." *Frontiers in Psychology* 5 (2014) 1–10.

Maslow, Abraham H. *Motivation and Personality*. New York: Harper and Row, 1954.

Mathews, Susan F. "All for Not: My Servant Job." In *The Bible on Suffering: Social and Political Implications*, edited by Anthony Tambasco, 51–71. New York: Paulist, 2001.

———. "When We Remember Zion: The Significance of the Exile for Understanding Daniel." In *The Bible on Suffering: Social and Political Implications*, edited by Anthony Tambasco, 93–119. New York: Paulist, 2001.

Maynard, Elizabeth A., et al. "Religious Coping Style, Concept of God, and Personal Religious Variables in Threat, Loss, and Challenge Situations." *Journal for the Scientific Study of Religion* 40 (2001) 65–74.

McAdams, Dan. "The Role of Narrative in Personality Psychology Today." In *Narrative, State of the Art*, edited by Michael Bamberg, 17–26. Philadelphia: John Benjamins, 2007.

McCubbin, Hamilton I., et al. "Families Under Stress: What Makes Them Resilient." *Journal of Family and Consumer Sciences* (1997) 2–11.

McDonald, Patrica M. "The View of Suffering Held by the Author of 1 Peter." In *The Bible on Suffering: Social and Political Implications*, edited by Anthony Tambasco, 165–87. New York: Paulist, 2001.

McFarlane, Alexander C. "The Severity of the Trauma: Issues About its Role in Posttraumatic Stress Disorder." In *Beyond Trauma: Cultural and Societal Dynamics*, edited by Rolf J. Kleber et al., 31–54. New York: Plenum, 1995.

McFarlane, Alexander C., and Rachel Yehuda. "Resilience, Vulnerability, and the Course of Posttraumatic Reactions." In *Traumatic Stress: The Effects of Overwhelming Experiences on Mind, Body, and Society*, edited by Bessel A. Van der Kolk et al., 155–81. New York: Gilford, 1996.

McGrath, Alister. *Christian Theology an Introduction*. Malden: Blackwell, 2001.

McKenzie, Steven. *How to Read the Bible: History, Prophecy, Literature—Why Modern Readers Need to Know the Difference and What it Means for Faith Today*. Oxford: Oxford University Press, 2005.

McMillen, J. Curtis. "Better for it: How People Benefit from Adversity." *Social Work* 44 (1999) 455–68.

McNally, Richard. "Panic and Posttraumatic Stress Disorder: Implications for Culture, Risk, and Treatment." *Cognitive Behavioral Therapy* 37 (2008) 131–34.

McNeal, Reggie. *A Work of Heart: Understanding How God Shapes Spiritual Leaders*. San Francisco: Jossey-Bass, 2000.

McWilliams, Warren. *Where is the God of Justice?: Biblical Perspectives on Suffering*. Peabody, MA: Hendrickson, 2005.

Meler, John. "Biblical Reflection: The Conflict at Antioch." *Mid-Stream* (1996) 471–75.

Miersma, Patricia. "Understanding Missionary Stress from the Perspective of a Combat-Related Stress Theory." *The Journal of Christianity and Psychology* 21 (1993) 93–101.

Mills, Mary. *Alterity, Pain, and Suffering in Isaiah, Jeremiah, and Ezekiel*. New York: T. & T. Clark, 2007.

Miner, Maureen, and Martin Dowson. "Spirituality as a Key Resource for Human Flourishing." In *Beyond Well-Being: Spirituality and Human Flourishing*, edited by Maurcon Miner et al., 5–31. Charlotte, NC: Information Age, 2012.

Miner, Maureen, et al. "Attachment to God, Psychological Need Satisfaction, and Psychological Well-Being Among Christians." *Journal of Psychology and Theology* 42 (2014) 326–42.

Minirth, Frank, and Paul Meier. *Happiness is a Choice: The Symptoms, Causes, and Cures of Depression*. Grand Rapids: Baker, 2007.

Moberg, David. "The Development of Social Indicators of Spiritual Well-being for Quality of Life Research." In *Spiritual Well-being: Sociological Perspectives*, edited by David Moberg, 1–13. Washington, DC: University Press of America, 1979.

Mobile Member Care. "Crisis Intervention." www.mmct.org.

Moffitt, Elizabeth. "Improvisation and Guided Imagery and Music (GIM) With a Physically Disabled Woman: A Gestalt Approach." In *Case Examples of Music Therapy for Event Trauma*, edited by Kenneth E. Bruscia, 12–19. Barcelona: Barcelona, 2014.

Monat, Alan, et al. "Anticipatory Stress and Coping Reactions Under Various Conditions of Uncertainty." *Journal of Personality and Social Psychology* 24 (1972) 237–53.

Monat, Alan, and Richard S. Lazarus. "Stress and Coping—Some Current Issues and Controversies." In *Stress and Coping: An Anthology*, edited by Alan Monat and Richard S. Lazarus, 1–12. New York: Columbia University Press, 1977.

Mucci, Clara. *Beyond Individual and Collective Trauma: Intergenerational Transmission, Psychoanalytic Treatment, and the Dynamics of Forgiveness.* London: Karnac Books, 2013.

Mukherjee, Preetika P., and Judith L. Alpert. "Overview of Psychological Interventions in Acute Aftermath of Disaster." In *Bereavement-Related Depression and PTSD: Evaluating Interventions,* edited by Laura Barbanel, and Robert Sternberb, 3–35. New York: Springer, 2006.

Myers, David G. *The Pursuit of Happiness: Discovering the Pathway to Fulfillment, Well-being, and Enduring Personal Joy.* New York: Quill, 1992.

Nolan Fewell, Danna, and David M. Gunn. *Gender, Power, & Promise: The Subject of the Bible's First Story.* Nashville: Abingdon, 1993.

Norris, Fran H. "Epidemiology of Trauma: Frequency and Impact of Different Potentially Traumatic Events on Different Demographic Groups." *Journal of Consulting and Clinical Psychology* 60 (1992) 409–18.

O'Collins, Gerald, and Edward Farrugia. *A Concise Dictionary of Theology.* Mahwah, NJ: Paulist, 2000.

O'Donnell, Kelly. "Member Care on the Field: Taking the Longer Road." In *Too Valuable to Lose: Exploring the Causes and Cures of Missionary Attrition,* edited by William Taylor, 287–302. Pasadena: William Carey Library, 1997.

O'Malley, William J. *Redemptive Suffering: Understanding Suffering, Living with it, Growing Through it.* New York: Crossroad, 1997.

O'Rourke, Norm. "Psychological Resilience and the Well-Being of Widowed Women." *Ageing International* 29 (2004) 267–80.

Ogden Bellis, Alice. *Helpmates, Harlots, and Heroes: Women's Stories in the Hebrew Bible.* Louisville, KY: Westminster John Knox, 2007.

Opoku, Onyihab. "God's Grace, Healing, and Suffering." *International Review of Mission* 95 (2006) 117–27.

Osborne, Travis L., and Brian Vandenberg. "Situational and Denominational Differences in Religious Coping." *The International Journal for the Psychology of Religion.* 13 no. 2 (2003) 111–22.

Palucka, Anna M., et al. "Social and Emotional Intelligence: Contributors to Resilience and Resourcefulness." In *Wayfinding Through Life's Challenges: Coping and Survival,* edited by Kathryn M. Gow, and Marek J. Celinski, 47–62. New York: Nova Science, 2011.

Papousek, Liona, and Gunter Genullter. "Don't Take an X for a U: Why Laughter is Not the Best Medicine, but Being More Cheerful Has Many Benefits." In *Psychological Well-Being,* edited by Ingrid E. Wells, 1–75. New York: Nova Science, 2010.

Pargament, Kenneth I. *The Psychology of Religion and Coping: Theory, Research, Practice.* New York: Gilford, 1997.

―――. "Religious Methods of Coping: Resources for the Conversation and Transformation of Significance." In *Religion and the Clinical Practice of Psychology,* edited by Edward P. Shafranske, 215–39. Washington, DC: American Psychological Association, 1996.

Pargament, Kenneth I., et al. "The Brief RCOPE: Current Psychometric Status of a Short Measure of Religious Coping." *Religions* 2 (2011) 51–76.

―――. "The Brief RCOPE: Current Psychometric Status of a Short Measure of Religious Coping." https://creativecommons.org/licenses/by/3.0/.

———. "God Help Me!: The Relationship of Religious Orientations to Religious Coping with Negative Life Events." *Journal for the Scientific Study of Religion* 31 (1992) 504–13.

———. "The Many Methods of Religious Coping: Development and Initial Validation of the RCOPE." *Journal of Clinical Psychology* 56 (2000) 519–43.

———. "Patterns of Positive and Negative Religious Coping with Major Life Stressors." *Journal for the Scientific Study of Religion* 37 (1998) 710–24.

———. "Red Flags and Religious Coping: Identifying Some Religious Warning Signs Among People in Crisis." *Journal of Clinical Psychology* 59 (2003) 1335–48.

———. "Religion and the Problem-Solving Process: Three Styles of Coping." *Journal for the Scientific Study of Religion* 27 (1988) 90–104.

Pargament, Kenneth I., and Crystal L. Park. In "Times of Stress: The Religion-Coping Connection." In *The Psychology of Religion: Theoretical Approaches*, edited by Bernard Spilka and Daniel N. McIntosh, 43–53. Boulder, CO: Westview, 1997.

Park, Crystal L. "Meaning, Coping, and Health and Well-being." In *The Oxford Handbook of Stress, Health, and Coping*, edited by Susan Folkman, 227–41. New York: Oxford University Press, 2011.

Park, Crystal L., and Susan Folkman. "Meaning in the Context of Stress and Coping." *Review of General Psychology* 1 (1997) 115–44.

Parker, Jane, and Michael Zakour. "Triumph Over Tragedy: Transformation Through the Aftermath of Disaster." In *Trauma Transformed: An Empowerment Response*, 279–99. New York: Columbia University Press, 2007.

Peres, Julio F. P., et al. "Spirituality and Resilience in Trauma Victims." *J Relig Health*. 46 (2007) 343–50.

Perren-Klingler, Gisela. "The Integration of Traumatic Experiences: Culture and Resources." In *Posttraumatic Stress Intervention: Challenges, Issues, and Perspectives*, edited by John M. Volanti et al., 43–64. Springfield, IL: Charles C. Thomas, 2000.

Philippe, Frederick, et al. "Ego-Resiliency as a Mediator Between Childhood Trauma and Psychological Symptoms." *Journal of Social and Clinical Psychology* 30 (2011) 583–98.

Phipps, Warwick D., and Charl Vorster. "Narrative Therapy: A Return to the Intrapsychic Perspective?" *Psychological Society of South America* 39 (2010) 32–45.

Pierce, Kathryn. "A Holistic View of the Missioning Process." *Missiology: An International Review* 36 (2008) 33–51.

Pines, Ayala M. "Burnout." In *Handbook of Stress: Theoretical and Clinical Aspects*, edited by Leo Goldberer and Shlomo Breznitz, 386–402. New York: Free, 1993.

Polman, Remco, et al. "Type D Personality, Stress, and Symptoms of Burnout: The Influence of Avoidance Coping and Social Support." *British Journal of Health Psychology* 15 (2010) 681–96.

Powell, John. "Short-term Missionary Counseling." In *Missionary Care: Counting the Cost for World Evangelization*, edited by Kelly O'Donnell, 123–35. Pasadena: William Carey Library, 1992.

Pulley, Mary Lynn, and Michael Wakefield. *Building Resiliency: How to Thrive in Times of Change*. Greensboro: Center for Creative Leadership, 2001.

Quick, James C., et al. *Stress and Challenge at the Top: The Paradox of the Successful Executive*. New York: John Wiley & Sons, 1990.

Rambo, Shelly. *Spirit and Trauma: A Theology of Remaining*. Louisville: Westminster Jons Knox, 2010.

Rance, DeLonn. "The Empowered Call: The Activity of the Holy Spirit in Salvadoran Assemblies of God Missionaries." PhD diss., Fuller Theological Seminary, 1999.

Raphael, Beverley. "The Interaction of Trauma and Grief." In *Psychological Trauma: A Developmental Approach*, edited by Dora Black et al., London: The Royal College of Psychiatrics, 1997.

Rassieur, Charles. *Stress Management for Ministers: Practical Help for Clergy Who Deny Themselves the Care They Give to Others*. Philadelphia: Westminster, 1982.

Rauschenbusch, Walter. *A Theology for the Social Gospel*. New York: Macmillan, 1922.

Regehr, Cheryl, et al. "Previous Trauma Exposure and PTSD Symptoms as Predictors of Subjective and Biological Response to Stress." *The Canadian Journal of Psychiatry*. 52 (2007) 675–83.

Rendon, Jim. *Upside: The New Science of Post-Traumatic Growth*. New York: Touchstone, 2015.

Richards, Scott P., et al. "Religious and Spiritual Assessment of Trauma Survivors." In *Spiritually Oriented Psychotherapy for Trauma*, edited by Donald F. Walker et al., 77–102. Washington, DC: American Psychological Association, 2015.

Richardson, Jarrett. "Psychopathology in Missionary Personnel." In *Missionary Care: Counting the Cost for World Evangelization*, edited by Kelly O'Donnell, 89–109. Pasadena: William Carey Library, 1992.

Riley, Kristen E., and Crystal L. Park. "Problem-Focused vs. Meaning-Focused Coping as Mediators of the Appraisal-Adjustment Relationship in Chronic Stressors." *Journal of Social and Clinical Psychology* 33 (2014) 587–611.

Roetzel, Calvin. *Paul: The Man and the Myth*. Minneapolis: Fortress, 1999.

Rogers, Everett, and Thomas Steinfatt. *Intercultural Communication*. Prospect Heights: Waveland, 1999.

Roop, Eugene. *Believers Church Bible Commentary: Genesis*. Scottdale, PA: Herald, 1987.

———. *Believers Church Bible Commentary: Ruth, Jonah, Esther*. Scottdale, PA: Herald, 2002.

Rosmarin, David H., et al. "Incorporating Spiritual Beliefs into a Cognitive Model of Worry." *Journal of Clinical Psychology* 67 (2011) 691–700.

Ross, Keisha, et al. "The Relationship Between Religion and Religious Coping: Religious Coping as a Moderator Between Religion and Adjustment." *J Relig Health* 48 (2009) 454–87.

Ruddick, Frederick. "Promoting Mental Health and Wellbeing." *Art and Science* 27 (2013) 35–39.

Rynearson, Edward K. "Introduction." In *Violent Death: Resilience and Intervention Beyond the Crisis*, edited by Edward K. Rynearson, 2–3. New York: Routledge Taylor & Francis Group, 2006.

Salloum, Alison, and Edward K. Rynearson. "Family Resilience After Violent Death." In *Violent Death: Resilience and Intervention Beyond the Crisis*, edited by E. K. Rynearson, 47–64. New York: Routledge, 2006.

Sammis, John H. "Trust and Obey." http://library.timelesstruths.org/music/Trust_and_Obey.

Sande, Ken. *The Peacemaker: A Biblical Guide to Resolving Personal Conflict*. Grand Rapids: Baker, 2004.

Savicki, Victor, et al. "Intercultural Development." In *Developing Intercultural Competence and Transformation: Theory, Research, and Application in International Education*, edited by Victor Savicki, 150–72. Sterling, VA: Stylus, 2008.

Schaefer, Frauke. "Resources for Effective Support: Healthy Stress Management." In *Trauma and Resilience: A Handbook*, edited by Frauke C. Schaefer and Charles A. Schaefer, 2293–533. Fresno, CA: Corderopress, 2012.

Schaefer, Frauke, et al. "Traumatic Events and Posttraumatic Stress in Cross-Cultural Mission Assignments." *Journal of Traumatic Stress* 20 (2007) 529–39.

Schaefer, Frauke, and Charlie Schaefer. "Resources for Effective Support: Spiritual Resources in Dealing with Trauma." In *Trauma and Resilience: A Handbook*, edited by Frauke C. Schaefer and Charles A. Schaefer, 2867–3744. Fresno, CA: Corderopress, 2012.

Schaefer, Jeanne A., and Rudolf H. Moos. "The Context for Posttraumatic Growth: Life Crises, Individual and Social Resources, and Coping." In *Posttraumatic Growth: Positive Changes in the Aftermath of Crisis*, edited by Richard G. Tedeschi et al., 99–125. Mahwah, NJ: Lawrence Erlbaum Associates, 1998.

Schlotz, Wolff, et al. "The Perceived Stress Reactivity Scale: Measurement Invariance, Stability, and Validity in Three Countries." *Psychological Assessment* (July 2010) 1–15.

Schottenbauer, Michele A., et al. "Attachment and Affective Resolution Following a Stressful Event: General and Religious Coping as Possible Mediators." *Mental Health, Religion and Culture* 9 (2006) 448–71.

Schottenbauer, Michele A., et al. "Religious Coping Research and Contemporary Personality Theory: An Exploration of Endler's (1997) Integrative Personality Theory." *British Journal of Psychology* 97 (2006) 499–519.

Schottroff, Luise, et al. *Feminist Interpretation: The Bible in Women's Perspective*. Translated by Martin and Barbara Rumscheidt. Minneapolis: Fortress, 1998.

Schuettler, Darnell, and Adriel Boals. "The Path to Posttraumatic Growth Versus Posttraumatic Stress Disorder: Contributions of Event Centrality and Coping." *Journal of Loss and Trauma* 16 (2011) 180–94.

Schwandt, Joanne, and Glendon Moriarty. "What Have the Past 25 Years of Member Care Research Taught Us?: An Overview of Missionary Mental Health and Member Care Services." *Missiology: An International Review* 36 (2008) 317–26.

Segerstrom, Suzanne, et al. "Optimism is Associated with Mood, Coping, and Immune Change in Response to Stress." *Journal of Personality and Social Psychology* 74 (1988) 1646–55.

Shaffer, Thomas. *Faith and the Professions*. Albany, NY: State University of New York Press, 1987.

Shalev, Aarieh Y. "Stress Versus Traumatic Stress: From Acute Homeostatic Reactions to Chronic Psychopathology." In *Traumatic Stress: The Effects of Overwhelming Experience on Mind, Body and Society*, edited by Bessel A. van der Kolk et al., 77–101. New York: Guilford, 1996.

Sheed, Frank. *Theology and Sanity*. San Francisco: Ignatius, 1993.

Skinner, Ellen A., and Melanie J. Zimmer-Gembeck. "Perceived Control and the Development of Coping." In *The Oxford Handbook of Stress, Health, and Coping*, edited by Susan Folkman, 35–59. New York: Oxford University Press, 2011.

Slattery, Jeanne M., and Crystal L. Park. "Spirituality and Making Meaning: Implications for Therapy with Trauma Survivors." In *Spiritually Oriented Psychotherapy for Trauma*, edited by Donald F. Walker, et al., 127–46. Washington, DC: American Psychological Association, 2015.

Smith, Amy. "The Buffering Role of Social Support on the Effects of Perceived Stress and Traumatic Stress Events among International Relief Workers and Missionaries." PhD diss., Fuller Theological Seminary, 2004.

Smith, Bruce W., et al. "Noah Revisited: Religious Coping by Church Members and the Impact of the 1993 Midwest Flood." *Journal of Community Psychology* 28 (2000) 169–86.

Solcova, Iva, and Vladimir Kebza. "Personality Characteristics Related to Resilience: Seeking for a Common Core." In *Wayfinding Through Life's Challenges: Coping and Survival*, edited by Kathryn M. Gow and Marek J. Celinski, New York: Nova Science, 2011.

Stead, Louisa. "Tis So Sweet to Trust in Jesus." http://library.timelesstruths.org/music/Tis_So_Sweet_to_Trust_in_Jesus.

Steffen, Tom, and Lois McKinney Douglas. *Encountering Missionary Life and Work: Preparing for Intercultural Ministry*. Grand Rapids: Baker Academic, 2008.

Steveson, Peter A. *Psalms*. Greenville, SC: Bob Jones University Press, 2007.

Stills, Michael. *The Missionary Call: Finding Your Place in God's Plan for the World*. Chicago: Moody, 2008.

Stone, Arthur A., and Christopher Mackie. *Subjective Well-Being: Measuring Happiness, Suffering and Other Dimensions of Experience*. Washington, DC: National Academies, 2013.

Stourton, Edward. *Paul of Tarsus*. New Jersey: HiddenSpring, 2005.

Sultana, Raheela, et al. "Outcomes of Belief in Just World Among Victims of Natural and Man-Made Disaster: Moderating Role of Resilience." *Pakistan Journal of Psychological Research* 30 (2015) 39–64.

Sutton, Julie. "A Flash of the Obvious: Music Therapy and Trauma." In *Case Examples of Music Therapy for Event Trauma*, edited by Kenneth E. Bruscia, 65–75. Gilsum, NH: Barcelona, 1991.

Sweetland, Dennis M. "Suffering in the Gospel of Matthew." In *The Bible on Suffering: Social and Political Implications*, edited by Anthony Tambasco, 120–43. New York: Paulist, 2001.

Tan, Siang-Yang. *Rest: Experiencing God's Peace in a Restless World*. Vancouver: Regent, 2000.

Taylor, Courtney. "What is ANOVA?" https://www.thoughtco.com/what-is-anova-3126418.

Taylor, Shelley E. "Affiliation and Stress." In *The Oxford Handbook of Stress, Health, and Coping*, edited by Susan Folkman, 86–100. New York: Oxford University Press, 2011.

———. "How Psychosocial Resources Enhance Health and Well-being." In *Applied Positive Psychology: Improving Everyday Life, Health, Schools, Work, and Society*, edited by Donaldson Stewart et al., 65–77. New York: Psychology, 2011.

Taylor, Shelley E., et al. "Culture and Social Support: Who Seeks It and Why?" *Journal of Personality and Social Psychology* 87 (2004) 354–62.

Taylor, William. "Challenging the Missions Stakeholders: Conclusions and Implications." In *Too Valuable to Lose: Exploring the Causes and Cures of Missionary Attrition*, edited by William Taylor, 341–60. Pasadena: William Carey Library, 1997.

———. "Introduction: Examining the Iceberg called Attrition." In *Too Valuable to Lose: Exploring the Causes and Cures of Missionary Attrition*, edited by William Taylor, 3–14. Pasadena: William Carey Library, 1997.

———. "Revisiting a Provocative Theme: The Attrition of Longer-Term Missionaries." *Missiology* 30 (2002) 67–80.

Tedeschi, Richard, and Lawrence Calhoun. *Trauma and Transformation: Growing in the Aftermath of Suffering*. Thousand Oaks, CA: Sage, 1995.

Theodoret. *Theodoret of Cyrus Commentary on the Psalms: Psalms 1–72*. Translated by Robert Hill. Washington, DC: The Catholic University of America Press, 2000.

Thompson, Suzanne C. "Finding Positive Meaning in a Stressful Event and Coping." *Basic and Applied Social Psychology* 6 (1985) 279–95.

Tillich, Paul. *Systematic Theology*. Chicago: The University of Chicago Press, 1957.
Tucker, Ruth. *From Jerusalem to Irian Jaya*. Grand Rapids: Zondervan, 1983.
Tucker, Ruth, and Leslie Andrews. "Historical Notes on Missionary Care." In *Missionary Care: Counting the Cost for World Evangelization*, edited by Kelly O'Donnell, 24–36. Pasadena: William Carey Library, 1992.
Tugade, Michele M. "Positive Emotions and Coping: Examining Dual-Process Models of Resilience." In *The Oxford Handbook of Stress, Health, and Coping*, edited by Susan Folkman, 186–99. New York: Oxford University Press, 2011.
Ungar, Michael, et al. "Unique Pathways to Resilience Across Cultures." *Adolescence* 46 (2007) 287–310.
Ursano, Robert J., et al. "Prevention of Posttraumatic Stress: Consultation, Training, and Early Treatment." In *Traumatic Stress: The Effects of Overwhelming Experience on Mind, Body, and Society*, edited by Bessel A. van der Kolk et al., 441–62. New York: Gulford, 1996.
van der Kolk, Bessel A. "The Body Keeps the Score: Approaches to the Psychobiology of Posttraumatic Stress Disorder." In *Traumatic Stress: The Effects of Overwhelming Experience on Mind, Body and Society*, edited by Bessel A. van der Kolk et al., 214–41. New York: Guilford, 1996.
———. "The Complexity of Adaptation to Trauma: Self-regulation, Stimulus Discrimination, and Characterological Development." In *Traumatic Stress: The Effects of Overwhelming Experience on Mind, Body and Society*, edited by Bessel A. van der Kolk, et al., 182–213. New York: Guilford, 1996.
———. "The Psychological Consequences of Overwhelming Life Experiences." In *Psychological Trauma*, edited by Bessel A. van der Kolk, 1–30. Washington, DC: American Psychiatric Press, 1987.
van der Kolk, Bessel, et al. "History of Trauma in Psychiatry." In *Traumatic Stress: The Effects of Overwhelming Experience on Mind, Body, and Society*, edited by Bessel A. van der Kolk, et al., 47–74. New York: Guilford, 1996.
van der Poel, Cornelius. *Wholeness and Holiness: a Christian Response to Human Suffering*. Franklin: Sheed & Ward, 1999.
Van Horn, Patricia, and Alicia F. Lieberman. "Early Intervention with Infants, Toddlers, and Preschoolers." In *Early Intervention for Trauma in Adults: A Framework for First Aid and Secondary Prevention*, edited by Brett T. Litz, 112–30. New York: The Guilford, 2004.
Verbin, N. Divinely. *Abused: A Philosophical Perspective on Job and His Kin*. New York: Continuum International, 2010.
Voorwinde, Stephen. *Jesus' Emotions in the Gospels*. New York: T. & T. Clark International, 2011.
Vrana, Scott, and Deah Lauterbach. "Trauma Events Questionnaire." http://web.a.ebscohost.com/ehost/search.
Vrana, Scott, and Dean Lauterbach. "Prevalence of Traumatic Events and Post-Traumatic Psychological Symptoms in a Nonclinical Sample of College Students." *Journal of Traumatic Stress* 7 (1994) 289–302.
Walsh, Froma. *Strengthening Family Resilience*. New York: Guilford, 2006.
Waltner, James H. *Believers Church Bible Commentary: Psalms*. Scottdale, PA: Herald, 2006.
Weathers, Frank W., et al. "The PTSD Checklist (PCL): Reliability, Validity, and Diagnostic Utility." *Society for Traumatic Stress Studies*, 1993.

WebMD. "Depression Health Center." http://www.webmd.com/depression/guide/default.htm.

Werdel, Mary Beth, et al. "The Unique Role of Spirituality in the Process of Growth Following Stress and Trauma." *Pastoral Psychology* 63 (2014) 57–71.

Westphal, Maren, and George A. Bonanno. "Posttraumatic Growth and Resilience to Trauma: Different Sides of the Same Coin or Different Coins?" *Applied Psychology: An International Review* 56 (2007) 417–27.

Whiteman, Darrell. "Integral Training Today for Cross-Cultural Mission." *Missiology: An International Review* 36 (2008) 5–16.

Wilkinson, Vera. "The Management and Treatment of Disaster Victims." *Psychiatric Annals* 15 (1985) 174–85.

Williams, Kenneth. "A Model for Mutual Care in Missions." In *Missionary Care: Counting the Cost for World Evangelization*, edited by Kelly O'Donnell, 46–60. Pasadena: William Carey Library, 1992.

Wintermyer, Carol. *Weaving a Tapestry: Loneliness, Spiritual Well-Being, and Communal Support*. Lanham, Maryland: University Press of America, 1993.

Wise, Judith. "Introduction: Empowerment as a Response to Trauma." In *Trauma Transformed: An Empowerment Response*, edited by Marian Bussey and Judith Wise, 3–12. New York: Columbia University Press, 2007.

Wittenbach, H. A. "The Training of a Missionary." *International Review of Missions* 49 (1960) 405–10.

Wohlgelernter, Devora K. "Death Wish in the Bible." *Tradition: A Journal of Orthodox Thought* 19 (1981) 131–40.

Wong-McDonald, Ana, and Richard L. "Gorsuch. Surrender to God: An Additional Coping Style?" *Journal of Psychology and Theology* 28 (2000) 149–61.

Woolfolk, Robert, and Frank Richardson. *Stress, Sanity, and Survival*. New York: Signet, 1978.

Wright, H. Norman. *Beating the Blues: Overcoming Depression and Stress*. Ventura: Regal Books, 1988.

Wright, Josephine. "Recognizing and Understanding Troubled Children." In *Healing the Children of War: A Handbook for Ministry to Children Who have Suffered Deep Traumas*, edited by Phyllis Kilbourn, 31–50. Monrovia: Marc, 1995.

———. "T = Talk and Time: Reaching the Troubled or Traumatized Child." In *Healing the Children of War: A Handbook for Ministry to Children Who have Suffered Deep Traumas*, edited by Phyllis Kilbourn, 157–74. Monrovia: Marc, 1995.

Yalom, Irvin, and Molyn Leszcz. *The Theory and Practice of Group Psychotherapy*. New York: Basic, 2005.

Yeh, Christine J., and Mayuko Inose. "International Students' Reported English Fluency, Social Support Satisfaction, and Social Connectedness as Predictors of Acculturative Stress." *Counseling Psychology Quarterly* 16 (2003) 15–28.

Young, E., and A. Korszun. "Sex, Trauma, Stress Hormones and Depression." *Molecular Psychiatry* 15 (2010) 23–28.

Zwickel, Steven. *Workplace Stress*. Milwaukee: Families International, 1994.